MARGO HENDRICKS CASEBOOK

MARGOH

Copyright © 2024 by Margo Hendricks

All rights reserved.

No part of this book may be reproduced in any form or by any electronic or mechanical means, including information storage and retrieval systems, without written permission.

ILLUSTRATIONS

- Costume design for the Indian boy, created by B. Modern for the 1991 Shakespeare Santa Cruz production of *A Midsummer Night's Dream*, directed by Danny Scheie.
- The Indian boy (actor Jaime Paglia) in *A Midsummer Night's Dream*, Shakespeare Santa Cruz, 1991. Photograph by Ann Parker.
- Aaron the Moor (actor Harry Lennix), *Titus* (2020), director Julie Taymor.
- Tybalt, Prince of Cats (actor John Leguizamo), *Romeo + Juliet* (1996), director Baz Luhrmann.
- Tish and Han (actors Aaliyah and Jet Li), *Romeo Must Die* (2000), director Andrzej Bartkowiak.

INTRODUCTION

Why <u>Margo Hendricks Casebook</u>?

After requests for copies of essays printed a few decades ago or having discussions about my work, I realized for most readers interested in my academic publications the essays were often inaccessible, hidden behind a press or database paywall. As someone who believes knowledge should not be private nor capitalized on except by the creator, and at the urging of a dearest friend, I collected most of my essays into a single book. Originally this collection was playfully titled *The Margo Hendricks Experience, A Casebook*. Realizing the original title was a bit unwieldy and there will only be one book of essays, it seemed a kindness to shorten it.

This book comes a t a time when I'm deeply heartsore, mourning the deaths of my first nephew and my sister-in-law. I have become a parent of a teen for a second time and so the idea of perfecting this book (every i dotted and every t crossed) is a waste of emotional energy since I will inevitably fall into the well of revising. So I chose to give you what's here and ask that you attend to the words, not the format. I'm a tad exhausted, y'all. So what you see is what you get.

<u>What you can expect to find inside</u>

I was once asked about my intellectual and imaginative creativity. The question surprised me because I rarely give thought to my writing process, whether it's academic or fiction. I have ideas, digressions, and meanderings that I allow to hold sway until an essay or a novel emerges in print form. Like many academic publications, these essays appeared first as talks. They were amorphous beings that took form in print when I was asked to contribute to a collection or journal. Like me, I view my writings as "walking chaos," in the world as reflections of a historical past, an academic present, and a writerly future. These are speculative essays rather than intellectual pronouncements; the what if, the why, and the perhaps. What if we explore gender in early modern English literature as a class configuration? Why does the ideologies of race-making shift from the premodern to the early modern and set the stage for settler colonialism, imperial colonialism, and modern racial capitalism? Can I love the literature and despise the socio-economic system that gave rise it?

Over the years, I've accepted the final question. I adore pre/early modern literature. The experimentation with form, language, and voice. The emergence of a mode of theater suited to redefinitions of nationalism in an international/global context even as it sought to entertain. I despise the rising colorism that feeds a redefinition of "race." The advent of European settler colonialism and enslavement of non-European peoples. While the majority of enslaved people were from regions of Africa, we shouldn't forget in the early stages of settler colonialism indigenous peoples were subject to enslavement until that project failed, to be substituted with genocide. I despise the patriarchal inflections of capitalism, its systems of gender oppression calculated in terms of "racial" taxonomies. The theft of cultural objects and funerary remains as part of conquest and collecting should be abhorrent to everyone of us.

My scholarly voice insists that we recognize what stands behind the Humanities, behind Literature, behind pre/early Modern English literature, behind cultural capitalism. My political voice is very much shaped by my subjectivity and the racial identity imposed by modern capitalism. I'm a Californian, a state constituted on the subjugation of and efforts to eliminate indigenous peoples. To know this is to recoil at the celebration of the Spanish and English "explorers" as historical icons worthy of adulation. Thus, I cannot ignore the complex history of conquest and settlement that has shaped much of the world's population. The egregious actions of tribes, political entities, and individuals should never be forgotten. However, the stolen land where I was born, where my "Anglo-Americanness" was formed, and where I continue to reside is inflected in my writings.

Land Back!

There is no purposeful intent to the organization of these essays other than theme (somewhat) and chronology, sorta. This is an academic book released outside of academia. The first section represents some of my early work on gender and drama, with a dash of race thrown in. The second section explores the matter of race-making as part philology and nuanced ideology (at least as I envisioned it), attending to all the parts that make up the concept of race in early modern English culture. What's left are essays that lengthen my musings on the ideas that have shaped my intellectual and academic career. Thus, readers are free to meander through the maze of MargoH's thoughts as they wish. I write to question not to answer, to push boundaries not to set limits, to engage in reflection and introspection not to seek accolades. I write for me and hope you'll find these musings to your liking. These pieces are exactly as they were originally published, no revisions or postscripts. They are indicative of a particular time and place in my career and I would not change a single word. In compiling these documents, I realized I am truly not a fan of traditional citational practices. Some essays have reference notes in the form of endnotes and others…welp. If you find a typo or silent emendation, consider it an Elizabethan printer's error or choice or I just can't with this book any longer.(smiles in MargoH).
Finally, I want to speak of scholarly joy, something crucial to my essays. I write from a place of curiosity which in turn produces a joy in my "shaping fantasies" about race, gender, genre, and literary culture. I laugh as I write. I talk back to the authors who form the context for my intellectual musings. I give them nicknames (Willie S, John D,

Eddie Spenser, Lizzie the First and so on). I take possession of their words and stand them on their heads, amused at what I see and what I didn't see. I loved writing these essays despite…

despite the sorrow and trauma the original texts generated, despite the use of the literary works for systems of oppression, for the negative connotations of peoples whose cultures, skin color, and sex/gender differed from the writers. Mostly, I despise the underlying white supremacist logic embedded in early modern texts. And yet, I love the literature of Chris M, Willie S, John D, Eddie S, Philip S, Mary W, and so many other pre/early modern writers. Most of all, thank you to all the silenced or unvoiced peoples whose lives were represented without their permission. Intuitively, these essays were attempts to project your inescapable histories.

Settler colonialism has wronged the planet

ACKNOWLEDGMENTS

This casebook would not have come into existence without the gentle exhortations (some less gentle then others) of people I've come to know, love, and respect within the academy, early modern English literature, and, specifically, within Premodern Critical Race Studies. Thank you, Ambereen Dadabhoy, Yasmine Hamachi, Ruben Espinosa, and all those who asked about an essay or discovered an essay. I will never be able to repay the intellectual, personal, and emotional debt I've received from Kim F. Hall, Arthur Little Jr., and Ayanna Thompson. Y'all have kept me in your hearts, supported and loved me through some very difficult times. Y'all also wouldn't let me disappear quietly into Romancelandia, reminding me there was still work to be done in academia. I love you all.

It goes without saying that throughout my career there were those white scholars who enabled my flights of intellectual fantasy and who are no longer with us (in their works, there is still wisdom to uncover) or who no longer write scholarly stuff. Thank you academic ancestors Terence Hawke, Janet Adelman, Harry Berger Jr., Hayden White, Leeds Barroll, and John M. Steadman III. You accepted that I could not be a clone and supported me as I pursued a job in academia (with all the trimmings). I cannot thank Jean Howard and Peter Erickson enough as they exemplified what an accomplice/ally to marginalized scholars ought to be.

My deep gratitude to the presses that granted me license to reprint these essays goes without saying. Thanks to the artists and creatives who allowed me to share their work the first time around and now once again.

The greatest debt owed is to Zeola Culpepper Jones, my great-grandmother, who worried about my soul even as she accepted my Aquarius mind, and to Patricia Parker whose friendship, love, and generosity of spirit has sustained me over my career. She is the epitome of an academic accomplice, ally, and friend.

Margo Hendricks aka MargoH

FEMINISM AND ME

IN THE BEGINNING WAS MARGO

A PAINTER'S EYE: GENDER AND MIDDLETON AND DEKKER'S THE ROARING GIRL

> There's a wench
> > Called Moll, mad Moll, or Merry Moll, a creature
> > So strange in quality, a whole city takes
> > Note of her name and person…. *(Prologue to The Roaring Girl)*[1]

To write of the characterization of Moll Cutpurse is much like crossing a swiftly moving river; one can quickly be swept under by the differing waves of feminist discourse. In recent studies of literary crossdressing in seventeenth century England Moll, the central protagonist in Middleton and Dekker's *The Roaring Girl,* has often been viewed as an occurrence of a sex/gender system under siege.[2] She is perceived as a woman whose masculine garments and independent behavior appear to represent an open challenge to existing structures of social power that demand men and women adhere to rigid codes of differentiation. More importantly, Moll Cutpurse is also perceived as enjoying an extraordinary amount of independence for a woman. In her role as man-woman/woman-man, Moll appears to move freely across the boundaries of gender ideologies. However, in light of her function within *The Roaring Girl,* if her appearance is subversive, Moll's depiction also raises the specter of collusion. Is it possible that her representation, contrary to current perceptions, functions not as a resistance but a recuperation and containment of its own critique of women's situation in Early Modern England?[3]

In recent discussions of the theoretical practices of new historicism, a number of American feminist scholars have been critical of the failure of new historicists to include an analysis of gender relations in their studies of Renaissance literary texts.[4] A common thread in this feminist critique is the view that the effect of new historicism has been a continuation of oppressive strategies against women. The absence of strategies for analyzing the paradigms of gender relations and ideologies, as feminists have argued, raises serious questions as to the usefulness of new historicist discourse for gender studies.

As a counter to an apparent masculine orthodoxy in new historicism, American feminists argue the necessity of over-reading texts: to read literary and historical documents in light of gender, to articulate gendered subjectivity and its significance for sexual oppression, as well as the possibilities of resistance or subversion. This theoretical position takes a new historicist practice of reading legal, political and social power relations to its logical next step, a determination of the way in which sexuality is historically and culturally constructed in Early Modern England.

What I intend to investigate in this essay is the way this imposition of power results in Moll colluding in her own oppression and that of women in general. Without question, Moll Cutpurse makes visible the contradictions of gender ideologies in seventeenth-century England, yet she does so without truly transforming the gender/power relations which constructed her social identity in the first place. What this essay will question is how Moll's apparent independence has come to occlude the collusive nature of Moll, both in her own containment and that of women in general, in the power relations which construct gender ideologies. In addition) I propose to examine the way in which theoretical strategies based on sexuality obscure the fact that in *The Roaring Girl* gender relations, not sexual desire, is the issue.

I

Teresa de Lauretis cogently argues that the use of sexual differences is marked with limitations: "it constrains feminist critical thought within the conceptual frame of a universal sex opposition"[5] Such constraints, in de Lauretis' view, obscure the differences among women, and thus render all women "different embodiments of" an archetypal essentialism.

> An additional limitation is the tendency to "re-contain or recuperate the radical epistemological potential of feminist thought" (2). The value of feminist epistemology in the 1980s, for de Lauretis, is the possibility of conceiving of the social subject and "the relations of subjectivity to sociality in another way: a subject [and "subjectivity"] constituted in gender" (2).

Specification of this subject begins with a notion of gender not "coterminous" with sexual difference. de Lauretis sees gender not as a "property of bodies or something originally existent in human beings" but "the representation of a relation, or. . .gender constructs a relation between one entity and other entities which are previously constituted as a class, and that relation is one of belonging" (4). Conceptualizing gender in this manner becomes a useful theoretical strategy for venturing outside the boundaries of current feminist practices where sexuality, rather than gender, appears to determine an individual's position within a particular social relation. In addition, analyses based upon conceptualizations of gender illuminate the way in which sexual differences and sexuality become ideological impositions of power relations.

The representation of Moll Cutpurse, therefore, can best be explored not by addressing the question of whether women cross-dressed or not, but by seeking to comprehend what may have lead some women to shun what seventeenth-century moralists and theologians argued was the single most important responsibility of a woman, marriage. Despite her garments, Moll is most definitely an unmarried woman and, as such, a potential threat to social order.

At the conclusion of *The Roaring Girl* Moll says to Lord Noland, "Heard you this jest, my Lord? .. ./ He was in fear his son would marry me, / But never dreamt that I would ne'er agree" (5.2. 210-14). Moll's decision not to marry is conceivably less important than the fact that she appears to have the freedom to make that decision. Recent historical studies of marital relations in Early Modern England seem to suggest that Moll's response to Sebastian Wengrave's declaration of affection, "Sir, I am so poor to requite you, you must look for nothing but thanks of me . . .," was not unusual for a woman of her status (2.2. 35-36).

Women in particular were more likely to be concerned about property and wealth since, upon her marriage, a woman ceased to exist as a legal individual and was subject to the authority of her husband. Consequently, what a woman brought to a marriage was just as important as the affection between a couple; the latter might ensure the couple's harmony but the former guaranteed the family's economic survival. More importantly, given the class-consciousness of seventeenth-century English society, Moll's words imply an awareness of the disparity between Sebastian's position within society, as a member of a gentry family, and her own as a single woman of questionable origins and very little wealth. Thus, while she alone can choose whether to wed or not it is her class position which informs Moll's refusal to even consider the possibility of marriage with Sebastian.

Moll's rejection of marriage draws attention to another issue of concern in seventeenth-century England. If a woman did exercise her freedom not to marry, what did she face in pursuing her independence? Historian Vivien Brodsky Elliott suggests that these unmarried women faced a difficult time, since London provided single women very few opportunities for employment. Elliott argues that women such as Anne Porter, who was "'at her own government and keeps a flax shop for herself and hires servants and so has done these 4 years or so'," were the exception rather than the rule. Unmarried women were more likely to end up as seamstresses or servants in a London household.[6]

Elliott's study examines the parish registers for London between the years 1598 and 1619, and her findings suggest two important patterns. First, there appears to have been a remarkable uniformity in mean age of first marriage, despite the status of a woman's parents. Among London-born single women that age was 20.5 years and for migrant women the mean age was 24.2 years. This difference, Elliott argues, is attributable to the second pattern she noted in reviewing marriage records and spousal documents. This second pattern revealed that the migrant woman's later age of marriage and the correspondent smaller age difference between partners were largely due to the absence of parental involvement and the woman's economic position.

Most unmarried women who travelled to London did so for economic reasons; they came in search of employment. These young women (usually between the age of 17 and 19) were often employed in households and businesses for periods of at least four to seven years. Thus, marriage was generally postponed until they had completed their service and accumulated enough income to begin a family. And, as Elliott infers, this factor may have granted these woman "greater freedom of choice of spouse and a more active role. . .in the courtship and marriage process" (89).

The involvement of the father in marriage decisions was greater for the single London-born woman than for her migrant counterpart. For the woman recently arrived to London the loss of a father, coupled with the absence of kin in the city, afforded her a greater degree of control over her marital status; a freedom which very few London-born women seem to have possessed (90). Migrant women, any one of whom could be Moll Cutpurse, were more likely than their London counterparts to marry late or not at all.

There has been a perception which presumes that much of what Elizabethan and Jacobean romantic comedy documents is the ideological transformation of marriage relations to reflect the emerging Puritan belief in companionate marriage. Yet, as historians have shown, the significance of external influence was just as strong in seventeenth-century England as in the sixteenth century. Couples were allowed freedom in making marital decisions but, should the marriage be one of serious inequality, family, community and the law were just as likely to intervene as not: an unstable or problem marriage could *very* easily become an economic burden on the community.[7]

Economics and the absence of familial influence can begin partially to account for the existence of women like Moll in London. However, we must follow another path if we wish to account for Moll Cutpurse's appearance on the Jacobean stage. Middleton and Dekker's *The Roaring Girl* offers an interesting ideological intersection of Early Modem England's gender relations. For any woman, but especially an unmarried woman, sexuality came to dominate the strategies of gender relations in seventeenth-century English social practices. One result was that gender ideologies came to be read as manifestations of sexual differences.

Gender relations, under the guise of sexual differentiation, historically have been shrouded with an immutability that seems to defy human intervention. Marilyn Williamson has argued that "nature," as it was conceptualized in Early Modern England, seemed to ". . . comprehend both the innate character and disposition of people and animals and the inherent creative power operating within material objects and phenomena."[8] Among men and women, their "innate character and disposition" were articulated as sexual differences, and ultimately evolved into gender differentiations.

The literary text, as a construct of ideology, becomes implicated in this hegemonic discourse of sexual difference. The tensions, contradictions and duplicity of constructing gender roles solely on the basis of sexual differences blur the relations of power dominating gender. Literary texts, therefore, tend to obscure these underlying power relations in their representation of gendered subjectivity and social roles. It is the transgression of these roles which renders Moll Cutpurse such a disturbing figure. Generally, cross dressing symbolizes an act of social and sexual transgression which requires intervention or suppression at the particular site of conflict.[9] In Renaissance literature, especially romantic comedies, this site was usually found in apparel. Clothing was a constructed demarcation of class and gender, supported by cultural and legal codes, and the appropriation of masculine apparel by women was viewed as an attempt to appropriate the power of men. In the majority of the comedies involving transvestism, the dramatist resolves the subversive implications of a masculine-garbed female by restoring her to her natural garments and, by extension, her natural role. It is not difficult to concur with Mary Beth Rose's assessment of the significance of sumptuary codes in seventeenth-century comedy. The restoration of women to women's garments, she argues, suggests that social stability, as the inherent purpose of "(the] romantic comic form, is at the heart of such dramatic resolutions."[10]

The disruptive function of the disguised female becomes, consequently, neither a radical critique of gender practices and strategies nor an interrogation of the inequality of power relations extant in society. On the contrary, "it is the temporary nature of the heroine's disguise which contains the formal solution to the potential psychological and social problems it raises" (389-390). Rose is correct in her perception of the conservative quality of romantic comedy; social order and stability are achieved through the unified family and symbolized by the marriage of the no longer disguised heroine, with its implicit affirmation of gender ideologies.

It is this affirmation which makes Moll Cutpurse, the central figure of Middleton and Dekker's *The Roaring Girl,* such an intriguing paradigm. Brought into the play to aid Sebastian Wengrave's intrigue, Moll becomes a visible articulation of an independent woman. Despite the fact that Moll apparently is not lascivious, she is perceived as such by most men in her world. Consequently, when Moll comments that a woman who "has wit and spirit/ May scorn / to live beholding to her body for meat / Or apparel, like your common dame *I* That makes shame get her clothes to cover shame" she offers a critique of the position women often find themselves in (3.1. 132-135). Moll argues that a woman of intelligence and resource can reject the legal prostitution many women come to know when they marry for wealth or position.

Ironically, only moments before Moll chastises Laxton for his misreading of her:

> In thee I defy all men, their worst hates,
>   And their best flatteries, all their golden witchcrafts,
>   With which they entangle the poor spirits of fools.
>   Distressed needlewomen and trade-fallen wives,
>   Fish that must needs bite or themselves be bitten,

> Such hungry things as these may soon be took
> With a worm fastened on a golden hook: (III.i.91-96)

Her words paint an image of a harsh reality for women who follow her advice. What they discover is that they are members of a society which is slowly making their pursuit of independence exceedingly difficult. For Moll, the contradictions engendered by the material reality of a woman's life are not born of a woman's sexuality but the result of gender-defined power relations which says that her only social value is her sexual or reproductive role.

The swordplay between Moll and Laxton (both verbal and actual) under scores this paradox gender relations have configured for women. When he initially sees Moll, Laxton observes, "I would give but too much money to be nibbling with that wench;. . .I'll lay hard siege to her, money is that aqua fortis that eats into many a maidenhead" (II.i.169-177). Laxton, and later Trapdoor, reads Moll's appearance within a discourse of female sexuality: one that envisions her as a sexual challenge to be met, an enclosure to be scaled, a commodity to be purchased.

It is in this marginality where Moll seeks to step across the boundaries of Laxton's assumptions "to teach [his] base thoughts manners. . ." and [to question] "how many of our sex, by such as thou/Have their good thoughts paid with a blasted name / That never deserved loosely or did trip / In path of whoredom beyond cup and lip?" (III.i.70-82). Moll recognizes that a woman's reputation is intricately intertwined with her chastity, or the appearance of chastity. The effect of a woman's loss of reputation reaches beyond just the individual. An increase in defamation suits by women attest to the seriousness with which seventeenth-century women took their reputations. Approximately sixty to seventy percent of defamation cases for slander were initiated by women.[11] Many of these complaints concerned accusations of infidelity, adultery, and fornication yet, as Martin Ingram discovers, "the most striking feature of cases brought by women was the high proportion which involved very unspecific slanders" (302). The majority of women who filed suit (50- 60%) sued for "such generalities as 'whore', jade' and 'quean'. (All these words signified a sexually immoral female, without necessarily implying prostitution.)" (302).

Nevertheless, it is this type of generalization which Moll abhors, and her victory over Laxton becomes symbolic, even if ineffectual. In actual practice, Moll would have sued Laxton in an ecclesiastical court, yet her behavior and garments would have lost her the case. And, Laxton's fundamental assumptions about women remain unchanged; an unmarried woman is nothing more than her apparent value as an object of sexual desire. She is a commodity. Thus while Moll's expertise with the sword gains her an apology, the gender relations which gave rise to the assumptions Laxton makes remain intact.

The Roaring Girl ends, as do most seventeenth-century comedies, with a marriage. Sebastian has achieved his goal, marriage to Mary Fitz-Allard. Moll, despite her vigorous protestations against the oppressive quality of marriage, assists in bringing about the marriage of Sebastian and Mary. Clearly, the characterization of Moll Cutpurse poses a paradox not easily resolved by simply talking of her as a "site" of sexual desire or oppression. How, then, are we to see Moll Cutpurse?

One possibility is to comprehend Moll as a determined and a determining social subject. As a determining subject Moll, in light of her decision not to wed and her masculine garments, raises the possibility of conflict within the gendered meaning of the text. However, as the determined subject woman, Moll is successfully contained by a gender ideology which appears to circumscribe her potential by embedding it in the loss of her reputation, and consequently restricting her subjectivity to that of a sexual commodity.

In relation to the conventional strategies of romantic comedy, the representation of Moll Cutpurse is an idiosyncratic and potentially subversive challenge to power relations which held that ungoverned women posed a serious threat to social stability.[12] Moll's "freedom," moreover, is limited to a decision on marriage, and that freedom is easily granted by the structures of power to one who obviously is least able to challenge the actual power relations in Early Modern England.

Middleton and Dekker's appropriation of Mary Frith (the historical Moll Cutpurse) may be viewed as the displacement of constructed subjectivity. The inclusion of a historical figure whose sole function is to bring about a marriage, I would argue, reconstructs the conventions of the text, and the historical contradictions, tensions, and conflicts of social discourse must necessarily intrude upon the discursive practices of literature.

The Roaring Girl positions itself as a compass point in any understanding of the context of Renaissance crossdressing. Moll Cutpurse exists as an antithesis of gender division: she is a unified masculine/feminine social identity. Moreover, as do others who challenge sexual roles, she soon realizes that merely assuming masculine attire does not significantly alter the economic and cultural power relations which require a system of inequality based upon sexual differences, nor does her attire modify the effect that such relations have upon her daily life. Ultimately, she is Moll the anomaly - unmarriageable and unmarried.

Unmarried women like Moll Cutpurse represented an aberration in seventeenth-century English society. Their presence enacted a potential resistance to ideologies of sexual difference enacted to regulate gender relations within the economic structure.[13] The effect of economic depression and contraction, agricultural transformations and an increasing market oriented society was producing a disruption in Early Modern England. Women like Moll, unable to marry or find the means to support themselves in their villages, migrated to London. The situation strikingly parallels that which occurred in England during the 1970s when young people, unemployed and unlikely to find employment, gave birth to the "punk movement." Both seventeenth-century "roaring girls" and twentieth-century British "punks" externalize their marginality by assuming aberrant forms of behavior and speech (for the punks this involved dying or "spiking" one's hair, clothing, aggressive music and behavior within the immediate social group) to demarcate the boundaries of their world. Problems of under- and unemployment, social dysfunction, political upheaval and religious dissent generated historical conditions that gave voice to these marginalized subjects, allowing them occasionally to cross the boundaries which keep them marginalized within the dominant discourse.

Moll Cutpurse's depiction resonates with the contradictions between her apparent independence and the actual limitations imposed by the gender relations of her time. The presence of women who transgress codes constructed on the basis of sexual differences often exposed those codes for what they were, power relations based upon material conditions. The appearance of women such as Moll creates a potential rupture in the strategies of gender relations in seventeenth-century England and must be contained.

Moll's containment is more subtle than usual in Renaissance crossdressing. And, consequently, often leads to problems of reconciling such behavior's ambivalence. Moll is a problematic form of resistance to gender ideologies and power relations in Early Modern England. Jean E. Howard argues that Moll's representation is "[a] resistance to patriarchy and its marriage customs."[14] About *The Roaring Girl*, Howard argues:

> in few cases . . . plays of female crossdressing were more than sites where creative accommodations to a demystified patriarchy were enacted. Instead they protested the hierarchical sex-gender system and the material injustices that, in conjunction with other social practices, it spawned. The obvious case in point is Middleton and Dekker's *The Roaring Girl*, a work based on an actual London woman's life and a work traversed by discourses of social protest not found in most of the plays I have so far examined (436).

Although I am in agreement with the spirit of Howard's argument, it is difficult to envision Moll as a form of "social protest" when her actions seem to reify particular ideologies which configured gender relations. Moll, despite her garments and her awareness (or possibly because of them), becomes a collusive mending of the tear her inclusion in the play creates.

II

Finally, I should like to reflect upon the significance of *The Roaring Girl* for analyses concerned with the relationship between gender, sexuality and material conditions. Although feminist theory has begun to articulate a distinction between sex and gender, in literary practice, particularly in Renaissance studies, this distinction often becomes obscure. The basis for such conceptualizations lies not in an inherent antithesis between sex and gender, but in failing to articulate gender as a historically-specific power relation.

Ideologies based upon sexual difference become a mask for the tensions, contradictions and multiplicities of the construction of gender in the power relations of a particular social structure. Thus, in his discussion of Moll Cutpurse, Harold Weber offers a mis-reading of the actual site of Moll's position within her society and, importantly, misappropriate the significance of Moll's victory over Laxton. Weber argues that "[by] donning the apparel of a man, Moll. . .may question the double standard that defines relations between men and women, but her effectiveness in doing so depends on her refusal *to* indulge her sexual appetites."[15] It is not her refusal to pursue her sexuality which constructs Moll but her failure to recognize that the gender ideologies which govern her world circumscribe her independence regardless of her actions.

As someone whose attire suggests that she is outside the boundaries of traditional seventeenth-century gender roles, Moll is a dislocation of gender based categories of social identification, and as such she becomes a configuration which limits yet makes visible the representation of gender relations on the stage. In other words, Moll is best understood in terms of the ambivalence her actions impose upon the text: she is constructed by and constructs a particular representation of gender. Consequently, without laboring the point, I would direct critics like Weber to de Lauretis' theoretical premise that sexuality enables gender ideologies but does not constitute the basis of gender relations in a social structure. Even Moll concedes the power material conditions have over women's existence; something critics like Weber have overlooked.

At the play's conclusion Moll addresses the audience with these words:

> A painter having drawn with curious art

> The picture of a woman (every part
> Limned to the life) hung out the piece to sell:
> People who passed along viewing it well,
> Gave several verdicts on it: some dispraised. . . [Epilogus]

Like the painter, Middleton and Dekker framed their dramatic representation within the cultural paradigms which structured their society, and, although *The Roaring Girl* conforms to traditional comic resolutions, the literary text appears unable to obscure completely the paradigms of gender.

Critical discourse, I believe, shares a similar intent: offering a theoretical frame for constructing and re-constructing meaning in a text. Yet many critics tend to approach *The Roaring Girl* in the same manner as the painter's commentators - with varied and often fragmenting "verdicts" with an eye towards "[mending] it/ In hope to please all."

All too often, the interrogation of gender contradictions and tensions involves the imposition of sexuality on what is instead the construction of a power relation. What occurs, then, in their efforts to elaborate meaning in a literary text, is that critics have come to lose sight of the fact that gender, not sexuality, is the discourse of power relations.

The Roaring Girl, I would argue, makes possible an understanding into the way in which gender relations are constructed and the importance of sexual difference in constituting the social and cultural practices which inform gender ideologies. The play offers a demystification of the essentialism of sexual difference and identifies it for what it truly is: the social and cultural articulation of power relations in seventeenth-century England.

Finally, feminist critics must begin to evaluate their own ideological imperative and collusion. Is it possible that, like Moll's painter, we too have fallen prey to making sexual what is a historically constructed meaning of power? Have we too often sought to re-configure women's history according to patriarchal ideologies without dismantling the gender conceptualizations which inform those ideologies? To begin to address these questions feminist theorists and critics must begin to reevaluate the position of privilege granted to sexuality and sexual difference.

Such privileging places limitations on our understanding of the historicity of gender representations and the position of sexual differences within gender relations. In Moll's world, sexual difference begins to mask the prescriptive role being constructed for a woman. Her social and personal identity is increasingly being defined by her marital status and her reputation; and, in the absence of either, but particularly a woman's reputation, will inevitably lead to a position of marginalization with society.

The Roaring Girl stands at an unusual intersection in studies of Renaissance crossdressing and its implications for gender struggle. On the surface, women like Moll appear to face a position of marginality and powerlessness against which the only challenge is sexuality.[16] Yet, Moll shows that such perceptions are both limited and deceptive. Her situation makes visible that the locus of power is not in sexual difference or sexuality, but in the way gender is constructed and the forces concealed by that construction.

Moll's participation in her own containment arises as much from her acquiescence to patriarchal ideologies as it is born of her bifurcated subjectivity. Even as she strives for a freedom few women of her time might know, she is hampered by the perceptions and assumptions which signal what her position is to be. For all that she infers a social disruption, a semiotic site of resistance to gender ideologies, Moll is the containment of that struggle. She is what no Renaissance woman would be. Perhaps, to recast Moll's admonition, it is time for feminist theory to cease "striving to please all, [while pleasing] none. . .," and begin to view the portrait of gendered subjectivity as it has been, and is being, painted.

"A WORD, SWEET LUCRECE": CONFESSION, FEMINISM, AND THE RAPE OF LUCRECE

The story of Lucrece would have been well known to Elizabethan audiences. Its passive / active linking of her rape/suicide was left largely unquestioned. The presumed choice presented in the poem between death or shame was a foregone conclusion. The theological position counseled choosing shame, of which one could be shriven, over suicide, a mortal sin. Preferring death implied that rape was necessarily, regardless of the purity of mind, a pollution of the body's chastity, an effect which could not be undone. (Carter, 1995: 212).

Produced in a society that considered itself deeply Christian, William Shakespeare's *The Rape of Lucrece* poses an intriguing dilemma for those moralists who would evoke the Roman wife Lucretia as an emblem of feminine chastity.[1] As Stephen J. Carter's observation, noted above, illustrates, the audience "could imagine, and perhaps praise, a woman's choosing a public transformation of unchastity through death, over the private shame of bodily pollution, however technically virtuous of mind she remains" (1995: 212). The effect, according to Carter, is a deployment "of a secular discourse within the larger theological context. The former produces a reading of female space as that which needed to be kept enclosed, unseen, pure – within a larger, allegedly protective male space." The "theological context," Carter asserts, produces a reading that condemns Lucrece's actions as, in St. Augustine's view, a failure to see "that while the sanctity of the soul remains even when the body is violated, the sanctity of the body is not lost; and that in like manner, the sanctity of the body is lost when the sanctity of the soul is violated, though the body itself remains intact" (Carter 1995:212). Shakespeare's "anticipation" and conflation of these two positions, Carter observes, seem to imply that "Lucrece's choice of suicide is not presented as the automatic secular choice it was assumed to be" (1995: 212). In the end, Carter contends, the narrative's Elizabethan audience becomes "aware of [the text's] emphatically split reading: that she courageously chose and acted on a theologically incorrect reading, for which she could not be held responsible given the Roman setting of the story" (1995: 212–13).

I begin with Carter's somewhat problematic commentary on the spatial and theological significance of Lucrece's suicide because, in many ways, her suicide has been a thorny issue for feminist criticism. Over the course of the narrative, Lucrece is transformed from a silent object of male gaze to an iconographic model of feminine subjectivity, the latter idealized in her death and the use of her lifeless body as a symbol of Roman unity against the Tarquins. For feminist critics seeking to find some definitive source of political power and agency in Lucrece, the narrative seems not to aid such an endeavor. The problem that faces any feminist reader of *Lucrece* is that any analysis must find a way to come to terms with the contradictory representations Shakespeare's retelling of the myth of Lucretia engenders. Thus feminist readings appear caught in a theoretical position of having to "stress the extent to which the idea of woman which it [*Lucrece*] represents is one overdetermined by patriarchal ideology, and [have] typically interpreted Lucrece herself as a sign used to mediate and define men's relationships to men" (Berry 1991: 33). To illustrate this point, I want to summarize a few of the recent feminist positions on *Lucrece*.[2]

In a cogent and insightful essay, Katharine Eisaman Maus explores the relationship between the "use and abuse of tropes" by both Lucrece and Tarquin as part of a "literalizing" tendency in the narrative. "Shakespeare's poem," Maus argues, "is essentially an account, punctuated by terrible violence, of two people making important decisions" (1986: 67). For both characters "their decision-making process becomes not the activity of a moment but a continuously repeated process." As a result, the "difficult process of decision-making is, for both characters, inseparable from their employment of a few crucial metaphors" (1986: 67). Ultimately, Maus suggests, the use of tropes, by both Lucrece and Tarquin, becomes intricately linked to the moral choices the characters make and occasional critical frustration with Shakespeare's excessive and elaborate rhetorical technique.

Like Maus, Joyce Green MacDonald is interested in Shakespeare's "poetic technique" and its relation to Lucrece's "voice," but with aims quite different from Maus. In her persuasive reading of *Lucrece*, MacDonald explores the "varieties of female speech and silence as they help shape Shakespeare's familial Roman ethos." For MacDonald, "Lucrece finds her desperate voice only to encounter its limitations in a poem deeply informed by Renaissance assumptions about silence and segregation as indices of chastity; contradictions and oppositions between modes of speech and silence mark the boundaries of her crisis" (1994: 78–9). Lucrece thus becomes doubly marked: a classically derived moral exemplum and an articulation of early modern gender and patriarchal ideologies. Despite its Roman setting, MacDonald finds the narrative depiction of Lucrece's "voice" to be thoroughly informed by the patriarchal ideologies that govern Shakespeare's England.

Similarly, Philippa Berry's insightful essay "Woman, Language, and History in *The Rape of Lucrece*" contends "that Lucrece is represented in the poem as an important but unorthodox example of Renaissance *virtù*" and "this quality is given most powerful expression in the poem, not through her actions, but through her private use of language – a use which implicitly stresses its performative, even magical powers" (1991: 34). Like MacDonald, Berry sees Lucrece's "secret and powerful eloquence" as an "indication of republican political ideals in the poem" (1991: 34), yet Berry differs as to the role this eloquence plays in terms of the overarching signifier of the narrative, the politics of family. It is, for Berry, in the end, the dynamic of political "history" and not "social" (and thus, to some degree, the personal) history that allows

Lucrece to find a voice (1991: 34). Berry, like MacDonald and Maus, seeks the key to a feminist reading of Lucrece in terms of rhetoric and the politics of speech. The final essays I wish to highlight pursue a slightly divergent path in their analyses of Shakespeare's poem; a path which redirects attention to questions of space and the female body in Shakespeare's narrative.

In a chapter titled "The Sexual Politics of Subjectivity in *Lucrece*," Coppélia Kahn seeks to balance the seemingly competing, and at times oppositional, issues of language and body. In her discussion, Kahn considers the relationship between the "problematic of rape" of Lucrece through an examination of the "language of power and the power of language with regard to the poem's two main characters, Lucrece and Tarquin" (1997: 27). Kahn contends that, in "giving Lucrece a tongue, Shakespeare perforce works *against* the patriarchal codes that, at the same time, he puts into her mouth" (1997: 28). What "fascinates and moves" Kahn is that Shakespeare "tries to fashion Lucrece as a subject not totally tuned to the key of Roman chastity and patriarchal marriage and to locate a position in which he as poet might stand apart from those values as well" (1997: 82). Yet, according to Kahn, Shakespeare "fails" and "his attempt reveals how narrowly the rhetorical traditions within which he works are bounded by an ideology of gender in which women speak with the voices of men" (1997: 82).

Georgianna Ziegler, on the other hand, looks to the "domestic architecture" of Elizabethan and Jacobean England as a way of adumbrating meaning in *Lucrece*. Briefly tracing the emerging sense of "private space," Ziegler outlines the role this concept plays in the cultural discourse on femininity. Women, she argues, become localized in the household, and definitions of a woman's "self" were articulated in the rhetoric of inside/outside or, as it has come to be labeled in current critical theories about early modern households, private/public. In an analysis that looks at three Shakespearean female characters, Lucrece, Desdemona, and Imogen, Ziegler writes, "in all of these works the woman's chamber has represented her 'self': both her physical body and mental/spiritual nature" (1991: 87). As Ziegler notes, Lucrece is the only one who does not leave her home, "and, thus, coming out of the genre of classical history, she fits most precisely the ideal of the 'normative Woman', and indeed by Shakespeare's time she had become a type of such women" (1991: 80).

Reading Lucrece's body metaphorically as a "chamber" (which, Ziegler rightly notes, is how Lucrece refers to herself during her attempts to persuade Tarquin not to pursue the rape), Ziegler observes, for Tarquin, "Lucrece is not so much a private chamber to be entered as a public edifice to be stormed" (1991: 80). "Only by making another violent entry into this house or closet [Lucrece's body] and letting the soul go free can Lucrece conceive of redeeming her own honour and that of her husband," Ziegler argues (1991: 81). In the end, Ziegler concludes,

> I think that Shakespeare seems almost to be asking if the patriarchy has not set up this classic, enclosed female icon *because* it is afraid of what it sees as the uncontrollable, unstable functions of the female body and nature. And once having formulated its own ideal, it never quite trusts even the women who seem to fit it. (1991: 87)

Each of these essays plays an important role in shaping the argument that follows. In reading these analyses, I found myself saying, yes *but*. Yes, the poem's narrator is in effect the mediator of Lucrece's voice and thus imposes a "silence" upon her, *but*; yes, her body is mutilated figuratively and literally, first by Shakespeare's use of the blazon (as Nancy Vickers so brilliantly illustrated), and then by Lucrece herself, *but*; and yes, Renaissance patriarchal ideology governs both how Lucrece "sees" herself and how the reader reads/sees that seeing, *but*. I am not entirely certain whether my *but* is a factor of the peculiarities of Shakespeare's narrative poem (which I increasingly suspect is the case), or my belief that female agency manifests itself in a multitude of ways, some not necessarily in accord with a set of feminist prescriptions. Nonetheless, I shall set out to add another feminist voice to the discussion of Shakespeare's *The Rape of Lucrece*.

In this essay I will consider the politics of the narrative in light of two concerns: the first is the tradition of reading Lucrece's suicide as a reflection of Christian ideologies on sexuality and on suicide, specifically as articulated in the writing of St. Augustine. Through a reading of Lucrece's actions and speech leading up to and resulting in her death, I will argue that her behavior is consistent with the two competing early modern Christian discourses (Catholic and Protestant) about the nature of "private confession." Thus, unlike other critics of the narrative poem, I read her speeches as reflections of the discourse of the confessional. The second concern that guides this reading is the place of race in Shakespeare's narrative poem. Race, I shall argue, is intertwined with Shakespeare's use of the confessional mode to represent female subjectivity. The conception of race I shall be working with in this discussion is not the current semantics of race, however. Instead, I shall be looking at an earlier notion whereby race signified primarily lineage but, increasingly, was being adapted to new and more geopolitical concerns.

It is my contention that Shakespeare's *The Rape of Lucrece* is an attempt to mediate the tensions (and contradictions) generated by competing discourses of race: race as defined by genealogy or lineage, and race as defined by ethnicity. In this imprecision, as an expression of fundamental distinctions, race's meaning varied depending upon whether a writer wanted to specify difference born of a class-based concept of genealogy, a psychological (and often essentialized) nature, or group typology. In effect, Shakespeare's narrative reproduction and (re)presentation of the Lucretia myth gives life to a more complex meaning of race, one which defines itself not only in terms of lineage but also in terms of ethnicity.

In my reading of *Lucrece* I make use of Louis Althusser's notion of "interpellation" and Michel Foucault's observations on confession in *The History of Sexuality* to explore what are two of the most effective discourses for constituting subjectivity, and by extension agency – racial identity and religion. Lucrece's confessional moments incorporate, as part of its truth-telling, an early modern racial ideology in the articulation of her subjectivity. My aim in linking the act of confession and the concept of race as features of the narrative representation of Lucrece's subjectivity is to highlight the relationship between speech and a gendered notion of "self" as part of the process of identity-making. And, as I hope to illustrate, confession, gender, and race can work to produce female agency even as they are deployed to prevent it.

The Conduct of Confession

The "confession," Michel Foucault reminds us, is "one of the main rituals [Western societies] rely on for the production of truth. [In effect, confession] came to signify someone's acknowledgment of his own actions and thoughts" (1980: 58). What this acknowledgment entails, however, differs according to the political, cultural, gender, and ethnic dictates of subjectivity. Yet, as Foucault argues, confession

> frees, but power reduces one to silence; truth does not belong to the order of power, but shares an original affinity with freedom: traditional themes in philosophy, which a "political history of truth" would have to overturn by showing that truth is not by nature free – nor error servile – but that its production is thoroughly imbued with relations of power. The confession is an example of this. (1980: 60)

On the surface, Shakespeare's *Lucrece* might seem an unlikely place to go looking for Shakespeare's possible engagement with the theological controversies surrounding the role of confession within late sixteenth-century Christian practice. Yet, attending carefully to the language Shakespeare uses, we find the exchanges between Lucrece and Tarquin to be replete with the Judeo-Christian language of sin, especially in the extended use of words such as "guilt," "sin," "shame," and "conscience." Moreover, Shakespeare's deployment of less generic terms, such as "convertite," "remission," and "absolution," further localizes the poem's depiction of Lucrece and Tarquin's introspection, respectively, within a clearly delineated Catholic paradigm. As Tarquin declares, "Thoughts are but dreams till their effects be tried; / The blackest sin is cleared with absolution" (lines 354–5).[3] Though these are Tarquin's words, it is Lucrece who becomes the narrative's focus for exploring the implications of this very "Catholic" assumption.

Tarquin's words make reference to two matters of concern in Christian doctrine: the relationship between thought and action or deed, and the possibility of forgiveness or absolution for one's sins.[4] Since the latter constitutes our understanding of the former in *Lucrece*, it will be useful to outline the workings of the pre-Reformation "system of forgiveness of serious sins and reconciliation with the body of the faithful" (Tentler 1977: 4). Thomas Tentler argues that confession is an "ecclesiastical ritual to restore baptized Christians who have committed serious sins, fallen from grace, and forfeited their right to full participation in the body of the faithful." Tentler contends that

> there is … a rough continuity between the institutions of forgiveness in the early church and those that were known on the eve of the Reformation. Throughout the history of this ritual of forgiveness four substantive elements persist, even though they receive varying emphasis from century to century. First, to be forgiven, sinners have always been required to feel sorrow at having lapsed. Second, they have consistently made some kind of explicit confession of their sins or sinfulness. Third, they have assumed, or had imposed on them, some kind of penitential exercises. And fourth, they have participated in an ecclesiastical ritual performed with the aid of priests who pronounce penitents absolved from sin or reconciled with the communion of believers. (1977: 3)

Succinctly, these elements became manifested in the early Church's canonical process of "penance" whereby the sinner admitted sin (confession) to a member of the clergy (confessor), was ordered to perform public penitential acts (satisfaction) in order to prove "true contrition," and then received absolution for the sin.

In its emergence as part of the early Christian Church's doctrine for governing its members' social and private behavior, penance had a very "public character." According to Tentler, the development of ecclesiastical penitential institutions was to "insure discipline" and "to exercise control" (1977: 13). More explicitly, he contends, "the first function of ecclesiastical penance is discipline, or social control. The penitent was accepted by society and in turn was expected to accept and conform to society's rules";

> the second function is directed more to the individual: it is the cure of a guilty conscience… If the first function is social control, the second is reconciliation with the self and with those social norms that the penitent has internalized. Its purest and simplest formulation is in the language of religion: "How do I know my sins are forgiven me?" (Tentler 1977: 13).

The answer to this question was found in the notion of "contrition." According to Tentler, during the twelfth and thirteenth centuries "contrition" became an acceptable and "principal part of the forgiveness of sins," displacing "satisfaction," as a result of the move toward a more private mode of seeking forgiveness. Contrition, it was thought, indicated an "internal sorrow" which stems "from the love of God" (Tentler 1977: 19). "But," as Tentler rightly queries, "if contrition is the principal part of the Sacrament of Penance, is there any need for confession?" (1977: 19). As Tentler illustrates in his study, despite the theological tensions created by this query, the Church's canonical doctrine remains resolute in the necessity of the confession of sins to a priest.

For pre-Reformation Christians, confession was an obligation. It was the priest who stood as the intermediate between the sinner and God in the display of "the remission of guilt" (Tentler 1977: 23). Thus the Church doctrine, following the argument of St. Thomas Aquinas, insisted "that contrition does not produce forgiveness apart from the sacramental absolution of the priest" (Tentler 1977: 25). What is important to note in this doctrinal position is that contrition, or "perfect sorrow," no matter how great, is incapable of generating forgiveness. Only confession can achieve that. The "necessity of confession" became inextricably part of social controls wielded by the pre-Reformation Christian Church. With allusions to specific scriptural sources, Church canons articulated the ecclesiastical laws that required every adult to attend confession and that the jurisdiction for confession belong to the Church. Not until the second half of the sixteenth century did this assumption about confession receive its most rigorous challenge.

Tentler argues that "it is [Martin] Luther, ironically, who must take primary responsibility for the situation in modern Christianity that allows a theologian to assert, by way of definition, 'a Protestant doesn't confess'" (1977: 351). Though not opposed to confession per se, Luther was opposed to the system of confession. Luther insisted on "the hidden sinfulness of man" and that "only sins that entail full consent to the deed and are universally recognized as serious sins should be confessed; and the examples he gives are murder, lying, stealing, and adultery" (Tentler 1977: 353). Even so, Luther did not advocate the absolute dismantling of the confession; rather, he argued for its modification. It was left to reformers such as Calvin and Zwingli to take Luther's position even further and argue for the complete abolition of the ecclesiastical confession in favor of the more private, individual, and unmediated relationship with God. As Jeremy Tambling suggests, the "Protestant outline certainly does not involve less confession than before: simply the mode alters in which that discourse takes place" (1990: 45). Both pre- and post-Reformation doctrine recognized confession as an opportunity to "offer a complete account of the self" (Tambling 1990: 46). The distinction between "Catholic" and "Protestant" modes of confession can be summarized as simply the difference between "a performance confession (Catholic) and the 'real,' or interiorized, confession (Protestant)," with "the latter manifesting itself in silence" rather than the public speech of the former (Tambling 1990: 55).

This minor "difference" does not render the Protestant confession any less controlling than its Catholic counterpart, however. On the contrary, in ways not possible within Catholic doctrine, the Protestant confessional interiorizes all four of the elements that Tentler associates with the Christian idea of divine forgiveness and insists on the individual subject as the agent of his own confessional process. Significantly, all four elements, in some manner, can be said to describe the behavior of Lucrece as she responds to Tarquin's rape, despite our "historical" awareness that the events surrounding her suicide reflect a pre-Christian Roman history.[5] In the next section of this essay I wish to explore the possibility and implications of viewing Lucrece as just such a confessing subject.

Lucrece's Confession

One of the subtly provocative issues that Lucrece raises in her voiced and frantic reaction to Tarquin's assault is whether Tarquin's rape has caused her to sin. Specifically, she questions whether, as a result of the sexual act, she has committed adultery and thus sinned. On the surface, the logical answer is no; a perspective reflected in the attitudes of her husband and father: "With this they all at once began to say / Her body's stain her mind untainted clears" (lines 1709–10). While her response, "'No, no,' quoth she, 'no dame hereafter living / By my excuse shall claim excuse's giving'" (lines 1714–15), indicates an awareness of the import of her family's absolution, I want to suggest that the confessional self-examination that Lucrece undertakes prior to her husband's arrival indicates a different assumption on her part; that in fact, she believes her stained body to be a reflection of an inner stain – the sin of adultery.

The question of whether Lucrece commits adultery as a result of Tarquin's actions is one taken up by St. Augustine in his commentary on Lucretia's rape and suicide. Augustine writes:

> What shall we say about her? Must she be judged an adulteress or chaste? Who can think it necessary to ponder over the answer? A certain declaimer develops this theme admirably and accurately: "A wonderful tale! There were two and only one committed adultery." Very striking and very true! For he, taking into consideration this intermingling of two bodies the utterly foul passion on one side and the utterly chaste will of the other, and paying attention, not to the union of the bodies, but to the variance in the souls, says: "There were two and only one committed adultery." (1957: 85)

Augustine then goes on to suggest that

> perhaps, however, she is not there [in attendance before a tribunal of Roman judges] because she slew herself, not innocently, but conscious of her guilt? What if – but she herself alone could know – she was seduced by her own lust and, though the youth violently attacked her, consented, and in punishing that act of hers was so remorseful that death seemed to be due expiation? (1957: 85)

Augustine makes these comments as part of a larger exploration of what he considers the true sin committed by Lucretia, her suicide. Yet, in raising the possibility of Lucretia's complicity in her rape, Augustine draws attention to a number of troubling questions that moralists, who offer Lucretia as an icon of chastity, either ignore or overlook: "If she was made an adulteress, why has she been praised; if she was chaste, why was she slain?" (1957: 89).

It is this point that Augustine sees as the paradox facing those who view Lucretia as an exemplum for Christian women who were raped. Moralists, Augustine observes, give tribute to Lucretia by declaring, "'There were two and only one committed adultery'" (1957: 89). Augustine counters this argument by stating, "in that case her killing herself, because, though she was not an adulteress, yet she endured the act of an adulterer, proves, not her love of chastity, but her irresolute shame" (1957: 89). And, he concludes, "for this reason she thought that she must present evidence before men's eyes to show what was in her heart – the evidence of that self-punishment, since she could not exhibit her conscience to them" (1957: 89).

While we may wish to dismiss Augustine's comments as indicative of a rather severe Christian patriarchal ideology about women and sin, his perspective does provide insight into the problematic that is Shakespeare's representation of Lucrece. In his expanded version of the Lucretia myth, Shakespeare creates a figure far more psychologically complex than his predecessors; and part of this complexity, I would argue, is imbued with the ideological assumptions that Augustine outlines in his commentary on Lucretia. Furthermore, Shakespeare's Lucrece explicitly struggles with the paradox that underscores the complex Christian attitude toward married women's sexuality: *any* sexual relations with a man other than one's husband *de facto* constitutes an act of adultery. The problem with this assumption, of course, is typified by Lucrece's situation. Is this notion to be held true in the case of a woman who is raped? Is adultery to be found only in "consensual" sexual relations between a married woman and someone else? How do we discover the *truth* as to whether a married woman's sexual relation with someone other than her husband is consensual or forced?

There are no clear-cut answers to these questions, especially within the contours of Christian doctrine about the innate sinfulness of women. Augustine's reflections on Lucretia, therefore, cannot help but waver between the two positions articulated in his writings: if she did not commit adultery there was no need for suicide; if in the course of the rape she experienced pleasure in the sexual act then she is an adulteress. Augustine does not believe that Lucretia is an adulteress and thus only condemns her act of suicide (which he views as the greater sin). This moral dilemma informs much of Shakespeare's Lucrece's confessional meditation. In the end, as Shakespeare's representation establishes, it is not what others think but what Lucrece believes herself to be.

When Tarquin's rape of Lucrece comes to an end, the narrator describes the behavior of both characters:

> He like a thievish dog creeps sadly thence;
> > She like a wearied lamb lies panting there.
> > He scowls, and hates himself for his offence;
> > She desperate, with her nails her flesh doth tear.
> > He faintly flies, sweating with guilty fear;
> > She stays, exclaiming on the direful night. (lines 736–41)

From this point on, the stage, as it were, belongs to Lucrece. In the speeches that follow, which I call Lucrece's moment of "confession," the raped woman not only resists the silence imposed upon her by Tarquin's threat to proclaim her an adulteress, but also his actual silencing of her voice with "the nightly linen that she" wore (line 680). These confessional speeches, I would argue, reflect the process of self-examination, contrition, and penance that informs early modern Christian confession in both its Catholic and its Protestant forms.

Immediately after she is raped by Tarquin, Lucrece gives voice to her despair. Shifting between rage, self-pity, shame, and despair, she simultaneously resists and acknowledges the confessional interiority that has come to be associated with "Christian" guilt: "'O unseen shame, invisible disgrace! / O unfelt sore, crest-wounding private scar! / Reproach is stamped in Collatinus' face" (lines 827–9). Railing against Tarquin, "Night," and "time," Lucrece finally abandons her lament and acknowledges that there is a "remedy" for her "foul defilèd blood" (line 1029). Determined to be "the mistress of my fate," she vows that "with my trespass never will dispense / Till life to death acquit my forced offence" (line 1070). A few lines later, she declares she will not "fold my fault in cleanly coined excuses. / My sable ground of sin I will not paint / To hide the truth of this false night's abuses" (lines 1074–5). Three points are crucial to Lucrece's thinking here: first, that Tarquin's rape has forced her to commit a sin; second, this sin, whether forced or consensual, and despite a presumption of secrecy, inevitably leaves its surface mark – a mark that can easily be read; and third, that she does have agency.

Interestingly, Lucrece's initial, and almost unconscious, reaction is to view her rape as affecting her familial and marital bonds, especially the latter. Without ever once using the term "race," Shakespeare manages to invest his narrative rendering of Lucretia's rape with all of the semiotic traces of early modern anxiety about defining a concept of race. Race is envisioned as something fundamental, something immutable, knowable and recognizable, yet we only "see" it when its boundaries are violated. It is this "seeing" that Shakespeare's narrative engenders in its rendering of Lucrece's confessional discourse. As the reproductive site for the continuation of her husband Collatine's line, Lucrece completely understands the immediate and future consequences of Tarquin's action – an accusation that she committed adultery and the possibility of pregnancy. She vows that Collatine "shalt not know the stained taste of violated troth"; that, in a noble gesture, she "will not wrong [his] true affection so, / To flatter thee with an infringed oath" (lines 1058–60). Promising that Tarquin's "bastard graff shall never come to growth," that he "shall not boast who did thy stock pollute / That thou are doting father of his fruit," Lucrece concludes that her only recourse is suicide. As she reasons, death will not only serve to expiate the immediate shame created by Tarquin's rape, but also will extirpate any potential offspring.[6] What is worth noting in Lucrece's words is her belief that Tarquin's rape has left its "racializing mark," on both her and Collatine's bodies.

The ironic paradox, of course, is that this sign is invisible except as it affects the imaginative threads of that locus of racial identity – heraldry. In Lucrece's mind, once the rape has been committed its inscription becomes indelibly etched on her body and by extension on Collatine's lineage. Where this sign becomes visible, as both Lucrece and Tarquin make clear, is in the heraldic depiction of their individual racial history. This illustrative signifier of race is understood to be the site where a nobleman's lineage, honor, and, importantly, acts of dishonor are publicly displayed. Tarquin's complicated self-reflexivity just prior to his rape of Lucrece explicitly draws attention to this belief. In a tense private moment, Tarquin confronts the "public" dimension of his "private" act: "O shame to knighthood and to shining arms! / O foul dishonour to my household's grave!" (lines 197–8). Tarquin is fully aware that should he carry out the rape, and should he die, the "scandal will survive" as "some loathsome dash the herald will contrive / To cipher me how fondly I did dote" (lines 204–6). This concern for family honor will surface once more when Tarquin acknowledges that "he [Collatine] is my kinsman, my dear friend, / The shame and fault finds no excuse nor end" (lines 237–8). Significantly, what Tarquin evokes in his words is his awareness that he should be thinking as a "racial" subject. That is, his consanguinity to Collatine and his own lineage are constitutive of his racial identity and bind him to action that respects those ties. In other words, his place within a race should be a sufficient deterrent to Tarquin's rape of Lucrece. Yet, as both this moment of voiced meditation and his later explanations to Lucrece demonstrate, lust recognizes no racial boundaries.

Though similarly deploying the rhetoric of heraldry in confronting the full implications of Tarquin's crime, Lucrece, in her moment of confession, sets the stage for a redefinition of racial identification. However, I want to argue that not until she acts to interpellate herself as a differently understood racial subject can Lucrece resolve the ideological dilemma created by Tarquin's rape.[7] The narrative mode deployed by Shakespeare in his poem intriguingly positions Tarquin and Lucrece as subjects capable of "hailing" not only each other but also themselves. For Lucrece, an alternative "interpellation" begins when she declares, "Let my good name, that senseless reputation, / Collatine's dear love be kept unspotted" (line 820). It is her name that enables her to act to expiate the "unseen shame," the "invisible disgrace," that marks both her body and Collatine's race as a result of Tarquin's rape. Lucrece's "hailing," however, is not just an interpellation of herself. This "hailing" also interpellates the readers of Shakespeare's narrative, effectively making them "agents in the reproduction of a violated body" on which a "narrative of liberation"[8] and an ideology of race become simultaneously (re)inscribed in history and, literally, on Lucrece's body, once "white," now marked by Tarquin's "racial stain." Importantly, it is in light of this "racial" marking that Lucrece's "reading" of the tapestry depicting the destruction of Troy can best be understood.

Searching for the face where "all distress is stelled" (line 1444), Lucrece finds solace in the painter's "anatomized" depiction of Hecuba: "In her the painter had anatomized / Time's ruin, beauty's wreck, and grim care's reign" (lines 1450–1). Hecuba's plight is the catalyst, the analogue, for Lucrece's own grief. Furthermore, her identification with the women of Troy, I would argue, also reminds the narrative's readers of another link between Rome and Troy: the commonplace mythography that the descendants of the Trojan Aeneas founded the city of Rome. However historically inaccurate, the literary tradition that linked Rome's genealogy to the fallen city of Troy and Aeneas and the mythography of his grandson Brutus as founder of Britain proved a useful trope for the emerging sense of national and ethnic consciousness in early modern England.

The poem's ekphrasis serves to illuminate not so much a cultural historiography as Lucrece's movement from one form of racial consciousness (and thus subjectivity) to another. While Lucrece condemns the presumed agent of Troy's fall, Helen—"show me the strumpet that began this stir / That with my nails I may tear" (lines 1471–2) – it is clear that Lucrece's condemnation is directed principally at the perpetrator of the heinous crime which directly concerns her. It is Tarquin Lucrece has in mind when she utters the fateful words, "for trespass of thine eye, / The sire, the son, the dame, and daughter die" (lines 1476–7). Yet none of this is evident when she questions, "why should the private pleasure of some one / Become the public plague of many moe? / Let sin, alone committed, light alone / Upon his head that hath transgressed so" (lines 1479–82). Lucrece's words eventually will prove prophetic when, as a result of her suicide, Rome is plunged into civil war.

Though Lucrece has committed no sin, in her despair and shame she finds in the image of the chaos that is the fallen Troy the subjectivity she will need to castigate the potential sin engendered by Tarquin's rape, his "bastard graff." Drawing upon the emotions stirred by the painting of the fallen Troy, Lucrece moves from silence to speech: "And now this pale swan in her wat'ry nest / Begins the sad dirge of her certain ending" (lines 1611–12). Later, in the presence of her husband and her kin, she conducts her own disciplinary ritual of forgiveness: "confessing" the narrative of Tarquin's rape, displaying her contrition by "castigating" the polluted body that continues Collatine's line, and finding "absolution" in the vow sworn by her husband and kin to redress the wrong against her honor. Like the ekphrasis on the destruction of Troy, Lucrece's "confession" renders visible the invisible stain of sin that is her dishonor. Though assured that she is blameless, Lucrece refuses absolution, saying "'No, no … no dame hereafter living / By my excuse shall claim excuse's giving'" (lines 1714–15).

This image is further instantiated when Lucrece sheaths "in her harmless breast/ A harmful knife, that thence her soul unsheathed" (lines 1723–4). In her attempt to exorcise Tarquin's violation of her body, Lucrece takes her own life. Yet the use of the word "sheath," with its obvious erotic signification, subtly undermines the high tragedy of this suicide, shadowed by the image of Tarquin's "gaze" which also rendered her breast a site of erotic desires. Lucrece's body, therefore, suffers penetration not once but twice. Once more involving the reader in a prurient gaze, Lucrece's self-inflicted wound is intended to purify, to "tear" away, the flesh that bears not only disgrace but the very real possibility that Tarquin's "momentary joy" might breed "months of pain" (line 690). Surrounded by her husband, father, and kin, Lucrece elicits from these men a vow to revenge her violated body. What Lucrece's demand entails is more than familial revenge, however; the vow the men make binds them as a "gens" or "ethnos" against Tarquin. Her confession heard and her shame absolved by the men who stand before her, Lucrece's body becomes the figurative and literal site where one meaning of race and racial identity ends and another begins.

Early modern readers of Shakespeare's *Rape of Lucrece* would, most likely, have been familiar with the ethnic mythology signified in the poem's ekphrasis. Whether or not this audience would have linked the final image of the narrative, where Lucrece's body is "paraded" through Rome as a testament to the tyranny of Tarquin, to an emergent notion of race as constituted in ethnicity is a matter of speculation. This sixteenth-century encounter with the political and ideological semiotics associated with the rape of Lucrece denotes, in a striking and persistent articulation, the necessary engendering of one's ethnicity through violence against the colonized (and generally female) body. What emerges in the aftermath of Lucrece's suicide is the embodiment of the Roman Republic and unified ethnos, and ultimately the Roman Empire; even as that suicide enacts the deracination of Tarquin's own lineage, what emerges in Shakespeare's retelling of the rape and suicide of Lucrece is the continued necessity to retell the rape to maintain the boundaries of that racial ideology. English imperialism required such a narrative.

Lucrece's Voice

For nearly a thousand years, the culture and politics of the Roman Republic and Empire have provided institutions and ideologies for developing nation states. The most influential of these phenomena, without doubt, is Christianity (despite its genesis within Judaism,

Christianity takes hold in the Roman Empire); the other was ethnos.[9] Early Christianity, in turn, set into motion the complex and contradictory, theological and patriarchal ideologies that came to govern societies such as the one Shakespeare inhabited and the empires they set out to create. My reading of Shakespeare's *Rape of Lucrece* through the double lens of confession and race has been an attempt to acknowledge these two powerful institutions as crucial to an understanding of his retelling of the Lucretia myth. Though Shakespeare ventriloquizes Lucrece's voice, he offers her a psychological complexity not evident in his source texts. This complexity, in my view, is achieved through the deployment of an interiority that can only be produced within the confessional mode of discourse.

This interiority, in turns, is also instrumental in Lucrece's perception of herself as a racial subject. It is this latter self-awareness that strikes me as potentially useful for recognition of Lucrece's act of resistance. If Tarquin's rape functions to "interpellate" her as an adulterous subject, then her suicide is a refusal to acknowledge that "hailing."[10] This act of agency, therefore, is a feminist one. In this light, Lucrece's suicide, and the rationale behind it, is analogous to the actions of African women who took their own lives rather than allow themselves to be raped or made slaves. As feminists we may deplore such actions, but such dislike should not blind us to the fact that the actions are self-determined acts of power and thus female agency.

Shakespeare's *The Rape of Lucrece* implicitly links the Roman Lucretia to early modern England's conceptualization of its participation in the humanist project, which in turn becomes a central tenet of modern imperialism and colonialism. Recognition of this, and the syncretic ways this tenet continues to require interrogation, must become part of feminist theorizing. The icon of Lucretia serves not just as a strategy of acculturation and assimilation; it equally functions to create a complicated relationship between self-sacrifice and femininity, politics and ethnicity, rape and progress. In what loosely might be termed "border theorizing," postcolonial critics and theorists have isolated a conceptual space where, as Françoise Lionnet argues, "all of our academic preconceptions about cultural, linguistic, or stylistic norms are constantly being put to the test by creative practices that make visible and set off the processes of adaptation, appropriation, and contestation that govern the construction of identity in colonial and postcolonial contexts" (1995: 111).

Lionnet's observation, while made in reference to francophone women writers, has bearing on the issues which concern feminism in general, and as considerations of race and post-colonialism continue to make inroads in early modern studies, feminist readings of Shakespeare's canon. Feminist considerations of *The Rape of Lucrece* might inquire whether, as part of Shakespeare's importance to English colonialism, especially in Africa and India, his *Rape of Lucrece* played a role in the development of feminist social consciousness among indigenous women, despite the narrative poem's tragic ending. Does the distinction between private and public blur the fact that Lucrece's body is a confessional political body? How did indigenous Western-educated ("subaltern") women "read" Lucrece's rape? Did Lucrece's rape and "confession" become unsettled in the modern colonialist project? Did these indigenous women see Lucrece's suicide as an exemplary model of "feminist" resistance to English hegemony and their own country's liberation? Did these women view the politics of Lucrece's confession and suicide as the female body literally and/or figuratively (as the idealized mother country or female territory) being transformed from victim to political agent in the pursuit of national liberation? Are there postcolonial rewritings of this master narrative of female chastity and sacrifice that challenge not only the humanistic ideology that has kept *The Rape of Lucrece* symptomatically part of cultural capital, but also the imperialist ideology that privileges only one definition of race?

The questions outlined above require more than this brief excursion can allow. Shakespeare's narrative poem, however, does offer feminist scholarship an opportunity to continue to define the terrain of Shakespeare scholarship. And, in taking up the challenges posed by these queries and the problematic Lucrece, feminist critics will once more see that her voice is always political.

ALLIANCE AND EXILE
APHRA BEHN'S RACIAL
IDENTITY

[Passing is] hazardous business . . . this breaking away from all that was familiar and friendly to take one's chance in another environment, not entirely strange, perhaps, but certainly not entirely friendly. What, for example, one does about background, how one accounted for oneself. (Nella Larsen, *Passing*)

Exilio

In May 1660, Charles II ended a decade-long period of exile, and with him returned a group of courtiers whose patronage would enable Aphra Behn not only to embark on a career as a professional writer but also to sustain that endeavor. Yet this return did not end the psychological effects that exile had on the returning royalists. In spite of a concerted effort to resume life as if the "rebellion" had never occurred, Charles and his court were never entirely able to put this moment of alienation and displacement to rest. In much of the writing produced during the Restoration, exile was a recurring theme or trope. This theme persisted despite the cynicism, secularism, and hedonism that came to be trademarks of Charles's reign. The irony, of course, is that these writings were not produced in exile, but in the very space from which the writer was initially exiled—England. In effect, what transpires is that the formerly exiled subject writes poignantly and tellingly about the experience of exile after the fact. From a psychological perspective, writing about the exile may have functioned as a cathartic exercise for the writer, as well as an attempt to conjure a sense of community with other former exiles. Exilic writing thus serves a strategic political purpose, bringing about unity among those who had shared the King's exile and setting them apart from the rest of the King's court—especially those who had remained in England.

In what follows I will argue that the writings of Aphra Behn contributed to the period's exploration of exile; as a woman writing, she implicitly and explicitly engages exile and the pressure toward community from both a gendered and a racial subject position. For the woman writer, as Behn's pastoral lyric, "Our Cabal," and her poetic epistle, "To Mrs. Price," illuminate, the isolation of exile is intensified as is the need for a community of readers. Deploying gossip as an instrument of community building among the personas within the lyric and poetic epistle, Behn offers a gendered-specific means to resolve the isolation of exile for the woman writer. Yet, when considered in relation to Behn's other work on exile, *Oroonoko,* we realize that the problem of exile is not so easily redressed through the motif of gossip; in using these tropes of exile (isolation and need for community), Behn represents them in extreme forms of slavery and "racial" difference. Strikingly, in this quasiautobiographical writing the effect of such representations is to direct the reader's gaze to the possibility of racial passing, which demands the most absolute of exiles: an exile where there is no possibility of a return home—an exile chosen to avoid the oppression associated with the color of one's skin. If Maria Rosa Menocal is correct in suggesting that the "lyric is invented in bitter exile. And not just the normal and conventional and essentially metaphoric exile that is, perhaps, the condition of all poetry and of its reading" (pp. 91-92), then intuitively reading Behn's "Our Cabal" and "To Mrs. Price" (as well as *Oroonoko*) as exilic texts may make possible the decryption of a passing subjectivity.

. . .

Solace in Exile

Bartlett Giamatti notes, in his discussion of the centrality of exile to Petrarch, that exile is less a narrative strategy than an ontological state. Giamatti contends that Petrarch's "sense of identity depended on being displaced, for only in perpetual exile could Petrarch gain the necessary perspective on himself truly to determine, or create, who he was. Only by being eccentric, could he center, or gather in and collect, his self" (p. 13). Only by being "eccentric" "Other" can the poet achieve that distance required to embark on the revision of his marginality. Marginality, displacement, alienation, loss, desire, nostalgia—these are the tropes of exilic writing. Aphra Behn's pastoral lyric, "Our Cabal," reflects an engagement of this psychological complexity inherent in exilic writing with its representation of authorial voice and the problem of isolation. The poem opens with a lighthearted exhortation to two friends, "Come, my fair Cloris, come away,/ Hast thou forgot 'tis Holyday? / And lovely Silvia too make haste" (Behn, 1993, p. 47). For the remainder of the lyric, the reader is presented with an intimate gaze into a controversial discursive space—gossip.

Behn's use of the pastoral convention to frame her handling of gossip resonates with Patricia Meyer Spacks's suggestion that we think of "gossip" as a version of pastoral. Not just any gossip: the kind that involves two people, leisure, intimate revelation and commentary, ease and confidence" (p. 3). In this context, gossip is valued for "the opportunity it affords for 'emotional speculation'" (p. 3). Gossip provides a continuum where exchanges both private and public can be made. These exchanges can, as Spacks contends, have significant effect outside its original context. Yet, because gossip "insists on its own frivolity," it frequently reifies the tendency to view it as a morally or socially suspect form of discourse and thus dismissible. What needs to be iterated here is that gossip also is predicated on the notion of absence and on the creation of an "in-group" (a concept that will become clearer as this essay evolves).

Thomas Parrot's satire "The Gossips Greeting: Or, A new Discovery of such Females Meeting" (1620) illustrates this problematic tendency and the serious social implications of gossip that its "frivolity" masks. "The Gossips Greeting" depicts a conversation between two women (Doll and Bess) who have embarked on a visit to a woman who has just given birth. Their discussion centers on the circumstances of different women in the town or village where Doll and Bess live. In particular, the women's talk focuses on the situation of "gossip Kate," a woman whose husband, "whilst all the weeke at home poore heart she toyle, …doth abroad live of the spoyle." According to one of the women, Kate's husband "beates and spurnes her" and "doth keepe a Queane e'ne vnderneath her Nose." While Parrot's purpose in depicting the exchange is to "censure" these "proud, peevish, pavltry, pernicious, she-pot companions, those curious, careless, craft, carping, curtizanicall gossips," his tale engenders a very different portrait than his vituperative comments presuppose.

What becomes obvious in Parrot's characterization of gossip is that the women seem to recognize the importance of alliances and communities generated within, yet distinct from, those instituted by the larger social order, namely marriage and family. Doll and Bess (and others) apparently come together to exchange information, to participate in rituals associated with childbirth (including banquets), and to condemn the anti-female behavior exemplified in Kate's husband. These women's relationships and connections with other women seem to play an important part in not only the social aspect of their lives but also in their individual self-awareness. The alliance of women who form the gossip's network in Parrot's work resists the arbitrary delineation of gossip as trivial. Rather, they illustrate the ways in which this discursive act engenders a range of possibilities for women to function as social agents. For example, upon hearing of Kate's predicament, Doll declares that "were I to chuse againe, I ne're would loue / A ciuill man; a man to all mens sight, Louing and courteous." For, Doll reflects, "I see, and do perceiue it now, . . . / That countenance and conscience seldome gree." Doll's words, even if contradictory to Parrot's intent, attest to the power of the gossips' network; the lesson of Kate's fate, for all women, is to beware of what floats on the surface, for it just may be that—superficial.

Behn's "Our Cabal" similarly reveals the protean quality of gossip, yet with a somewhat different revelation. Transgressing the boundaries between literacy and orality, the poem figuratively "gossips" into existence a complex series of alliances: between reader and poem, reader and speaker, and reader and the women of the poem. As Spacks argues, "gossip speaks in the world's voice and elucidates the world's operation" (p. 8); this world, however, is embodied in one person, the narrator. Images of triviality, solidarity, and self-representation are textured by the readers' knowledge of the writer's isolation and, at the same time, her figurative centeredness in the lyric. As privileged spectators, the reader and the poet's companions thus become implicated in the speaker's act of gossip and the images she creates: "'Tis Philocles, that Proud In grate,/ That pays her Passion back with Hate" *(Works,* 55-56). Most of the speaker's comments, however, are intended to foster a link between the three women gathered in the room—"yes, Silvia, for sh'l not deny/ She loves, as well as thou and I"—or to convey a compassion toward those women abused by a lover, "Poor Doris, and Lucinda too." Even when the narrator sympathetically recounts the difficulties facing one lover, Martillo, there is an absence of condemnation for the object of Martillo's desire. Gossip thus serves not as a malicious force in Behn's lyric, but also as a powerful intervention in the larger world.

In the course of her narrative, the speaker tells Cloris about Philander's "passion" for Lycidas: "So innocent and young he is,/ He cannot guess what Passion is./ But all the Love he ever knew,/ On Lycidas he does bestow" (183-86). Earlier, Lycidas had been described as a "haughty Swain," who "Barely returns Civility" to the "Beauties" to whom he once vowed "much Love" (149-54). More important, as the speaker confides, Lycidas's fickleness is truly reprehensible because he "pays his Tenderness" to Philander (Mr. Ed. Bed.)" in a manner the speaker labels "too Amorous for a Swain to a Swain" (187-88). The frivolous intimacy established at the poem's inception gradually gives way in light of Cloris's disclosure of her affection for Philander. Warming to her account of Lycidas's perfidy, the speaker details his manner and record of abusing women's "hearts." Yet her words appear to be of no avail as, she reveals, she (and others) often have heard

Cloris "Vow, If any cou'd your heart subdue, / Though Lycidas you nere had seen, / It must be him, or one like him" (202-4). Her concern prompts the speaker to warn Cloris to "keep your heart at home" (200). Yet, realizing that her efforts are ineffectual, the speaker decides to try another tack and exhorts Cloris to "try thy power with Lycidas; / See if that Vertue which you prize,/ Be proof against those Conquering Eyes" (221-22).

The trace of scorn in these words sits uneasy against the sense of alliance that I am suggesting exists between the women in the chamber, yet I would argue that the speaker's challenge resonates with affection and friendship. Our ability to see the bond between the speaker and Cloris is heightened if we take seriously the significance of the poem's title, since the word cabal generally evokes images of secrecy, intrigue, and political coteries, usually comprised by men. Behn's use of the word to describe the group of three women gathered in the chamber, therefore, only serves to heighten the ironic disjunction between the poem's title and its contents, especially since the poem seems concerned not with state affairs but the affairs of women. Even so, by labeling the three women a cabal Behn resists the reification of her poem as merely frivolous. While the orality of the poem's gossip infers its place as part of a private exchange of information, the textuality of the poem emphasizes the importance of gossip to the formation of alliances. The small community of women depicted in the poem functions in the interest of female homosociality. These women gather to share information and offer advice and warnings. Alliance, not competition and rivalry, becomes the frame of reference for the three women who make up Behn's cabal. Gossip and "cabal," as both contradictory terms and social paradigms, work to engender a radical rewriting of the politics of both speech and agency among women.

Amid the seemingly trivial details of contradictory love affairs, heartless men, stunning beauty, and alliances recounted in "Our Cabal" is an image of exile so unassuming that it is easily overlooked: the poet writing. If exile is "a lifelong scenario of estrangement," then what enables the writer to come to terms with exile is her ability to create "not only a new space to exercise one's being but a medium through which to re imagine one's beginnings" (Seidel, p. 5). The idea of the pastoral thus powerfully aids this poetic exercise; its laconic and simple frames of reference (shepherds and shepherdesses, rural topography, and emphasis on the idea of retreat) mark the linguistic intersections where the poet can find, if only temporarily, the means to ease the loss by constituting new alliances. In "Our Cabal," Behn's idealization of alliance conceals the fact that the figure who sits at the center of the alliance, the speaker, is in fact alienated from that which she narrates. Yet the poem itself reminds us that exiles do work in isolation, to create a "psychic space" in order to "weave their web of story." The illusion of conversation, of gossip, is what points to the exile of the represented authorial voice in "Our Cabal." Behn's use of gossip incorporates the writer and reader as speaking and listening subjects, respectively, thereby implicating both as sharers in the communal narrative under construction. Yet, because she is both speaker and writer, Behn mediates the ways this representation can be understood. As Spacks rightfully argues, in gossip the "presence of even a single observer would change the conversation's character: no longer true gossip, only a simulacrum" (p. 8). The creation of a spectorial position that encompasses reader and writer as one masks this fact in Behn's poem.

"Our Cabal" is indeed a simulacrum, one shaped by the self-reflexivity of the writing poet, shadowing its ghostly images of exile in visions of alliance and community. Gossip permits the poet to indulge in a retreat into the idyllic world of the pastoral poem, where loss is defined only in terms of hearts. The poem purposely yet subtly refracts our gaze from its own exilic condition by highlighting the alliance between the three women, thereby concealing the alienated position of the writer who figures herself as simultaneously a member and an outsider of the figurative alliance imagined in "Our Cabal." The lyric is never free of the intrusive presence of its own constitutive moment; there is, after all, the specificity of a woman, Aphra Behn, writing a poetic account of an intimate exchange between friends long after the moment has passed. What "Our Cabal" reveals is the dialectics of writing the defense against the exilic condition; to frame a representation of community, especially through the trope of gossip, the poet must also frame its opposition: isolation and disconnectedness.

   Like "Our Cabal," the poetic epistle "To Mrs. Price" figuratively instantiates a pastoral defense against exile, though one which more explicitly elucidates the poet's sense of isolation and her desire to constitute a community to which she can belong. The letter writer begins by celebrating the absence of "noisy Factions of the Court" from the "peaceful Place where [she] gladly" resorts (1). This site is sylvan; the only sounds heard are the "gentle Sighs of Love" as "Nymphs and Swains" prepare for "rural Sports" (6-7). In such a world, the writer notes, any deviation from the norm is quickly redressed: "if by Chance is found a flinty Maid, / Whose cruel Eyes has Shepherds Hearts betray'd," she in "other Climes a Refuge . . . must find, / Banish'd from hence Society of Kind" (9--12). The epistle ends with the writer evoking images of union, of calm, of peace, and exhorting the addressee, "kind Aemilia," to "flie that hated Town, / Where's not a Moment thou canst call thy own," and "share the Pleasures I count only mine" (19--22). What floats to the surface of the epistle is the idyllic, the "retreat" of the poet into what is an acceptable form of exile-the pastoral economy. Yet the poet's own status as a lover (or beloved) in this economy is curiously ambiguous. As in "Our Cabal," the writer alludes to an involvement in an amorous relationship, but the language of the poem and epistles suggests that this relationship is long past and there is no indication that she is involved in a new one. The locus of the writer's attitude is one of detachment; she is, in effect, the unmarked observer in this tranquil community: part of, yet alien from, the "Society of Kind." Poignantly, she writes that "ev'ry Object adds to our Delight, / Calm is our Day, and peaceful is our Night," even as she sits in solitude penning an epistle to Aemilia.

   Benedict Anderson has argued that "communities are to be distinguished, not by their falsity / genuineness, but by the style in which they are imagined" (p. 16). The "imagined community" in "To Mrs. Price" is *one* where exile is an explicit condition of existence, but it is a condition that is idealized and desirable. In the interstices of the poet's meditation, however, we realize that what seeps to the surface of her exuberance is the emotional and psychic *state* that the lyric's pastoral conventions cannot entirely obscure. We, as privileged readers, discover what the exile comes to understand as the episteme of exile: there is no adequate replacement for what has been lost. In fact, what makes this epistle more revelatory than Behn's "Our Cabal" is that it paradoxically *engages* and avoids its own condition of existence. And, in an oft-repeated sign of deferral, the writer seeks not the society that surrounds her but the so ace of an already constituted alliance—in effect, seeking the "familiar and friendly."

"To Mrs. Price" illuminates the longing of the subject to resolve the psychic crisis of exile. Despite the pastoral setting, the easy congress among nymphs and swains, the tranquil days and peaceful nights, the writer *seems* uneasily reconciled with the "Happiness divine" which she claims to have found. Beneath the pastoral language and the air of calm is the suggestive unspoken: the psychic upheaval created by exile. The pastoral world our poet has turned to is a mixture of "tuneful Anger" and "Sighs of Love," of "Cruel *eyes,*" "flinty" maids, and "Nymphs and Swains." The epistle's language is replete with images of death, betrayal, and difference. What we discover upon closer scrutiny is that embedded in the pastoral imagery is a moving plea for succor, for relief from exile. Discord, betrayal, banishment, cruelty, flight, and death are constant reminders of the inadequacy of the pastoral epistle as a defense against exilic loss. As Isis and Thame join, "mixt, embracing, they together flie, / They Live together, and together Die," (15-16) the reader is aware that the joining is temporary, already anticipating its own demise. The word "Die" hovers over the lyric, a sign of mortality and loss, and perhaps despair, a striking contrast to the image of concord that directly follows. In the end, despite the writer's initial praise of the "peaceful Place where I gladly resort," one cannot help but wonder if there isn't a bit of self-mockery in the epistle's final words: "Haste for to meet a Happiness divine, / And share the Pleasures I count only mine" (21-22).

The epistle leaves the reader with an image of a female alliance that is all the more significant when we consider that the epistolary form is an attempt to bridge the disconnectedness and the isolation of the writer, and the loss (even if temporarily) of community or alliances. The epistle is framed in solitude and inflected by the loss of a lover and the potential loss of a friend even as its discourse harkens to an alliance. The epistle's writer makes use of Aemilia's absence to consider the effects of the loss of connection by revisiting the moment in which the connection was engendered. Even so, Behn's epistle reveals none of the sadness or the emotional sorrow associated with exile; for in the moment when the writer must confront her loss, she defers the inevitable reckoning by dealing with another's passions. Exile is deferred but not erased.

"Ego in exilio genitus, in exilio natus sum"

"Was Aphra Behn passing?"

    This question was put to me during a brief conversation with African-American scholar Frances Smith Foster concerning Behn's personal and professional history. Foster's question clearly implied color passing and my reply was a decisive "no," for it seemed to me, at the time, that Behn's biographers were quite thorough and the evidence indisputable. However, as I pursued my consideration of Behn's writings and the cultural milieu in which she lived, Foster's softly spoken query haunted my reflections. Questions multiplied, leaving their liminal traces in every opinion, every sentence, every paragraph of what I read.

    The word "passing" has a curious and complex sociolexical history in Anglo-American culture. According to *Webster's International Dictionary*, the definition of pass is, "to move or be transferred from one place, state, or condition to another; to change possession, condition or circumstances, to undergo transition or conversion." The word, in both its noun and verb forms, has also come to signify death; that is, rather than say a person died, one might use the verbal phrase "he passed away" or "he passed on" or, simply, "he passed," or "his passing was unexpected." There is another definition of "passing" that has its genesis in all these definitions and yet is distinctive in its own right. This "passing" marks the process whereby a person self-consciously enters into an identity made possible by the instability and uninhabitability of the very ideologies created to prevent such entries. Once entering into this identity, however, the passer must maintain the boundaries of this identity, vigilantly guarding against the slippages, erasures, and exposures that once defined her/him in terms of another identity. The objective is never to be found out.

In one of the most cogent and intelligent discussions of racial and sexual passing, Amy Robinson writes that "sexual preference and race [provide modern racial theorists] . . . with a simple schema of optic dichotomies. That is, subjects were presumed to be either white or black, either straight or gay, as visual paradigms of racial and sexual identity manufactured presumption as a choice between legible social identities" (pp. 717-18) And, she continues, in "such an economy of readable identity, the successful passer only disappears from view insofar as she appears (to her reader) to be the category into which she has passed" (p. 718). Optic knowability, which is rooted in a simple paradigm of either/or identity and is "visible as an epistemological guarantee" to both the passer and the "dupe," is what makes the successful pass. Finally, according to Robinson, what enables passing is "the multiple codes of intelligibility," where an "in-group" ("the group from which one has passed") has intuitive recognition of the "prepassing identity," and a "duped" group sees the "manufactured presumption" of identity in terms of a simple paradigm of social identity. The result, Robinson cogently demonstrates, is a set of "competing rules of recognition," that is, rules predicated upon an opposition to a set of normative standards associated with epidermal, behavioral, or cultural difference.

If Behn was a "passer," from which parent did she inherit her black African ancestry? How did that ancestor end up in Canterbury, if the parish records cited by Behn's biographers are accurate? If she were of "mixed heritage" would there be a cultural necessity for her to engage in "racial passing"? Lastly, what clues, what sort of "evidence," did she leave behind for an inquisitive reader, and can her writings be used to decipher the enigma? What if Behn intended her writings to be read as a "passing" narrative? What if the psychic trauma of conformity to a dominant paradigm of racial identity in early modern English culture engendered in the subject Aphra Behn a hypersensitivity to the contradictions between the passer's ethnicity and the dominant culture into which she assimilates? How would she go about inscribing codes of intelligibility that aid the "reading" of the pass? To explore these and other questions, one would need to argue for a textual and biographical history that if Behn did pass the pass would not be documented—at least not in conventional ways. The reason is obvious: for the individual who engages in color passing, there is always the danger of being found out, of being exposed as a passer. One fears the birth of children, the chance meeting with someone from the old community, the invisible traces of blackness. Passing clearly was not something one did on a whim.

Rather than attempt to prove definitively that Behn may have had a black African ancestor and that, as a result, she was engaged in color passing, I propose to explore the semiotic "machinery" that triggers for an "in-group" the very question Foster asked of me. The problem in the analysis is that in order for a pass to be known there has to be a relationship of complicity between the passer and an "in-group," usually on the part of anyone who knew the passer before the pass. This person (or persons) generally acquiesces to the pass by not revealing it. The epistemological difficulty in my analysis is that Behn and anyone constituted as a contemporaneous member of an "in-group" died three hundred years ago. However, there is another way of "knowing" the pass, of establishing one's status as a member of the "in-group" intuition. By "intuition," I am invoking Robinson's deployment of the word: "If the action of sight requires a subject, then intuition summons a denotation of unmediated access to a truth whose function is the fortification of the subject who looks. It is thus no accident that the eyes are named as the privileged vehicle of intuitive knowledge" (p. 720). What intuition enables, in Robinson's words, is the "visibility of the apparatus of passing literally the machinery that enables the performance. What the in-group sees is not a stable prepassing identity but rather the apparatus of passing that manufactures presumption (of heterosexuality, of whiteness) as the means to a successful performance" (p. 721).

Throughout this discussion, the possibility of a "passing" Aphra has stood quietly, a cultural wraith hovering at the margins of my reading and, I would argue, who stood looking over the poet's shoulder, guiding her quill as she embeds the codes of intelligibility and the traces of her passing in her literary writings. In the conflicting signifiers of alliance and estrangement, the question of racial subjectivity dances tantalizingly on the margins in an illusory (and at times elusive) gesture of remembrance until it finds release in the writing subject's most explicit narrative of exile, the novella *Oroonoko*. What I propose to do in the final pages of this essay is to position my reader as a member of the "in group" that forms part of the triangular condition of Behn's pass, and to guide this reader through an act of intuition to literally discern the pass.

Published in 1688, *Oroonoko* ostensibly recounts the biographical history of an African prince forcibly taken from his homeland and sold into slavery in the English colony of Surinam. The story of Oroonoko's exile is purportedly told to the author, who in turn localizes that narrative in print form. In the telling of Oroonoko's history, the narrator also instantiates her own, producing what Margaret Ferguson notes are complex and multivalent representations of early modern colonial subject positions. In this and other recent feminist discussions of *Oroonoko*, readings of the racial dimension of the novella have centered on the complicated figuration of author and narrative object (Behn and Oroonoko), white woman and black man (again Behn and Oroonoko), and white woman and black woman (Behn and Imoinda). Because the narrator represents herself as a member of the dominant class, and because this representation is taken as "true," the possibility of a third racial paradigm is rarely considered: namely, that the racial triangulation may not be white/black/black, but black/black/black. To explain this provocative hypothesis I want to focus on two often noted yet narrowly read descriptions in the novella. The first is the complicated description of Oroonoko's racial identity. According to the narrator, Oroonoko was:

> pretty tall, but of a shape the most exact that can be fancied; the most famous statuary could not form the figure of a man more admirably turned from head to foot. His face was not of that brown, rust black which most of that nation are, but a perfect ebony, or polished jet. His eyes were the most awful that could be seen, and very piercing; the white of them being like snow, as were his teeth. His nose was rising

and Roman, instead of African and flat. His mouth, the finest shaped that could *be seen;* far from those great turned lips, which are *so* natural to the *rest* of the *Negroes.* The whole proportion and air of his face was so noble, and exactly formed, that, bating his colour, there could nothing in nature more beautiful, agreeable and handsome. (Behn, 1992, p. 81)

Interestingly, Margaret Ferguson does not make much of this description in her otherwise excellent analysis of *Oroonoko.* Laura Brown, on the other hand, argues that, in describing Oroonoko, "Behn's narrator seems to have only two choices: to imagine the other either as absolutely different and hence inferior, or as identical and hence equal" ((Laura Brown, "The Romance of Empire: Oroonoko and the Trade in Slaves," in *The New Eighteenth Century,* ed. Laura Brown and Felicity Nussbaum (New York: Methuen, 1978), p. 48). Thus Brown views the description of Oroonoko as the "failure of Behn's novella to see beyond the mirror of its own culture [that] here raises the question of Behn's relationship with the African slave" (p. 48).

Brown's observation points tantalizingly to what is an intriguing depiction in Behn's novella: the inverse mirroring implied in that relationship when the novella is read as a text of passing. In other words, what the novella may position the "knowing" reader to do is to ignore the optical illusion and "intuit" that Oroonoko is constitutive of the authorial subject, just as the authorial subject contains the black African. To read Behn's novella in this fashion, of course, undermines not only assumptions about Behn's racial identity but also our own complicity in the "false promise of the visible as an epistemological guarantee" (Robinson, p. 716). I want to argue that Behn's novella, coming as it does at the end of her life, schematizes an optic dichotomy whereby the passer reveals herself to an "in-group." It is this suggestive but unexamined possibility, latent but unexamined in any of the recent criticism of *Oroonoko,* that Behn invites "us to see and ponder the fact that we are not seeing the 'whole truth' about her white or non-white characters, including herself" (Ferguson, 1994, p. 189).

Nearly two-thirds into the narrative the narrator remarks:

My stay was to be short in that country, because my father died at *sea*, and never arrived to possess the honour was designed him (which was lieutenant-general of six and thirty islands, besides the continent of Surinam), nor *the* advantages *he* hoped to reap by them, so that though we *were* obliged to continue on our voyage, *we* did not intend to stay upon the place. (Behn, 1992, p. 115)

This interjection, of course, serves two purposes: first, it validates the authenticity of the narrative by concretizing the author's presence in both the story and Surinam; and second, it allies the author to the governing structure of the slave society that is Surinam. In addition, the passage also establishes the involuntary exile to Surinam of both narrator and Oroonoko. Both individuals have been brought to an alien world; the difference is that one enters this world as a slave and the other as, ostensibly, a member of the conquering class.

What is interesting about this "biographical" statement is that nowhere before or after are readers made privy to the Christian names of the narrator or her father. This oversight(?) takes on greater importance when one considers that, since the initial publication of *Oroonoko*, the novella has been used as an evidentiary site in the historical excavation of Aphra Behn's life. One explanation for this absence of patronymic detail is, of course, the fact that Behn is writing a fictional narrative and such details are not necessary for plotting. Another, and more controversial, reason may well reside in the notion that the passage is intentionally ambiguous; that Behn chooses not to name her father or, more relevant to this discussion, her mother. It is this latter possibility that intrigues me. Were we to read *Oroonoko* as the passing subject's "subtle claim of telling in the absence of knowing-[or] 'it takes one to know one'"-we might discover a more complex enunciation of the racial subjectivity of an author in exile. (See Amy Robinson, "It Takes One to Know One: Passing and Communities of Common Interest." *Critical Inquiry* 20 (Summer 1994), pp. 721.)

Central to my reading is the supposition that it is in exilic writing that we find the codes that would reveal the pass. Though not often described as such, the phenomenon of passing is literally a form of exile. As the passage from Nella Larsen's novel *Quicksand and Passing* cited at the opening of this essay indicates, the passing subject breaks away from "all that is familiar and friendly" and constitutes a new identity and a new life "in another environment, not entirely strange, perhaps, but certainly not entirely friendly" (pp. 186-87). Part of this constitution involves replacing old alliances with new ones, finding ways to negotiate the very real possibility that one can never return to the pre-passing environment without revealing the pass. For the passing subject, as this essay's epigram suggests, the pass is not without costs. In writing about the exile, one becomes acutely and often painfully aware of the intricate liability of her or his identity, for exile allows time, ever so much time to reflect on what it means even to conceive of oneself as an individual, as a subject, as an exile.

What deep secrets about her identity would Behn desire to conceal in the fictive anonymity of her genesis? Is there more to her "exile" than she tells? The possibility that there may be a more direct tie linking the novella's author and Oroonoko—a link forged not in Surinam but in that miscegenous space of the early modern European slave trade—has not been explored. What if the narrator's grandmother was of African ancestry and, given the dire situations facing any person of African bloodlines in early modern English colonies, the novella's author was engaged in racial passing? How might the narrator discursively constitute Oroonoko's identity in light of anxiety associated with her own possible pass? To broach these questions (and attempt to address them) is to insist upon a critical awareness that, in the early modern English colonial spaces, not all relations of miscegenation necessarily ended as *Othello* or *Titus Andronicus*. Despite George Best's assertion that "blackeness proceedeth of some natural infection of the first inhabitants of that Countrey, and so all the whole progenie of them descended, are still polluted with the same blot of infection ... by a lineall discent they have hitherto continued thus blacke" (Hakluyt, vol. 7, pp. 262--63), time proved this assumption a genetic fallacy: within four generations of miscegenation, the "White Ethiop" was a very real possibility, and with it the passing subject. And, it is this porous aspect of genetics, complicating the ideology of race, that marks the narrator's complex and troubling representations of self and Oroonoko.

In his study of writing and exile, *Transgressions of Reading: Narrative*

Engagement as Exile and Return, Robert D. Newman argues that what exiled writers do is "continually define themselves in relation to what is absent, their homeland, which they simultaneously embrace and deny. Their recreation of that homeland, necessarily infused with irony, demonstrates memory as a revisionary act and history as an exercise in narrative memory" (pp. 1-2). As a consequence:

> their mental [or, I would posit, poetic] returns are guided by the necessity of making that home, which was once an extension of Self, Other, in part so as to preserve the home that now is. This necessitates alienation from oneself, the Self that was and that still is present as an influence upon and aspect of the present Self. (p. 2)

For Newman, "irony" becomes a "natural vehicle for the writer as exile. The authorial Self is extended into the character functioning within a setting that recalls a previous Self of the author through a present interpretation, and thus must be ironically distanced as Other" (p. 2). And Newman concludes, "readers engaged by a text function much like exiles, viewing the narrative as a type of homeland in which they can no longer live." Persons who engage in racial passing must leave the community of their birth, their families, and, most important, all social and cultural traces of a "pre-passing" identity. What is not discarded (as passing literature demonstrably illustrates) are the "mnemonic traces" of connection, kinship, and belonging, which form the basis of a desire to recreate if not the originary community itself at least a simulacrum. What these exiles discover is that substitute can never stand in for the original. There is no return home.

In the silent space of the poet's room, did the poet's subjectivity come into existence as a memoir of a moment that is a remembrance of a racial past? Did Behn glance out a small window overlooking a busy street in St. Bride's Parish and see a woman of African ancestry struggling to deal with the life of servitude engendered by the color of her skin? Did Behn mentally strip the blouse from the woman's back and see the evidence of a maternal ancestor's resistance to slavery, to rape? Did she see the African man who had fathered the woman's first child and died trying to prevent both from becoming property of the

Portuguese, Dutch, or English slaver? Did Behn unconsciously perceive in the woman the liminal figure of a mother whose *mestizaje* (mixedness) drew the sexual attention of a white planter in Barbados? Are these the constitutive images, the "secret ciphers," along with her own passing, inscribed in the representations of self and Oroonoko, in the depiction of non-royal black Africans? Is the African prince the self who constitutes Behn's 'other,';an abject display of the psychic trauma of passing?

There are no definitive answers to these queries; not enough evidence exists even to establish with absolute certainty Behn's parentage, let alone her ethnicity. What the questions allow me to do is to engage Behn's texts and her position as an authorial subject in early modern England in a manner that permits an epistemological rethinking of the early modern concept of race. It is most often in exile that racial memories can condition the poetics of writing. More significant, it is the resemblances of new alliances to earlier ones that often force the poet to revisit continually the painful memories of what has been lost and, in the process, to return to the moment which triggered the memory. This circularity of remembrance becomes, as it were, a tabula rasa for a "plausible history." Struggling to erase from memory the painful refrains of the *canzoniere di razza,* the *chanson de race,* or the *cantar de raza,* the poet seeks but fails to castigate from her soul the knowledge of her exile.

Writing from and in exile, the passer creates with an aim to "feign telling the truth by feigning to feign" (Derrida, pp. 84-85). The secret cipher of the author's race becomes intelligible when read not only through *Oroonoko* but, more important, through each of Behn's other works as well. However, this intelligibility can only occur when exile ceases to be metaphoric and becomes actual: that is, when alliances and communities fragment, and the narrator can no longer poetically mediate the condition of her exile. Although "Our Cabal," "To Mrs. Price," and *Oroonoko* were published, they resonate as private exchanges, a confidential diary left open for the invading reader, revealing the extraordinary psychic price of exile and passing. The passer must create new alliances and a new identity in an alien world. And although Behn's poetic writings reveal that, for a woman in exile, the creation of alliances with women may somewhat alleviate the sense of loss, the pain of exile never truly disappears. It is not implausible that, in the "secret ciphers" that mark her texts, Aphra Behn has left behind the inscriptions of the genealogy of her exile, her passing, for the intuitive reader. Perhaps, in the figure of Isis (with its dual allusion to the English river near Oxford and the Egyptian goddess, both of which Behn would have known) Behn writes the double histories of her origins and exile. Perhaps, in writing women's alliances into her poetic meditations on exile, Behn came to understand the painful irony that forever escapes women such as Irene Redfield in Larsen's *Quicksand and Passing:* when passing, a person can never fully account for herself until the two halves of her divided self "live together, and together Die."

WORK CITED

"A Painter's Eye: Gender In Middleton and Dekker's *The Roaring Girl*."

Originally published in *Women's Studies: An inter-disciplinary journal* (1990) Vol. 18, pp. 191-203. Copyright 1990. Reproduced with permission of the Licensor through PLSclear.

1. Thomas Middleton and Thomas Dekker, *The Roaring Girl*, ed. Andor Gomme (London: Ernest Benn Limited, 1976). All other quotations will refer to this edition.
2. See, for example, Jean E. Howard, "Crossdressing, The Theatre, and Gender Struggle in Early Modern England," *Shakespeare Quarterly* 39, 4 (1988), 417-439; Mary Beth Rose, *The Expense of Spirit: Love and Sexuality in English Renaissance Drama* (Ithaca: Cornell University Press, 1988), particularly 43-93; and Phyllis Rackin, "Androgyny, Mimesis and the Marriage of the Boy Heroine on the English Renaissance Stage," *PMLA*, 102 (1987) 29-41.
3. Most studies of Renaissance women's social history begins with Lawrence Stone's *The family, sex and marriage in England, 7500-7800* (New York: Harper & Row, 1977). For revisions of Stone's assessment see Martin Ingram, *Church Courts, Sex and Marriage in England, 7570-7640* (Cambridge: Cambridge University Press, 1987) and Susan Dwyer

Amussen, *An Ordered Society: Gender and Class in Early Modern England* (London: Basil, Blackwell, 1988).

4. The discussion began with Louis Adrian Montrose's essay "Renaissance Literary Studies and the Subject of History," and Jean E. Howard's "The New Historicism in Renaissance Studies" both in *English Literary Renaissance* 16 (1986), 6-7; 27-35. The best articulation of the feminist position is seen in Lynda E. Boose, "The Family in Shakespeare Studies; or - Studies in the Family of Shakespeareans; or - The Politics of Politics" *Renaissance Quarterly* 40 (Winter, 1987), 707-742, and Carol Thomas Neely, "Constructing the Subject: Feminist Practice and the New Renaissance Discourses" *English Literary Renaissance* 18 (1988), 5-18. I think the most cogent position on the argument is to be found in an essay of Judith Newton, "History as Usual? Feminism and the 'New Historicism'" *Cultural Critique* (1988), 87-121.

5. Teresa de Lauretis, *Technologies of Gender: Essays on Theory, Film, and Fiction* (Bloomington: Indiana University Press, 1987), 2. Current feminist discourse, particularly in the United States, has a peculiar sexual bias which often overlooks the material conditions of women's existence and history. The theoretical dichotomy, between issues of sexual differences and the material conditions of gender, has recently been addressed in an essay by Tori! Moi, "Feminism, Postmodernism, and Style: Recent Feminist Criticism in the United States" *Cultural Critique* (1988), 3-22.

6. Vivien Brodsky Elliott, "Single Women in the London Marriage Market: Age, Status and Mobility, 1598-1619," *Marriage and Society: Studies in the Social History of Marriage*, ed. by R.B. Outhwaite (New York, St. Martin's Press, 1981), 91.

7. For a discussion of the role of family and community in marital relations see Martin Ingram, *Church Courts, Sex and Marriage in England, 7570-7640*, 189-218.

8. Marilyn L. Williamson, *The Patriarchy of Shakespeare's Comedies*. (Detroit: Wayne State University Press, 1986), 119.

9. See Margaret W. Ferguson, Maureen Quilligan, and Nancy J. Vickers, *Rewriting the Renaissance: The Discourses of Sexual Difference in Early Modern Europe* (Chicago: University of Chicago Press, 1986), particularly the introductory discussion. For an insightful discussion of

Elizabeth I as a "gendered subject" see Louis Adrian Montrose, "The Elizabethan Subject and the Spenserian Text" in *Literary Theory/Renaissance Texts,* edited by Patricia Parker and David Quint (Baltimore: Johns Hopkins University Press, 1986), 303-340.

10. Mary Beth Rose, "Women in Men's Clothing: Apparel and Social Stability in *The Roaring Girl." English Literary Renaissance* 14 (1984), 389-390.

11. Martin Ingram, *Church Courts, Sex and Marriage in England, 7570-7640,* 302-319.

12. Both Martin Ingram and Susan Dwyer Amussen discuss the use of community and ecclesiastical pressure to regulate social behavior. For additional discussions see G.R. Quaife, *Wanton Wenches and Wayward Wives: peasants and illicit sex in early seventeenth century England* (New Brunswick: Rutgers University Press, 1979) and Keith Wrightson, *English Society, 7580-7680(London:* Hutchinson & Co., 1982).

13. Mary Prior, ed. *Women in English Society 7500-7800(London:* Methuen, 1985).

14. Jean E. Howard, "Crossdressing, The Theatre, and Gender Struggle in Early Modern England," *Shakespeare Quarterly* (vol. 39 no. 4, 1988) 439.

15. Harold Weber, *The Restoration Rake-Hero: Transformations in Sexual Understanding in Seventeenth-century England* (Madison: University of Wisconsin Press, 1986), 133. I single out Weber's essay on *The Roaring Girl* as it, in my view, exemplifies current discussion on the sexual subject of Moll Cutpurse. Feminist analysis of *The Roaring Girl* remains, with occasional exception, still quite rare.

16. 14.Susan Dwyer Amussen, *An Ordered Society: Gender and Class in Early Modem England* (London: Basil, Blackwell, 1988), 68.

"A word, sweet Lucrece: Confession, Feminism and *the Rape of* Lucrece.

. . .

An earlier version of this essay appeared in Orkin and Loomba (1998). I am 1 An earlier version of this essay appeared in Orkin and Loomba (1998). I am grateful to Martin and Ania for their judicious interventions and generosity. Dympna Callaghan is to be lauded for her patience and never-ending support. "This essay appears in *A Feminist Companion to Shakespeare* ed., Dympna Callaghan. 2nd edition. John Wiley & Sons Limited, copyright 2016. Reproduced with permission of the Licensor through PLSclear.

1. I do not take up what are probably the two seminal pieces of writing on Shakespeare's narrative poem, Nancy Vickers's two essays on Lucrece (Vickers 1985a; 1985b), as nearly every recent essay on Shakespeare's narrative poem engages Vickers's work and thus it need not be rehearsed here.
2. All references to *The Rape of Lucrece* are from *The Complete Oxford Shakespeare*, edited by Stanley Wells and Gary Taylor (1987).
3. In the discussion that follows, I am heavily indebted to Thomas N. Tentler's study *Sin and Confession on the Eve of the Reformation* (1977) for providing a general history of the system of penance and confession prior to the Reformation. Tentler's work provides a more easily accessible overview than the foundational work of Henry Charles Lea's *A History of Auricular Confession and Indulgences in the Latin Church* (1896).
4. I make this point because of the critical tendency to elide the chronological and historical boundaries that separate Shakespeare's "construction" of his narrative of the rape of Lucretia and those written by Livy and Ovid. This tendency has the effect of generating a problematic essentialism whereby there are no fundamental distinctions, culturally or ideologically, between Roman gender ideologies and those of early modern England.
5. Abercrombie, Hill, and Turner argue that "the insistence on chastity and virtue for wives as a condition for the economic strength of the feudal family was also closely connected with the ideology of chivalry. Since noble birth was a crucial feature of knighthood, only true-born sons would be brave and worthy of their families ... Confusion of blood produced unreliable men" (1980: 90).

6. According to Althusser, interpellation occurs when "ideology 'acts' or 'functions' in such a way that it 'recruits' subjects among the individuals (it recruits them all), or 'transforms' the individuals into subjects (it transforms them all) by that very precise operation which I have called interpellation or hailing, and which can be imagined along the lines of the most commonplace everyday police (or other) hailing: 'Hey, you there!'" When the individual turns to acknowledge the hailing, "he becomes a subject. Why? Because he has recognized that the hail was 'really' addressed to him, and that 'it was really him who was hailed' (and not someone else)" (1971: 174).

7. Jed observes that "every encounter with a representation of the rape of Lucretia is an encounter with a literary topos of Western civilization. And, as a topos, the meaning of this rape is constructed as universal, transcending historical conditions: in every age and place, Lucretia had to be raped so that Rome would be liberated from tyranny" (1989: 49).

8.This statement is not to deny the importance of Greece as the ideological genesis of "ethnos." It is important to recall that Rome, not Greece, has the most influence over Western Europe in the early modern period. 10 See Althusser (1971: 174).

"Alliance and Exile: Aphra Behn's Racial Identity"

"Alliance and Exile: Aphra Behn's Racial Identity," *Maids and mistresses, cousins and queens : Women's Alliances in Early Modern England* ed., Frye, Susan, and Robertson, Karen. copyright 1996. Oxford UP. Reproduced with permission of the Licensor through PLSclear."

RACE AND GENDER

THE POLITICS OF INTERSECTIONALITY: GRADUATE SCHOOL

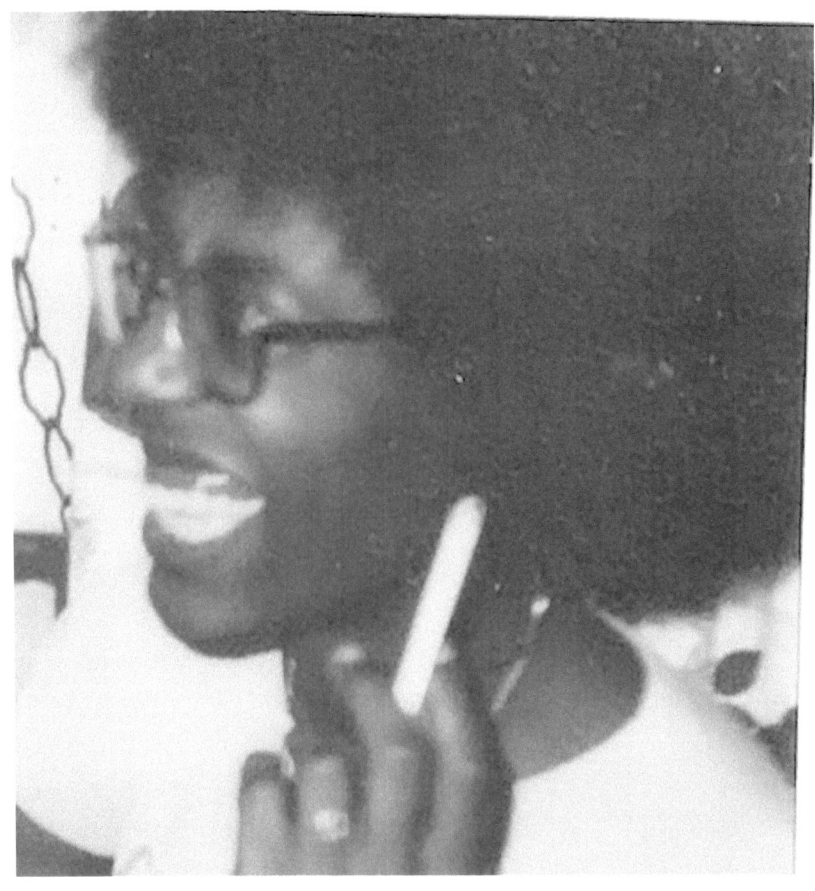

A FEMINIST HISTORIOGRAPHY

The choice of narrative implies that behind the vicissitudes of every narrative there are a set of a priori values – regarding time and materiality – that will emerge naturally from the 'natural' mode of narration. (Kearns 1997: 121)

The historian's decision to write about one facet of human experience and not another gives that aspect permanence and significance. For history represents a people's, a society's, a culture's way of remembering itself. Jacob Burckhardt described history to his nineteenth-century readers as 'the record of what one age finds worthy of note in another'. The recorded is saved, and conversely, the unrecorded is lost. (Zinsser 1993: 117)

Lorenzo: I shall answer that better to the commonwealth than you can the getting up of the Negro's belly. The Moor is with child by you, Lancelot.
Lancelot: It is much that the Moor should be more than reason, but if she be less than an honest woman, she is indeed more than I took her for. (*The Merchant of Venice*, 3.5.35–40)

The Problem of History

Since the publication of Jacob Burckhardt's *Civilization of the Renaissance in Italy* (1860) modern historiography about Renaissance cultures has been shaped by Burckhardt's insistence on the importance of the individual to these cultures. Apart from a few aristocratic females, women seemed to have played virtually no role in the 'civilizing' of cultures that (for Burckhardt) marks the 'Renaissance'. Furthermore, given the aims of 'traditional historiography', women as a group appeared to have only a tangential connection to the events and relations of power that produced 'History', with a few notable exceptions like Elizabeth I and Mary Stuart. For academic women interested in writing about ordinary ('common') women's lives, the place of such women in the grand narrative of 'English History' was a rather contested one. First, these historians faced the difficult challenge of proving that there was a history to tell, and that its telling required new methodologies. Second, because the majority of historians in the academy were male, any woman seeking to write women's history was likely to face criticism for wanting to deal with such supposedly trivial issues. Thus these early women historians often either acquiesced in the rules of traditional historiography – telling the story of major events, peoples, civilizations and ideas – or broke from the ranks and suffered marginalization and/or trivialization for their insistence on researching 'women's' histories.

The publication of Alice Clark's *Working Life of Women in the Seventeenth Century* (1919, reprinted 1982) marked a major turning point for the study of women's history. For the first time, the historian's concern with women as a group intruded itself into the telling of 'English History' and, by extension, into the question of historiography itself. Clark's book made the study of working-class English women's lives a legitimate and necessary component of labour historiography. Clark's book was followed by studies such as Carroll Camden's *The Elizabethan Woman* (1952), Ruth Kelso's *Doctrine for the Lady of the Renaissance* (1956) and Lawrence Stone's *The Family, Sex, and Marriage in England 1500–1800* (1977). These studies increased awareness of women's lives in Renaissance and early modern England, yet none represented itself as 'feminist historiography'. Not until Joan Kelly asked, 'Did Women Have a Renaissance?' did the problem of historiography become a feminist concern to scholars of Renaissance cultures. Kelly's essay, first published in 1977 (and reprinted in 1984), served as a clarion call for feminist historians (literary as well as social or cultural) to rethink their assumptions about the period called the Renaissance (Kelly 1984).

As Kelly argues, 'one of the tasks of women's history is to call into question' the accepted view of women's equality with men during the Renaissance (ibid.: 19). Furthermore, as she aptly demonstrates, the Italian Renaissance worked to foster a 'new division between personal and public life . . . and with that division the modern relation of the sexes made its appearance' (ibid.: 47). Since then historians have redefined the theoretical and historical tapestry of Renaissance and early modern cultures. Women's lives have been solidly woven into the narrative fabric of history – economic, political, social/cultural, intellectual and artistic. Historians of literature, culture, politics, philosophy and economics no longer ignore the role of women in helping to shape the contours of Renaissance English history.

Insisting that women's lives and activities were critical to Renaissance and early modern English social formations and their histories worth telling, feminist social historians helped to redraw the boundaries of historiography, thus prompting feminist scholars to reconsider not only their political relationship to the telling of history but women's role in making history. This 'second wave' of feminist historiography includes such works as Susan Amussen's *An Ordered Society: Gender and Class in Early Modern England* (1988), Keith Wrightson's *English Society 1580–1680* (1982), Margaret R. Sommerville's *Sex and Subjection: Attitudes to Women in Early-Modern Society* (1995), Martin Ingram's *Church Courts, Sex and Marriage in England, 1570–1640* (1987) and Anthony Fletcher's *Gender, Sex and Subordination in England 1500–1800* (1997). It has engineered a shift in the imperatives guiding historiography concerned with early modern English history. Hence, while it is possible to write a history of early modern England without 'attending to women', it is difficult to imagine that such a study will be accepted without some form of criticism.

Feminist and radical historiography, in its attempt to address

Kelly's provocative (at the time) question, 'Did Women have a Renaissance?', has fundamentally altered what constitutes normative historiography. Moreover, in tracing the history of labouring women, unruly women, women writers, mystics, rebellious women, as well as wives, mothers, daughters, sisters, whores, courtesans, tribades and 'spinsters', feminist cultural, social and literary historians have facilitated historicist approaches to literary texts and have broadened the basis of evidence that constitutes sites of discursive engagement. For example, Elaine Hobby's *Virtue of Necessity: English Women's Writing 1649–88* (1989) and Margaret Ezell's *Writing Women's Literary History* (1994) prompted a similar project in literary studies. Seeking to "re-vision" women's literary past and to reveal some of the assumptions embedded in the current model of feminist historiography concerning the connections between gender and modes of literary production and about historical conditions of authorship', these two very different works challenged traditional assumptions about our ability to 'recover' a past or a 'women's tradition' (Ezell 1994: 5–6).

We now take for granted the publication of anthologies such as *Kissing the Rod* (1989) and *Renaissance Drama by Women* (1996). Critical anthologies such as Early Women Writers: 1600–1720 (1998), *Re-writing the Renaissance* (1986), *Women, 'Race', and Writing in the Early Modern Period* (1994), *Feminist Readings of Early Modern Culture* (1996), *A Feminist Companion to Shakespeare* (2000), *Maids and Mistresses, Cousins and Queens* (1998) and *Rereading Aphra Behn* (1993) have forever changed the theoretical and intellectual landscape of Renaissance Studies. Editions of texts written by Renaissance and early modern women writers are no longer on the 'unavailable list'. We now have access to the collected works of Aphra Behn, Mary Wroth and Mary Sidney; individual editions of works such as Aemilia Lanyer's *Salve Deus Rex Judaeorum*, Elizabeth Cary's *The Tragedy of Mariam* and Anna Weamys's *A Continuation of Sir Philip Sidney's 'Arcadia'* (published under the auspices of the Women Writers Project at Brown University) have expanded our literary horizons and made us acutely aware of the contributions Renaissance women made to 'the Renaissance'. Recent technological innovations helped to generate Brown University's

'Renaissance Women Online' – a resource that continues to place more texts by women in the hands of students and scholars alike.

Like Joan Kelly's ground-breaking query, these timely interventions have triggered, among feminist scholars of Renaissance culture, a rethinking of theoretical and historical methodologies. Women's literary practices did not reside in a single genre, but rather emerged in a myriad of forms. And, importantly, authorial voice was not one of feminine singularity among pre-1700 women writers but one as varied as the experiences of the women writing. In particular, Margaret Ezell's *Writing Women's Literary History*, while not the only work to critique modern historiographical assumptions about pre-1700 women, was one of the few studies to interrogate a branch of feminist historiography and its relationship to the past. Since these pioneering studies, revisionary literary histories are being written that resist prescriptive categorization of women writers into 'feminist' or 'non-feminist' camps. Significantly, gender studies, queer studies and cultural studies have effectively redefined the terms of literary historiography.

Questions about the relationship between gendered identities and sexual identities and about the role of race and colonialism in the construction of history have begun to redefine the practice of cultural historiography. Similarly, since the publication of Alan Bray's *Homosexuality in Renaissance England* (1982), the complex (and often problematic) place of sexuality in Renaissance and early modern English culture has made us crucially aware of the significance of erotic desire not only in the lives of men but also in the lives of women. Women's challenges to patriarchal ideologies regarding female sexuality have been explored in feminist literary studies such as Susan Zimmerman's *Erotic Politics: Desire on the Renaissance Stage* (1992) and Ferguson's, Quilligan's and Vickers's *Re-Writing the Renaissance* (1986). Similarly, attention to the discourses of 'race' and colonialism in Renaissance English literary culture has grown by leaps and bounds. Within these studies women are of especial interest given the social constraints imposed by imperialist and colonialist social formations. Yet in all that is 'new' it is intriguing that feminist historiography continues to reflect an unconscious complicity in positing a portrait of early modern English culture that is singularly homogeneous and white. In other words, it is both ironic and troubling that, despite the current critical engagement with ethnicity and race in early modern English studies, the histories of non-European (and even some European) women residing in England (especially in the larger towns and cities) remain untold or under-told. Did all immigrant women so easily assimilate into English culture as to erase their 'ethnic' presence in the nation? While the personal history of Aemilia Lanyer provides some insight into one immigrant family's assimilation, Lanyer's musician family moved in social circles unavailable to the thousands of women settling in England. What about those women fleeing persecution, or seeking a better socio-economic existence, or forcibly brought to England? Where do these women fit in the historical paradigm of early modern English culture? How do we 're-vision' their histories, to use Margaret Ezell's chosen term?

Renaissance London, in its own way, was as diverse in its population as the Venetian world represented in *The Merchant of Venice*. Yet we know little of that England. Who are the immigrant women who resided outside the city, in Spitalfields, Moorfields, in Southwark? Who are the ethnic women who worked in the 'stews' and brothels of Renaissance London? What place do these immigrant women have in our 'readings' of Shakespeare's women? While much has been done on 'blackness' of late, our sight has been directed at the manor house and not the 'public' house. In other words, we've studied the master's house, not the servant's.

Over the course of the past five to ten years new voices have confronted these problems in feminist historiography and scholarship. The year 1992, the quincentenary of Columbus's voyage to the Americas, proved especially significant in terms of a reappraisal of Renaissance culture. 'New World studies', postcolonial studies and 'ethnic studies' renewed interest in the dynamics of colonialism and imperialism. Feminists of colour began to question the grand narratives of feminist theory and historiography, which not only generalized or essentialized 'women' according to a single paradigm but also seemed to elide non-European and non-white feminist issues from those grand narratives. In an astute commentary on the critical and theoretical practices of Western feminism, Chandra Talpade Mohanty writes: 'Western feminists who sometimes cast third world women in terms of "ourselves undressed" (Michelle Rosaldo's [1980] term), all construct themselves as the normative referent in such a binary first world/third world] analytic" (Mohanty 1991: 56). The problem, in Mohanty's view, is that this positions women as 'somehow socially constituted as a homogeneous group prior to the process of analysis' (ibid.).

Women, 'Race' and Writing in the Early Modern Period (Hendricks and Parker 1994) was an epistemological attempt to redress some of the problematic issues noted by Mohanty. A collection of essays written by women scholars and reflective of the interdisciplinarity of contemporary feminist scholarship, *Women, 'Race' and Writing* marked a sea-change for feminist historiography; Woman suddenly became woman, and Women became women individuated by ethnicity. A new generation of feminist historians of early modern culture has begun cogently to interrogate the universal woman model and to outline ways of illuminating women's heterogeneity in terms of ethnicity, class and sexuality in sixteenth and seventeenth-century England. The tendency to speak of women in universal terms has not entirely disappeared, however. In part, the epistemological difficulty inheres in the terms of the debate; women across the globe and temporalities, regardless of class, ethnicity, education and sexuality, do share a common set of experiences. But the elision of fundamental differences born of cultural and economic specificity that accompanies the subsuming of all women under the category Woman not only marginalizes those differences but occludes the privilege that accrues to some women as a result of their affiliation with a colonial or imperial power.

With the publication of Ania Loomba's *Race, Gender, and Renaissance Drama* (1989) and more recently of Kim Hall's *Things of Darkness: Economies of Race and Gender in Early Modern England* (1996), with its excellent attention to the 'archive', we may now have a theoretical and/or historiographical paradigm for bridging the 'gap' between literary history, cultural studies and social historiography. As Hall illustrates, within the epistemology and historiography of Renaissance

Studies (whether literary, historical or visual), non-European women play an important role in the definitions) of the category of Woman. Hall, in particular, has shown us how to investigate the gender and ethnic contours of Shakespeare's England without sacrificing theoretical concerns. The women of Shakespeare's plays have ethnic and racial identities that are drawn not just from the imagination; these representations are indicative of the complex and multi-ethnic environs that foster that imagination.

These scholarly and historiographical developments make clear that Renaissance and early modern England was neither ethnically homogeneous nor inexorably heterosexual. Ironically, much of this work has been undertaken by literary historians; many social and political historians dealing with Renaissance and early modern England continue to represent sixteenth and seventeenth-century England as if none of this new historiography exists. In other words, issues of race, sexuality, ethnicity and immigration are curiously absent from these historians' publications. This absence, in turn, engenders a curious interpretive window for literary and cultural historians interested in investigating, for example, the English context for play texts such as *Othello*, *Titus Andronicus*, *The White Devil* or *The Merchant of Venice*, or for proclamations such as Elizabeth I's authorization of the 'deportation of negars, negroes, and blackamoores' from England. Was there 'just cause' for Elizabeth's action? Was there a significantly large population of people of African ancestry in England, and were a large number of these individuals becoming a 'drain' on society? Was the visit of the Moroccan ambassador to Elizabeth I's court the only possible context for Shakespeare's *Othello* and *The Merchant of Venice*, or were there a number of mixed marriages or sexual unions (like that suggested between Lancelot Gobbo and the Moorish female in *The Merchant of Venice*) evident in the London boroughs for the playwright to draw upon?

Similar questions can be asked, and perhaps more fruitfully answered, about the influx of other European non-aristocratic women into England, especially Dutch, Flemish, Spanish, German, Italian and eastern European women. Was there extensive migration of labouring women from these areas? Were these women single or married? What types of labour activities did they engage in, especially if they were not attached to a household? Did women who were not attached to households become assimilated into English culture, and if so, how? Did any of these women become involved in the sex trade in London? If so, did ethnic and national enclaves develop? What place did [Roma] women have in this world? Is it possible to reconstruct these histories? And if so, what type of historiography is required? Do historians (social, political, literary, economic and cultural) have the requisite tools and theories to discover/uncover these histories?

I must confess that, other than raising the questions, I can only suggest possible ways of beginning to 'balance' our historical enquiries into women's lives in Renaissance England. Perhaps the most important way is one advocated by social historians: archival investigations. If there are evidentiary materials that can provide answers to my questions, these materials are not going to be found easily, nor are they necessarily easily comprehensible. We may have to redefine the parameters of our expectations and perceptions of what constitutes 'factual evidence' and 'truths' about Renaissance societies and their cultural practices. We may have to exercise a 'necessary suspension of disbelief' in order to practise a feminist historiography that acknowledges not only the diversity of women in Renaissance and early modern England but also the politics of patriarchal historiography when dealing with these women.

The first step, however, is a traditional one: into the archives. There is a wealth of unexamined materials awaiting the intrepid cultural detective. Feminist historiography has not yet begun to exhaust the rich archival materials residing in major libraries and resources such as the Bodleian and British Libraries, the Public Records Office, the London Metropolitan Records Office, and local and county archives throughout England. We cannot, however, go into these archives looking for the 'usual suspects'. We must begin to read these documents with an air of defamiliarization – as if we were coming to Renaissance English history for the first time. This does not mean that we project some vision of 'objectivity' onto our endeavours: far from it, for 'objectivity', like 'truth', has always been the bane of women's histories and feminist historiography. Rather, we must read archival materials with the expectation that they will conceal as much as they reveal, and our task is to account for both.

To illustrate this point I want to focus on two accounts dealing with women's lives that have not yet made their way into the scope of feminist historiography dealing with Renaissance and early modern England. The first discussion focuses on an incident brought to my attention by Kim Hall concerning the activities of Sir Francis Drake during his travels in the Pacific. The second account seeks to highlight some of the intriguing histories extant in the archives. Both accounts are intended to serve as an indication of the possibilities for feminist historiography and its aims.

A Matter of History/Historiography

> The Negress Maria stared unblinkingly at the retreating white sails of the English ship, her belly slightly swollen against the thin linen shift the English captain preferred her to wear. To her right stood the Mandingo, to her left the Bambara. Her own people no more than the shadowy image associated with the faint whisper of remembered voices in a language she no longer used. Don Francisco had called her María, but that was not her name. The Anglo Captain had called her Mary each time he had taken her to his bed, though in her tears and passion she had whispered her true name. When she could no longer see the white spectre of the English ship, she turned and looked to the bare encampment the English had left on the barren island. She vowed that the niño in her womb would leave this island and seek the land of his father.

The above account of the Negress Maria is a fictional 'narrative' [mine] based on a historical account describing an event that took place in 1577–8 (Nuttall 1967). In 1577 Francis Drake sailed along the coast of Central America, near Panama, towards Guatulco. On the way, he captured a Spanish vessel bound for Lima. On board the ship was a gentleman named Don Francisco de Zarate. Drake held the Don for three days, showing de Zarate 'much favour' and giving him 'the poop to sleep in' (Nuttall 1967: 31). De Zarate travelled with a black woman, apparently his mistress. According to John Drake's report, Drake 'took from Don Francisco a negress named Maria, and the pilot of said ship' (ibid.). Drake continued his journey to Guatulco where he released Don Francisco and the other hostages he had taken before reaching Guatulco. After replenishing his vessel, Drake 'set sail with men of [his] own nation only, the said negress Maria, a negro whom they had taken at Païta, and another they took at Guatulco, besides one they had brought with them from England' (ibid.). From Guatulco, Francis Drake sailed westward, eventually reaching the Indian Ocean. Reaching the Moluccas islands, Drake 'took in a supply of meat and provisions and lightened their ship by reducing their company to sixty men' (ibid.: 32). From the Moluccas the ship sailed north until it reached an uninhabited island, where, because of contrary winds, it remained for approximately six weeks. When the ship departed three people were left behind: 'the two negroes and the negress Maria, to found a settlement' (ibid.). In his generosity, the Englishman Drake left the three 'rice, seeds and means of making fire' (ibid.).

According to the accounts used by Zelia Nuttall (which form the basis of my discussion), Maria was the mistress of a Spanish nobleman (Zarate) and, when he is captured and held for ransom by Francis Drake, made part of the ransom payment (apparently at the insistence of Drake). A pregnant Maria is abandoned by Drake some few months later, along with two male slaves, on a deserted island in the Indian Ocean. Maria was by no means the only woman of African ancestry to have been abducted from her homeland, nor was she the first to become (whether by force or choice) the sexual partner of a European. On the contrary, like Maria, thousands of young women forcibly taken from Africa's west coast became subject to sexual exploitation and rape by European sailors. Some, in recognition of the limited power that might become available to them, became the mistresses of European men such as Zarate or Francis Drake. The story of the Negress Maria occurs in two Renaissance narratives: Francis Fletcher's *The World Encompassed* (1628) and John Drake's testimony to an inquisition court in Lima, Peru. My 'version' of the Negress Maria's situation is a deliberate attempt, on my part, to minimize the Anglo-Spanish conflict and emphasize the undocumented details of an African woman forcibly taken from her family, community and homeland. Such an intrusion, and a fictive one at that, is a direct response to the historian Zelia Nuttall's handling of the incident, which gives no significance either to Drake's appropriation of the slave woman or to the fact that he kept her on board his ship for months, and then left her, and two male 'negroes', on an 'uninhabited' island. Granted Nuttall's edition was published in 1967; yet the type of historiography practised by Nuttall remains intact even now. Published in 1995, reprinted in 1997, John Cummins's *Francis Drake: Lives of a Hero* reproduces the 'historicity' of Nuttall's account, along with his own masculine interpretation. As Cummins writes, 'Drake retained from Zarate's ship a good-looking black girl called María, "which was afterward gotten with child between the captain and his men pirats, and sett on a small iland to take her adventure"' (Cummins 1995: 111). The very next sentence, ironically, is 'Drake's business with the Spanish was now almost done' (ibid.). Cummins's 'business' with Maria, however, was not yet 'done'. Later in the chapter he returns to her story. This time, however, Cummins's language lacks the inflection of familiarity that marks his earlier account: 'When they sailed on 12 December they left behind the black woman María, now pregnant, and two negroes, "to start a population"' (ibid.: 121).

The historiography exemplified in Cummins's celebratory biography of Francis Drake and in Nuttall's translation of the Spanish documents and her editing of the English accounts dealing with Drake's abduction and abandonment of Maria is the mode of historiography that feminists need to challenge. Cummins's description of Maria as 'good-looking' serves to trivialize and, seemingly, justify Drake's taking her from the Spanish ship. We need to resist reaffirming with our silence this problematic exemplum of Renaissance English heroism. Feminist historiography engaged in critiques of patriarchal exploitation of women cannot ignore this example of one of the more extreme forms of that exploitation.

Eighty years after Drake abandoned Maria, Richard Ligon composed his *A True and Exact History of the Iland of Barbadoes* (1657), creating titillating images of women of African ancestry as part of

English imperial attitudes towards women in English colonial space. While Ligon's experiences and actions differ radically from Drake's, Ligon too finds himself drawn to the 'dark' body of the African woman. Ligon's story, however, is told in his own words. Confined at Upper Bench Prison, Ligon decided to write an account of his 1647 journey from England to the Caribbean island of Barbados. Ligon's *A True and Exact History of the Iland of Barbadoe*s is far more than just a travel diary, however. In his text, Ligon offers his readers an ethnographic, topographical and social portrait of places and peoples he found along the way. One of the more interesting segments of Ligon's account concerns his adventures on the Cape Verde island of St Jago. Like most ethnographers, Ligon is concerned to set down in as detailed a fashion as possible all that he sees so that anyone reading the narrative will gain as accurate a likeness of the inhabitants, customs and social relations on the island as his words can convey.

In his description of Vagado, the Portuguese Governor of St Jago, for example, Ligon writes: 'though he were the chiefe Commander of the Iland: yet by his port and house he kept he was more like a Hermite then a Governour. His familie consisting of a Mollotto of his own getting, three Negroes, a Fidler, and a Wench' (Ligon 1657: 11). When invited to dine at Vagado's house, Ligon continues his profile of the governor's household, dwelling at length on the physical appearance of the governor's black mistress. In the course of his account Ligon reveals to the modern reader a side of seventeenth-century English history that was, until recently, rarely investigated within the context of early modern English literature. As he concludes his description of Vagado's household, Ligon finally comes to the one figure conspicuously absent from the earlier details of the Padre's hospitality, the female presence which marks domestic space. Until this point, it is not clear whether Vagado's mistress was present during the dinner or whether she joins the group at precisely the moment Ligon indicates in his narrative. Regardless, the presence of this woman apparently so affected Ligon that he felt compelled to include a detailed exposition of her person and manner, and of his attempts to engage her in polite conversation. The passage begins with Ligon declaring the woman to be a 'Negro of the greatest beautie and majestie together: that ever I saw in one woman. Her stature large, and excellently shaped, well favoured, full eyed, and admirably graced' (ibid.: 12). From his description, the woman's garments clearly denote her privileged status, for she is adorned in costly fabrics and materials. Richly attired in buskins of silk, a mantle of 'purple silk', 'pearls' and 'large pendants', Vagado's mistress stands before Ligon, 'the rarest black Swanne' (ibid.).

Ligon's description of Vagado's mistress conveys the same erotic register as Cummins's remarks on the attractiveness of Drake's Maria. Because these women are registered narratively merely as sites of erotic pleasure, their subjectivity remains an enigma in the historical narratives crafted in celebration of early modern colonization. Given the general perception of women as primarily breeding sites, it is intriguing to note that rarely is there any mention made of the offspring generated by these momentary sexual encounters, especially those in England. What about the children of second and third-generation relations of miscegenation? How did they fare in a cultural climate in which increasingly blackness was linked to slavery? As social historians of American slavery have shown, when English colonial slave codes began to figure lineage in terms of skin colour, mandating that '"Mulatto" children . . . born of slave mothers, were categorized as slaves irrespective of their fathers' social status', the aim was not only to confront the disruptive sexual dynamics of a new social formation but, more importantly, to shore up the rifts accruing to patriarchal property relations (Beckles 1989: 133). The question we may want to ask is whether these new 'Europeans' disturbed or undermined patriarchal ideologies about racial identity in Renaissance and early modern England as well.

In 1555, when John Lok returned from Africa accompanied by five Africans, London's total population was approximately a quarter of a million. Of this number an estimated five thousand inhabitants were 'aliens'. This figure is misleading as it only represents the 'registered alien' population and thus fails to account for those 'undocumented aliens' that have plagued governments since the inception of the modern nation-state. The complexity of immigration into England is not by any means new; rather, as Laura Hunt Yungblut demonstrates in *Strangers Settled Here Amongst Us* (1996), xenophobia has long plagued England's perceptions of itself. Throughout the sixteenth century, surveys, legislation and royal proclamations became recurring reactions to increasing immigration and its attendant problems. As Yungblut illustrates, an influx of Italians, Germans, Dutch, French and Mediterranean peoples provides insight into the effect immigration had on native English people. Yet people of African ancestry are routinely ignored as a contributor to this documented history of immigration.

Yungblut, for example, directs our attention to a 1567 London survey on immigrants to England:

> By Easter (March 30) 1567, authorities found 3,324 aliens in London, the liberties, and Westminster. The point of the survey was clear, since the aliens were questioned primarily about nationality and length of residence in England. Of these immigrants, 156 had come in the past twelve to twenty-four months, and 232 had arrived within the last year. A survey dated December 15 of that same year reported 3,758 aliens in London and the adjoining liberties, with 1,059 of them citing a length of residence of one year or less. (Yungblut 1996: 21)

In the footnote where she provides the source for her citation, Yungblut remarks: 'interestingly, two "blackmores" were [reported] living in London at the time of this survey' (ibid.: 134). Yungblut's comment is significant not just because it provides some 'evidence' of a black presence; it is also important for its revelation that these 'blackmores' were clearly viewed as part of the foreign-born immigrant population in London.

Yungblut's decision to relegate the 'two blackmores' to a footnote rather than include them in her general discussion of ethnic immigrants into England sadly reflects the tendency by most historians to marginalize the place of blacks in England's history. Even more problematic is the fact that Yungblut's book was published in 1996 – nearly a quarter of a century after James Walvin's *Black and White: The Negro and English Society 1555–1945* and Folarin Shyllon's B*lack People* *in Britain, 1553–1833*; over a decade after Peter Fryer's *Staying Power: The History of Black People in Britain* and Nigel File's and Chris Power's anthology, *Black Settlers in Britain, 1555–1958*; and fewer than four years after the anthology *Essays on the History of Blacks in Britain*, edited by Jagdish S. Gundara and Ian Duffield. What is missing in Yungblut's analysis (and most of the recent social histories of sixteenth and seventeenth-century England) is an acknowledgement that a small group of historians have made us very much aware of Renaissance and early modern England's black immigrant population. Yungblut's oversight is indicative of the degree to which race and ethnicity truly do not register on historians' methodological and intellectual radar.

Despite the work of Walvin, Fryer, Shyllon, File and Power, and Gundara and Duffield, academics such as Anthony Appiah and Ivan Hannaford can still make sweeping generalizations about the question of an African presence in Renaissance and early modern England. The idea that sixteenth and seventeenth-century England lacked a sufficiently large population of African/English to warrant anxiety about race continues to influence the theoretical and historical analysis of race. So endemic is this assumption to traditional historiography, that I have often jested that perhaps it is time we literary critics who work on race temporarily abandon the 'literary' (i.e. the texts of Shakespeare and company) and expand our archival efforts on behalf of the Renaissance and early modern English/Africans who are denied a presence in the world in which they lived. My point here is that historiographers have been shown a path for such investigations; they need only follow it.

Given the increased presence of scholarly discourse about the significance of race and colonialism to Renaissance and early modern English literary culture, it is surprising that a concomitant discussion is not taking place among social and cultural historians about the presence of non-Europeans residing in English cities and towns, especially London. The histories of these individuals are intricately interwoven into the history of England's ethnic diversity and, if one looks closely, residing in the very archives that social and cultural historians privilege. One such individual is Martin Francis, an African/Englishman whose name appears in public records. I discovered Francis by accident during a recent visit to the London Metropolitan Archives. As I perused a reference book filled with cases selected from the Middlesex Sessions Registers (in search of references to gypsies and courtesans for another project) I came across a brief account of a complaint filed by Francis against Katherine Hutchins. The case, recorded on 21 October 1658, was both a find and a puzzle. According to the accusation, Hutchins, along with Elizabeth Simpson and Mary Biggins, pretended 'to make a marriage between the said Martin Francis (a Blackmoore) and the said Elizabeth Simpson; thereby defrauding him of seventeen pounds in money' (Middlesex County Sessions of Peace Roll, 1658: 1189/117, 281). The full entry in the Sessions book also suggests that this was not the first time the three women had undertaken such a pretence.

The record of Martin Francis's complaint is significant for two reasons. The brief entry serves as further 'proof' of the presence and assimilation of people of African ancestry into early modern English culture. Second, the entry is complete enough to give us some insight as to the degree of assimilation on the part of individuals like Francis. Francis clearly understood that he had recourse to English law when the agreed-upon marriage failed to occur. Moreover, he was apparently financially sound enough to be the target of a marriage scam, suggesting that perhaps money and not colour might have carried greater weight within the communities where English/Africans resided. What remains a puzzle are the same queries that we should ask about 80 per cent of England's population during the period: where did Francis earn his income (his trade is not indicated in the Sessions entry); what was the final disposition of the case? Did Martin Francis eventually marry? How and when did he arrive in England, or was he native born? Were his parents native born, or immigrants? Martin Francis appears on very few historical radars in the renewed attention to matters of race in Renaissance and early modern English culture. One reason is that records such as the Middlesex Sessions Registers are generally not among the archival starting points for the study of the African presence in England. Another, and more troubling explanation, is the pervasiveness of assumptions about the size of the

English/African population in sixteenth and seventeenth-century England.

Martin Francis has shown us that English/Africans did not have a propensity for celibacy, nor were they isolated into a single ethnic community. While some English/Africans probably married among themselves, others often married or became sexually involved with non-black English men and women. In other words, English/Africans most likely lived the same lives as their peers whatever their social status. The Martin Francis case warrants further investigation (as does the case of Drake's Maria) by feminist historians. These cases document the place of ethnic women and men as part of the English social fabric; Elizabeth Simpson and Katherine Hutchins exploit a man for money; that he happens to be a 'blackamoore' appears not terribly significant if we recognize that the parentheses that surround the term in the Sessions Roll may be there solely to distinguish this Martin Francis from another man of the same name. In addition, as the document indicates later, this is not the first time the two women have been brought before the courts on this type of charge.

My own interest in this case is generated by the obvious interactions between peoples of different ethnic groups within the communities of London, and by the fact that the women appeared to exploit brilliantly a major patriarchal institution that circumscribed women's agency. The activities of women such as Hutchins and Simpson lead me to wonder how many immigrant women, including those of African ancestry, may have used similar ploys to survive in Renaissance and early modern London? Were Hutchins and Simpson preying on some anxiety of Martin Francis related to his presence in London, or did they merely see a victim? Interestingly, there is no indication in the Sessions Roll account of Francis's age, occupation, and whether he had been previously married. Such information would make Hutchins's and Simpson's deception even more intriguing matters for historical study, especially in the light of George Best's observations about the offspring produced by such 'mingling' (in Hakluyt 1903–5: 1589–90).

Instances such as these ought to serve as prompts for greater scrutiny of archival materials by social, political and cultural historians interested in the lives of women in Renaissance and early modern England. Furthermore, literary historians writing about issues of race and ethnicity must begin to expand the categories of textual analysis on the topic; that is, these scholars must begin to look beyond the literary text. The type of cross-fertilization I am suggesting here is reflected in works such as Hall's *Things of Darkness* and Imtiaz Habib's *Shakespeare and Race: Postcolonial Praxis in the Early Modern Period* (1998). In both studies, woman becomes a decentered category of analysis, and ethnicity is as much a paradigm as sex. Importantly, as a result of the increasing significance of postcolonial theories to the study of the past, ethnicity becomes a dynamic force in the study of gender relations in Renaissance and early modern England. What has to happen, in my view, is that as we use the term 'ethnic' in our historiographical practices we must begin to include women of African ancestry in the definition of what constitutes ethnicity. English-African women need to be viewed under the same microscopic conditions as their English-Italian or English-Irish counterparts, especially if these women were born in England.

As always, there are an infinite number of questions which dance at the edge of cultural criticism, especially of the sort I attempt here. The most pressing ones include: how do feminist scholars of early modern English culture understand the immigrant woman's position in a world which symbolically exploits her 'otherness' as a literary and cultural foundation for the construction of a particular form of womanhood at the same time as it literally conceals her presence in Renaissance England? How do we 'discover' this archived history in the light of this concealment? Moreover, what are the dynamics between these women and other immigrant women? I believe answering these queries may shed epistemological light on the literary representation of immigrant women in Renaissance and early modern England. To what degree does the behaviour of women such as Elizabeth Simpson and Katherine Hutchins speak to the problems facing indigenous English women in cosmopolitan London? How many Negress Marias find their way to London, pregnant by some Englishman or another European male? Do they link up with the Katherine Hutchinses and Elizabeth Simpsons to survive in a city that affords them an opportunity to 'disappear' into its communities and archives?

Feminist historiography has as its theoretical and political obligation the imperative to redress traditional historiography's gendered oversights. Feminist historians of Renaissance and early modern English culture also have the added imperative of redefining the parameters of feminist historiography so that it is truly representative of 'women's histories'. In essence, feminist historiography cannot afford to generate totalizing narratives about women's existence in Renaissance and early modern England, particularly when a number of these women were from diverse ethnic and social backgrounds. It is important that feminist social historians take the lead in reshaping and redefining the categories of analysis in modern historiography. Literary historians have brought the non-English female body from obscurity to visibility in their readings of Renaissance and early modern literary texts. It is time social and cultural historians incorporate that visibility into their own historiographical methods and investigations.

Ernst Breisach (1994: 410) writes: 'no other endeavour fits as well as history does with the peculiar needs of human beings, to whom the temporality of life allots the roles of emigrants from the past, inhabitants of the present, and immigrants into the future'. If there is one major task remaining for feminist historiography it is the positing of how best to undertake this project. And, without question, uncovering the complex and diverse history of Renaissance and early modern England affords feminist historiography a continuing opportunity to demonstrate Breisach's postulation. In the university settings of England, the United States and member nations of the English Commonwealth, feminist social, literary and cultural historians should not sit complacently and assume that someone else will take up the task of writing and interpreting the histories of immigrant women, of ethnic women, of women involved in the sex trade, or migratory women. Alice Clark's *Working Life of Women in the Seventeenth Century* should not stand as the *sine qua non* of research on labouring women in Renaissance and early modern England. Nor should aristocratic, middle-class and poor women be collapsed into the general category of 'Renaissance or Early Modern Woman'. Finally, we should not wait for (nor expect) these accounts to be written by someone who 'identifies' with one or any of these categories. Having accepted the wisdom of a feminist revision of history, we must continue practicing what we preach.

MANAGING THE BARBARIAN: THE TRAGEDY OF DIDO, QUEEN OF CARTHAGE

In 1589 one of the more eloquent yet self-consciously anxious readings of early modern English nationalism surfaced in the preface to Richard Hakluyt's *The Principal Navigations, Voyages, Traffiques & Discoveries of the English Nation*. Hakluyt explains that the purpose of the collection of narratives is

> to speak a word of that just commendation which our nation does indeed deserve: it cannot be denied, but as in all former ages, they have been men full of activity, stirrers abroad, and searchers of the most remote parts of the world, so in this most famous and peerless government of Her most excellent Majesty, her subjects, in compassing the vast globe of the world more than once, have excelled all the nations and people of the earth. (*Voyages* 33)

Hakluyt's need "to speak a word of that just commendation" is, as Richard Helgerson argues, not "merely to record" English achievements but to reinvent "both England and the world to make them fit for one another" (153).

The paradox of this written "reinvention," however, was that it frequently localized and rendered visible the principal source of English anxiety over its place in early modern geopolitics, namely the threat posed by imperial Spain. With its extensive overseas territories, its wealth, its hegemony in Europe, and its Catholic militancy, Spain was the major obstacle to English imperial aims and political autonomy. As early as 1553, with the publication of Richard Eden's "A briefe description of Afrike," printed accounts of England's contentious relations with Spain in the Americas, with Portugal in Asia, and with both Iberian nation-states in Africa record a growing sense of national consciousness and a perceived need to define and defend "Englishness."[1] One of these defenders was the playwright Christopher Marlowe. Yet, unlike Hakluyt, Marlowe did not compose his defense in terms of England's present "glory" but in terms of its glorious "past."[1]

Marlowe's *The Tragedy of Dido, Queen of Carthage* re-presents a mythic narrative quite familiar to an Elizabethan audience conversant with Virgil's *Aeneid*. Additionally, to the educated spectators who patronized the Elizabethan theaters, the historical subtexts traced in the antithesis of Dido and Aeneas would also have been common knowledge: that is, these viewers would have been familiar with historical narratives of the Rome/Carthage conflicts (the Punic Wars), such as Polybius's *The Rise of the Roman Empire* and Livy's *Lives*. Furthermore, this audience would have been cognizant of the cultural mythology surrounding the genesis of England's racial origins (the founding of Britain by Ascanius's son, Brutus) and the complex historical and cultural links between Africa and Spain.

For a variety of reasons, most having to do with Marlowe's revision of Virgil's *Aeneid* and the play's dramatic disruptions, very little attention has been paid to these mythic and historical subtexts which mark Marlowe's text as a political allegory.[2] In what follows I will explore the significance of Christopher Marlowe's response to the "reinvention" of England. What I hope to make clear is the way gender and a particular meaning of race (genealogy) mark a new boundary for how "Englishness" (and by extension the concept of race) was to be defined. I also hope to illuminate how sixteenth century geopolitics becomes allegorically situated in light of this racial discourse.

Of course, in suggesting that *The Tragedy of Dido, Queen of Carthage* may have been written as a political allegory, that Troy and Carthage serve as gendered racial tropes for England and Spain, I realize that I am perched precariously on the fragile bough of authorial intention. However, I believe my reading may not be so implausible given the acute anxiety about Spanish hegemony we so frequently find in some Elizabethan writings. As Philip Wayne Powell writes in his study of the ideology called "Leyenda Negra":

> The basic premise of the Black legend is that Spaniards have shown them selves, historically, to be *uniquely* cruel, bigoted, tyrannical, obscurantist, lazy, fanatical, greedy, and treacherous Thus, Spaniards who came to the New World . . . are contemptuously called cruel and greedy . . . or other opprobrious epithets virtually synonymous with "Devils"; but Englishmen who (came to the] New World . . . are more respectfully called "colonists." (11; emphasis in original)

The circulation of the "Leyenda Negra" in early modern English texts reminds us that too narrow a definition of race can obscure one of the principal targets of English racism. From Edmund Spenser's *A Short View of the Present State of Ireland* to the translation and publication of Bartolome de Las Casas 's *Brevissima relación de la destruyción de las Indias,* Spain quickly became the standard of barbarity and racial inferiority.[3]

Just as important to this ideological representation is the interlocking history of Spain and Africa. The eight hundred years of African (Moorish) rule in Spain inevitably was called into play further to racialize the Spanish and to substantiate their inferiority:

> (Spain) is and ever hath bene the sinke, the puddle, and filthie heape of the most lothsome, infected, and slavish people that ever yet lived on earth. . ... This wicked race of those half Wisigots This demie Moore, demie Jew, yea demie Saracine What shall those Marranos, yes, those impious Atheistes reigne over us kings and Princes? . . . [Those Spaniards with) theyr insatiate avarice, theyr more than Tigrish cruelty, theyr filthy, monstruous and abominable luxurie . . . theyr lustfull and

inhumaine deflouring of their matrones, wives, and daughters, theyr matchless and sodomiticall ravishings of young boyes, which these demi-barbarian Spaniardes committed (Qtd. in Powell 76)

If my dating of *Dido, Queen of Carthage* is accurate (between 1588 and 1592), then the dramatic binarism mapped by the gendered history of Dido and Aeneas gestures toward this racial discourse.

For England, in the last decades of the sixteenth century, the cultural image of racial difference often wore the face, manner, and customs of Spain; and, as Marlowe shows, this face could also be drawn female, powerful, and African. In the discursive process of "reinventing" England, Marlowe's text stands as a testament to the effect Anglo/Spanish geopolitics had on early modern English racial thinking. My purpose, in the end, is to muddy the waters of current thinking on the question and "appearance" of race in Renaissance literary discourse.

II. The Absence of Race

Sometime during the four years following the English defeat of the Spanish Armada in 1588, Christopher Marlowe translated the first four books of Virgil's *Aeneid* and crafted a dramatic text, *The Tragedy of Dido, Queen of Carthage* (hereafter *Dido*). *Dido* opens with a stunning tableau that, on first reading, seems to have little to do with early modern English and Spanish political relations: "Here the curtains draw; there is discovered Jupiter dandling Ganymede upon his knee, and Mercury lying asleep" (1. l.s.d.). This first scene meanders, for forty-nine lines, through the vagaries of the personal relationship between Jupiter and Ganymede, and the audience is made privy to Jupiter's outrage at Juno's abuse of Ganymede, to Ganymede's manipulative and seductive petulance, and to Jupiter's erotic desires for the young man. Finally, just as Jupiter becomes reconciled with Ganymede, an infuriated Venus disrupts this intimate moment, "Ay, this is it: you can sit toying there, / And playing with that female wanton boy, / Whiles my Aeneas wanders on the seas" (1.1.50-52). From this point onward, the first act of *Dido* deals primarily with a recitation of the immediate events which led to Aeneas's arrival at Carthage.

In her censure of Jupiter's neglect of Aeneas, Venus reminds Jupiter that he has patriarchal responsibilities to Aeneas, her son and Jupiter's grandson. Jupiter defuses Venus's anger by reiterating the prophecy concerning Aeneas: "[his fate is) firm," and "in stout Hector's race, three hundred years / The Roman sceptre royal shall remain" (1.1.83, 104-05). Calling Aeneas "th' offspring of our kingly loins," Jupiter essentially confirms Aeneas's lineage and the future that he represents (1.1.116). This public proclamation of Aeneas's genealogy legitimates not only a male heir but also Aeneas's right to claim divine and royal racial origins. A member of both Jupiter's "race" and "Hector's race," Aeneas becomes the genesis for a future race "[w)ho will eternish [immortalize] Troy in their attempts" (1.1.108). Having made her point, Venus departs-satisfied that patriarchal power will be expended on behalf of her son.

What is striking about this opening gambit is that even before he begins his dramatization of the "tragedy" of Dido, Marlowe chose to rehearse the lineage of Aeneas. Strategically, this move quickly establishes the boundaries of identification in the play. Our empathy is immediately drawn to the tragic events that have befallen the hapless Trojan hero, and it is his situation which seems most compelling. While on the surface this dramatic device implicitly makes Aeneas appear more human than divine, it also persistently produces a problematic image of Dido, an image at times so critically overdetermined that it has prompted a number of scholars to dismiss the politics of gender and race inscribed in Marlowe's representation and see Dido as a woman who invites derision because of her passions (Leech 36). If we are to understand this critical reaction, we need to reconfigure a politicized racial history that, on the surface, appears disconnected from Marlowe's dramatic text. Only then can we grasp the assumptions which serve to trivialize Dido's situation.

At first glance, Aeneas's arrival at Carthage is remarkably unremarkable. The image that shadows the hero is of a man so consumed by personal grief that he is virtually immobilized; however, once Aeneas enters Carthage his demeanor visibly shifts. Dido's initial inquiry, "What stranger art thou, that dost eye me thus?" (2.1.74), immediately draws attention to what is a painful concern for the Trojans, the erasure of their identity with the destruction of Troy. Aeneas's reply confirms this sense of absence or erasure: "Sometime I was a Trojan, mighty queen, / But Troy is not: what shall I say I am?" (2.1.75- 76). The intentional ambiguity of Aeneas's words attests to a concern for a sense of identity. If there is no Troy, how are he or his men to display themselves to others? What is not articulated in Aeneas's words but which sits at the core of the Trojan's purpose is the need to restore the identity of himself and his men. Aeneas is in Carthage not because he has chosen to be, but because his ships were deflected from their primary goal—the colonizing of Italy. Literally, Aeneas is free to name himself even as his fate drives him to protect his Trojan lineage.

    Once Aeneas's identity is known to her, Dido exclaims, "Warlike Aeneas, and in these base robes!" (2. 1.79). She then orders that Aeneas is to be clothed in the "garment which [her husband] Sichaeus ware," and offers the Trojan the seat at her side. Aeneas declines the seat, claiming " . . . though my birth be great, my fortunes (are) mean, / Too mean to be companion to a queen" (2.1.88-89). As a member of a royal (and divine) family, Aeneas has the right to occupy the chair offered by Dido. However, he resists the implicit subservience involved in being a supplicant. It is only when the queen reassures him that his "fortune may be greater than (his) birth" (2.1.90), that Aeneas, wearing Sichaeus's garment, finally accepts the royal seat at her side.

    In an attempt to explain Aeneas's puzzling behavior, Roger Stilling writes that "Aeneas' mind, when he reaches Carthage, is a hell of dreadful, unmanning images, and these remembered scenes have great effect on his actions in Carthage" (42). On the surface, this reading would not be problematic had Marlowe not complicated the image of a distraught, befuddled Aeneas by having the Trojan make a remark that seems coldly calculating. When Dido approaches the group of men surrounding Aeneas, Ilioneus remarks, "Look, where she comes! Aeneas, view her well" (2.1.72). Aeneas replies, "Well may I view her; but she sees not me" (2.1.73). Given Aeneas's apparent despair only moments before, we might well ask, what prompts this remark? Extratextually, we might also ask, what inspires Marlowe to retain this less than obvious allusion to Virgil's *Aeneid,* where Venus has shrouded her son and his companions in invisibility as they approach Carthage, without duplicating the scene? In other words, what is the significance of Aeneas's comment?

If we juxtapose Aeneas's remarks with the gods' discussion in act 1, then his baffling remark becomes less enigmatic. What is at stake in this exchange of gazes is the ideological validity of Aeneas's lineage. As Marlowe's act 1 highlights, Aeneas can trace his patrilineal and matrilineal history (his "race") in divine and royal genealogies; he is the son of Venus, and his father, Anchises, was cousin to Priam king of Troy. Yet Aeneas's appearance gives no clue to his identity: he is dressed in "base robes." Dido's lack of recognition, therefore, is not surprising. To the queen, the man standing before her is simply a man whose fortunes have fallen; for Aeneas, however, the queen's failure to "see" him only affirms the absence, the loss, of his identity. The Trojan is a man who accepts his racial destiny, and for whom Carthage is little more than an opportunity to restore the honor of Trojan masculinity. Thus Aeneas's remark bespeaks an ironic subtext that does not disappear until the Trojan has imposed his identity, his will, on Carthage. Despite the certainty of his mother and his men, as the one responsible for securing the Trojan heritage Aeneas must exercise greater caution before accepting the pledges of an unknown and powerful political entity. He has, after all, faced enormous obstacles in his efforts to reach Italy. Aeneas has very strong motives for his initial self-effacement; while he has lost Troy, Aeneas has not lost his political sense and his sense of destiny.

Dido's acknowledgment of Aeneas's status signals the Trojan's emerging ascendancy over the Carthaginian queen, for Aeneas's acceptance of the robe and royal seat of Sichaeus allows Aeneas to rename himself temporarily without giving up his patrial identity. In fact, his acceptance of Dido's offer initiates the recuperation of Aeneas's masculinity, restoring a "manhood [which] would not serve" (2.1.272) in Troy but which will serve in female-ruled Carthage. In effect, Aeneas *becomes* Sichaeus-without being Sichaeus-to restore his "manhood." Sichaeus's robe and his seat at Dido's side empower

Aeneas in a way the status of Dido's guest could not. Both the chair and the robe symbolize the power of a husband, not a guest; and as such, they represent a powerful incentive for Aeneas. The wealth and power of Carthage permits not only the repair of his fleet but also, when he elects to remain in Carthage, the construction of a New Troy:

> Then here in me shall flourish Priam's race;
>   And thou and I, Achates, for revenge
>   For Troy, for Priam, for his fifty sons,
>   Our kinsmen's lives and thousand guiltless souls,
>   Will lead an host against the hateful Greeks. (4.4.87-91)

Though these words come much later in the play, they reflect the attitudes and perceptions of a man whose imperial ambitions are paramount.

The whole of *Dido,* from its stage directions to its final scene of immolation, is intended to rehearse the significance of Aeneas, his race and his fate. But, in the attempted recuperation of his "manhood," Aeneas nearly loses more than he had at Troy. Clearly, as Achates remarks, "Aeneas, for his parentage, deserves / As large a kingdom as is Libya" (4.4.79-80). But, for Aeneas, the question is not so easily resolved. Achates' observation comes at a moment when Aeneas faces conflicting desires rooted in the prophecy that drove him from Troy and in the status and power he has acquired in Carthage. From the moment he accepts Sichaeus's robe, Aeneas benefits from and participates in the divinely inspired exploitation of Dido and Carthage. He accepts the power Dido offers, ostensibly to rebuild his ships and continue on to Italy. However, with the same blindness that obscured his ability to recognize Venus, Aeneas apparently fails to see beyond the generosity of the Carthaginian queen to the seductive effeminacy of Carthage.

Consumed by desires for the exotic and the feminine, Aeneas neglects his duties to his men, to the memory of Troy, and, most importantly, to his son, Ascanius. In the eyes of his men and the gods, Aeneas has truly come to exemplify what his initial words to Dido only hinted at-"Sometime I was a Trojan, mighty queen, / But Troy is not: what shall I say I am?" (2.1.75-76). Not surprisingly, this question proves to be the crux of Marlowe's dramatic narrative. Attired in Sichaeus's robe, wearing Dido's jewels, and building a Carthaginian Troy, Trojan Aeneas is once again concealed by the power of the feminine. Only this time, the source of the Trojan's "invisibility" is a mortal woman who threatens the racial prophecy Venus so assiduously seeks to preserve.

What Marlowe does to alleviate this troublesome moment is to construct a different racial narrative for the Carthaginian queen, and that narrative is largely comprised of allusions and references to geographic rather than patrilineal (racial) origin. For example, when a disguised Venus approaches Aeneas, the goddess advises him to "haste thee to the court, / Where Dido will receive ye with her smiles" (1.1.233-34). Only moments earlier, the goddess had described Carthage as "the Punic Kingdom, rich and strong, / . . . / The kingly seat of Southern Libya, / Whereas Sidonian Dido rules as queen" (1.1.210-13). Even when there is an allusion to Dido's pre-Carthaginian past, the reference is to a city, Sidon, rather than to a family. All in all, the name Sichaeus is the only reference to a person Marlowe makes in the telling of Dido's history.

Marlowe's handling of Dido's lineage is additionally problematic when we consider, if we look at a contemporary translation of the *Aeneid,* that there is no obvious justification for the playwright's erasure of Dido's lineage. For example, in the 1584 translation of the *Aeneid,* Thomas Phaer and Thomas Twyne duly retain Virgil's genealogy: the writers vividly recount the death of Dido's father, the treachery of Pigmalion (Dido's brother), who ruthlessly murdered Sichaeus, and the dangers which forced Dido to flee Tyre. Clearly, in the case of the Phaer-Twyne translation an exact reading is the ultimate goal. Marlowe's text, on the other hand, requires more unpacking if we are to understand the logic in his elision of Dido's lineage.

Strategically, the absence of any patrilineal identification in Marlowe's version can be viewed as a radical refiguring of patriarchal political authority. Dido's independence forces Iarbas and the other African kings to deal directly with her. In a moment of despair, Iarbas provides insight into Dido's character as he recounts how she, "st[r]aying in our borders up and down, crav'd a hide of ground to build a town" (4.2.12-13). Iarbas's words offer an impression of a resourceful and shrewd woman, despite the terms "straying" and "crav'd": especially when we consider that Dido received from the African ruler, in addition to the "hide of ground," a division of "laws and land, / And all the fruits that plenty else sends forth" (4.2.14-15). Under Dido's rule, Carthage appears to have prospered to such an extent that Dido can vow to place at Aeneas's disposal "as many Moors *I* As in the sea are little water drops" (4.4.62-63). Moreover, when Anna voices concern over the growing Carthaginian opposition to Dido's political elevation of Aeneas, the queen responds that the "ground is mine that gives them sustenance, / The air wherein they breathe, the water, fire, / All that they have, their lands, their goods, their lives" (4.4.74- 76). Though his tone is often ironic, Marlowe makes clear the power that Dido has achieved is a factor of her determination. Nonetheless, in light of the careful attention given to retelling Aeneas's lineage, Marlowe's decision to omit or partially allude to Dido's patrilineal history seems especially suspect.[4]

Marlowe's intentional erasure of Dido's lineage weaves a different pattern in the discourse of race articulated by *Dido,* for it makes geography, Africa and Carthage, the origins of Dido's racial history. After the initial reference to Sidon, Dido is referred to mostly in terms of Africa-the "queen of Afric," or the "queen of Libya," or the "queen of Carthage." Denied a racial identity based upon lineage, Dido's history becomes constituted solely in her identification not just with Carthage but with the whole of Africa. Thus localized, Dido's character is subject to and would be read in light of existing sixteenth century assumptions about the behavior and disposition of the peoples of Africa. In other words, the spectators would view Dido, as a result of the allusions to Libya, Africa, and Carthage, exactly as they might view a sixteenth-century African. Indistinguishable from any other inhabitant of Africa, Dido would be subject to the same behavioral deficiencies: sexual promiscuity, heathenism, an inability to maintain a civil government, and a tendency toward irrational and degenerate behavior.[5]

Even though Venus does instruct Cupid to intervene on Aeneas 's behalf, "Now, Cupid, . . . go to Dido, . . . touch her white breast with this arrow head, / That she may dote upon Aeneas' love" (2.1.323-27), Dido's racially inferior "nature" makes her especially vulnerable.6 What is apparent in Marlowe's depiction of Dido, who oscillates between her inability to control her erotic desire and her political self-consciousness, is an image which valorizes an emerging cultural tendency toward reductive caricatures of both women and Africans. As Marlowe traces her, Dido is a political power reduced to an irrational and destructive gendered and racial schizophrenia:

> Then never say that thou art miserable,
>   Because, it may be, thou shalt be my love.
>   Yet boast not of it, for I love thee not,
>   And yet I hate thee not.-O, if I speak,
>   I shall betray myself!-Aeneas, come:
>   We two will go a-hunting in the woods;
>   But not so much for thee,-thou art but one,
>   As for Achates and his followers. (3.1.169-76)

The emotional instability of the Carthaginian queen is a powerful element in our reading of *Dido*, at times eliciting a modicum of sympathy or, at other times, evoking a dismissal of a problematic portrait, as one critic does:

> What primarily emerges is a fierce portrait of a woman avid for loving, with a complementary one of a man who would, if he could, have things both ways but who pines principally for Italy and the New Troy it offers. The woman may . . . excite our derision, as she struggles against her feelings, as she makes her overtures to Aeneas, as she tries to believe that her lover will come back, as she tumbles herself into the fire of death. . .. (Leech 36).[6]

In this reading, Dido appears as much a victim of the critic's romantic misogyny as she is the symbolic sacrifice to a notion of race that I have been arguing is at the center of Marlowe's narrative. For this critic and others, Dido's descent into madness and suicide is little more than melodrama.[7]

One question these critics might well ask is, what is at stake in Dido's capitulation to eros? Is Venus's intervention necessary to ensure Aeneas's racial survival? As both Marlowe and Virgil make clear, Venus acts to guarantee that Dido aid Aeneas. However, as a monarch apparently sympathetic to the Trojans, Dido, of her own volition, most likely would have provided Aeneas with the "means [to] repair his broken ships, / Victual his soldiers, give him wealthy gifts, / And he, at last, depart to Italy" (2.1.328-29). Given Jupiter's prophecy, what anxiety warrants the ruin of someone who is sympathetic to Aeneas's cause? As Marlowe represents the answer, it is Dido's independence, power, and desirability, as well as her African femaleness, which mark her as a different threat to Aeneas.

These qualities prove stronger than the divine prophecy, keeping Aeneas at her side and in Carthage. And it is this anxiety which prompts Achates to admonish Aeneas to

> Banish that ticing dame from forth your mouth,
>   This is no life for men-at-arms to live,
>   Where dalliance doth consume a soldier's strength,
>   And wanton motions of alluring eyes
>   Effeminate our minds, inur'd to war. (4.3.31-35)

Hence, it is as much an anxiety about Dido's power as it is the prophecy which drives Aeneas to abandon his plans to "build a statelier Troy / Than that which grim Atrides overthrew" (5.1.2-3) and, with his son and his men, to sail to Italy.

Clearly, the histrionics of Dido's behavior are intended to invoke racial images of the irrational, and thus emasculating, female. Yet the effort completely to enclose Dido's identity in a racial paradigm based on geography or gender is only partially successful. Dido does not go quietly into the arms of love; on the contrary, the queen struggles to retain her imperial authority over both Carthage and Aeneas. And in doing so, she becomes the threat to Aeneas that no man could ever represent. More importantly, as long as Dido's imperial power remains intact, Carthage stands as a political wild card in Aeneas's colonizing endeavors. A spurned Dido threatens more than just the imminent departure of Aeneas; she poses a serious political and military danger to the well-being of the Trojans in Italy. We need to remember that, despite the pathetic portrait Marlowe sketches at the play's conclusion, it was Dido who made Carthage a military force.

Marlowe's representation of Dido's "love" for Aeneas, and its all or nothing quality, has generally overshadowed the racial and gender discourses being sorted out in *Dido*. African Dido disturbs the patriarchal order signified by Aeneas, and that threat has to be contained or destroyed; there is no room for mediation. Dido's containment, not surprisingly, comes in a familiar misogynist pattern of feminine vacillation, disintegration, and death. In a moment distinctive for its self-reflective introspection, she demands of Aeneas,

> Hast thou forgot how many neighbour kings
> > Were up in arms, for making thee my love?
> > How Carthage did rebel, Iarbas storm,
> > And all the world calls me a second Helen,
> > For being entangled by a stranger's looks? (5.1.141-45)

What is striking about this portrait is that Marlowe's depiction of events leading to Dido's death and Carthage's collapse cannot completely contain the sense that it is Aeneas who, Helen-like, is the source of Carthage's fall.[8] Thus it is not Dido who is "a second Helen" but Aeneas who mirrors the "ticing strumpet." Where we might expect a traditional vision of a "world turned upside down," in which the rule of woman can only result in civil unrest and chaos, Marlowe subtly inverts the paradigm, and Carthage proves the exception to tradition.

In other words, Aeneas's behavior recalls all of the traits normally associated with women—fickleness, inconstancy, and duplicity. From the play's beginning it is Aeneas who vacillates at strategic moments, who evades rather than confronts Dido with the knowledge that he has decided to leave Carthage. In one of the central contradictions in his representation of Aeneas, Marlowe is unable to reconcile the image of a man who is to be the genesis of an imperium and the image of an effeminate man who cannot make up his mind. In the end, it is the destruction of Dido and Carthage that resolves this contradiction and effectively legitimates Marlowe's surreptitious "gender inversion . . . because it is directed against a supposed ethnic inversion" (Stallybrass 212).

Marlowe's staging of this destruction has presented difficulties for scholars of the text. On the one hand, we cannot deny the theatricality of watching the spectacle of multiple suicides on the stage. On the other hand, as a number of critics have argued, the scene tends to trivialize the tragic implications of what has befallen Dido.[9] What are we (the audience) supposed to think of this sovereign whose death is framed by the ridiculous? Can we dissociate Dido's death from those of Anna and Iarbas, or, as I believe is the case, are we forced to maintain the connections that Marlowe establishes? And, how are we to read these connections?

In Dido's thinking, suicide represents the only option to an untenable situation: the only means to "rid (her) from these thoughts of lunacy" (5.1.273). Marlowe, on the other hand, seems to envision the three deaths as expected outcomes to the political narrative his play is weaving. When Dido pleads, "from mine ashes let a conqueror rise, / That may revenge this treason to a queen / By ploughing up his countries with the sword" (5.1.306-09), the potential threat to Aeneas's well-being is quite real, since both Anna and Iarbas are alive. With the subsequent deaths of the two people who would have the motive and the resources to carry out this threat, the one possible thread establishing a racial lineage for Dido is erased. Moreover, the death of Anna is a particular effacement of Dido and what she created in Carthage. As Dido's nearest blood kin, Anna would inherit the royal seat of Carthage. More importantly, from a familial standpoint, Anna would have the strongest motive to seek revenge. The death of Anna ensures that from Dido's lineal race no one can rise to fulfill the dying queen's curse. When a conqueror does "rise" from Dido's "ashes," he will paradoxically be of Dido's *race* but not of her *race;* and here, I am referring to Hannibal, who is African but to my knowledge is not lineally related to Dido.

Anna's death, therefore, enacts final closure to a carefully articulated image of racial difference. In the wake of Aeneas's newfound masculinity, feminine "Carthage . . . vaunt[s] her petty walls no more" (5.1.4). The principal threat to his "manhood" consumed by fire, the only "conqueror" to rise from Dido's and Carthage's ruin is the Trojan himself. Having already *managed* one "barbarian," Aeneas can set sail for Italy where "full three summers likewise shall he waste / In managing those fierce barbarian minds" (1.1.91-92).

III. Race and Nation: The Authenticating of English Imperialism

In 1564 John Hawkins sailed to the west coast of Africa, where he "dispatched his business, and so returned with two caravels, laden with negroes" (Hakluyt, *Voyages* 106). Hawkins's action, done in defiance of Iberian "rights" to control the African coastline, in the long run proved a catalyst for later "adventurers" such as Francis Drake and Walter Raleigh.[10] For the remainder of Elizabeth's reign, English privateers used the west coast of Africa to attack and plunder Spanish ships making their way to and from Spain. Additionally, through a series of strategic alliances with Morocco and Tunisia, England attempted to exploit the contentious relationship between Spain and Islamic North Africa by drawing these Islamic states into the English military and economic campaign against Spain.

When England was successful against Spain, the effect on the English national consciousness was evident in the cultural posturing that came to mark printed accounts of these activities. For example, the chronicler of Francis Drake's success at the Spanish port of Cadiz writes,

> And here by the way it is to be noted, that the taking of this carrack (Sir Francis Drake's battle at Cadiz] wrought two extraordinary effects in England: first, that it taught others, that carracks were no such bugs but that they might be taken, and secondly in acquainting the English nation more generally with the particularities of the exceeding riches and wealth of the East Indies: whereby themselves and their neighbours of Holland have been encouraged, being men as skilful in navigation and of

no less courage than the Portuguese to share with them in the East Indies: where their strength is nothing so great as heretofore hath been supposed. (Hakluyt, *Voyages* 312)

In a master stroke of irony, England's conflict with Spain takes place in the one geographic region that paradoxically produced Spain's cultural greatness and, to the English mind, its racial inferiority. Before I look at the way this paradox is mapped in *Dido,* I wish to reiterate briefly what is often forgotten when Spain's African history is discussed: the fact that Africa played a role in Spanish history long before Islam established its hegemony in Africa.

As early as 500 BCE, Carthage began laying the foundation for its hegemonic control of the territory we call Spain. At some point in Carthage's emergence as an imperial power, the Spanish outpost of New Carthage was built and fortified. For most of the Punic Wars, New Carthage was a strategic military and mercantile site second only to African Carthage. When the Roman army and navy successfully supplanted the Carthaginians, New Carthage became a Roman outpost, retaining its historic name and character. By the end of the sixteenth century there was a third city named Carthage; one located neither in Africa nor Spain, but in Spanish territory in the Americas, Cartagena. Just as its classical counterpart, this "Carthage" proved to be politically significant. As the site for transporting the wealth of the Americas to Spain (and then to the rest of Europe), Cartagena became for the English the symbolic quest for imperium. In light of the 1585 conquest and sacking of Cartagena, Marlowe's audience would have recognized immediately the allegorical parallels between that event and *Dido,* envisioning this third defeat of Carthage as a prophetic confirmation of England's racial and imperial heritage.

In his discussion of *Dido,* Roger Stilling observes that Ascanius "serves throughout [the play] as a symbolic reminder [for Aeneas] of the past and the future that must come from the past" (44). I believe we can also argue that Ascanius "serves" as Marlowe's "symbolic reminder" of England's reinvention of a Trojan past in order to undertake its imperial future. The need to invent an imperial, racial history was not unique to the English. But, and this is the salient point, sixteenth-century England had neither an indigenous imperial history to draw upon (as did, for example, the French with Charlemagne or the Italians with the Romans) nor an existing hegemonic history (as did Spain with its control of extensive territories outside its geographic boundaries) to proclaim itself an empire. Thus, even though the belief that Aeneas was the patrilineal genesis of the English people was vigorously repudiated by sixteenth-century historians, the idea continued to circulate. The sixteenth-century literary production of England's racial origins, in essence, becomes the reiteration of a longstanding imperial prophecy that began with Aeneas in Carthage. The narrative of Aeneas and his son provides a cultural memory, albeit fictional, for English resistance to the imperial expansion by (African) Spain. Such a reminder, of course, also bears with it the recurring need to dispel doubts as to the validity of the reminder, especially one whose foundation itself is mythic invention.

Implicit in Marlowe's allegory is the impression that the racial hierarchy between the English and the Spanish grows out of a prophecy. For the most part, critical attention has been focused on Aeneas. The prophecy most important to English racial history, the one concerning Ascanius, often becomes overlooked. Both Jupiter and Hermes make clear that Aeneas's fate is to ensure that Ascanius's prophecy is fulfilled: " . . . think upon Ascanius' prophecy, / And young Iulus' more than thousand years" (5.1.38-39). What goes unspoken in Marlowe's text, but is always already intrinsic to the discourse, is the belief that Ascanius's grandson, Brutus, was the founder of Britain. It is in the son, not the father, that the real genesis of the English empire will emerge. I make this point because it is directly related to another Marlowe innovation in *Dido*.

Just before Aeneas departs, Dido makes what on the surface is a rather odd request given her situation: "Had I a son by thee, the grief were less, / That I **might** see Aeneas **in** his face" (5.1.149-50). Not surprisingly, Aeneas responds, "If words might move me, I were overcome" (5.1.154). As Dido begs, the Trojan goes silently from her presence "[with] haste unto Lavinian shore, / [To] raise a new foundation to old Troy" (5.1.78-79). In this exchange, *Dido* concludes in much the same manner that it begins, with a concern for the preservation of lineage. But, and this is both the paradox and the point of *Dido*, it is not Dido's race that is the focus of Marlowe's treatment but that of Aeneas (and by extension the English race).

Aeneas's refusal to accede to Dido's plea, of course, resolves the troubling scenario created by the dramatist's invocation of a familiar patriarchal ideology. However, what does become obvious in Dido's plea is that the implicit assumptions about race that Marlowe works from cannot conceal the artificiality of the racial boundaries articulated. In Renaissance patriarchal ideology, lineal descent is derived not from the mother but from the father; thus, any child of Dido and Aeneas would claim descent not from Dido but from its father, Aeneas. Had Aeneas consented to Dido's plea, the political implications are such that power relations between Carthage and Trojan Italy could become, to say the least, problematic, especially when Aeneas's Carthaginian son reached adulthood.

Dido's racial heirs, whether lineally or ethnically, pose a significant threat to the colonizing project and general welfare of the Trojans and their descendants. Any offspring of Aeneas must unquestionably be racialized according to patrilineal descent, which means that Dido's "son" could not be an African. Though staged as an apparent act of feminine collaboration with patriarchy, Dido's plea effectively forces Marlowe immediately to negate the racial paradox that his gesture signifies. Resolutely, Marlowe has Aeneas deny Dido's request, and the danger posed by this fantasy disappears into the illusion that is Dido's tragedy. Or does it? Why did Marlowe raise the specter of a Carthaginian-Trojan child when there was no apparent need? And, on a more topical note, how does this threatening moment of miscegenation figure in England's need to revive, to articulate, a genesis of racial origins at precisely the moment when Spain, its cultural and racial history the result of miscegenation, is at the height of its imperium?[11]

The answer to these questions, quite simply, is that the ideological implications of Marlowe's gesture in no way interfere with the political allegory he maps. Dido's plea for a child reveals that patriarchal notions of racial identity can be disrupted. When Dido makes her request, we need to understand that her gesture signals her status as a childless woman, a blot on her femininity. Even so, the racial implication of her request should not be ignored. Within Dido's womb, Aeneas's race can be appropriated, absorbed, and redefined.

If, as I believe is the case, Marlowe's allegorical trajectory has been to sanction the racial histories of England and Spain in the bodies of Aeneas and Dido respectively, then the specter of a Trojan Carthaginian child suggestively (if only textually) and problematically links English and Spanish racial histories. In the teleology of European history, the cultures of Spain and Africa are inseparable: from the establishment of an African settlement called New Carthage, which was to play a strategic role in Hannibal's invasion of Italy, to the Moorish control of Spain for centuries, to the establishment of Cartagena in America for the transportation of slaves to Spanish colonies and the shipment of silver to Spain. In its culture, its people, and its history, Spain is the (dis)seminator of cultural and ethnic "miscegenation." And, because Aeneas's lineage is perceived to be constitutive of English racial history, Dido's request generates an anxiety that Marlowe must alleviate in the face of the political implications of his dramatic gesture. Consequently, while Marlowe's imagination came dangerously close to rewriting the mythic scope of English racial history, in the end the play's originary narrative intervenes, restoring patriarchal and racial order, leaving behind an image of a dying, powerless, and barren woman who pleads for a "conqueror to rise from (her] ashes" to avenge her denigration.

In the "real" geopolitics of sixteenth-century Europe no such figure would arise to prevent the *race* of Aeneas from continuing the mission of Trojan imperialism. Despite its wealth and power, early modern Spain appears to be just as vulnerable to the racial prophecy promulgated in *Dido* as its African progenitor. In 1585 the American city Cartagena, "which cannot be denied to be one of the chiefe places of most especiall importance to the Spaniard of all the cities which be on this side of the West India," was attacked and briefly held by an English fleet of privateers under the command of Francis Drake:

> This towne of CARTAGENA we touched in the out parts, and consumed much with fire, as we had done S. DOMINGO vpon

discontentments, and for want of agreeing with vs in their first
treaties touching their ransome, which at the last was concluded
betweene vs, should be a hundred and ten thousand Duckets
for that which was yet standing. (Keller 258)

Drake's victory against the heavily fortified Cartagena, though not
as successful as his other exploits, would become a cultural memory of
racial superiority not to be surpassed until 1588. Once again trapped in
the seemingly endless circle of fate, Carthage was *managed* a third time
by one of Aeneas's race.[12]

IV. *The Tragedy of Dido, Queen of Carthage*

Throughout my analysis of *Dido*, I have explored the concept of race as
it informs the political allegory of Marlowe's play. Particularly, it has
been in the interstices of gender ideologies that my discussion of *Dido*
has sought to explore the complexities of racial theorizing and racial
consciousness in early modern English society. What I have not done is
to explain the theoretical context for my reading of race, and I would
like to do so at this juncture by exploring briefly what I will call the
"problem of race" in early modern English studies. It seems to me that
an important query (and one deserving of exploration) is to ask, when
scholars identify a racialized representation (Othello, for example), are
they working from the same definition as early modern peoples? In
other words, is the twentieth-century definition of race identical to that
used or understood by early modern English writers?

To pose these questions as I have is to imply that the contours of
race may not be as fixed, as transcendental, as universal as critical
practices and postmodern social discourses about race seem to infer.
Since the late nineteenth century, theories of race generally have been
articulated in terms of biological (and thus immutable) differences
traceable to genetics. Privileging some characteristics over others
(blue eyes over brown, fair skin instead of dark, tall rather than
short), this form of explanation "encouraged people to think of
themselves as belonging to races and paved the way for the
elaboration of a form of classification which assigned all peoples of

the world to racial categories" (Banton, *Idea of Race* 27).[13] Until recently, race was viewed as a "natural" and therefore transcendent category of social distinction. But, as one social theorist writes, challenges to such essentialism have emerged, recognizing that other possible meanings—class, status, lineage, or group affiliation-have played a significant role in the genealogy of the concept of race.[14] Consequently, if we are to grasp the primacy of racial thinking in early modern England, we must first expand the conceptualization of race to accommodate the multiple meanings that the word has often signified.

Historically, the definitions and the usage of the word *race* have been imprecise, possessing meaning only in a particular moment and within a given set of circumstances. Within the early modern English lexicon, for example, the word *race* appeared to have had far more fluidity in its signification than it currently has in late-twentieth century parlance. In its earliest and most common usage *race* simply signified patriarchal lineage.[15] In a broader political context, *race* was employed interchangeably with *nation* to signify a people (e.g., the Spanish nation or the Spanish race). At times, *race* was used to denote class affiliation; that is, property and its transmission often deter mined whether a person belonged to a race or not. However, by the end of the sixteenth century, *race* was beginning to bear more and more its modern sense, that is, alluding to a national or biological typology.[16]

I am not arguing that the crucial feature of modern racist attitudes (skin color or phenotype) did not appear in early modern English writings; one has only to look at the ease with which early modern commentators naturalized the hierarchal differences between Africans, American Indians, and Asians on the one hand, and Europeans on the other hand, as causally linked to variations in pigmentation to recognize a familiar pattern of social exploitation.[17] What I do want to argue is that we need to expand the parameters of the concept of race to take into account the contradictory assumptions about nation-states such as Spain (or Ireland) that led the English to construct racist ideologies about a people who are, for the most part, phenotypically similar to the English. What is quite discernible in this early modern conceptualization is that social customs, geography, and degree of civility become the visible predicate of racial difference whenever the term *race* is used.[18]

If scholars are to "see" the racializing of Renaissance society, then we also need to realize that our primary category of definition may be ill-equipped to handle the assignment. *The Tragedy of Dido, Queen of Carthage* reminds us that race is not a seamless narrative of color but an occasionally ill-fitting garment generated in the historical context of English nationalism and empire-building. Furthermore, as the text illustrates, lineage, once the primary marker of racial identity, was giving way to a new matrix: a matrix where geography, phenotype, and culture racialized regardless of lineage. Hence, we need to visualize English(ness), Spanish(ness), and especially Irish(ness) as multivalent racial categories, in addition to looking at the ways in which "white" and "black" begin to serve as taxonomic descriptors for conceptualizing the idea of race.

The *Tragedy of Dido, Queen of Carthage,* thus, is not to be found in Dido's resolute fidelity to Aeneas, nor in the honor presumably attendant upon her suicide, but in her racial identity. Though Dido's suicide is quite melodramatic, bordering on the ludicrous, it serves only to concretize the absolute racial differences between Dido and Aeneas. Marlowe's dramatic text, like the writings of Hakluyt, Spenser, and others, participates in the re-writing, the "reinvention," of Englishness. In the end, it is Aeneas who gives England its tint of superiority, and it is Dido who marks Spain as a space of African inferiority. And it was to sixteenth-century English writers such as Christopher Marlowe that the task fell to ensure that England understand its place in the prophecy of Aeneas: as a "race of kings" descended from Aeneas's "stock," and through whose imperial enterprise "the round circle of the whole earth [would become) subject to them."[19]

CIVILITY, BARBARISM, AND APHRA BEHN'S THE WIDOW RANTER

> We have been unable to address questions of race to any adequate degree **in** this book, and we are not exonerated in this deficiency by the most visible complexion of European Renaissance society. Rather, it is its very whiteness that we need to learn to see.[1]

As one of the small but growing number of scholars of color engaged in the study of Renaissance English culture and colonialism, I am heartened by the current attention being paid to early modern European racialism and racism. Yet implicit in Valerie Wayne's comment cited above is an uncomplicated assumption about what "race" means in the early modern period. Intrinsic to this type of reasoning is a perception that early modern English people equated "race" with color in the same way that citizens of the United States currently do. In this presumption, "race" is used as if it were a universal paradigm rather than a mediated social practice.

In his introduction to *The Bounds of Race,* Dominick LaCapra obliquely refers to this particular linguistic inflection, arguing that "race" has come to be a "valorized and often unmarked center of reference"; and consequently, [it becomes] decidedly difficult to overcome the tendency to privilege whiteness as the master-text ... and to identify the nonwhite as "other" or "different." It is equally difficult to avoid the growing tendency to substitute a commercialized exoticism or an anodyne, commodified discourse on race for problems of racial stereotyping and oppression. [2]

Recognition of critical complicity in the transmission or reification of such ideological tendencies has generated an incipient awareness of the complex history of the idea that we call "race." To resist concomitantly the "commercialized exoticism" attendant upon "race" *and* "make the categories of race [as well as those of class and gender] ... historically contingent and relational rather than foundational concepts,"[3] feminist and cultural scholars cannot limit their readings to seeing the "whiteness" of Renaissance studies. Such a move will only make more precise the ideological binarism produced by racial categories, not undo it. Rather than marking "whiteness," the imperative that faces cultural and feminist scholarship is theoretically and historically to map the discursive and social practices that prompted seventeenth-century Englishmen and women to define themselves not only in terms of nationalism but also, increasingly, in terms of color.

This imperative, then, is the context of my reading of Aphra Behn's *The Widow Ranter.* One of the earliest professional women writers, Behn actively participated in the literary construction of late seventeenth century English ideologies of cultural and social identity. Her relationship to the court of Charles II, as well as her own lived experiences, resulted in Behn's complex and often contradictory assumptions about race, class, and gender. Though she was politically conservative (Tory), Behn's writings reveal a social consciousness deeply affected by the colonial infrastructure of early modern capitalism. As a colonial subject and a writer complicitous in the production of English hegemonic discourses, Behn (and her writings) represents a particular resonance in early modern English culture. At a moment when "questions of race" were complicated by English overseas expansion, Behn dramatizes the politics of a particular notion of race and its effect on English colonialism.

Behn's play *The Widow Ranter* (c.1688-9) (despite, or perhaps because of its problematic idealization of American Indians) serves as a useful starting place to begin addressing the question of "race." The play is a tragi-comedy which comically maps the travails of impoverished gentlemen who travel to the Virginia colony in search of wealth, and the sexual relations which play a part in that process. *The Widow Ranter*, however, is an unusual text in that it is also a fictional revision of a historical event.[4] In 1676 Nathaniel Bacon, in defiance of the ruling oligarchy in the Virginia colony, organized a volunteer army of indentured English servants, African slaves, dissatisfied soldiers, and the laboring poor to wage war against the American Indians who resisted English hegemony. The success of Bacon's efforts to extirpate the American Indians created difficulties for the ruling council: his militarism was successfully containing the American Indian threat to English safety in the colony; yet Bacon's hubris in defying government orders to cease his activities could not be allowed to go unchecked. On October 26, 1676, Nathaniel Bacon died "of the 'Bloody Flux' and 'Lousey Disease,' only a month after having successfully captured Jamestown.[5] With his death, the rebellion collapsed and a number of Bacon's officers were put to death.

Aphra Behn's "dramatic revision" of Bacon's rebellion significantly rewrites the historical narrative: first, in its depiction of members of the Virginia Council the text inverts the class affiliation of the ruling oligarchy of Virginia; second, the text significantly marginalizes the brutality of Bacon's militarism; and third, Behn creates a tragic triangular relationship between Bacon and two American Indian monarchs. What is striking about this third "alteration" is that it displaces Bacon's relationship with his actual English-born wife, Elizabeth Duke, and constructs in its stead a fictional "star-crossed" miscegenous romance between Bacon and the American Indian Queen. In its integration of literary conventions, historical narrative, and the problematic sexual politics that seems to surface in much of Behn's canon, *The Widow Ranter* participates in what I shall call a racialized discourse of civility. The argument of this chapter, therefore, is that in its representations of the American Indians *The Widow Ranter* maps a central paradox of the concept of civility: the more the native becomes assimilated, the more her/his alienness becomes culturally reified. Essentially, though the American Indian may come to accept the values, customs, and ideologies of the English, ultimately and fundamentally s/he is not English; s/he will always be an Indian. Civility does not erase difference but, in fact, serves to emphasize difference. The play convincingly reminds its audience of what, in the last instance, links the English in Virginia—the perception of ultimately belonging to the same race.

The Idea of Civility

From its earliest engagement with the "New World," England strategically invoked the binarism of civility to carry out its imperial mission. In his study *Savagism and Civility*, Bernard Sheehan argues that, conceptually, this binarism construed a civilized society as definable by its sense of discipline, its religious morality, a legal system, and political authority.[6] Thus, as a value judgment, the discourse of civility always articulates a paradigm where native cultures exist as a "primal state" in which "savages might be either noble or ignoble, either the guardians of pristine virtue or the agents of violent disorder" but always different, always alien.[7]

In its articulation in English cultural discourses, the trope of civility draws upon very specific yet ambivalent ethnographic images of what English colonizers might expect to find in the New World.[8] On the one hand, these narratives represented the native peoples as treacherous, lazy, religious idolaters, ignorant of civil government, and sexually licentious. On the other hand, Arthur Barlow could write in 1584, "We found the people most gentle, loving, and faithful, void of all guile and treason and such as lived after the manner of the Golden Age."[9] It is Thomas Harriot's view, however, which seems to reflect the habit of mind of the English who traveled to the New World:

> In respect of us they [the natives] are a people poor, and for want of skill and judgement in the knowledge and use of our

things do esteem our trifles before things of greater value...
And...so much the more is it probable that they should desire
our friend ships and love and have the greater respect for
pleasing and obeying us. Whereby may be hoped, if means of
good government be used, that they may in short time be
brought to civility and the embracing of true religion.[10]

The imposition of this value system, intricately intertwined with English imperial expansion, onto the native peoples of the English colonies was not without its contradictions. As Karen Kupperman writes,

> Discussion of the Indian character is complicated by the assumption that there was a native hereditary class system. The praise of Indian courtesy, dignity, and trustworthiness was often restricted to the Indian nobility What all this means is that status, not race, was the category which counted for English people of the early years of colonization. Put in its most direct form this means that it was not the case that the "savage" was forever set apart from civilized mankind by qualities which were peculiar to him. The "meaner sort," the low-born, whether Indians or English, were set apart by qualities peculiar to them.[11]

English attitudes toward the American Indians in the first few decades of the colonizing project (1580s to 1620s), according to Kupperman, were shaped by the class affiliation of the narrator; thus, the ability to "bring" the native to "civilization" was largely dependent upon the native's social position. Kupperman goes on to argue that this view linked "in roughly the same terms English people of low status" and "the rank and file Indians."[12]

Though I am in general agreement with Kupperman's overall analysis, it seems to me that she ignores the centrality of "race" to discussions of status in England's colonial discourses. In his pioneering study *The Idea of Race,* Michael Banton observes that within Western history we can map the multiple ways in which "race" has been employed to describe personal identity—lineage, nation, typology, biology, and status. According to Banton, as a particular culture's social relations and practices changed or as nation-states from Europe extended their territorial claims across oceans, "race" proved an effective polyseme in the process of constituting and authenticating an official explanation for social, cultural, and phenotypical differences. What becomes obvious, if the scholar steps outside her own particular historical consciousness, is the fact that a genealogy of "race" reveals that the concept has never had a fixed meaning, but has been variable.

In its conceptual shifts, "race" often leaves residues of previous significations to inflect current usage.[13] Kupperman's insistence that "status" was "the category which counted for English people," however, seems to elide the presence of these residues. Conceptually and politically, "race" permitted the English to explain hierarchies of lineage, status, or typology without changing the language. In other words, a writer could describe the inferiority of the Irish "race" and the superiority of the aristocratic "race" in the same text with little concern for conflicting meanings, since the text's audience would be expected to supply the requisite definition of the word "race." In this manner, the literary circulation of "race," unlike that of "status," infuses a more concrete and definitive resonance to the discourse of civility.

In a trenchant essay on "the other question," Homi K. Bhabha argues that it "is the force of ambivalence that gives the colonial stereotype its currency: ensures its repeatability in changing historical discursive conjunctures; informs its strategies of individuation and marginalization."[14] It is in the margins of such "ambivalence" that Behn locates her dramatic depiction of Bacon's rebellion. Though Behn ends with an image of a self-consciously unified English settlement, she begins with the drama of a class-based division among the English. And this "drama" is displayed along a familiar early modern racial grid—an anxiety about lineage.

For many of the characters in *The Widow Ranter,* arrival in Virginia necessitated a lineal history, a genealogy to authorize their new identity. Initially, especially among the lower-class immigrants, this was done by fabricating a gentry or aristocratic heritage out of the rubble of the English Civil War. For example, Mistress Flirt, in an effort to mute skepticism about Parson Dunce's lineage, claims, "but methinks Doctor Dunce is a very edifying Person, and a Gentleman, and I pretend to know a Gentleman; for I *my* self am a Gentlewoman: *my* Father was a Baronet, but undone in the late Rebellion" (l.i). The irony of this defense is that the very hierarchy which produced the social conditions that resulted in the parson's and Mistress Flirt's transportation to Virginia ends up being invoked in the construction of a new identity.

In the minds of the transported, the colonies represented an opportunity to "fashion" an identity. Behn captures this practice in her characterization of the Justices who share power in Virginia. Formerly men whose lives in England had resulted in their transportation for criminal activities, the Justices struggled to efface their past identities as "tinkers, excise-men, pickpockets, and farriers"—men of the "common Rank."[15] In an age preoccupied with identity, needless to say, the ability to "put on" an identity as easily as one puts on a coat is troubling. The success of men such as the Justices visibly undermines the class-based assumptions about who is capable of ruling. And, as if to militate against these early modern "Horatio Alger" narratives, Behn depicts these men as incompetent, foolish, cowardly, and driven by greed (this in stark contrast to the actual class origins of most of the Virginia oligarchy, a group of men with either aristocratic or gentry lineage).

Behn stages this heterogeneity to three effects: first, it individualizes her hero Bacon; second, it normalizes the class hierarchy which must accompany social order; finally, it harnesses racial consciousness against the threat posed by the American Indians. This final reason is the most significant in Behn's representation. If the English colonizers are to be successful in subjugating the American Indians, it can only happen under the administrative and military superiority of a particular form of English masculinity. The embodiment of "courtesy, liberality, decorum, ... compassion," and honor, this man attests to the heroic ideal of Restoration militarism, the warrior prince.[16] In effect, Behn's text articulates a desire for a central figure to reaffirm the distance between the English and the "savages," as current English behavior seems dangerously close to denying any "difference."

In Behn's dramatic fantasy, Nathaniel Bacon, the embodiment of the warrior prince, points to the degeneracy, the barbarity, and thus the incivility of the "common Rank." He is a man who exercises power to sustain the authority of England's colonial project. Bacon is also an aristocratic figure who exudes a powerful romantic image in his respectful treatment of the women taken hostage, his solicitous concern for the wounded American Indian King, and his wooing of the American Indian Queen. Behn's depiction insists that the measure of English colonial masculinity is not acquired through wealth or social power but through birth.

In many respects, the contrast between Bacon and the ruling oligarchy stresses a conservative belief that the absence of aristocratic power in the colonies constitutes a significant threat to the entire project. Virginia is seen as a "Country ... [that needs to be] peopled with a *well-born Race*, to make it one of the best Colonies in the World" (1.1, my emphasis). Like many of the reactionary narratives that emerged in the wake of the Civil War, Behn's rhetoric inextricably links the "race" problems surfacing within the colonial enterprise to the emergence of a powerful class that derives its wealth and power from trade and financial ventures, yet demonstrates little of the nobility fashionably expected of an early modern ruling class. Furthermore, in contrast to the Flirts, Parson Dunces, and Boozers, the truly "civilized" immigrants to Virginia have no need for a manufactured genealogy to explain their behavior. Clearly, the success of the American Indians' resistance arises from the dissension that marks English colonial society.

Civility - Race

In her explanation of what assumptions lay at the center of English colonialist discourse, Karen Kupperman writes that it "was a commonplace that the English would perform for the Indians the same function as the Romans once performed for the English—the bringing of civilization and Christianity."[17] What is often evident in the social and discursive practices of English colonists, however, is an ambivalence about the strategies of the mission to civilize the American Indian. In 1623 John Robinson wrote:

> Concerning the killing of those poor Indians, of which we heard at first by report, and since by more certain relation. Oh, how happy a thing had it been, if you had converted some before you had killed any! Besides, where blood is once begun to be shed, it is seldom staunched of a long time after. You will say they deserved it. I grant it Methinks one or two principals should have been full enough, according to that approved rule, The punishment to a few, and the fear to many.[18]

Thomas Morton, though criticized by the colonial oligarchy in Plymouth, Massachusetts, for his intimacy with the American Indians, shares this view - "I cannot deny but a civilized Nation, has the preheminence [sic] of an uncivilized, by means of those instruments that are found to be common amongst civile people…"[19] While Morton views the American Indians as living a "contented life," he nonetheless perceives them to be an "uncivilized" people.

By 1676, this "civilized" ambivalence had erupted into full-fledged racism and genocide. Nathaniel Bacon, the heroic figure of *The Widow Ranter*, wrote in his "Manifesto" requesting a commission to wage war against the American Indians:

> Whether or no wee ought not to judge his Majesty's title prerogative good here, and his claime better than that of all Indians whatsoever, and whether since his Majesty hath been possessed of this part of America, wee have not been invaded, and his Territories claimed, and his subjects barbarously murdered, his Lands depopulated and usurped by those barbarous Enemies, whose outrages, wrongs and violences offered to our Soveraigne and his subjects have been soe cunningly mixt among the severall Nations or familyes of Indians that it hath been very difficult for us, to distinguish

how, or from which of those said Nations, the said wrongs did proceed.[20]

Though denied his commission, Bacon nonetheless embarked on his campaign.

The Widow Ranter assimilates much of this militaristic and polemical rhetoric in its characterization of Bacon: "Should I stand by and see *my* country ruin'd, my King dishonour'd, and his Subjects murder'd, hear the sad Crys of Widows and of Orphans?" (I1.4.). Yet, overall, Behn's treatment of Bacon is deliberately sentimentalized by his romantic attachment to Semernia, an American Indian woman. Furthermore, using the romantic escapade of the Widow Ranter (who boldly pursues and "captures" her man) as a parodic contrast to the relationship between the Englishman and the American Indian woman, Behn trivializes the genocidal implications of the use of the American Indian woman as a vehicle for the "bringing of the savages" to civility.

In their discussion of the English genocidal practices in Ireland, Ann Rosalind Jones and Peter Stallybrass observe that "civility ... does not emerge through cultural evolution but through military conquest."[21] Nowhere is this hypothesis more acutely demonstrated than in the relationship between Bacon and the American Indian monarchs. In constructing this dramatic relationship, Behn directs attention away from the political drama taking place in Virginia, guiding the spectator's gaze through a sentimental lens of high romance. In this instance, Kupperman's reading (that the English viewed the American Indian through the spectrum of status and not race) appears valid; in a gesture of ideological elision, Behn rhetorically assimilates the characters Cavernio and Semernia into the civilized world of the English aristocracy. In almost every conceivable way, the Indianness of the monarchs is subsumed by their identification with Bacon.

Though at war, Cavernio and Bacon enact the ritualized discourse of aristocratic power:

KING Yet though I'm young, I'm sensible of Injuries; and oft have heard my Grandsire say, That we were Monarchs once of all this spacious World, till you, an unknown People, landing here, distress'd and ruin'd by destructive Storms, abusing all our charitable Hospitality, usurp'd our Right, and made your Friends your Slave. (2.1)

BACON: I will not justify the Ingratitude of my Fore-fathers, but finding here my Inheritance, I am resolv'd still to maintain it so, and by my Sword ... defend each Inch of land, with my last drop of Blood. (2.1)

Neither man will suffer a loss of honor; and as Cavernio recognizes, the differences between them are "better disputed in the Field."

As with Bacon, Cavernio's words and deeds are consistent with the heroic formulae Behn makes use of in her dramatic narratives. For example, in the duel that eventually costs him his life, Cavernio continually displays the honorable behavior of the "civilized" man: from his expressed concern that Bacon "bleed[s] apace" to his request that Bacon "Commend me to her [Semernia]" (4.2). Behn consciously manipulates the elision of difference between Cavernio and Bacon, making of both characters men who are "indeed above the common Rank, by Nature generous, brave, resolv'd and daring." (1.1) Thus, when Cavernio is murdered by Bacon, the audience is made witness to the death of a man who is "governed absolutely by [an] allegiance to the conventional aristocratic code of love and honor."[22] The mirroring of these two characters is consistent with Behn's dramatic technique. In her insightful analysis of *Oroonoko*, Laura Brown argues that "Oroonoko is ... not only a natural European and aristocrat, but a natural neoclassicist and Royalist as well."[23] As Cavernio resists the invasion of his lands, he exemplifies the English warrior prince, and is an admirable match for his aristocratic counterpart, who "first taught ... [Cavernio] how to use a Sword" (4.2).

Not until Act IV is there an explicit allusion to an inherent difference between the American Indian King and the Englishman. In the stage directions to a scene that can only be viewed as a stereotypical representation of the "barbaric" theology of the American

Indians, Behn reminds her audience of the futility of any attempt to bring "civility" to the natives:

> A Temple, with an Indian God placed upon it All bow to the Idol, and divide on each side of the Stage. Then the Musick playing louder, the Priests and Priestesses dance about the Idol with ridiculous Postures, and crying (as for Incantations) thrice repeated, Agah Yerkin, Agah Boah, Sulen Tawarapah, Sulen Tawarapah. (4.1)

In evoking this image, Behn openly draws upon a cultural difference to mark racial inferiority. And, in this moment of non-Christian paganism, Cavernio and Semernia become visibly disengaged from the trope of civility.

Like Oroonoko, Cavernio falls victim to English imperialism and in the process his death, just as Oroonoko's, is linked to a classical heroic heritage—"He's gone—and now, like Caesar, I could weep over the Hero I my self destroyed" (4.2). What becomes obvious at this point is the paradox of the discourse of civility: to exercise an ideological strategy that erases all differences (i.e., makes of the American Indians "civilized" English) calls into question the continued immigration of English men and women. On the other hand, to abandon the ostensible "mission" of the colonizing project (i.e., "civilizing the savages") is to admit that territorial ambition and empire-building are the real motivation behind the English invasion of the American Indians' lands. In either case, the "civilized" American Indian remains a problem, since he poses untold legal and political contradictions for the English settlers, particularly in the acquisition of land. Once "civilized," the native becomes an equal competitor for property, and by extension control of the colony; and, given her/his a priori natal claim to the lands, such a competition is the last thing that imperialist hegemony desires. In the end, the English colonialists abandon the principle of bringing the American Indians, as a "race," to civility.[24] And despite his "civility," Cavernio dies alongside the other "savages" who "fall to massacring [the English] wherever [they] lie exposed to them" (Li).

Before concluding my reading of *The Widow Ranter*, I want to look at the interlinking of miscegenation and the idea of civility in Behn's play.[25] Early in the play the audience learns that Bacon's "Thirst of Glory cherish'd by sullen Melancholy ... was the first motive that made him in love with the young Indian Queen, fancying no Hero ought to be without his Princess" (1.i). On the one hand, literary convention can help us understand why Behn consciously elects not to represent Bacon's actual wife in the play: romantic love in Restoration comedy rarely takes place in marriage since the phenomenon is about courtship. On the other hand, however, literary convention cannot explain why Behn chooses to construct a miscegenous relationship. Behn's construction of the fantasy of Semernia, I believe, serves to deflect a very real anxiety in the racial ideology of English colonialism —unrestrained English female sexuality.

In an instance of form(al) mediation, Semernia, as an American Indian, displaces the unmarried upper-class English woman as the object of upper-class masculine erotic desire. In much of colonial English ethnography, American Indian women were stereotyped as sexually active and aggressive. In *A Map of Virginia,* one of the narrators reports that the women of Powhatan's nation "solemnly invited [John] Smith to their lodging; but no sooner was he within the house but all these nymphs more tormented him than ever with crowding and pressing and hanging upon him, most tediously crying, 'Love you not me?'"[26] William Strachey reported that American Indian men permitted their wives full sexual freedom, arguing "uncredible yt is, with what heat both Sexes of them are given over to those Intemperances, and the men to preposterous Venus, for which they are full of their owne country-disease (the Pox) very young."[27]

It is this "baggage" which Behn cannot displace in her representation of Semernia, though the Englishwoman tries. As Behn draws her, Semernia's "Indianness" is concealed by the rhetoric of a conventionalized version of English femininity. Semernia is virtuous, attractive, loyal, honorable, and she is in love with the heroic Bacon. Confiding in her servant Anaria, the Queen gives expression to the struggle between her passions and her reason: "Twelve tedious Moons I pass'd in silent Languishment; Honour endeavouring to destroy my

Love, but all in vain" (5.3). Though married to Cavernio, Semernia is not unaffected by the presence of Bacon. When the Englishman describes, with a "faltring" tongue, the effects of love— "It makes us tremble when we touch the fair one; . . . the Heart's surrounded with a feeble Languishment, the eyes are dying, and the Cheeks are pale" (2.1) —Semernia's reaction mirrors Bacon's words: "I'll talk no more, our Words exchange our Souls, and every Look fades all my blooming Honour" (2.1).

As a married woman, Semernia recognizes the "symptoms" as something to fear, and she quickly seeks the protective standard of virtuous distance. In fact, to guard her "honour," Semernia exhorts Bacon to take "all our Kingdoms—make our People slaves, and let me fall beneath your conquering Sword: but never let me hear you talk again, or gaze upon your Eyes" (2.1). By the play's conclusion, Bacon's desire to possess Semernia does exact the enormous toll her prophetic words bespeak. In the end, her husband-king dead, her people dispossessed and slaughtered, Semernia's dilemma is resolved when Bacon mistakenly kills the Queen. The American Indian woman's body has channeled male interest until the Englishwomen can be safely engaged or wedded.

With Semernia's death, Behn effectively brings to closure her narrative of the romance. Bacon's death is somewhat anti-climactic: he commits suicide after successfully routing the Jamestown forces allied against him. Nonetheless, the play ends with two significant articulations. The first is the imposition of a class hierarchy among the English settlers. The army which pursued Bacon was composed of both gentry and lower-class men, and their class differences become resolved in pursuit of a common enemy. Even so, the play concludes with the Acting Governor dislodging Justices Whiff and Whimsey—" your Places in the Council shall be supplied by these Gentlemen of Sense and Honour" (5.5).

The second articulation of Behn's narration occurs just after Bacon slays Semernia. The General claims, "There ends my Race of Glory and of Life" (5.3). Behn's ambiguous use of the word "Race" produces two parallel readings. In the first instance, "Race" straightforwardly signals the end of Bacon's ambitious endeavor. On a second and more ideological level, Bacon's words are much more revealing of a cultural anxiety about miscegenation if we read "Race" as a reference to lineage. In what follows I want to make a case for the second reading in light of the discourse of civility.

Bacon's rhetoric dramatizes the anxiety concerning the acquisition and transmission of property that circulates within the discourse of "race." In an earlier statement, Bacon declared that Semernia was "the dear Prize, for which alone he toil'd!" (5.3). If we link his use of the word "toil'd" with his earlier declaration to "defend every inch of Land," Bacon's pursuit of Semernia takes on the rhetoric of property. Symbolically, Bacon's pursuit is about the English efforts to acquire American Indian lands. In a letter, John Winthrop argued, "That which lies common, and hath never beene replenished or subdued is free to any that possesse and improve it."[28] If we read Bacon's pursuit of Semernia as parallel to his efforts to possess American Indian lands, then it is not inappropriate to extrapolate a reading that sees both the woman and the lands as the "property" of another person, in this case Cavernio.

The acquisition of Semernia not only would signify Bacon's mastery of the American Indians (including their enslavement) and what they control but also the English man's right to lay claim to the American Indian female body. In Bacon's colonialist endeavors, Cavernio stands between the Englishman's accumulation of property —whether lands or the object of his erotic desire, Semernia. Given that Semernia is the wife of Cavernio and, in the context of early modern English ideologies regarding marriage, "belongs" to him, Bacon's actions represent an encroachment upon the property of the American Indian. The "warrior prince," far from being civilized, symbolizes social disorder and immorality. Yet from the English perspective, Bacon's position is typical of a general colonialist attitude.

It is this ambivalent racial inscription which makes Behn's *The Widow Ranter* a deeply troubling text. By framing the discourse of civility in a miscegenous romance, Behn doubly insures the eradication of the American Indians, but at the expense of obscuring the problematic paradox of Bacon's undertaking. Should Semernia become the "property" of Bacon (whether as his wife or his mistress), any offspring are of Bacon's "Race." What better way to shift the balance of power in the New World than by increasing dramatically the number of sympathetic natives who identify with a patrilineal authority and culture? More importantly, what better way to achieve this goal than through sexual and marital relations with American Indian women?

In her able study, Mary Dearborn argues that one of the "single most important received metaphor[s] of female ethnic identity" is "the story of Pocahontas."[29] This myth lies at the very center of Behn's depiction of Semernia, altered, however, to meet the objectives of the late seventeenth-century colonizing project. What this "metaphor of female ethnic identity" tells us is that, from the standpoint of the civilizing mission propounded by the English, miscegenation is both desirable *and* dangerous. And, given the overall objective of early modern English colonialism, the danger far outweighed the pleasures.

Miscegenation threatens the idea of assimilation that lies at the heart of civility. Unlike genocide, miscegenation can (and often does) result in the proliferation of "natives" who reject "civility."[30] What is more frightening, from the standpoint of the colonizers, is the possibility that the "savage" would come to dominate both in numbers and in culture.[31] If miscegenation could "civilize," could it not also create "savages" who preferred polygamy or a communal existence based on the absence of competition and greed?[32] Furthermore, if miscegenation erases the boundaries between the English and the American Indians, what then becomes of the ineradicable measure of "difference" required to justify the colonizing project?

Ultimately, it was the loss of "Englishness" within an erotic, miscegenous space of "civilized conquest" that most alarmed the colonizers. As Bacon pursues Semernia, is he civilized man or "savage" native? Do we excuse Bacon's blatant disregard of the Christian prohibitions against adultery, lust, and murder because the individuals who provoked this behavior were considered "savages"? Or, do we condemn him for his failure to remain a "true" Englishman? Finally, when Bacon takes his own life for love of an American Indian woman—"Come, my good Poison, like that of Hannibal; long I have born a noble Remedy for all the Ills of Life. I have too long surviv'd my Queen and Glory" (5.4)—has he succumbed to "Indian savagism"? Or is his death the return of his "English civility"?

As Behn writes it, what seemed most important to the colonial project was unity among the English, as Bacon's last words indicate: "Now while you are Victors, - make a Peace with the English Council, and never let Ambition, - Love, - or Interest, make you forget, as I have done, your Duty and Allegiance" (5.5).

Afterword

> I have sought to ensure that the integrity of the evidence was respected at all times, for this has always to be demanded from those who practise the writing of history. Beyond that, the interpreter is himself nothing but a spokesman for historical forces.[33]

Like others of her circle, Aphra Behn was deeply implicated in colonial politics; if Behn's account is to be believed, her father was, after all, appointed Lieutenant-Governor of the English Surinam colony. Yet there are clear traces of uncertainty in *The Widow Ranter* about the morality of English colonial actions in seventeenth-century Virginia. As Laura Brown and Margaret Ferguson have shown in their discussions of Behn's *Oroonoko*, the historical does not easily coexist with the romantic idealization that Behn's discourse produces.[34] Despite the romanticization of both Cavernio and Semernia, their cultural identity is always inscribed by their Indianness. Even as Cavernio responds to Bacon's courtesy with courtesy, it is clear that even the aristocratic or royal American Indian is not (and cannot be) fully assimilable.

The discourse of civility allowed Behn to invent an "American Indian" who is both assimilable and unequivocally alien. Behn drew upon existing racialist ideologies and, in incorporating them into the discourse of civility, produced a new discourse that spoke to unalterable differences that were not easily exoticized. In creating *The Widow Ranter,* she unconsciously exposes the principal contradiction of her class-based discourse of civility: aristocratic civility is incompatible with colonialism and imperialism. However, when the discourse of civility is constructed upon a racialized binarism, as is the case with *The Widow Ranter*, then the justifications for genocide, cultural hegemony, and slavery become more easily enunciated and defensible.

Homi Bhabha argues, "the objective of colonial discourse is to construe the colonized as a population of degenerate types on the basis of racial origin, in order to justify conquest and to establish systems of administration and instruction."[35] As "race" becomes imbricated in the geopolitics of early modern England, then the moral impetus of ideologies such as civility becomes a sailor's knot, tightening its hold not on the American Indians but on the English immigrants. The "most visible complexion" of "race" in the early modern English discourse, to return to Valerie Wayne's observation, is indelibly etched not in color but in the paradox of civility. Only when the concept of civility proves to be an ideological contradiction in the colonial project does the idea of "race" shift its meaning.

In the end, while the African woman's body became the primary locus for the economic enactment of English imperialism in the Americas from the eighteenth century onward, the American Indian woman functioned as the initial register for a discourse of "race" where color fixed difference. Thus, while the phenotypical differences between the American Indians and the English, in the English racial consciousness, were not as stark as the differences between Africans and English, they were important to the construction of a newer racial ideology. Essentially, and this is where I diverge from scholars such as Kupperman, the differences were enough to produce a binarism of inferiority/superiority.

Ultimately, the task that faces Renaissance scholars is not just to make visible the "whiteness" that is presumed to be the center of the concept, as Wayne has argued. Rather, we must begin to question the implicit racial assumptions being reread as a homogeneous society attempts to extend its hegemony beyond its own geographic boundaries. How does that society mark itself as different from the peoples it wishes to conquer? What effect does this marking have on the conquerors' own sense of identity? Only when we address these issues shall we begin to see the real property of the idea of "race." And perhaps, there will no longer be a need to "exonerate."

'TIS NOT THE FASHION TO CONFESS' 'SHAKESPEARE—POST-COLONIALITY JOHANNESBURG, 1996

> For truths to become the basis of national policy and, more widely, of national life, they must be believed, and whether or not whatever new truths we take from the West *will* depend in large measure on how we are able to manage the relations between our conceptual heritage and the ideas that rush at us from worlds elsewhere. (Appiah 1992:5)

Post-colonial confessions

Following four days of papers, conversations, debates and performances, 'Shakespeare-Post-coloniality-Johannesburg, 1996' concluded with an open forum. Participants were invited to offer their thoughts, critiques and ideas on the issues that had preoccupied the international gathering of cultural critics (many of whom were, in one way or another, involved in Shakespearean studies). The moment soon became what one participant termed 'the confessional' as people spoke eloquently, whether in praise or criticism, about the conference which was in the final stages of conclusion. Tensions had hovered, wraith-like, throughout much of the conference and, in the final hours of the conference, made their presence fully known as the varying cultural, political and ethnic points of reference surfaced; on a fundamental level, although not for the first time, the theory and praxis of 'post-coloniality' itself was subject to interrogation. Was it not indicative of the continued legacy and hegemony of colonialism that many of the speakers at this post-apartheid Shakespeare conference in South Africa were not South Africans? Can expatriates from former colonies, now living in the metropolis or its surrogate (England or the United States) speak for those who remain in the former colonized spaces that marked the boundaries of the British Empire? Is it appropriate for black Americans to express kinship with the black South African? Should there even have been a conference on Shakespeare and post-coloniality, given the uses to which Shakespeare's writings have been put throughout the history of English/British imperialism? That these issues came at the end of the conference is neither surprising nor, importantly, problematic. In fact, it would have been deeply troubling had the conference not ended on this note. What was noteworthy was the role 'confession' or, more properly, 'testimony' played in the process, simultaneously heightening and disrupting theoretical and cultural differences.

The 'confession,' as Michel Foucault reminds us, is 'one of the main rituals [Western societies] rely on for the production of truth. [In effect, confession] came to signify someone's acknowledgment of his own actions and thoughts' (Foucault 1980a: 58). What this acknowledgment entails, however, differs according to the political, cultural, gender and ethnic dictates of subjectivity. Yet, as Foucault understood, confession

frees, but power reduces one to silence; truth does not belong to the order of power, but shares an original affinity with freedom: traditional themes in philosophy, which a 'political history of truth' would have to overturn by showing that truth is not by nature free— nor error servile —but that its production is thoroughly imbued with relations of power. The confession is an example of this. (Ibid.: 60)

That my own contribution/confessional narrative to 'Shakespeare-Post-coloniality-Johannesburg, 1996', was figured as a reading of William Shakespeare's *Rape of Lucrece* and the significance of Lucrece's 'confession' as a complex interpellation of racialization is not without irony—a point to which I will return later in this discussion. For now, however, I want to explore the argument that, upon reflection, like the 'drive'/desire compelling Lucrece to 'politicize' Tarquin's rape of her body through confession (which leads to suicide), any attempt to theorize and or come to terms with the ideological assumptions compelling post-colonial theorization must also comprehend the significance of confession as a 'ritual' deeply implicated in the identity politics which often constitutes the impulses of post-colonial theorizing.

The contention of this essay is that the confession functions simultaneously as a counter-hegemonic strategy for racial liberation and as a dangerous problematic in Shakespeare's *Rape of Lucrece*. My aim is twofold: first, as part of long-term attempt to destabilize traditional assumptions about 'race' in early modern English culture, I propose to read *The Rape of Lucrece* as a text constitutively implicated in the emergence of the modern notion of race. Race, as I have argued elsewhere, was neither stable nor transcendental in its signification; rather, the word and concept was quite variable in its semantics and semiotics (Hendricks 1992; 1996). Consequently, instead of beginning with the assumption that 'race' exists as an unchanging, transcendental category of social identity, one ought to begin with the supposition that, in each historical and cultural context, race is a newly minted coin whose terminus ad quem is always yet to be codified. Second, and largely in response to a recurring theme during the Johannesburg conference, I hope to illustrate the continuing necessity for post-colonial studies in relation to Shakespeare's canon: in particular, to call attention to those works that are not readily identifiable as works bearing colonialist ideologies. Ultimately, this essay seeks to advocate a recognition of the necessity of not only interrogation but also confession as theoretical strategies important to post-colonial theoretical interventions.

Lucrece's rape/race

In an informative study of the varied cultural (re)presentations of Lucretia's rape, Ian Donaldson traces the long history of artistic and literary treatments of the rape of Lucretia. Of particular note is his discussion of Titian's painting, which represents this most interesting icon of Western culture. In his 'reading' of Titian's work, Donaldson remarks that,

> despite the high color of her face, Lucrece is pale beside Tarquin's darker skin—a tonal contrast which possibly hints at the racial, as well as purely sexual, oppositions of the story: Lucrece is a Roman, Tarquin an Etruscan. (Donaldson 1982:13)

For Donaldson, this politicized commentary is intended to provide not only a semiotic register for comprehending Titian's painting but also a specifically modern ideological framework for understanding the significance of Lucrece's rape. Yet, having made this rather provocative statement, Donaldson immediately abandons it. In part, because he is dealing with painting, Donaldson can only draw attention to what is evident in Titian's painting. However, by invoking a specific 'historicity' to Lucrece's rape—the different ethnic backgrounds of Lucrece and Tarquin—Donaldson suggestively reminds his readers that there is, significantly, a dual cultural/historical context to the image before us: the colonized Roman and the colonizing Etruscan.

On one level, Donaldson's notation of the contrasting lightness and darkness of the two figures in Titian's painting evokes the tropic association of light and dark with good and evil and it is not difficult read Donaldson's observations as simply reiterating the type of fetishistic moralizing of color employed in so much early modern discourse concerned with gender relations, sexuality and Christianity. Add to this ideological mix the political idealization of Lucrece's rape as the genesis of Rome's rise to republicanism (and eventually imperial and colonial power), and Donaldson's analysis of Titian's painting bespeaks a familiar post-Enlightenment notion about 'race' based on skin color. Beyond this, Donaldson's remark on the color difference between Lucrece and Tarquin seems almost gratuitous (though his comments do have broader implications for inquiry into Donaldson's 'reading' Titian's reading of the Lucrece/Tarquin narrative). We might well ask: were there actual color differences between Romans and Etruscans? If so, did these color distinctions come into play in the political struggle between the ruling Tarquins and their subjects and, thus, were indelibly etched in the narratives recounting the struggle? Or, is the 'racial opposition' that Donaldson 'sees' an anachronistic reading of Titian's painting—an illusion brought on by the aging of paint pigmentation, for example, or Donaldson's own twentieth-century subjectivity seeking to substantiate color differences where there may have been none? Accustomed as we are to looking for 'familiar markers' (skin color, physical features, code words and so on), it is easy to arrive at the same conclusions as Donaldson.

What discoveries would Donaldson have made had he framed his inquiry with slightly different assumptions about what signified race in Renaissance and early modern visual representations and literary discourses? That is, if he had turned his gaze from one perspectival position to another, would the racial inscriptions be as readily (or as easily) 'readable'? Furthermore, may it not be argued that, when one turns from painting to literary works, the art of representing the racial identities of Lucrece and Tarquin may have a radically different complexity; a complexity not easily reducible to shades of coloring, i.e., 'paleness' and 'darkness'; that race is much more ambiguously rendered because it has not yet stabilized into one dominant signification? It is this mode of inquiry, I would contend, that must be brought to bear on readings of literary and visual 'encounters' with the narrative history of the rape of Lucretia.

William Shakespeare's literary 'encounter' with the narrative account of Tarquin's rape of Lucretia provides a useful exemplum for the complicated figuration of race that I am suggesting. Drawing upon the two major Roman texts recounting the story of Lucretia's rape (Livy's *History of Rome* and Ovid's *Fasti*), Shakespeare's narrative poem shows itself to be part of that process which Stephanie Jed describes when she remarks:

> every encounter with a representation of the rape of Lucretia is an encounter with a literary topos of Western civilization. And, as a *topos*, the meaning of this rape is constructed as universal, transcending historical conditions: in every age and place,

Lucretia had to be raped so that Rome would be liberated from tyranny. (Jed 1989:51)

What I would add, or state more categorically, is that Shakespeare's *The Rape of Lucrece* also reveals that every encounter is also an encounter with an ideology of race. What distinguishes Shakespeare's telling of the narrative from the texts that interest Jed is that republicanism is (I would argue) of less concern than the ideology of racial identity. Without ever once using the term 'race,' Shakespeare manages to invest his narrative rendering of Lucretia's rape with all of the semiotic traces of early modern anxiety about defining a concept of race.

It is my contention that Shakespeare's *The Rape of Lucrece* is an attempt to mediate the tensions (and contradictions) generated by competing discourses of race: race as defined by genealogy or lineage and race as defined by ethnicity. In this imprecision, as an expression of fundamental distinctions, race's meaning varied depending upon whether a writer wanted to specify difference born of a class-based concept of genealogy, a psychological (and essentialized) nature, or group typology. Nonetheless, in all these variations, race is envisioned as something fundamental, something immutable, knowable and recognizable, yet we only 'see' it when its boundaries are violated. It is this 'seeing' that Shakespeare's narrative engenders in its rendering of Lucrece's confessional discourse.

In the aftermath of Tarquin's rape, Lucrece engages in an extraordinary lamentation for her lost virtue. Nicholas Abercrombie, Stephen Hill and Bryan S. Turner have argued that

> the insistence on chastity and virtue for wives as a condition for the economic strength of the feudal family was also closely connected with the ideology of chivalry. Since noble birth was a crucial feature of knighthood, only true-born sons would be brave and worthy of their families. …Confusion of blood produced unreliable men. (Abercrombie, Hill and Turner 1980:90)

Shifting between rage, self-pity, shame and despair, Lucrece simultaneously resists and acknowledges the interiority associated with guilt: "O unseen shame, invisible disgrace!/O unfelt sore, crestwounding private scar!/Reproach is stamped in Collatinus' face' (827–9). Unable completely to absolve herself of some degree of complicity, 'yet I am guilty of thy honour's wrack;/Yet for thy honour did I entertain him' (841–2), she embraces the role of both judge and executioner to expiate her 'crime'—even though she must rely on her husband, father and kin to punish Tarquin for his actions.

What is central to Lucrece's logic here is her awareness that unlawful sexuality, despite its initial invisibility, inevitably surfaces. What is noteworthy, however, is that when this surfacing occurs, it is described as marking both the body of Lucrece and that of her husband. This 'sign,' ideologically figured as the loss of honor, is linked to a fear not of the act itself but what the act threatens to produce—the illegitimate child. Where this inscription becomes visible, of course, is in the semiotics of genealogy, and more specifically, as Shakespeare depicts it, in the discourse of heraldry. For both Lucrece and Tarquin, heraldry is the place where a nobleman's lineage is figured; the images and shapes to be publicly noted (his shield) provide the metonymic site for revealing the effects of Tarquin's desire. In other words, Shakespeare uses heraldic language to mark the graduated shift from one form of racial thinking to another.

Tarquin's complicated self-reflexivity just prior to his rape of Lucrece marks the first half of this narrative strategy, exemplifying the logic of racial identity as a matter of genealogy. In a tense private moment, Tarquin confronts the 'public' dimension of his 'private' act: "O shame to knighthood and to shining arms!/O foul dishonour to my household's grave!' (197–8). Tarquin is fully aware that should he carry out the rape, and should he die, the 'scandal will survive' as 'some loathsome dash the herald will contrive/To cipher me how fondly I did dote' (204–6). This concern for family honor will surface once more when Tarquin reflects on the fact that 'he [Collatinus] is my kinsman, my dear friend,/The shame and fault finds no excuse nor end' (237–8). Kinship or family should have been sufficient to prevent Tarquin from carrying out his rape, yet, as both his disputation and subsequently his words to Lucrece demonstrate, lust recognizes no lines of kinship.

Lucrece, in her disputation, also recognizes the significance of her rape as a matter of familial ties. As the reproductive site for the continuation of Collatine's line (race), Lucrece completely understands the immediate and future import of Tarquin's action (miscegenation and possibly a child). Her initial reaction is to vow that Collatine 'shalt not know the stained taste of violated troth'; that, in a noble gesture, she 'will not wrong [his] true affection so, / To flatter thee with an infringed oath' (1058–60). Of course, what Lucrece is alluding to is the threat of pregnancy that may ensue as a result of Tarquin's rape. Promising that Tarquin's 'bastard graff shall never come to growth,' that he 'shall not boast who did thy stock pollute / That thou are doting father of his fruit,' Lucrece concludes her 'disputation,' resolved to commit suicide. For Lucrece, suicide will not only serve to expiate the immediate shame created by Tarquin's rape but also will extirpate any potential offspring.

Though similarly employing the rhetoric of heraldry in confronting the full implications of Tarquin's crime; Lucrece, in her moment of confession, conjoins the two significations of race. However, I want to suggest that not until she 'interpellates' herself as a racial subject can Lucrece resolve the ideological dilemma created by Tarquin's rape. Louis Althusser offers the following explanation of interpellation:

> ideology 'acts' or 'functions' in such a way that it 'recruits' subjects among the individuals (it recruits them all), or 'transforms' the individuals into subjects (it transforms them all) by that very precise operation which I have called *interpellation* or hailing, and which can be imagined along the lines of the most commonplace everyday police (or other) hailing: 'Hey, you there!' (Althusser 1971:174)

When the individual turns around, 'he becomes a *subject*. Why? Because he has recognized that the hail was "really" addressed to him, and that "it was *really him* who was hailed" (and not someone else)'(ibid.).

The disputational mode deployed by Shakespeare in his narrative poem positions, intriguingly, Tarquin and Lucrece as subjects capable of 'hailing' not only each other but themselves. For Lucrece, 'interpellation' occurs when she declares, "Let my good name, that senseless reputation, / Collatine's dear love be kept unspotted' (820). It is her name which enables her to act to expiate the 'unseen shame,' the 'invisible disgrace,' that marks both her body and Collatine's as a result of Tarquin's violation of racial lines. Lucrece's 'hailing,' however, not only interpellates her, but also interpellates the readers of Shakespeare's narrative, effectively making them 'agents in the reproduction of a violated body, a prod to prurience in a humanistic peep show,' from which the 'narrative of liberation' (Jed 1989:49) and an ideology of race become simultaneously (re)inscribed in history and, literally, on Lucrece's body, once 'white' now marked by Tarquin's racializing 'stain.' It is against this 'stain' that the ekphrasis on the destruction of Troy must be read. Searching for the face where 'all distress is stelled' (1444), Lucrece finds solace in the painter's 'anatomized' depiction of Hecuba: 'In her the painter had anatomized / Time's ruin, beauty's wreck, and grim care's reign' (1450–1). Hecuba's plight is the catalyst, the analogue, for Lucrece's own grief. Furthermore, her identification with the women of Troy, I would argue, also reminds the narrative's readers of another link between Rome and Troy: the commonplace mythography that the descendants of the Trojan Aeneas found the city of Rome.

The ekphrasis serves to illuminate not so much a cultural historiography but rather Lucrece's movement from one form of racial consciousness (and thus subjectivity) to another. Thus, while Lucrece condemns the presumed agent of Troy's fall, Helen—'Show me the strumpet that began this stir / That with my nails I may tear' (1471–2)—Lucrece's condemnation is really directed at the perpetrator of the heinous crime which directly concerns her, viz. Tarquin. It is, I would argue, Tarquin that Lucrece has in mind when she utters the words, 'for trespass of thine eye, / The sire, the son, the dame, and daughter the' (1476–7). Yet none of this is evident when she asks

Why should the private pleasure of some one

Become the public plague of many moe?
Let sin, alone committed, light alone
Upon his head that hath transgressed so (1479-81)

Lucrece's words eventually will prove prophetic when, as a result of her suicide, Rome is plunged into civil war.

Though Lucrece has committed no sin, in her despair and shame she finds in the image of the chaos that is the fallen Troy the subjectivity she will need to castigate the racial possibility of Tarquin's 'bastard graff.' Drawing upon the emotions stirred by the painting of the fallen Troy, Lucrece moves from silence to speech: 'And now this pale swan in her wat'ry nest/Begins the sad dirge of her certain ending' (1611–12). In the presence of her husband and her kin, she performs her own eulogy, 'confessing' the narrative of Tarquin's rape, binding her husband and kin to redressing the wrong against her honor, 'castigating' the pollution created by Tarquin's desire. Like the ekphrasis on the destruction of Troy, Lucrece's 'confession' renders visible the invisible stain of her dishonor. Though assured that she is blameless, Lucrece refuses absolution, saying '"No, no...no dame hereafter living/By my excuse shall claim excuse's giving"' (1714–15). From a feminist perspective, Lucrece's words are deeply troubling; in effect, one hears the rape victim blaming herself for the rape.

This image is further instantiated when Lucrece sheaths 'in her harmless breast/A harmful knife, that thence her soul unsheathed' (172 23–4). In her attempt to exorcize Tarquin's violation of her body, Lucrece takes her own life. Yet the use of the word 'sheath,' with its obvious erotic signification, subtly undermines the high tragedy of this suicide, shadowed by the image of Tarquin's 'gaze' which also rendered her breast a site of erotic desires. Lucrece's body, therefore, suffers penetration not once but twice. Once more involving the reader in a prurient gaze, Lucrece's self-inflicted wound is intended to purify, to 'tear' away, the flesh that bears not only disgrace but also the very real possibility that Tarquin's 'momentary joy' might breed 'months of pain' (690). Surrounded by her husband, father and kin, Lucrece elicits from these men a vow to revenge her violated body. What Lucrece's demand entails is more than familial revenge, however; the vow the men make binds them as a 'gens' or 'ethnos' against Tarquin. Her confession heard and her shame absolved by the men who stand before her, Lucrece's body becomes the site where the meaning of race and racial identity shifts.

The poem's audience would have been quite familiar with the ethnic mythology signified in the ekphrasis and linked to the final image of the narrative where Lucrece's body is 'paraded' through Rome as a testament to the tyranny of Tarquin. Rome's heritage (genealogy) was understood to have its very genesis in the fallen city of Troy; Aeneas, escaping the destruction of Troy, made his way to Italy where his descendants and those of other Trojans eventually found the city of Rome. Furthermore, though recognized as historically inaccurate even among early modern English historiographers, the mythography of Aeneas' descendant Brutus as progenitor of England's people proved a useful trope for the legitimization of incipient imperialist and colonialist endeavors. In essence, Shakespeare's narrative reproduction and (re)presentation of the Lucretia myth gives life to a new ideology of race; an ideology which defines itself not only in terms of lineage but also in terms of ethnicity. This sixteenth-century encounter with the political and ideological semiotics associated with the rape of Lucrece denotes, in a striking and persistent articulation, the necessary engendering of one's ethnicity through violence against the colonized (and generally female) body. What emerges in the aftermath of Lucrece's suicide is the embodiment of the Roman Republic and unified ethnos, and ultimately the Roman Empire, even as that suicide enacts the deracination of Tarquin's own lineage; what emerges in Shakespeare's retelling of the rape and suicide of Lucrece is the continued necessity to retell the rape to maintain the boundaries of that racial ideology. English imperialism required such a narrative.

Lucrece's rape revisited, 1997

For nearly a thousand years, the Roman Republic has provided the foundational ideology for Western political institutions; and, as Jed's study (Jed 1989) illuminates, the rape of Lucrece sits at the apex of this ideology, even though the politics of republicanism has rendered this presence virtually invisible. What Jed sought to do in her engagement with the narrative was to shift the perspectival position of readers/viewers of Lucrece's rape, so that Lucrece's violated and mutilated body no longer lies on the margins of republican idealism but is the territory upon which that idealism (and Tarquin's rape) is inscribed and continuously rehearsed every time the narrative is retold. Shakespeare's narrative participates in this rehearsal even as it works, I would argue, to conjoin the mythography of Lucrece's rape to a newly emerging ethnos. In subtle ways, the myth comes to serve a didactic purpose in the formation of English nationalism and, markedly, imperialism. Along with the other texts of Shakespeare's canon, *The Rape of Lucrece* performs in both theory and in practice the colonialist impulses that continue to haunt those spaces, cultures and peoples once subject to British rule.

As Jed so astutely demonstrates in her study, every reading, rewriting, and scholarly or critical engagement with the narrative of Lucretia's rape continues the transmission of ideologies central to the development of modern social institutions, and, I would add, modern imperialism as part of the topos of constituting 'civilized man.' Shakespeare's *The Rape of Lucrece*, like the other texts that form his 'canon,' though not necessarily one of the more celebrated works, circulates as part of the cultural hegemony extant in nineteenth-century English imperialism and remains, even today, one of the most pervasive artifacts left in the wake of English colonialism. We might well ponder whether the narrative informed the social consciousness of indigenous women (and men) in their struggles for liberation: did acculturated women see Lucrece's suicide as an exemplary model of resistance to English hegemony? Was the female body literally or figuratively (i.e., as the idealized mother country or female territory) raped and/or sacrificed as part of the struggle for liberation? How did indigenous, Western-educated ('subaltern') women 'read' Lucrece's rape? Did Lucrece's rape and 'confession' become unsettled in the modern colonialist project? Are there post-colonial rewritings of this master narrative of female chastity and sacrifice that challenge not only the humanistic ideology that has kept it in circulation but also the imperialist ideology that requires its continual circulation? Does the distinction between private and public blur the fact that Lucrece's body is a confessional political body?

From the margins

Shakespeare's *The Rape of Lucrece* implicitly links the Roman Lucretia to early modern England's conceptualization of its participation in the humanist project, which in turn becomes a central tenet of modern imperialism and colonialism. Recognition of this, and the syncretic ways this tenet continues to require interrogation, must become part of post- colonial theorizing. The icon of Lucretia serves not just as a strategy of acculturation and assimilation; it equally functions to create a false relationship between self-sacrifice and femininity, politics and ethnicity, rape and progress. Interrogating this and other Shakespearean texts not on Western terms but on those of indigenous cultures' resistance to British hegemony, using these texts as sites of 'cultural intercourse' (Lionnet 1995:115), using the text to 'write back' to the 'margins,' may be one of the possible and potentially radical strategies available to post- colonialist critics.

Perhaps similar to Lucrece's presence before the males of her family, my presence in South Africa was both a personal and public expression of historical kinship with black South Africans. Yet at the same time, I realize, ironically, that any invocation of the idea of kinship is at best symbolic, in as much as the material and cultural conditions of existence of the black Americans present at the conference were, in all likelihood, fundamentally different. Such are the dialectics of post-coloniality.

In what might be loosely termed 'border theorizing,' postcolonial critics and theorists have isolated a conceptual space where, as Françoise Lionnet argues, all of our academic preconceptions about cultural, linguistic, or stylistic norms are constantly being put to the test by creative practices that make visible and set off the processes of adaptation, appropriation, and contestation that govern the construction of identity in colonial and postcolonial contexts. (Lionnet 1995:111)

Lionnet's observation, while made in reference to Francophone women writers, has a bearing on the issues that concern this essay. Asked to explore the role of post-colonial theories in the 'business' of Shakespearean studies, the participants of 'Shakespeare-Postcoloniality- Johannesburg, 1996' found themselves 'tested' by not only their perceptions of Shakespeare's creative practices but also by the dilemma of continuing the valorization of Shakespeare. At the center of the discussions, debates and testing was the very real understanding of the uses to which Shakespeare and his writings have been put in colonized spaces. For some, Shakespeare became just another 'white' space, a point of reference on the continuum of producing the civilized native. The confessional moment which marked the final day of the conference, then, not only brought to the surface the narrative of the cultural struggles taking shape in South Africa, it also highlighted that the discourses and politics of post-coloniality have forever altered the ways in which Shakespeare's writings can be engaged.

By way of closure, I want to (re)present one last encounter. In an odd way, the moment was replete with the materiality of post-colonialism: a dozen or so individuals who had journeyed to Johannesburg, South Africa, for a conference on Shakespeare and post-coloniality and who either lived or were born in nation-states designated as 'post-colonial' spaces (India, New Zealand, Canada) or in the metropolis which engendered these spaces, packed in a Toyota van, hurtling away from Johannesburg and towards the black township known as Soweto. Only the driver and the student guide were native to South Africa. As the van moved inexorably toward the icon that had come to symbolize the protracted struggle of black South Africans and their white allies to dismantle the institutions of apartheid, a strange sense of familiarity floated fleetingly to my consciousness, not quite *déjà vu* yet not entirely foreign. The sensation passed as quickly as it came and, like the others in the van, I studied the arid, desert-like landscape between the two cities.

A few months after my return to the United States, I visited my birthplace of Riverside, California: a city of nearly 300,000 people located on the periphery of the largest desert in the United States and approximately 45 minutes from Los Angeles. As the car I drove reached the crest of a small hill and began its descent, images of the topography which divided Johannesburg and Soweto played in my mind, bringing with them memories of the conversations and debates that framed 'Shakespeare—Post-coloniality-Johannesburg, 1996.' The most interesting conversation occurred between Wonderboy Peters and myself not long after I had delivered my paper, when he spoke about his curiosity as to the term *mestizaje'*, a concept I used in reference to a discussion of Shakespeare's comedy *A Midsummer Night's Dream*. I explained that *mestizaje*, according to the *Diccionario de Uso del Español,* is defined as the *'cruzamiento de razas,'* (literally, cross-breeding of races) or the *'conjunto de mestizos'* (group of mestizos) and related to the verb *mestizar,* which is defined as *'adulterar la puerza de una raza por el cruce con otras'* (adulterating the purity of one race by mixing with others) (Molner 1984). Intrigued by my deployment of the notion of the Spanish term *mestizaje* as a post-colonial critique of early modern discourses of race, Wonderboy spoke of his own *mestizaje,* his status as a colored in South Africa (he is the son of a white father and a black mother) and the politics that inform such subjectivity in both the old and new South Africa. Neither white nor black yet both, Wonderboy considered the idea of thinking through the concept of race in terms of an idea of *mestizaje* as an epistemological, political and theoretical framework, one tied neither to a specific nation-state nor to a linguistic community, a useful theoretical tool. The irony of observing this appropriation of a Spanish word, initially used to frame a critical reading of two Shakespearean texts, one of which was the retelling of an ancient Roman narrative, to come to terms with one's subjectivity in post-apartheid Johannesburg, was not lost on me. On the contrary, if asked to locate an 'appropriate' site for such a deployment, I could not have chosen better. This essay, then, is dedicated to him and the other students who occupied both the center and the margins of 'Shakespeare–Post-coloniality-Johannesburg, 1996.'

WORK CITED

A Feminist Historiography

Published in *A Companion to Early Modern Women's Writing. ed. Anita Pacheco.* Wiley & Sons copyright 2002. Reproduced with permission of the Licensor through PLSclear.

References

Amussen, Susan (1988). *An Ordered Society: Gender and Class in Early Modern England.* New York: Columbia University Press.
Beckles, Hilary M. (1989). *Natural Rebels: A Social History of Enslaved Black Women in Barbados.* London: Zed Books; New Brunswick, NJ: Rutgers University Press.
Bray, Alan (1982). *Homosexuality in Renaissance England.* London: Gay Men's Press.
Breisach, Ernst (1994). *Historiography: Ancient, Medieval, and Modern,* 2nd edn. Chicago: University of Chicago Press.
Clark, Alice (1982) [1919]. *Working Life of Women in the Seventeenth Century.* London: Routledge and Kegan Paul.
Cummins, John (1995). *Francis Drake: Lives of a Hero.* New York: St Martin's Press.
Ezell, Margaret J. M. (1987). *The Patriarch's Wife: Literary Evidence and*

the History of the Family. Chapel Hill: University of North Carolina Press.

—— (1994). *Writing Women's Literary History*. Baltimore, MD: Johns Hopkins University Press. Ferguson, Margaret, Quilligan, Maureen and Vickers, Nancy (eds) (1986). *Re-Writing the Renaissance: The Discourses of Sexual Difference in Early Modern Europe*. Chicago: University of Chicago Press. File, Nigel and Power, Chris (1981). *Black Settlers in Britain, 1555–1958*. London: Heinemann.

Fletcher, Anthony (1997). *Gender, Sex and Subordination in England 1500–1800*. New Haven, CT: Yale University Press.

Fryer, Peter (1984). *Staying Power: The History of Blacks in Britain*. London: Pluto Press.

Gundara, Jagdish S. and Duffield, Ian (eds) (1992). *Essays on the History of Blacks in Britain: From Roman Times to the Mid-Twentieth Century*. Aldershot: Avebury.

Habib, Imtiaz (1998). *Shakespeare and Race: Postcolonial Praxis in the Early Modern Period*. Lanham, NY: University Press of America.

Hakluyt, Richard (1903–5). *The Principal Navigations, Voyages, Traffiques & Discoveries of the English Nation (1600)*, 12 vols, ed. Walter Raleigh. Glasgow: James Maclehose and Sons.

Hall, Kim F. (1996). *Things of Darkness: Economies of Race and Gender in Early Modern England*. Ithaca, NY: Cornell University Press.

Hendricks, Margo and Parker, Patricia (eds) (1994). *Women, 'Race' and Writing in the Early Modern Period*. London: Routledge.

Hobby, Elaine (1989). *Virtue of Necessity: English Women's Writing 1649–88*. Ann Arbor: University of Michigan Press.

Ingram, Martin (1987). *Church Courts, Sex and Marriage in England, 1570–1640*. Cambridge: Cambridge University Press.

Kearns, Katherine (1997). *Psychoanalysis, Historiography, and Feminist Theory: The Search for Critical Method*. Cambridge: Cambridge University Press.

Kelly, Joan (1984). *Women, History and Theory: The Essays of Joan Kelly*. Chicago: University of Chicago Press.

Ligon, Richard (1657). *A True and Exact History of the Iland of Barbadoes*. London.

Loomba, Ania (1989). *Race, Gender, and Renaissance Drama.* Manchester: Manchester University Press.

Maclean, Ian (1980). *The Renaissance Notion of Woman: A Study in the Fortunes of Scholasticism and Medical Science in European Intellectual Life.* Cambridge: Cambridge University Press.

Middlesex County Sessions of Peace Roll, 1189/117 (1658). London: Metropolitan Archives.

Mohanty, Chandra Talpade (1991). 'Under western eyes: feminist scholarship and colonialist discourses.' In Chandra Talpade Mohanty, Ann Russo and Lourdes Torres (eds), *Third World Women and the Politics of Feminism* (pp. 51–86). Bloomington: Indiana University Press.

Nuttall, Zelia (ed. and trans.) (1967). *New Light On Drake: A Collection of Documents Relating to His Voyage of Circumnavigation 1577–1580.* Reproduced by permission of the Hakluyt Society from the edition originally published by the Society in 1914. Nendeln/Liechtenstein: Kraus Reprint.

Orlin, Lena Cowan (1994). *Private Matters and Public Culture in Post-Reformation England.* Ithaca, NY: Cornell University Press.

Shakespeare, William (1988). *The Merchant of Venice.* In Stanley Wells and Gary Taylor (eds), *The Complete Works of William Shakespeare.* Oxford: Oxford University Press.

Shyllon, Folarin (1977). *Black People in Britain 1555–1833.* London, New York and Ibadan: The Institute of Race Relations, London by Oxford University Press.

Sommerville, Margaret R. (1995). *Sex and Subjection: Attitudes to Women in Early-Modern Society.* London: Arnold.

White, Hayden (1978). *Tropics of Discourse: Essays in Cultural Criticism.* Baltimore, MD: Johns Hopkins University Press.

—— (1987). *The Content of the Form: Narrative Discourse and Historical Representation.* Baltimore, MD: Johns Hopkins University Press.

Wrightson, Keith (1982). *English Society 1580–1680.* New Brunswick, NJ: Rutgers University Press.

Yungblut, Laura Hunt (1996). *Strangers Settled Here Amongst Us: Policies, Perceptions, and the Presence of Aliens in Elizabethan England.* London: Routledge.

Zimmerman, Susan (ed.) (1992). *Erotic Politics: Desire on the Renaissance*

Stage. New York: Routledge. Zinsser, Judith P. (1993). *History and Feminism: A Glass Half Full*. New York: Twayne Publishers.

Managing the Barbarian: *The Tragedy of Dido, Queen of Carthage,*

Published in *Renaissance Drama* ,New Series, Vol. 23, Renaissance Drama in an Age of Colonization (1992), pp. 165-188. copyright 1992. The University of Chicago Press for Northwestern University Reproduced with permission of the Licensor through PLSclear."

I want to thank my colleagues at the University of California, Santa Cruz, for their criticisms and willingness to read and re-read this essay. I especially wish to thank two readers, Jean E. Howard and Don E. Wayne. Without their intellectual intervention much of this discussion would have never been written. I also wish to thank Stephen Orgel for putting me onto this line of inquiry.

1. I am indebted to Stephen Orgel for suggesting that I look more closely at Anglo/ Hispanic relations at the close of the sixteenth century. For useful studies of the naval conflict between England and Spain, see Parry, *The Spanish Seaborne Empire* and *The Age of Reconnaissance*. For an overview of early modern European imperialism, see Scammell.
2. See Stilling.
3. As Powell notes, many of these pamphlets were based on Dutch pamphlets and the account of Las Casas. The political biases of both the English and the Dutch should not be ignored in readings of these documents.
4. What is noteworthy about this monarch is the similarity between her political status and that of Marlowe's monarch, Elizabeth I. Yet the cultural differences sufficiently mark Dido so that she exists not as an analogy to Elizabeth but as a particular emblem of alien femininity. See Jordan.
5. See John Pory's introduction to Leo Africanus's *A Geographical Historie of Africa*. For a recent study of the representation of Africans on the English stage, see D'Amico. See also Howard.

6. This is one of two statements alluding to a "white" Dido in Marlowe's text. The other occurs when Aeneas declares, "O queen of Carthage, wert thou ugly-black, / Aeneas could not choose but hold thee dear!" (5.1.125-26). For a discussion of the "trope of blackness," see Hall.

7. See Robert A. Logan's "The Sexual Attitudes of Marlowe and Shakespeare" and W. Craig Turner's "Love and the Queen of Carthage." In both essays, Dido's subjectivity becomes subsumed in such critical questions as Marlowe's Ovidian re-reading of Virgil's *Aeneid* or the dramatist's "passionate" treatment of tragic love. Without belaboring the minor differences, these essays do little more than reiterate the "reason versus passion" argument perceived in Renaissance discourse as gender difference; consequently, Logan's reading of Dido becomes virtually indistinguishable from Turner's. For an excellent corrective to these readings, see ch. 5 in Jankowski.

8. See Stallybrass.

9. See Judith Weil's *Christopher Marlowe*. Weil shares Turner's and Leech's perception of the comic overtones which accompany Anna's and Iarbas's suicides.

10. For incisive discussions of the European slave-trading period, see Rodney, *A History of the Upper Guinea Coast, 1545 to 1800* and *How Europe Underdeveloped Africa*.

11. I deliberately employ the word *miscegenation* to include cultural exchanges as well as sexual and marital relations between peoples allegedly of different races. Although the term is first used in 1863 to describe relations between Africans and "whites," I believe it can and does have broader implications beyond its usual application to "black" and "white" sexual relations.

12. The Roman general Scipio Africanus was the second "Aeneas" to sack Carthage. See Polybius, *The Rise of the Roman Empire,* for the historical accounts of the Punic Wars.

13. Banton, *The Idea of Race* 26. See also Banton's *Racial Consciousness*.

14. Banton, *Racial Theories*. This book is organized along this matrix.

15. Banton, *Racial Theories* 2. Banton notes that John Foxe's *Book of Martyrs* (1570), in which the author makes reference to "the race and

stocke of Abraham," was the earliest appearance in English of the word *race*.

16. I recognize that the use of the term *nation* is problematic; however, as early modern English writers continually employed the term, I shall follow their example and retain its usage in reference to England. For discussions of nations, and nationalism, see Bhabha and Anderson.

17. See Leo Africanus, *A Geographical Historie of Africa,* and Hakluyt, *Principal Navigations.*

18. See Jones and Stallybrass.

19. Geoffrey of Monmouth 65. This view is dealt with in the chronicles of British history written by Polydore Vergil, Stow, Holinshed, and Speed.

References

The Aeneid of Thomas Phaer and Thomas Twyne. Ed. Steven Lally. New York: Garland, 1987.
Anderson, Benedict R. O'G. *Imagined Communities: Reflections on the Origin and*
Spread of Nationalism. London: Verso, 1983.
Banton, Michael. *The Idea of Race.* London: Tavistock, 1977.
— *Racial Consciousness.* London: Longman, 1988.
— *Racial Theories.* Cambridge: Cambridge UP, 1987.
Bhabha, Homi K., ed. *Nation and Narration.* London: Routledge, 1990.
D'Amico, Jack. *The Moor in English Renaissance Drama.* Tampa: U of South Florida P, 1991.
Eden, Richard. "A briefe description of Afrike gathered by Richard Eden." Hakluyt,
Principal Navigations 6: 142-45.
Geoffrey of Monmouth. *The History of the Kings of Britain.* Trans. Lewis Thorpe. London: Penguin, 1986.
Hakluyt, Richard. *The Principal Navigations, Voyages, Traffiques* & *Discoveries of the English Nation.* 12 vols. Glasgow: MacLehose, 1914.
— *Voyages and Discoveries: The Principal Navigations, Voyages, Traffiques and Discoveries of the English Nation.* Ed. Jack Beeching. Harmondsworth: Penguin, 1972.

Hall, Kim F. "'I would rather wish to be a black-moor': Beauty, Race, and Rank in Lady Mary Wroth's *Urania*." *Women, "Race," and Writing in the Early Modern Period*. Ed. Margo Hendricks and Patricia Parker. London: Routledge, 1993.

Helgerson, Richard. *Forms of Nationhood: The Elizabethan Writing of England*. Chicago: U of Chicago P, 1992.

Howard, Jean E. "An English Lass amid the Moors: Gender, Race, Sexuality, and National Identity in *The Fair Maid of the West*." *Women, "Race," and Writing in the Early Modern Period*. Ed. Margo Hendricks and Patricia Parker. London: Routledge, 1993. Jankowski, Theodora A. *Women in Power in the Early Modern Drama*. Urbana: U of Illinois P, 1992.

Jones, Ann Rosalind, and Peter Stallybrass. "Dismantling Irena: The Sexualizing of Ireland in Early Modern England." *Nationalisms and Sexualities*. Ed. Andrew Parker, Mary Russo, A. Sommer, and Patricia Yeager. London: Routledge, 1991. 157-69.

Jordan, Constance. *Renaissance Feminism: Literary Texts and Political Models*. Ithaca:
Cornell UP, 1990.

Keller, Mary Frear, ed. *Sir Francis Drake's West Indian Voyage, 1585-86*. London: Hakluyt Soc., 1981.

Leech, Clifford. *Christopher Marlowe: Poet for the Stage*. Ed. Anne Lancashire. New York: AMS, 1986.

Leo Africanus. *A Geographical Historie of Africa*. Trans. John Pory. Amsterdam: Theatrum Orbis Terrarum, 1969.

Logan, Robert A. "The Sexual Attitudes of Marlowe and Shakespeare." *University of Hartford Studies in Literature* 19.2-3 (1987): 1-23.

Marlowe, Christopher. *Dido, Queen of Carthage*. Ed. J. B. Steane. London: Penguin, 1969.

Parry, J. H. *The Age of Reconnaissance*. Berkeley: U of California P, 1981.

— *The Spanish Seaborne Empire*. Berkeley: U of California P, 1990.

Powell, Philip Wayne. *Tree of Hate: Propaganda and Prejudices Affecting United States Relations with the Hispanic World*. New York: Basic, 1971.

Rodney, Walter. *A History of the Upper Guinea Coast, 1545 to 1800*. New York: Monthly Review, 1970.

— *How Europe Underdeveloped Africa*. Washington: Howard UP, 1972.

Scammell, G. V. *The First Imperial Age: European Overseas Expansion c. 1400-1715.*
London: Unwin Hyman, 1989.
Stallybrass, Peter. "The World Turned Upside Down: Inversion, Gender, and the State." *The Matter of Difference: Materialist Feminist Criticism of Shakespeare.* Ed. Valerie Wayne. New York: Harvester-Wheatsheaf, 1991. 201-20.
Stilling, Roger. *Love and Death in Renaissance Tragedy,* Baton Rouge: Louisiana State UP, 1976.
Turner, W. Craig. "Love and the Queen of Carthage: A Look at Marlowe's *Dido.*" *Essays in Literature* 11 (1984): 3-9.
Weil, Judith. *Christopher Marlowe: Merlin's Prophet.* Cambridge: Cambridge UP, 1977.

Civility, Barbarism, and Aphra Behn's *The Widow Ranter*

Published in *Women, 'Race' and Writing in the Early Modern Period* Routledge. Copyright 1994 Reproduced with permission of the Licensor through PLSclear.
1. Valerie Wayne, ed., *The Matter of Difference: Materialist Feminist Criticism of Shakespeare* (London: Harvester Wheatsheaf, 1991), 11.
2. Dominick LaCapra, ed., *The Bounds of Race: Perspectives on Hegemony and Resistance* (Ithaca: Cornell University Press, 1991), 2.
3. Margaret Ferguson, 'Juggling the Categories of Race, Class, and Gender: Aphra Behn's *Oroonoko,*" ch. 12, this volume (*Women, Race, and Writing in the Early Modern Period*).
4. One of the primary texts Behn may have used was *Strange News From Virginia: Being a full and True Account of the Life and Death of Nathanael Bacon Esquire, Who was the only Cause and Original of all the Late Troubles in that Country. With a full Relation of all the Accidents which have happened in the late War there between the Christians and Indians.* The pamphlet narrates Bacon's lineage, his settlement in the Virginia colony, his anger at the Virginia Council's refusal to grant him a commission, the ensuing discord between Bacon and the Council, his death, and the sentences meted out to his principal followers.
5. Wilcomb E. Washburn, *The Governor and the Rebel: A History of*

Bacon's Rebellion in Virginia (Chapel Hill: University of North Carolina, 1957), 85.

6. Bernard W. Sheehan, *Savagism and Civility: Indians and Englishmen in Colonial Virginia* (Cambridge: Cambridge University Press, 1980), 2.

7. Sheehan, *Savagism and Civility,* 2.

8. See Ann Rosalind Jones and Peter Stallybrass, "Dismantling Irena: The Sexualizing of Ireland in Early Modern England," in *Nationalisms and Sexualities,* ed. Andrew Parker, Mary Russo, Doris Sommer, and Patricia Yaeger (London: Routledge, 1992), 157-71.

9. Louis B. Wright, ed., *The Elizabethans' America: A Collection of Early Reports by Englishmen on the New World* (Cambridge, Mass.: Harvard University Press, 1965), 109.

10. Thomas Harriot, *A Brief and True Report of the New-Found Land of Virginia,* in *The Elizabethans' America,* ed. Louis B. Wright (Cambridge, Mass.: Harvard University Press, 1965), 129-30.

11. Karen Ordahl Kupperman, *Settling with the Indians: The Meeting of English and Indian Cultures in America, 1580-1640* (New Jersey: Rowman & Littlefield, 1980), 121-2.

12. Kupperman, *Settling with the Indians,* 122.

13. See Michael Banton's *The Idea of Race* (London: Tavistock, 1977) and *Racial Theories* (Cambridge: Cambridge University Press, 1987) for an incisive analysis of the history of "race." See also *Anatomy of Racism,* ed. David Theo Goldberg (Minneapolis: University of Minnesota, 1991).

14. Homi K. Bhabha, "The Other Question: Difference, Discrimination and the Discourse of Colonialism," in *Out There: Marginalization and Contemporary Cultures,* ed. Russell Ferguson, Martha Gever, Trinh T. Minh-ha, and Cornel West (New York: MIT Press, 1990), 71.

15. Aphra Behn, *Five Plays* (London: Methuen, 1990). All references to *The Widow Ranter* are to this edition, hereafter cited in the text.

16. Marvin B. Becker, *Civility and Society in Western Europe, 1300-1600* (Bloomington: Indiana University Press, 1988), xiii.

17. Kupperman, *Settling with the Indians,* 113.

18. John Robinson, "How Happy a Thing Had It Been, if You had Converted Some before You Had Killed Any!" in *The Indian and the White Man,* ed. Wilcomb E. Washburn (New York: New York University Press, 1964), 176-7. John Morton, *New English Canaan,* in *The*

Indian and the White Man, ed. Wilcomb E. Washburn (New York: New York University Press, 1964), 37-8.

19. Morton, *New English Canaan*, 37.
20. Jones and Stallybrass, "Dismantling Irena," 160.
21. Laura Brown, "The Romance of Empire: *Oroonoko* and the Trade in Slaves," in *The New Eighteenth Century*, ed. Laura Brown and Felicity Nussbaum (New York: Methuen, 1987), 48.
22. Brown, "The Romance of Empire", 58.
23. Sheehan, *Savagism and Civility*, 3.
24. *Webster's New Collegiate Dictionary* defines miscegenation as the "marriage or interbreeding of different races." Usage of the word occurs for the first time in 1863 specifically to describe sexual and marital relations between "whites" and "blacks." Thus, for me to employ the term to describe such relations between American Indians and Europeans is, of course, problematic given the linguistic history of the word. However, lacking a better descriptive term and believing that similar assumptions inform resistance to intermarriages or sexual relations, I feel justified in expanding the definitional boundaries of miscegenation to include sexual and marital relations between American Indians and English immigrants.
25. Wright, *The Elizabethans' America*, 185.
26. Quoted in Kupperman, *Settling with the Indians*, 59.
27. John Winthrop, cited in *The Invasion Within: The Contest of Cultures in Colonial North America* (Oxford: Oxford University Press, 1985), 137. What is not clear in this declaration is the English attitude toward cultivated "Indian" lands.
28. Mary Dearborn, *Pocahontas' Daughters: Gender and Ethnicity in American Culture* (New York: Oxford University Press, 1986), 97.
29. Here I am thinking of the literary and film trope of the "half-breed" who self-consciously rejects "white" culture for American Indian culture.
30. For example, the Maryland colony enacted one of the earliest prohibitions against English-African miscegenation: "any White man that shall beget any Negroe Woman with Child whether Free Woman or Servant, shall undergo the same Penalties as White Women." These penalties included indentured servitude for seven years for the man or

woman and thirty-one years for the child(ren) of such unions. Occurrences of English-African miscegenation in the Virginia colony in the first half of the seventeenth century were also generally punished. There is, however, no record of legal opposition to marital relations between Englishmen and American Indian women in the early stages of English colonialism in the Virginia colony. See also William Browne et al., eds, *Archives of Maryland* (Baltimore, 1883-1912), vol.1.
31. See Felicity Nussbaum, "The Other Woman: Polygamy, *Pamela,* and the Prerogative of Empire," ch. 8, this volume.
32. Walter Rodney, *A History of the Upper Guinea Coast 1545 to 1800* (New York: Monthly Review, 1970), ix.
33. See Laura Brown, "The Romance of Empire," and Margaret W. Ferguson, "Whose Dominion, or News from the New World: Aphra Behn's Representation of Miscegenous Romance in *Oroonoko* and *The Widow Ranter,"* in *The Production of English Renaissance Culture,* eds. David Lee Miller, Sharon O'Dair, and Harold Weber (Ithaca: Cornell University Press, 1994).
34. Bhabha, "The Other Question," 75.

''Tis not the fashion to confess' 'Shakespeare—Post-coloniality—Johannesburg, 1996'

Published in *Post-Colonial Shakespeares*. Eds., Loomba, Ania, and Orkin, Martin. London: Taylor & Francis Group, Ó1998 Reproduced with permission of the Licensor through PLSclear.

RACE AND NATION

A DICTIONARIE IN SPA-
NISH and ENGLISH, first published into the *English tongue by* Ric. Perciuale *Gent*. Now *enlarged and* amplified with many thousand words, as by this marke * to each of them prefixed may appeere; together with the accenting of euery worde throughout the whole Dictionarie, *for the true pronunciation of the language, as also for the diuers signification of one and the selfe same word:* And for the learners ease and furtherance, the declining of all hard and irregular verbs; and for the same cause the former order of the Alphabet is altered, diuers hard and vncouth phrases and speeches out of sundry of the best Authors explained, with diuers necessarie notes and especiall directions for all such as shall be desirous to attaine the perfection of the Spanish tongue.

All done by IOHN MINSHEU
Professor of Languages in London.

Hereunto for the further profite and pleasure of the learner or delighted in this tongue, is annexed an ample English Dictionarie, Alphabetically set downe with the Spanish words thereunto adioyned, as *also an Alphabeticall Table of the Arabicke and Moorish words now* commonly receiued and vsed in the Spanish tongue, which being dispersed in their seuerall due places throughout the whole Dictionarie are marked thus † : *by the same* Iohn Minsheu.

For the right vse of this worke, I referre you to the directions before the *Dictionarie*, contriued in diuers points differing *from other Dictionaries heretofore set foorth.*

Imprinted at London, by *Edm*. Bollifant.
1599

"THE MOOR OF VENICE," OR THE ITALIAN ON THE RENAISSANCE ENGLISH STAGE

A number of critics have read *Othello* principally with an eye toward illuminating the moral sense of the problematic racial and sexual politics engendered not only by the play's depiction of what is viewed as an interracial marriage but also by Othello's sensationalized murder of his wife, Desdemona. The obstacle facing all such critical readings, as Michael Neill astutely points out, is that the play itself conspicuously denies us (even as it denies Othello) an opportunity to enact "the funeral dignities that usually serve to put a form of 'moral] order upon such spectacles of ruins;' creating an "ending [that is] perhaps the most shocking in Shakespearean tragedy" (383-412). Neill concludes that it is the final tragic scene, where "white" Desdemona is murdered and her husband/murderer, "black" Othello, violently avenges her murder-"I took by th'throat the circumcised dog/ And smote him thus" (5.2.351-52) -which most "articulate[s] the [racial] anxiety evident almost everywhere in the play's history-a sense of scandal that informs the textual strategies of editors and theatrical productions is much as it does the disturbed reactions of audiences and critics" (384).

Feminist scholars have made clear that this "scandal" actually begins long before this most "unnatural" ending to the marriage of Othello and Desdemona. For example, Patricia Parker sees the "simultaneously eroticized and epistemological impulse to open up to show" the " 'fantasies' of race and gender" in *Othello* as an anxiety-ridden linkage of female sexuality and the exotic narratives of "African or New World discovery" (92), while Janet Adelman argues that the "whole of his exchange with Desdemona demonstrates Othello's terrible conflict between his intense desire for fusion with the woman he idealizes as the nurturant source of his being and his equally intense conviction that her participation in sexuality has contaminated her and thus contaminated the perfection that he has vested in her" (66-67). What has become obvious in these recent studies of *Othello*, as Valerie Traub contends, is that "Othello's anxiety is culturally and psychosexually overdetermined by erotic, gender, an racial anxieties, including ... the fear of chaos [usually] associate[d] with sexual activity." In what follows, I wish to reconsider the possibilities of reading the racial and sexual anxieties latent in Shakespeare's *Othello*. The focus of my discussion is not so much the personal relationships represented in the play as it is the cultural assumptions which may be coincident with the notion of race in *Othello*; in particular, I want to argue the possibility that the social site of Shakespeare's tragedy, Venice, is a much more significant player in the construction of early modern English racialist ideology than critics have hitherto illuminated. Simply stated, my purpose is to show that Venice is a crucial yet often critically neglected racial persona in *Othello*.

My reading builds upon and diverges from studies that examine Shakespeare's use of Italian city-states, in particular Venice, in his dramatic works—a usage which, according to these critics, highlights an Elizabethan "fascination" with Italian culture.[5] In the case of Venice, this fascination is rooted in, as David C. McPherson terms it, the "myth of Venice," wherein the city is perceived as a state whose wealth, political stability, justice, and civility set it above all others (27). This image, of course, has its origins in early modern Italian political theories whose principal goal was to conceptualize a model civil society that "was to be paradigmatic for [Italian] civic humanism" (Pocock 271). In these theories Venice is represented as an uncorrupted, tranquil, and stable state; in fact, "Venice appears, both physically and politically, 'rather framed by the hands of the immortal Gods, than any way by the arte, industry or inuention of men.' "[6]

Ultimately, as J. G. A. Pocock has shown, this "myth of Venice (at its most mythical) was to lie in the assertion that the Venetian commonwealth was an immortally serene, because perfectly balanced, combination of the three elements of monarchy, aristocracy, and democracy" (102).

It is my contention that this myth inheres in Shakespeare's *Othello* and exercises a "compulsive force on the imagination;' of both the characters within the play and the audience watching events unfold. But, because it is a mythology, "framed by the hands, ... arte, industry, [and] invention of men," the ideal of Venice is also a paradox which ultimately subverts its illusion of perfection by drawing attention not only to the dichotomies (pure/impure, black/white) it constructs but also to the interiority that the myth and it dichotomies seek to conceal (Pocock 102). In other words, while the myth extols an image of Venice as the idealized feminine body, beautiful, desirable, and virginal, it also vicariously projects an image of Venice as the imperfect body- corruptive, desiring, and easily violated. If, as Patricia Parker argues, "the gaze is a vicarious gaze, a substitution of narrative" (89), then our attempt to discern how this paradox works racially must make use of this vicarious perspective.

"The Cunning Whore of Venice"

Lewes Lewkenor's 1599 translation of Gasparo Contarini's *De Magistratibus et Republica Venetorum* (along with Thomas Coryat's *Crudities*) did much to circulate this particular variant of the "myth of Venice" in Elizabethan and Jacobean England. In his dedication to the reader, Lewkenor writes that visitors to Venice, at least those "of a grauer humor;'

> would dilate of the greatnes of their Empire, the grauitie of their prince, the maiesty of their Senate, the vnuiolablenes of their lawes, their zeale in religion, and lastly their moderation, and equitie, wherewith they gouerne such subiected prouinces as are vnder their dominion, binding them therby in a faster bond of obedience then all the cytadels, garrisons, or whatsoeuer

other tyrannicall inuentions could euer haue brought them vnto. (A2)

Lewkenor uses the dedication to set the context for his dilation of the greatness of Venice and to encourage his readers to gaze upon the book as if it were the city itself. Characterized as a "pure and vntouched virgine, free from the taste or violence of any forraine enforcement;' Venice is laid open for the "admiration" and entertainment of the book's English readers. Though not often viewed as a narrative of discovery, Lewkenor's text might well be included in that genre, as it has in common with other narratives of discovery what Patricia Parker calls "the language of opening, uncovering or bringing to light ... what had been secret, closed or hid" from the majority of the English reading public whose travels were limited to environs of London (87).

Of course, Venice is neither Africa nor the "New World," and Lewkenor's dedication to the reader of *The Commonwealth and Gouernment of Venice* is intended merely to set the stage for his translation of a work of political philosophy. Even so, the edition circulates conflicting images of the republic known as La Serenissima. In contrast to Lewkenor's praise of Venice's "unblemished" status, the commendatory poems written in praise of Lewkenor's endeavor convey a somewhat different vision of Venice. For example, one poem compares Venice to the "antique" cities of Babel, "fallen" "with the weight of their own furquedry." In another poem, though her "virgins state ambition nere could blot;' the "swarmes" from "forrein nation[s]" prompt the writer to proclaim Venice's "ruinous case" which, of course, is reflected in the city's "painted face." Ironically, what is intended to honor the celebrated myth of Venetian stability and invulnerability, Lewkenor's dedication and the commendatory poems, actually draws attention to what stands behind the myth—Venice's notoriety as a site of illicit sexuality, dangerous passions, violence, and extraordinary cunning.

Thomas Coryat's *Crudities* exhibits a similar ambivalence toward Venice. In the account of his travel to Italy in 1608, Coryat begins with a description of Venice as "the fairest Lady," a "noble citie" (311). After a rather detailed description of the magnificence of Venice's architecture, Coryat interrupts his narrative to warn his readers to be wary of the city's gondoliers, who are "the most vicious and licentious varlets about all the City" (311). Coryat's warning is typical of his tendency to juxtapose an image of Venice as "this thrice worthie city... yea the richest Paragon" with an image of Venice as a city whose blatant acceptance of sexuality (the seeming valorization of the courtesans and the touted infidelity of Venetian wives) and violence denotes the "Virgin's" corruptibility. Coryat's maneuver serves strategically, as Ann Rosalind Jones suggests, as both a lure and an admonition: "Coryat writes with a double agenda: to thrill his readers and to protect their morals, to sell his book with the promise of titillation and to dignify it by setting his ethical seriousness as an Englishman against the variety of 'Ethnicke' types he encounters" (104).

Jones rightly observes that the Venice "of English [writers such as Coryat] from the 1580s on was not a geographer's record but a fantasy setting for dramas of passion, Machiavellian politics, and revenge-a landscape of the mind" (no). For Coryat and others, within this "landscape of the mind" it is the "interplay of pleasure and danger" (Jones 102) posed by Venice's gendered and Janus-like status within European culture that must be castigated and the city reclaimed as the paradigm of cultural perfection. And it is this gendered "interplay" that Shakespeare distills in *Othello,* coupling the metaphoric blackness of Venice's reputation as a site of feminine sexual corruption and the literalness of Moorish Othello's black skin with the unstained honor of the Venetian military commander Othello and the symbolic whiteness of an uncorrupted Venice. Shakespeare's Othello joins these other early modern English texts in presenting a perspective of Venice that satisfies the desire to see encompassed in one racialized body, even if vicariously, both the virgin and the whore. And that body belongs, of course, to a woman.

Desdemona's Choice

From the play's inception, when Brabantio reprimands Iago for his indecent language and both Roderigo and Iago for their disruption of

Brabantio's peace—"What, tell'st thou me of robbing? this is Venice, my house is not a grange" (1.1.105-106)—the paradoxical "myth of Venice" is instantiated as a paradigm for reading the play's presumed sexual and racial deviances. Brabantio's words obviously are intended to correct what he perceives to be a misperception on the part of Iago, namely that there are no farm animals in his house. Significantly, Brabantio's rebuke conjures images of the Venice, La Serenissima, extolled in Lewkenor's translation, as the tone of Brabantio's declaration suggests that such a crime could never take place in Venice, and, more important, that Roderigo's and Iago's accusations of a barnyard theft would not have been brought surreptitiously to the victim's door in the middle of the night. Brabantio's reprimand indicates that he is a man possessed of the judicious gravity praised in Lewkenor's preface: a man whose "moderation and equitie" will lead him to behave rationally when confronted by what appears to be the irrational pranks of a spurned suitor.

Once he understands the implication of Iago's salacious words, however, Brabantio begins to exhibit the stereotypical irrationality which came to be a metaphoric staple of Jacobean dramatic depictions of Italians. Governed by his fury, Brabantio accuses Othello of sorcery or witchcraft even before the marriage is confirmed by the couple: "is there not charms, / By which the property of youth and maidhood, / May be abused? Have you not read, Roderigo, / Of such a thing?" (1.1.171-74) When we consider Brabantio's grave "This is Venice;' the sight of the rational "senator's" descent into illogic is somewhat surprising as he attempts to explain what he perceives to be unexplainable:

> My daughter, O my daughter, ...
>> She is abus'd, stol'n from me and corrupted,
>> By spells and medicines, bought of mountebanks,
>> For nature so preposterously to err,
>> (Being not deficient, blind, or lame of sense,)
>> Sans witchcraft could not. (1.2.60-64)

Brabantio's "My daughter, O my daughter" poignantly recalls

Solanio's account of Shylock's pained cry at Jessica's elopement with Lorenzo—"My daughter! O my ducats! O my daughter!"—and Shylock's own descent into irrationality (*MV* 2.8.15). Given Desdemona's position as only child and heir to Brabantio's estate, a situation analogous to Jessica's in *The Merchant of Venice*, it is not without significance that Shakespeare alludes to this earlier work in depicting a father's reaction to the news that his daughter has married without his approval and apparently to someone outside his ethnic community.

Shakespeare draws one other parallel between Brabantio and Shylock, in that both men seek to exploit the strict terms of Venetian law to extract justice from their perceived enemies. When he finally confronts Othello, Brabantio tells the general, "I therefore apprehend and do attach thee" (1.2.77). In this moment, the rational Venetian has displaced the irrational father who has roused his "kindred" to pursue the couple. Once he has Othello in custody, Brabantio is confident that he will be able to prove Othello guilty of witchcraft and that the Venetian legal institution will prove "pure and uncorrupted" as it evaluates the truth of his accusation. And, not unexpectedly, when Venetian law appears, in the persona of the Duke, it reaffirms Brabantio's faith in its exactitude:

> Whoe'er he be, that in this foul proceeding
>   Hath thus beguil'd your daughter of herself,
>   And you of her, the bloody book of law
>   You shall yourself read, in the bitter letter,
>   After its own sense, though our proper son
>   Stood in your action (1.3.65-69)

No matter the cost, Brabantio is being guaranteed that the "penal Lawes [will be] most unpardonably executed" (Pocock 325).

Whatever Brabantio's cause, when Othello is named the guilty party, the senators who have accompanied the Duke respond to Brabantio's accusation in a rather cryptic fashion: "We are very sorry for't" (1.3.73). This comment can, of course, be interpreted in one of two ways. First, it can be seen as an expression of regret that Othello's service will be lost to Venice, given the political tensions that exist between Venetians and Turks. Or it can be read as an expression of compassion for Brabantio and the loss of his daughter in the manner he has described. I would propose that the former reading (regret at the loss of Othello's service to Venice) is the more likely intent behind the senators' words. When Othello and Brabantio first come into the presence of the Duke and senators, one senator refers to Othello as "the valiant Moor." More telling of the esteem Othello has in Venice is the Duke's reaction after hearing Othello's narrative, when the Duke exhorts Brabantio to "Take up this mangled matter at the best; / Men do their broken weapons rather use, / Than their bare hands" (1.3.172-74). Brabantio's refusal to comply with the Duke's admonition is, as Lynda Boose argues, a refusal to "act out," to ritualize the symbolic transfer of his daughter to her husband not because Othello is necessarily unworthy but because the selection of Desdemona's husband was not Brabantio's: that right had been usurped by his daughter ("Father and Daughter" 327). Desdemona's choice of a husband has been the object of critical gaze ever since Thomas Rymer first questioned Shakespeare's use of a "Blackamoor" as the tragic protagonist in *Othello*: whether in M. R. Ridley's introduction to the Arden edition of *Othello*, where Ridley writes, "It is the very essence of the play that Desdemona in marrying Othello-a man to whom her 'natural' reaction should (her father holds) have been fear, not delight, has done something peculiarly startling" (liii), or in Stanley Cavell's careful explanation that, in choosing Othello, Desdemona has "overlooked his blackness in favor of his inner brilliance": in effect, "that she saw his visage as he sees it, that she understands his blackness as he understands it, as the expression (or in his word, his manifestation) of his mind" (129).

 Complicating these, and other, critical attempts to explain Desdemona's choice is the fact that Shakespeare's play presents a world whose very social codes are frequently contradictory and conflicting, thus enabling Desdemona to act as she does. On one level, Venice is a place where the contagious rhetoric of racialism can easily destroy lives and careers, as Iago's manipulation so aptly illustrates. Yet it seems that early modern Venice is also a society where a man such as Othello can achieve success and fame to such a degree that a duke is moved to declare, "I think this tale would win my daughter too" (1.3-171). Othello's status and position, that is, his "honours and valiant parts" (1.3.253), prove as desirable to Desdemona as the narratives for which "She gave ... a world of sighs" (1.3.159) and" ... lov'd [Othello] for the dangers [he] had pass'd" (1.3-167).

Though a Moor, Othello is perceived as a valuable member of Venetian society and his action as nothing more than "a *mischief* that is past and gone" [emphasis mine] (1.3.204). Emily Bartels rightfully argues that Othello's acceptance includes Iago, who "even as he attempts to prove Othello the outsider, ... represents him as an authorizing insider."[9] As Lewkenor's translation of Contarini's work documents and J. G. A. Pocock's study substantiates, Venice was often cited by early modern political theorists as a state to be commended for its successful handling of its imperial aims through the hiring of foreign nationals to provide its military force and to police the city. This long-standing practice, plus the city's mercantile zeal, created a cosmopolitan environment where "one sees in this city an infinite number of men from different parts of the world" (McPherson 30). Furthermore, according to Lewkenor, it was apparently not unusual for "forreyn mercenarie souldiers" to be "enabled, with the title of citizens & gentlemen of Venice" (S2).

Brabantio's cultivation and acceptance of Othello, therefore, may very well reflect this custom, so that when Othello explains that Desdemona's "father lov'd me, oft invited me" (1.3.128), we are reminded that it was Brabantio him self, as a senator, who first acknowledged Othello an "insider."[10] It is the senator Brabantio, and thus by extension Venice, who sets up contradictory notions about racial identity and social place within Venetian society. Desdemona's marital choice, therefore, may very well enact not only adherence to assumptions about appropriate spouses (Othello is, by birth, a prince, by merit a general, and through patronage wealthy) but, in addition, the transference of the daughter's love for her father to another Venetian father figure and not an "outsider." Thus we may want to ask not why Othello drew her love but what is it in the man that her father loved that moves a woman "So opposite to marriage, that she shunn'd

/ The wealthy curled darlings of our nation ... " (1.2.67-68) to set aside her reluctance to marriage and elope? And, whether Brabantio's reaction to the marriage, and Othello, is linked not to Othello's physical appearance but to that "thing ... to fear, not to delight" in (1.2.71), an incestuous desire for his daughter?

If we view Desdemona's choice as being consistent with Shakespeare's characterization of her, of Othello, of Desdemona's willingness to perform her symbolic role in the ritual expression of marriage, and the myth of Venice, then perhaps it is Brabantio who continually refuses to participate in the ritual by subverting the activities which would require that he allow himself to be dispossessed of his daughter, that he permit another Venetian to sexually claim the one female body that he himself cannot sexually possess.[11] Thus Brabantio's earlier rebuke of Iago becomes an ironic echo when Brabantio employs not only the language of theft to accuse Othello, "O thou foul thief," but also the language often associated with witchcraft, "chains of magic" and "foul charms;' in an effort to destabilize the ritualized exchange of the female body that marks the institution of marriage. And Brabantio's charges, like his censure of Iago, allude to the complex and often contradictory social attitudes in Venice which allow for an Othello and a Desdemona but which also demand that they adhere to the customs and laws which govern that society.

Jacques Lacan has argued that "in our relation to things, in so far as this relation is constituted by the way of vision, and ordered in the figures of representation, something slips, passes, is transmitted from stage, to stage, and is always to some degree eluded in it-that is what we call the gaze" (73). I have been arguing that throughout *Othello*, this "something" is Venice, and I wish . to conclude by looking briefly at the paradox that Shakespeare's play reveals Venice to be.

The Venetian Moor, or the Italian on the English Stage

One of the disturbing things about *Othello*, despite centuries of ideological intervention, is the play's ability to disrupt any attempt to make uneven the level playing field Shakespeare has created in his tragedy. This dilemma is further exacerbated by the crudely psychosexual dimensions engendered by Iago's rhetoric in the very first scene of the play:

> Zounds, sir, you are robb'd, for shame put on your gown,
>   Your heart is burst, you have lost half your soul;
>   Even now, very now, an old black ram
>   Is tupping your white ewe (1.1.86-89)

Iago's words neatly transform what is an act of elopement into an imagined cuckoldry; that is, in the double reference to Brabantio's nakedness (he lacks both property and his "gown"), Iago sets the stage for a further shaming of Brabantio by subtly naming what is lost as if it were a wife ("half your soul") and luridly localizing this pseudo-wife in a pornographic fantasy. And though this fantasy is momentarily displaced by the intrusion (in the person of Othello) of Lewkenor's Venice, its affective power to create and sustain its image of perversion is not altered one whit.

Ironically, Iago's thematization of an imagined (and bestial) cuckoldry insinuates itself not only in Brabantio's imagination but in his later displacement of that anxiety onto Othello: "Look to her, Moor, have a quick eye to see:/ She has deceiv'd her father, may do thee" (1.3.292-93). Predictably, Othello reenacts the violent passions that drove Brabantio to repudiate Desdemona, once again bringing to the surface the male anxiety about female sexuality (despite Desdemona's married state), considered the hallmark of "corrupt" Venice, that initiates the "tragedy of Othello." However, Othello's complete displacement of Brabantio can occur only when, I would argue, he takes to its ultimate, punitive conclusion (by killing Desdemona) Brabantio's disowning of his daughter. In effect, it is the Venetian Othello who must see to it that Venice's "penal Lawes [are] most unpardonably executed" when the virgin is shown to be a whore.

Representations of early modern Venice were always gendered feminine: it was a city "so beautiful, so renowned, so glorious a Virgin" and, at the same time, a " 'Circe's court; teeming with 'wanton and dallying' Calypsos and Sirens." [14] This allusion to the seductive women who delayed Ulysses' return to Ithaca finds its parallel in

Desdemona's "supersubtle" seduction of the warrior Othello: "she thank'd me,/ And bade me, if I had a friend that lov'd her,/ I should but teach him how to tell my story, / And that would woo her" (1.3-163- 66). Like Venice, Desdemona has the appearance of purity (and discretion) even as she boldly lays herself open to Othello's suit. Even so, when Iago calls into question Desdemona's virtue, Othello iterates his faith in his wife-"For she had eyes, and chose me" (3.3.193)-even as he leaves open the possibility of her infidelity: "No Iago, / I'll see before I doubt, when I doubt, prove, / And on the proof, there is no more but this: / Away at once with love or jealousy" (3.3-194-96).

Othello's insistence on "proof," of course, becomes the opening that Iago needs to "abuse Othello's ear" (1.3.393). It is not insignificant that both Othello and Desdemona initially are swayed by what is heard rather than what is seen. From its inception, the play luridly juxtaposes rumor and storytelling, on the one hand, and an emphasis on seeing, on the other. Brabantio must see for him self the truth of Roderigo's and Iago's report of Desdemona's elopement. Othello will not question Desdemona's virtue until he sees proof; but once rumor "abuses" his ear, Othello, as did Brabantio, begins the process of "bring ing to light" the blackness of his Venetian wife.[15] If the first act of the play serves to displace Othello's blackness into his Venetian identity, then the remaining acts serve to dilate Desdemona's.

Iago is the first to constitute Desdemona black when, in response to her question "what wouldst thou write of me, if thou shouldst / praise me" (2.1.118), he reiterates a familiar trope of femininity:

If she be fair and wise, fairness and wit;
   The one's for use, the other using it
   If she be black, and thereto have a wit,
   She'll find a white, that shall her blackness hit. (2.1.129-33)

Lines 132-33, not surprisingly, find their close interpretive echo in the adage "wash the Ethiop white:' If Desdemona is "black" and possesses a "wit;' Iago's advice to her is to seek that which will transform her, her opposite. Iago ends his "praise" of Desdemona by railing against even fair women, terming them "wight[s]" who "suckle fools, and chronicle small beer" (2.1.160).

This exchange, for all its seeming irreverence, finds its dramatic replay in act 4, scene 2. After a mournful lament for his "affliction," Othello turns his fury to Desdemona: "Turn thy complexion there; / Patience, thy young and rose-lipp'd cherubin, / I here look grim as hell" (4.2.63-65). Othello then goes on to say,

> O thou black weed, why art so lovely fair?
>   Thou smel'st so sweet, that the sense aches at thee,
>   Would thou hads't ne'er been born! (4.2.69-71)

Othello's language enacts the familiar Petrarchan opposition of fair/dark, yet it also perverts that rhetoric with its reluctance to further denigrate the object which it initially constitutes as undesirable (see Hall, esp.178-79). More important, this semantic instantiation of Desdemona's desirability registers the allure traditionally associated with Venice, and which prompts Othello later to name Desdemona that which no Englishman who has read Coryat would have failed to understand, "that cunning whore of Venice."

Once again, despite the domesticity of this bedroom scene, it is Venice which becomes the object of our gaze as both the symbolic virgin that the warrior Othello defends and the corrupted bride he has wed. In an emotionally charged accusation to Desdemona, Othello declares, "I took you for that cunning whore of Venice/ That married with Othello" (4.2.91). Othello's words become a distorted projection of Brabantio's caution that the mask of virginity hid a corruption. It is Venice itself which suffers the "dilation" of its exterior to reveal the blackness inside. Othello's search for "proof" must begin "in" Venice, and thus with himself. What is revealed is the sameness of the interior and exterior: the Moor without is the Venetian within, and the Venetian within is the Moor without. And, in a remarkable mimicry of Brabantio's incredulity over Desdemona's willing participation in the marriage, Othello stages himself as the innocent seduced by the wiles of the Venetian whore—aided and abetted by the plot's initial and careful delineation of Othello as a Venetian. We see mirrored in

Othello's rage that of Brabantio. Though born a Moor, in his irrationality Othello is very much a Venetian. And in an ironic though not surprising twist of fact, both the father and the husband, whose violations of the rites of marriage set into motion the tragic events of Shakespeare's tragedy, die as a result of their attempts to defend the illusion of perfection that is the myth of Venice.

"I took by th'throat the circumcised dog"

At the conclusion of *Othello*, Shakespeare leaves us with a disturbing dramatic tableau: the corpses of Othello, Desdemona, and Emilia upon the bed which has occupied (most likely) center stage for much of the final act; a (for once) silent Iago; and the Venetian lords as witnesses to this final tragic event. Just before he commits suicide, Othello says,

> And say besides, that in Aleppo once,
>   where a malignant and a turban'd Turk
>   Beat a Venetian, and traduc'd the state,
>   I took by the throat the circumcised dog,
>   And smote him thus. (5.2. 353-57)

This speech has often been read as, symbolically, a racialized confirmation of Othello's awareness of himself as an outsider—a Moor. But if my argument is valid, then such a reading is highly questionable and may point to the deployment of the "racial anxiety" that Michael Neill suggests is "everywhere" in the play's critical and cultural history rather than in Shakespeare's representation of Othello's self-consciousness.

I would argue that what Othello does is to draw upon the myth of Venice to re-create not just a racial image but also a political one where Venetian law is exact, swift, and inviolate-whether one is a Turk or, in the case of Othello, a Venetian. More important, as the symbol of Venetian law on Cyprus, it is Othello who must stand in for the Duke and affirm the "bloody book of law" against those who have violated that very law. It is Venetian Othello who judges and executes the Turk who assaulted a Venetian, and it's this same Othello who must judge and execute the murderer of another Venetian, Desdemona. The race of this judge cannot, therefore, be viewed in terms of his color but as identical to that of the Duke in whose stead Othello carries out Venetian law.

It seems imperative, therefore, not to overlook the complex history that the concept and the word race may project in early modern English discourses and its implications for interpretations of *Othello*. In a world where women were often described as a "race;' where the word race signified aristocratic or noble lineage, where race was often used as synonymous with nation, to argue that issues of race in *Othello* are easily reducible to one matrix, color, is a problematic misreading of an emerging taxonomic shift in the process of classifying human beings. In early modern Venice and England, where racial and social identities are formulated as much in genealogy as in ethnicity or geography, in gender as in color, the "illusion of perfection" cannot sustain itself as its own discourse points to the almost yet not quite invisible fractures that inevitably occur in the process of mythologizing "race." And it is this paradox which must be recognized in Othello rather than, as Jack D'Amico suggests, the idea that "Shakespeare revealed how a man could be destroyed when he accepts a perspective that deprives him of his humanity, ... Othello is debased by a role that he adopts and acts out on the *Venetian-Elizabethan* stage" (177). Ignoring, for the moment, the problematic collapsing of Venice and England, I want to call into question the implicit assumption that there is English identification with the Venetians as a homogeneous racial group. As I have suggested elsewhere, "the contours of race may not be as fixed, as transcendental, as universal as critical practices and postmodern social discourses seem to infer" ("Managing the Barbarian" 183). English writers, Shakespeare included, pointedly distinguished within the European community just as they did without (perhaps even more so given their more extensive knowledge of nations within Europe). One has only to recall Portia's mockery of her French, German, Scottish, and English suitors, or Shakespeare's depiction of the Welsh and French in *Merry Wives of Windsor* to know that D'Amico's "Venetian-Elizabethan" elides the powerful sense of national consciousness that encodes itself in the dramatic representation of other cultures (see Howard).

It seems to me that we might derive a better understanding of Shakespeare's tragedy if we recognize that the "lustful" Moor is the "whorish" Venetian. Behind Desdemona stands the duplicitous Venice, behind Iago the cunning "Machiavel;' and behind Othello the irrationality of Italian masculinity. What sets into motion the tragic events in Shakespeare's tragedy, and what makes Othello an ideological quagmire, is the Venetian ambivalence that accepts Othello as a well-born, honorable, successful military commander and courtier even as it insists that he remain an outsider, an alien who must resort to sorcery or witchcraft to become a part of the world he inhabits already. In the end, our interpretive and critical imperative, in addition to tracing the overdetermined markings formalized by the racialist rhetoric figured by the references to the color of Othello, should be one of exploring the multifaceted and often subtly nuanced discourse of race that aligns color, gender, geography as it sees fit. In this vein, we might also want to pose another query that Shakespeare's tragedy seems to invoke and which has bearing for our understanding of racial discourse in early modern English contexts. Who, symbolically, comes to be racialized as the "cunning whore" of Venice capable of causing nature to err from itself? The answer, not surprisingly, is all in how one defines the concept of race.

WHAT'S RACE GOT TO DO WITH IT? TEACHING SHORTER ELIZABETHAN POETRY

The emergence of a body of scholarship concerned with race in early modem English culture has generated much interest in pedagogical strategies for teaching race in literature classes. Newly available documents and changes in historiography have sparked debates about the "semiotics of race" (Hall, *Things of Darkness* 10) in the canon of early modem English literature. Students and scholars of Elizabethan literature not only have a wide range of critical studies to draw on but also have access to manuscripts and printed texts whose existence has been either unknown or elided. This expanded textuality has produced revisionary reinterpretations of canonical works in the light of the myriad textual and visual representations of Africans, Indians, and Native Americans.

Often contrasting the beloved's whiteness against the darkness of the Moorish, Indian, or Ethiopian body, a number of Elizabethan poems illuminate the significance of ethnicity and race to early modem English literary culture. These early modem lyrics frequently draw on different tropes (exoticism, blackness, whiteness, barbarity, savagery, and the erotic) to adumbrate idealized notions of Englishness, love, and beauty. Ultimately, these lyrics, as Kim Hall suggests, warrant "more sustained attention" (*Things* 269) than they have been given not only in scholarly studies of Elizabethan poetry but also, more crucially, in the teaching of early modem English literature.

In this brief pedagogical essay, I offer a framework for teachers interested in fostering discussions about race and shorter Elizabethan poetry. In doing so, I hope to illustrate that considerations of race in sixteenth-century English literature can be fostered through an examination of lyrics. In effect, this essay seeks to encourage teachers of Elizabethan literature to incorporate what is not always "black" and "white" in the Elizabethan conceptualization of racial identity. In what follows I outline a number of useful strategies to introduce students to the semiotics of race in early modem England. The course that provides the pedagogical context for this essay is titled The Idea of Poetry. In this course, students read a range of late sixteenth- and early-seventeenth century lyrics, traversing a variety of modes (odes, elegies, sonnets, and verse satires), Philip Sidney's *Apology for Poetry*, and a number of critical essays on race. Over the course of ten weeks, students write four to five analytical papers (3-5 pages in length) and an original lyric. For the purposes of this essay, John Donne's *Elegy 19* and Everard Guilpin's *Skialetheia*, satire 5, will illustrate the ways in which race can be made part of the study of Elizabethan poetry.

Introducing Race

One of the difficulties in teaching race as an aspect of shorter Elizabethan poetry is that students often protest the interjection of "politics" into what they see as an aesthetic appreciation of a literary work. Encouraged to appreciate the imagery, wordplay, assonance, and form of a poem, students view any attention to social or cultural issues as detracting from the beauty of the work and, in their writings or comments, often appear openly hostile to considerations of race. For these students, race evokes sometimes painfully contradictory and burdensome emotions. Is there no place where the complex social injustices or problems that shape much of their social consciousness can be set aside and the literary work appreciated solely on its own merits? Can we not read literature for its own sake without dragging into it the current polemics? Why can't we just view art as art without complicating it with all this social baggage? These and other questions have surfaced in my courses whenever the issue of race (or gender or class) is raised vis-a-vis a literary work whose imagery is not obviously racial, that is, in texts where characterizations or references are not of Africans, Indians, Moors, or Native Americans.

In these instances, works such as the poems reproduced in Hall's appendix can be introduced as depicting images of race, but texts such as Edmund Spenser's *Epithalamion* or William Shakespeare's *The Rape of Lucrece* cannot. Thus the first order of business in getting students to consider race in relation to Elizabethan poetry is to help them reevaluate their assumptions about the relation between art and ideology. In The Idea of Poetry students are invited to reframe the question of race so that the complexity of early modem notions of race is not occluded by modern ideologies. To stimulate their efforts, I give students a photocopied handout of the *Oxford English Dictionary*'s entry on race, photocopies of entries from sixteenth- and seventeenth-century dictionaries (Richard Percyvale's and John Minsheu's bilingual dictionaries are two favorites), and a brief lecture on lexicography. Students are asked to select a synonym of race (kind, lineage, nobility, and stock, for example) and to trace its lexical genealogy. This exercise encourages students to focus on the etymological origins and extant definitions of the word race and simultaneously destabilizes assumptions about the fixity of meaning. It is important that students become sensitive to the historical specificity a word may have in the sixteenth century that, as centuries pass, becomes occluded or even effaced.

Students are divided into small working groups and are given secondary readings that offer an overview of the concept of race in Western culture. In this particular course, I have found chapter 2 of Michael Banton's *The Idea of Race*, Kwame Appiah's entry on race in *Critical Terms for Literary Study*, and chapter 1 of Benedict Anderson's *Imagined Communities* quite useful. Each group is asked to summarize the arguments of these chapters, to assess their usefulness in relation to early modern English literature, and to ascertain whether the information provided by the students' examination of early mod em dictionaries complicates these very modern theoretical considerations. Each group then is asked to produce a brief position paper, which is circulated among the class for later discussion. Central to the strategies suggested here is a notion of race broadly construed as signifying not only color or phenotype but also nationality, ethnicity, genealogy, or typology. It should be noted that students have not engaged in readings of any lyric as yet. This is done deliberately. In other early modem English literature courses where the topic of race is introduced, I have found that the greatest resistance comes when students see themselves as having been forced to tum from aesthetic considerations of a work to political readings. The activities deployed in this course before close reading aid students as they examine theoretical and cultural assumptions about race, its meaning, and its historicity. Such strategies redefine the critical terrain so that when an intersection is postulated between a notion of race and early modem aesthetics students are less hostile to the idea.

Pleasures of the Text

Teaching John Donne's *Elegy 19* has long been both a pleasure and a bane. On the one hand, the lyric's evocative sensuality and imagery provide an excellent example of the complexities and logic of Petrarchism—Donne's opening exhortation is nothing more than an elaborate blazon. On the other hand, when read against Nancy Vickers's cogent essay "Diana Described: Scattered Woman and Scattered Rhyme," for example, Donne's elegy engenders in its readers a heightened sensitivity to the disturbing paradox produced by the blazon. Add to this mixture Donne's use of the trope America (usually figured as a site of enormous wealth that is female, chaste, and unguarded), and one finds a lyric that traverses the aesthetic-political divide that students often insist is necessary to appreciate a literary work.

In a carefully structured writing assignment, students are asked to make sense of Donne's request that his mistress "licence [his] roving hands, and let them goe I Behind, before, above, between, below" (lines 25, 26) in the light of the previous image in which she is likened to "Mahomets Paradise" (line 21). Students quickly comprehend that there are frequent shifts in Donne's imagery from angelic to terrestrial to textual. In discussions about the imagery, I guide students over

Donne's highly attenuated exotic landscape as the lyric's argument turns from the mistress's body to overt ethnic loci—Islam and America. As the lyric unfolds and the imagery of one stanza flows into the next, defining the mistress's body first as "Mahomets Paradise" and then as the speaker's "America, [his] new found lande" (line 27), the mistress subtly becomes identified with non-English and non-European cultures and spaces that, typically, are represented as alien, dangerous, exotic, and barbaric in early modem English writing.

Edward Guilpin's "Satire 5" similarly deploys non-European spaces and cultures as a point of departure for his satire on London. The poem invites its readers to accompany the satirist-narrator as he exposes the dis-ease that has infected London (and by extension England). The satirist guides the reader along a "flower bespangled walk," where he "may heare / Some amorous Swaine his passions declare !To his sun-burnt Love" (lines 33-35). The poet then describes London as the "mappe of vanities, / The marte of fooles, the Magazin of guiles" (lines 66, 67). And if the reader does "but observe the sundry kindes of shapes," he would "sweare that London is as rich in apes / As Afrricke Tabraca" (lines 68 71). A few lines later the poet observes that the city is overwhelmed by a "hotch-potch of so many noyses, [. . .] / That Chaos of rude sounds, that harmony, / And Dyapson of harsh Barbary" (lines 37-44). Throughout this section of the satire, Guilpin works with a dichotomy presumably familiar to his readers—Africa, with its "sun-burnt" women, apes, and "harsh Barbary," on one side, and London, with its "flower bespangled walk," on the other.

What becomes apparent to students is the subtle ways in which a very specific type of racializing begins to emerge in the two poets' use of imagery. In both texts, Africa, America, and Islam provide Donne and Guilpin the means to deploy a hierarchical system of contrasts based on a coded lexicon that defines each of these terms as barbarous and exotic and as sites of sensuality and sexuality. Furthermore, as I suggest to my students, such lexicons are implicated in the formation of a concept of race as they allow hierarchies of difference to be adumbrated, constituted, and reaffirmed. In the moment that Donne's mistress becomes "America" and Guilpin's "apes" appear in London, the poems cease to concern just a man's desire for his mistress or a satirist castigating his fellow citizens and become an evocation of a racializing discourse intended to foster early modem England's developing sense of racial identity.

In arguing that these two poems contribute to early modern conceptualizations of race, I endeavor to highlight the complex aesthetic, moral, and political dimensions invoked by the lyrics' associative juxtapositions of non-English and non-European geography and cultures. Students are encouraged to consider in their written assignments the ways Donne's elegy and Guilpin's satire create or add to a semiotics of race through the figurative use of terms such as "Barbary," "hatch-patch," "America," "sun-burnt Love," and "Afrricke." As part of their reflections on the poems, students are asked to identify and discuss, especially in Guilpin's work, other possible racializing terms or images and to relate this to the lexicographical and theoretical work done at the beginning of the course.

What transpires in the students' engagements with the poetry is a growing appreciation for the complexity of early modem conceptions of race, the contribution made by poetic writings to these conceptualizations, and the complex intermingling of social and aesthetic cultural assumptions attendant on the formation of racial identity. In the current academic climate, teaching race as integral to an understanding of Elizabethan poetry can be fraught with obstacles. For those of us whose scholarly writings seek to highlight the issue, teaching race to undergraduates can challenge even the most experienced. The strategies in "The Idea of Poetry" course provide students a matrix for examining both their presumptions about the function of literature and those of early modem English poets.

Not surprisingly, these strategies have their genesis in a traditional pedagogical technique—close reading. Once students discover that the language used to create images of pleasure in Elizabethan poetry is also the language used to create racial ideologies, they are more willing to consider the possibility (and plausibility) of reading race in works such as Donne's or Guilpin's. Moreover, students are more willing to assume responsibility early in the course for the pedagogical imperatives and strategies that will guide them through a work's racial inscriptions, and in doing so they also take responsibility for beginning the process of redefining what race means.

Ultimately, students must approach "the texts of Western culture as equals" and the professoriate must forego "the role of Prospero-teacher to passive students" (Hall, *Things* 268) when treating issues of difference (whether race, gender, sexual orientation, class, or religion) in the classroom.

As teachers of Elizabethan poetry we must begin to rethink our own assumptions about what constitutes a meaningful engagement with Elizabethan poetry, an inquiry that may perhaps be the most useful framework for introducing race into the classroom. For, as the poetry of Donne and Guilpin highlights, the lexicon of race recognizes few borders—whether temporal, historical, aesthetic, political, or philosophical. Our responsibility is not merely to teach the techniques of close reading but to "licence" our students' "roving hands" to begin the difficult work of uncovering the literary history of race in Western culture.

RACE: A RENAISSANCE CATEGORY?

In the beginning was the word, and the word was race.

For a four-letter word that has preoccupied and defined Anglo-American societies for nearly 400 years, the term 'race' remained until recently a somewhat under-theorised epistemological category within Renaissance English studies. Despite the inroads made by historians, literary scholars, students of cultural studies, sociologists, and philosophers, our knowledge of the complex and often problematic ways in which Renaissance England defined and understood the concept of race remains somewhat tenuous. On the one hand, this tenuous hold can be explained in part by the extraordinary semiotic malleability of the word 'race': it can mean whatever a social formation wants it to mean. In its literature, philosophy, art, theological debates, and politics, Renaissance England made use of the word 'race' to both define and differentiate itself from the rest of the world. The word was borrowed from French in the first half of the sixteenth century: it had appeared in various Romance languages and dialects as early as 1300. Its etymology is disputed – it seems that the word originally had to do with the breeding of horses (see OED s.v. n^6). Given that the OED distinguishes eight primary meanings and eighteen secondary meanings that had emerged by 1612, it is not surprising that 'race' provided English writers with a certain flexibility of meaning as they classified and ordered English society.

The OED (s.v. 2a) cites John Foxe's *Acts and Monuments* as an example of one of the earliest uses of 'race' and, as the dictionary notes, the meaning of the term, for Foxe, principally denoted genealogy or lineage: 'Thus was the outward race and stock of Abraham after flesh refused.' 'Race' also was used to differentiate the sexes: men and women were frequently described as being different races. The word 'race' is used seventeen times in the whole of Shakespeare's canon: with two exceptions, he uses it to refer to a person's genealogy, or their lineage in terms of social status. The exceptions occur in The Tempest (when Miranda refers to Caliban's 'vile race', 1.2.358) and *Macbeth* ('Duncan's horses – a thing most strange certain – / Beauteous and swift, the minions of their race', 2.4.14–15).

Over the course of the latter half of the sixteenth century and the first half of the seventeenth, however, the idea of race and the word's usage suffered a semiotic sea-change. As we shall see, this alteration in meaning occurred in large measure because of the ease with which the governing precepts behind a concept of race can be linguistically corrupted, disestablished, or rendered ambiguous. Moreover, it is obvious that the word was understood to be malleable as a signifier of classificatory hierarchy, particularly within human societies. And, I will argue, it is this malleability that generated increasing anxiety about the nature and meaning of race.

This essay does not aim to provide a comprehensive historical study of the complex origins of race in early modern cultures; rather, it seeks to offer a brief overview of race through the two conceptual threads that contributed to the formation of the Renaissance concept: the philological history of the word 'race' from its entry into the English language, and the Renaissance theory of 'generation', which attempts to explain away the problematics that surface in relation to the use of 'race' as a category of social identity. I have chosen this approach, rather than discussing the concept of 'colour', for a number of reasons. First, an abundant body of scholarship tracing the significance of race as colour in Renaissance English literature and culture already exists (for general studies dealing with the matter of colour as a racialising feature see Gillis 1995; Hall 1996; and Macdonald 1997). Second, shifts in semantics, semiotics, and usage are often shaped by the specific socio-economic and cultural needs of a given society, and the lexical history of the word 'race' appears to reflect just such a process. Finally, the Renaissance concept of race is based on an elaborate system of metaphors and synonyms whose rhetorical and interpretative strength lies in its fluidity and, as I hope to illustrate, Renaissance medicine and Renaissance philology are inextricably linked to the conceptualisation of race in Renaissance English culture.

Genealogy

The origins of the word 'race' are as ambiguous as the term itself. 'Race' appears to have entered written English sometime during the first half of the sixteenth century, though it is likely that its oral history can be traced to the Crusades. Even the word's etymological genesis is open to debate: some argue for a Latin etymology via Italian (ratio or generatio), others contend that the word is Germanic, and still others argue for a Spanish or Moorish heritage. Whatever the source, 'race' quickly became instantiated in the English tongue and culture by the end of the sixteenth century. Notably, it seems that the word was culturally significant enough to warrant inclusion in a number of Renaissance English dictionaries, both monolingual and bilingual. For example, John Florio, in his *World of Words* (1590) offers the following entry for the Italian term for race: 'Razza, Raza, as Raggia, a kind, a race, a brood, a blood, a stock, a name, a pedigree' (p. 309).

Richard Percyvale's *Biblioteca Hispanica* on the other hand, does not provide a separate entry for the Spanish term raza and the English equivalent 'race' (Percyvale 1591). It does, however, incorporate the term in other Spanish word entries – casta, abolengo, and abolorio – as a synonym. When Percyvale turns to English, however, not only does he include the English term 'race', but he also provides a list of synonyms: 'a race, a lineage, a breed, genus'. The absence of an entry for raza may be explained by looking to the word's problematic semantics in Spain. As a number of critics have shown, in Renaissance Spain raza already signified a complex (and often contradictory) classification system, which included ethnicity and phenotype (see Stolcke 1994; Smith 1992). For some unknown reason Percyvale deems a separate entry for the word raza unnecessary. After Percyvale's death, John Minsheu revised and expanded the *Biblioteca Hispanica*. Though Minsheu's 'augmentation' was not quantitatively substantial, careful scrutiny reveals that his additions are nonetheless far more significant entries to the Biblioteca Hispanica than his title page suggests (Minsheu 1613).

In his dictionary, Minsheu includes not only an entry for raza but also one for another term which would come to have major ideological consequences, mestizo. Minsheu's handling of the Spanish raza and English 'race' does indeed 'enlarge' on what is missing from Percyvale. For example, in the Spanish–English section, the entry for raza (or raca) is defined as 'a ray or beam shining through a hole. Also a race, stock, kind or breed'. Additionally, in the English–Spanish section, Minsheu writes, 'line or race – vide Casta, Raca', and under the entry 'race or stock' he directs the reader to 'Raca, caste, Abolorio, Abolengo'. In doing so, Minsheu creates a dictionary which offers its users as much information as they will need to comprehend all the vagaries of the Spanish language and its racial lexicon, even going so far as to provide definitions for subsets within entries. Yet every entry seems to reiterate a prevailing semantics; whatever Spanish word one uses – caste, raza, abolorio, abolengo – it will inevitably signify in English 'a race, a lineage, a breed, issue of one's body, a progeny, a stock an offspring' or 'pedigree, stock, or descent of kindred'.

The sudden florescence of dictionaries offering similar or exact English versions of this meaning of 'race' – John Baret's *An Alvearie or Triple Dictionarie* (1573, 1580), Claudius Holyband's *A Dictionarie French and English* (1570/1), and Thomas Wilson's *A Christian Dictionary* (1612) – suggests how pervasive the link between the word 'race' and the idea of Christian nobility was in English Renaissance culture: 'Race. The course of Christianity and godliness. Let us run [with patience] the race [that is set before us. Heb. 12:1, Geneva Bible]' (Wilson 1612: I, 387). These careful attempts to delineate (and limit) the meaning of race are not a coincidence. On the contrary, these dictionaries contribute to a major recalibration of the semantic possibilities of the word 'race' in the face of expanding internationalism within and beyond England, as well as of the growing social and economic power of a mercantile class. Between 1560 and 1660 England's political economy and social institutions underwent a radical realignment. Works such as William Harrison's *A Description of England* and John Stowe's *A Geographical History* testify to the gradual alteration of the English social hierarchy. Merchants, lawyers, and other professionals (especially as civil servants) were an important defining presence in Renaissance English culture. Though a portion of the merchants and financiers came from the nobility or the gentry (younger sons), the majority of this class were 'commoners'. The increased wealth of this emergent class produced fundamental changes in a social fabric once thought immutable. Money enabled these 'commoners' to live in a manner once thought solely the privilege of the nobility, to acquire the trappings of 'civility' (land, education, luxury goods), and, more importantly, to procure titles (either through service, purchase, or marriage).

In other words, economic changes effectively forced the redrawing of the taxonomic boundaries of one form of racial classification. It is, perhaps, this social and cultural reformation which may have prompted sixteenth- and seventeenth-century English lexicographers such as Percyvale, Minsheu, and Florio (among others) to undertake the onerous task of constructing a taxonomic system for the word 'race' that would be, paradoxically, exclusive but also, when necessary, inclusive. In this way early modern writers could deploy the word in a variety of ways without once having to evince concern for the ideological contradictions that may surface. Race, it seems was a semiotic category, best dealt with in ambiguities.

Familial Ties

For most individuals in Renaissance England, use of the word 'race' was tied to both ancestry (see OED s.v. 1a) and social status. For example, in an anonymous elegy on the death of Sir Philip Sidney, the poet describes Sidney in the following way:

> Drawn was thy race aright from princely line
> Nor less than such (by gifts that Nature gave
> The common mother that all creatures have)
> Doth virtue show, and princely lineage shine. (from Rollins 1954)

In his 'Verse in Praise of Lord Henry Howard, Earl of Surrey' George Tuberville similarly deploys the term:

> Though want of skill to silence me procures
> I write of him whose fame for aye endures
> A worthy wight, a noble for his race,
> A learned lord that had an earl's place. (from Rollins 1954)

Strikingly, the rhetoric of race becomes localised in key words: worth, learning, honour, valour, and courtesy. As James Casey notes, 'the cornerstone of nobility is religion, honour, talent and valour' (Casey 1989: 9) – to which we might also add loyalty, magnanimity, and courtesy. In addition, these attributes were considered transmittable from father to child (or, in those problematic situations, from mother to child) and would make themselves known at every instance.

What is readily apparent in the usage of the word race is that both word and concept become a crucial category of identity in Renaissance England because English patriarchy 'depends on the principle of inheritance in which the father's identity – his property, name, his authority is transmitted from father to son. ... But this transmission from father to son can take place only insofar as both father and son pass through the body of a woman' (Adelman 1992: 106). Furthermore, 'the insistence on chastity and virtue for wives as a condition for the economic strength of the ... family was also closely connected with the concern about lineage. Since noble birth was crucial feature of knighthood, only true-born sons would be brave and worthy of their families ... Confusion of blood produced unreliable men' (Abercrombie, Hill, and Turner 1980: 80). It is especially significant that, according to Huet, 'in a political culture where the notions of inheritance, name, title, and lineage [i.e. race] were reinforced by multiple rights (birthrights, rights to inheritance, entails, and so forth), the question of paternity had considerable urgency. The uncertainty of legitimacy also explains the success of a theory that attributed a lack of resemblance to the power of the mother's imagination'; this theory was called 'generation' (Huet 1993: 34).

Since Aristotle propounded his theory of generation in *De Generatione Animalium*, physicians and natural philosophers have debated one of the theory's central paradoxes: why it is that, occasionally, children do not resemble their fathers. Within Renaissance medical and scientific discourses, explanations were as varied as the people providing them – we find historians, poets, philosophers, and physicians all contributing to the discourse of generation. Without question the most influential Renaissance voice in this ongoing debate was the sixteenth-century French physician Ambroise Paré. Paré's *De la chirurgie* (1585) quickly became an encyclopaedic reference for English physicians and medical practitioners,[1] such as Helkiah Crooke. Like Paré's *Des monstres et prodiges* (1573), portions of Crooke's *Microcosmographia* (1613) are intended to provide an explanation for one of the more troubling anomalies in generation, the problem of resemblance. Aristotelian tradition held that, by virtue of the male seed's 'natural' superiority, a man's offspring should resemble him. Not surprisingly, all types of difficulties arose when a child bore little or no resemblance to the father – questions of legitimacy in particular. If the male seed was dominant (as Aristotelian theory held), then how was it possible for a man's offspring to resemble him neither in appearance nor sex? Either his wife had committed adultery or, if she was virtuous, then the answer lay elsewhere. Not surprisingly, theorists looked to Aristotle's concept of the malleability of 'seed' after conception to explain this conundrum.

In his discussion of the matter of resemblance, Helkiah Crooke implicitly seeks to assure the anxious father that the causes for the absence of paternal resemblance are both explicable and natural:

> The infant sometimes is altogether like the mother, sometimes altogether like the father, other sometimes like them both, that is, in some parts resembling the mother, in others the father. Oftentimes he resembleth neither the father nor the mother, but the grandfather or the great grandfather, sometimes he will be like an unknown friend, as for example, an Ethiopian or such like who never had hand in his generation. Of all these similitudes we have many examples in authors of approved credit. (*Microcosmographia,* Book 5, 26)

While Crooke alludes to classical authors such Herodotus, Pliny, and Aristotle as sources for his commentary, it is clear that he is deeply indebted to Ambroise Paré's *Des monstres et prodiges.*

Paré's text similarly draws upon 'many examples in authors of approved credit' in its efforts to address the problematics of resemblance (Paré 1982: xv). However, there is a marked difference between Paré's and Crooke's handling of the matter. Paré begins by adumbrating the difference between 'monsters' and 'marvels': 'Monsters are things that appear outside the course of nature (and are usually signs of some forthcoming misfortune), such as a child who is born with one arm, another who will have two heads, and additional members over and above the ordinary' (Paré 1982: 3). Prodigies, or 'marvels', on the other hand, are 'things which happened that are complete against Nature as when a woman will give birth to a serpent, or a dog, or some other thing that is totally against Nature' (1982: 3). In perhaps an unconscious parody of the Ten Commandments, Paré provides his readers with a list of the 'several things that cause monsters': the 'glory' or the 'wrath' of God; too much or too little 'seed', 'imagination', 'posture', 'hereditary or accidental illnesses', 'rotten or corrupt seed', or 'through mixture or mingling of seed' (1982: 4).

For Paré, as for Crooke, the principal causes of monsters and marvels is the human imagination, which Paré identifies as the 'fifth cause of monstrosity'. As part of his explanation, Paré first turns to Heliodorus' Aethiopica and an explanation that we would immediately recognise as racial in its semiotic register. According to Paré, Heliodorus 'writes that Persina, the Queen of Ethiopia, conceived by King Hidustes – both of them being Ethiopian – a daughter who was white and this [occurred] because of the appearance of the beautiful Andromeda that she [Persina] summoned up in her imagination, for she had a painting of her before her eyes during the embraces from which she became pregnant' (Paré 1982: 38). Paré then tells the story of Hippocrates saving the life of 'a princess accused of adultery, because she had given birth to a child as black as a Moor, her husband and she both having white skin; which woman was absolved upon Hippocrates' persuasion that it was [caused by] the portrait of a Moor, similar to the child, which was customarily attached to her bed' (Paré 1982: 38).

Paré cites these examples as 'true accounts' of the extraordinary power of the female imagination, and advises that 'it is necessary that women – at the hour of conception and when the child is not yet formed (which takes thirty to thirty-five days for males and forty or forty-two, as Hippocrates says, for females – not be forced to look at or to imagine monstrous things' (Paré 1982: 39–40). Paré's examples, of course, illuminate more than just an ancient belief. In reiterating Herodotus' tales of imaginative miscegenation, Paré highlights the impossibility of completely alleviating male anxiety about the legitimacy of his offspring. Race as lineage proved too permeable, too malleable a term for a society undergoing social and cultural change.

Race: A Renaissance Category?

I want to conclude by returning to John Minsheu's 'augmentation' of Percyvale's *Bibliotheca Hispanica*. As I noted earlier, the Bibliotheca does not provide entries for most of the Spanish racialising lexicon (raza, mestizo, mulatto). Minsheu adds two of the three; interestingly enough, he includes mestizo but not mulatto. Moreover, in his definition of mestizo Minsheu does not cross-reference other Spanish terms or offer English equivalents. Instead, he writes, 'mestizo, m. that which is come or sprung of a mixture of two kinds, as a black Moor and a Christian, a mongrel dog or beast'. What Minsheu's definition elides, or more accurately what it misrepresents, is that the word was coined to describe offspring of Spanish and American Indian unions and was rarely applied to anyone born of the sexual relations between African (or Moor) and Christian. Moreover, mestizo was not used to describe non-human animals. What Minsheu does to create his definition is to combine a number of different terms in the Spanish racial lexicon (mestizo, mestico, mulatto, and morisco) and offer his English readers a hybrid explanation. As Minsheu constitutes it, mestizo functions as a less than desirable term of reference. To categorise a person as a mestizo, then, is not only to point to a problematic genealogy but also to deny that individual a 'racial' history.

Ultimately, it was England's pursuit of power in the Americas that triggered the kind of redefinition reflected in Minsheu's translation of the Spanish racial lexicon.[2] Engendered by a combination of political unrest, economic dearth, and political oppression, the migration of Englishmen to the emerging colonies in the Americas wrought unexpected changes in the English social consciousness. In this brave new world, the aristocratic ideology that had given rise to the word 'race', and its social legitimacy, proved inadequate as a method of categorising in the colonial space. Sexual and marital unions across ethnic, social, and geographical lines created a group of individuals whose identities threatened to undermine the conceptualisation of race as solely based on patrilineal descent tied to social status. Moreover, those people born in the colonies who could claim an English father posed a singular difficulty for the prevailing discourse of race: what exactly was the race of the mulatto or mestizo if the father was 'nobly born'?

Certainly, the most significant factor in the changing definition of race as a category of identity during the sixteenth and early seventeenth centuries was the impact of colonialism and the African slave trade. The shift in race's meaning can be mapped in those Renaissance texts whose methodological impulses we would now classify as constitutive of cultural anthropology and physical anthropology: travel narratives, ethnographic writings, and writings that included specific references to Africa, America, and Asia. Texts such as Raleigh's *The Discoverie of Guiana*, Leo Africanus' *The Geographical History of Africa*, Richard Hakluyt's *Voyages and Discoveries*, and the myriad plays, ballads, official reports, and personal letters associated with the mercantile and colonising project signalled a radical change in the English consciousness. No longer looking inward, Renaissance England cast its gaze to the world and discovered that the world was decidedly not English.

In the end, the Renaissance usage of the word 'race' reveals a multiplicity of loci, of axes of determinism, as well as metaphorical systems to aid and abet its deployment across a variety of boundaries in the making (Hendricks 1996). As an expression of fundamental distinctions, race's meaning varied depending upon whether a writer wanted to specify difference born of a class-based concept of genealogy, a psychological (and essentialised) nature, or group typology. Nonetheless, in all these variations, race is envisioned as something fundamental, something immutable, knowable, and recognisable, yet it can only be 'seen' when its boundaries are violated, and thus race is also, paradoxically, mysterious, illusory, and mutable. As a classificatory category the Renaissance concept of race, it turns out, was riven with fault-lines, which human beings proved quite adept at exploiting.

Over the course of the sixteenth century race proved itself a useful social category. In its linguistic and ideological permutations, it allowed for the classification of all humankind, but with distinct variants according to political and cultural needs. A Renaissance category that once defined a person's ability to claim a noble heritage, race quickly proved useful as a generic typological term. Depending on context, audience, and gender, Renaissance writers moved freely between phrases such as 'the English race', 'the Irish race', 'race of women', 'black race', and 'white race'. Race became divorced from its strict genealogical semiotics and became increasingly associated with a colour-based taxonomy ('black race' or 'white race'). Furthermore, nation-states and continents became tied to this taxonomy, and lineage took on a different importance. Racial descent was no longer defined solely through the father, and 'seed' no longer determined the contours of racial identity. Although it would take two centuries for the word 'race' to be defined solely in terms of colour, it is in Renaissance English culture that the first steps were taken towards establishing race as an unquestioned detail of cultural identity. Race, indeed, is a Renaissance category.

RACE AND NATION

RACE AND NATION WERE familiar terms to pre-1700 English men and women. Individuals understood their "place" in society as a reflection of these two conceptual markers of subjectivity. The discourses of race and nation were founded on an elaborate system of linking metaphors whose rhetorical and interpretive strength lay in their fluidity. Yet, with the rapidly changing geopolitics that England faced, it became apparent that race and nation were rife with fault lines. Awareness that human beings proved quite adept at exploiting the fissures led to frequent recalibrations of the meanings of the terms. Even in the face of such exploitation, as William Shakespeare's usage of race and nation illustrates, English political and cultural institutions continued to rely on the concepts as ideological demarcations.

RACE

Although its dates are more suggestive than factual, the *Oxford English Dictionary (OED)* offers a useful etymological dateline for the importance of "race" as a concept and a descriptive word. It surfaces in English around the fifteenth century and, as the *OED* shows, maintains as its core definition the idea of descent and heredity even as it evolves toward its more modern usage:

group of people connected by common descent (c1480 as rasse), offspring, descendants (1496), subdivision of a species represented by a certain number of individuals with hereditary characteristics (c1500), time span of a generation (1552), origin, extraction (1558), set or class of people sharing the same profession or the same character (1564), group of animals born to the same mother (1611), subdivision of mankind which is distinguished from others by the relative frequency of certain hereditary traits (1684). (*OED*)

By the time William Shakespeare was born, both race and nation marked an individual's affiliation with or incorporation into a specific group; yet, depending on the particular circumstances, one concept (race) signified genealogy whereas the other concept (nation) denoted community or geographic belonging. But, not surprisingly, race had more cultural, ideological, and political valence for Tudor England. For example, use of the term "race" primarily evoked an ideology of "hereditary traits" associated with a person's patrilineal origins. As James Casey notes, "the cornerstone of nobility is religion, honour, talent and valour," to which we might add loyalty, magnanimity, and courtesy (Casey 19). These traits were perceived as biologically transmittable from father to child and, not surprisingly, will always be visible regardless of the social conditions that might prevent the person's racial identity from being initially recognized. In the non-dramatic writings of the sixteenth century and the first decade of the seventeenth century, "race" was routinely deployed in poems of praise or narratives that dealt with aristocratic or royal subjectivities. See, for example, the way the word is used in the Trevilian commonplace book shown in Figure 135. Its account of the lineage of James I is "A true description of the noble race of the Stewarts."

[135. Thomas Trevilian, "A true description of the noble race of the Stewarts." (1608). By permission of the Folger Shakespeare Library]

In an epitaph on the death of Sir Philip Sidney, Walter Raleigh describes Sidney in similar terms: "drawn was thy *race* aright from princely line / Nor less than such (by gifts that Nature gave / The common mother that all creatures have) / Doth virtue shew, and princely linage shine" (Rollins, emphasis added). At the center of pre-1700 semantics of race was an assumption about exclusivity, authority, ethical and moral character, and, most importantly, belonging. Race denoted membership in an elite "club"—the noble family, the gens, the polis, or the nation; membership, however, was limited to those whose claims of affiliation could be substantiated, and substantiation was inextricably tied to birth. By "birth" I mean both the literal act of being born and the ideological sense of rank and/or social position inherited from parents. Thus, an individual's first psychic affiliation is not to a place, a group, a color, or an idea but to her or his parents - and more specifically the mother because she is the locus of nourishment.

RACE AND WOMEN

Yet claiming a racial identity in pre-1700 Western cultures was rarely articulated through one's relationship to the mother. Patriarchal hegemony dictated that racial membership in terms of family, gens, polis, or nation was primarily (though not always) determined through patrilineal descent. One effect of the ideology of patrilineal descent as a predicate of race was the pathological drive for male control over the female body as the site of species reproduction. Marie-Helene Huet suggests that "in a political culture where the notions of inheritance, name, title, and lineage [were] reinforced by multiple rights (birth rights, rights to inheritance, entails, and so forth), the question of paternity [has] considerable urgency" (Huet 34). Importantly, as Janet Adelman observes, "patriarchal society depends on the principle of inheritance in which the father's identity—his property, his name, his authority is transmitted from father to son.... But this transmission from father to son can take place only insofar as both father and son pass through the body of a woman; and this passage radically alters them both" (Adelman 106).

Children whose legitimacy can be called into question cannot make claims for racial affiliation that would guarantee social status and/or financial success (see Chapter 82, "Birth, Marriage, and Death"). These individuals had no claim, under existing codes of law, to a name, political status (in some instances), marriage, and inheritance. And thus, race defined patrilineally became almost exclusively a matter of biology, specifically blood.

Nicholas Abercrombie, Stephen Hill, and Bryan S. Turner have noted that "the insistence on chastity and virtue for wives as a condition for the economic strength of the feudal family was also closely connected with the ideology of chivalry. Since noble birth was a crucial feature of knighthood, only true-born sons would be brave and worthy of their families. Confusion of blood produced unreliable men" (Abercrombie, Hill, and Turner So).

What this anxiety engendered was a concept that would be labeled "race" - the ability to distinguish one individual from another on the basis of a set of attributes connected to his or her birth. The idea that race is a biological category is not entirely inaccurate when we consider that a person is born with certain physiological or class characteristics shared with other individuals. It is important to note, however, that these characteristics do not de facto enact a hierarchy between individuals; a social and economic infrastructure is needed to do that. In other words, a flexible concept of race was necessary to a patriarchal society determined to ensure the legitimacy of its governing class.

Female chastity thus became a constitutive guarantee of patrilineal descent and by extension a surety in the transmission of property (including the patrilineal surname) (see Chapter 83, "Gender Relations and the Position of Women"). Furthermore, when we look at the myriad ways in which patriarchal societies attempted to quell their anxiety over unregulated female sexuality, we realize that the dialectical relationship between race and the female body is an ideological given. Marriage, female chastity, virginity, female obedience, and the presumption of male superiority are constituted to avert the "confusion of blood"—a metaphor for race—that may occur when women control their sexuality. Shakespeare's engagement with this problem occurs throughout his canon. In *Antony and Cleopatra,* for example, Antony remonstrates himself, "have I my pillow left unpress'd in Rome, I Forborne the getting of a lawful *race"* (*Ant.* 3,13.237, emphasis added), for his affair with Cleopatra. Implicit in his words is his awareness of what is lost by continuing his sexual liaison with the Egyptian queen. Interestingly, it is not the loss of political power that disturbs him but the potential loss of lineal history.

William Shakespeare's engagement with race operates on multiple levels, moving fluidly between race as a signifier of social status and as an emerging signifier of biophysical subjectivity. Yet Shakespeare's use of the word "race" is relatively uncommon. In all, there are sixteen instances where the playwright employs the term, nearly all occur in his dramatic works, and with a few exceptions they are indicative of lineage. This meaning is what the Earl of Suffolk has in mind when he tells the Earl of Warwick, "thy mother took into her blameful bed / Some stern untutor'd churl; and noble stock / Was graft with crab-tree slip, whose fruit thou art, / And never of the Nevills' noble *race"* (2H6 3.2.212-15, emphasis added).

Similarly, *A Winter's Tale* reiterates this interconnection of biology, social status, and appearance. Speaking to Perdita, Polixenes explains that marrying outside of one's lineage or social status has residual effects, both positive and negative:

> You see, sweet maid, we marry
> A gentler scion to the wildest stock,
> And make conceive a bark of baser kind
> By bud of nobler *race*: this is an art
> Which does mend nature - change it rather - but T
> he art itself is nature. (*WT* 4.4.92-97, emphasis added)

Despite the suggestion in Polixenes's words that noble and base can, in nature, blend and produce art, we need to recall that Perdita is still the daughter of a king and an appropriate match for Florizel. Even so, Polixenes's words reflect, in many ways, shifting values about marriage across class lines in seventeenth-century England—as well as the regulation of female sexuality.

What is important in these examples is that race is viewed as an internal (genetic) and external (appearance and behavior) sign that manifests itself through patrilineal descent and social class. This perception is what defines Shakespeare's *King Richard III* as an intriguing reflection of the changing semantics of race. At the end of the play, both Richard III and Richmond are visited by the ghosts of those Richard murdered. In Richmond's case, the visits are to bless his political and military enterprise. The dead princes visit Richmond in a dream and declare, "Live, and beget a happy *race* of kings! (*R3* 5.3.160, emphasis added). The blessing of Richmond by the dead princes illuminates the fluidity of the idea of race as a cultural concept in Shakespeare's world. The transmission of nobility, honor, and legitimacy from father to children instantiates race, in this instance, as a coded term of political, historical, and social significance. It is notable that whereas Richard Ill's characterization reflects the negativity associated with what can be considered mod ern notions of race (physical appearances, color, sin, and inferiority), Richmond's "race" is illustrative of the premodern idea of race linked to lineage, nobility, virtue, and superiority.

NATION

Etymologically derived from the Latin verb *natio,* to be born, nation describes the collective body of people born in a specific geographical location. Conjoining actual physical space and reproductive biology, nation becomes a socially defined principle to organize a diffuse collection of individuals whose interests diverged on the basis of social status, sex, customs, and sometimes religious views into a seemingly homogeneous political and cultural entity. This signification informs the *Oxford English Dictionary* (*OED*) definition of nation:

> An extensive aggregate of persons, so closely associated with each other by common descent, language, or history, as to form a distinct race or people, usually organized as a separate political state and occupying a definite territory.
>
> In early examples the racial idea is usually stronger than the political; in recent use the notion of political unity and independence is more prominent.

Two aspects stand out in the *OED* definition: first, the order of what links individuals in a nation—"common descent, language, or history'"—and second, the phrase "as to form a distinct race or people." If we accept the ordering principle outlined in this definition, the confusion that often arises when examining the intersection of race and nation in Renaissance and early modern English culture is understandable. However, as the definition implies, two crucial elements link both concepts—"descent" and "language." The discussion that follows looks first at the role of language in shaping concepts of nation and race, in particular the way a social formation instantiates its ideologies of natioiness and racial identity, before turning to the issue of what impact skin color would have on the idea of national identity.

Language, as Emma Smith illuminates in her essay "'Signes of a Stranger': The English Language and the English Nation in the late Sixteenth Century," is key to the development of the English sense of itself as a nation and a race in the modern sense. In her discussion, Smith describes a telling moment in *The Life and Death of Jack Straw,* where a "'Flemming', or Dutchman" faces a tribunal and is asked to pronounce the words "bread and cheese" (E. Smith 171). The Dutchman's failure to pronounce the phrase in "good and perfect English" results in his execution. As Smith argues, "the incident proposes that foreignness, and by inference therefore Englishness too, is inherent in speech: that the English language offers a clear and audible marker of national difference" (170). The idea that "an integral feature of English [is] that it cannot be pronounced correctly by foreigners," in effect, produces "its own shibboleth" (172). This point, Smith contends, is concretely evident in Richard Carew's *An Epistle concern ing the Excellencies of the English Tongue:*

> . . . so that a Stranger, tho never so long conversant amongst us, carrieth evermore a Watch-word upon his Tongue, to descrie him by; but turn an *Englishman* at any time of his Age into what Country soever, allowing him due respit, and you shall see him profit so well, that the imitation of his Utterance will in nothing differ from the Pattern of that native Language. (E. Smith 172)

Despite the Englishman's linguistic prowess, it is the foreigner's accent that is at issue, yet, as Smith rightly argues, "this assertion of the integrity of the English language as an absolute barrier to foreign infiltration was a hollow one" (E. Smith 172). Language becomes the first articulation of native or foreign, belonging or not belong ing, English or not English.

Even people living adjacent to England did not escape this classificatory test. In *Henry V*, Shakespeare highlights this bias in the dialects of Macmorris and Jamy: Macmorris's use of "ish" and Jamy's "guid" and "baith." However, it is the exchange between Fluellen and Macmorris in act 3 that most demonstrates the pervasive sense of language as a mark of national difference:

> FLUELLEN: Captain Macmorris, I think, look you, under your correction, there is not many of your nation—
> MACMORRIS: Of my nation! What ish my nation? Ish a villain, and a bastard, and a knave, and a rascal. What ish my nation? Who talks of my nation? *(H5* 3.3.59-63)

Whereas elsewhere Shakespeare has used linguistic pronunciation to articulate class differences (e.g., Dogberry in *Much Ado about Nothing* or Nick Bottom in *A Midsummer Night's Dream*), in *Henry V* he centers national identity as its core.

At the same time that language was emerging as a key predicate of nationness, a person's birthplace was also becoming a determinant of Englishness. Concern for what appears to permeate social, political, and cultural boundaries led Renaissance and early modern governments to aggressively pursue policies that allowed them to regulate immigration and concomitantly determine who constituted an English subject. Not surprisingly, the distance between rights and privileges accorded the native-born English and those granted the resident or newly arrived immigrant grew exponentially as internal politics warranted. However, the civic language used to describe a person's legal status—denizen—more often than not generated confusion. "'Denizen' could equally signify anyone, native or not, living in a place, or the category of foreigner ameliorated by a Letter of Denization from the Queen or her appointed agent," Smith notes (E. Smith 176). In the case of the immigrant, a Letter of Denization allowed him or her to escape alien status and with it the taxes and legal disabilities associated with foreignness. Even if a foreigner possessed the Letter of Denization, legal limitations were placed on the individual's ability to own property, the amount of taxes paid, the type of trade or labor he or she could conduct or pursue, and his or her ability to move about the land.

Such measures, of course, did not address all problems associated with immigration to England. For example, children born to English parents residing in another nation and who returned to England proved to be something of a dilemma. Traditionally, the geographic place of birth was used to signify national identity; that is, a person "born in, say Antwerp to Antwerper, English, or parents of any other nationality, was considered to be a native of Antwerp, and thus an alien under English law" (E. Smith 175). The "shift in the Tudor period from a concept of alien status based exclusively on place of birth to one which took some account of heredity and parentage" (ibid.) allowed children born of English parents residing outside of England to become naturalized as native English. Paradoxically, the status of English-born children of immigrant parents was always in question. Two efforts to ensure that these children were legally denoted foreign, despite having been born in England, failed as "the idea that the English-born children of strangers were themselves [to be] classified as strangers persisted" (ibid.). As Smith's essay suggests, late sixteenth- and seventeenth-century English writers such as Shakespeare sought to define national characteristics as paradigmatic to English political and legal policies, as well as fostering a sense of cultural investment in the process.

SHAKESPEARE AND ALIENS

Language was one measure used to define and regulate Englishness, but immigration policies also underwent revision to maintain differences between native and foreign. In a study of the effects of immigration on sixteenth-century England, Laura Hunt Yungblut suggests that there were approximately four thousand to five thousand immigrants or "aliens" living in England by the end of Elizabeth's reign (Yungblut 13). Before 1588, most of these aliens were of German and Italian extraction, primarily merchants and traders, and generally temporary residents. After 1588, with growing religious intolerance spreading across Europe and the Mediterranean, England suddenly became a haven for refugees and immigrants. Yungblut's projection of the number of immigrants or "aliens" residing in England in 1604 may well reflect a rather conservative figure, as it likely represents the "registered alien" population and not the "undocumented aliens" that have plagued governments since the inception of the idea of a nation. England's ongoing tensions with Spain often prompted the English government to pursue diplomatic ties and expand trade relations with Islamic and African nation-states such as Morocco and Turkey. The effect of such political activity increased, even if temporarily, the presence of non-Europeans in London and other major urban centers so that once solid "English" neighborhoods soon began to reflect the various "nations" of Europe, Africa, and Asia.

This growth prompted Elizabeth's government in 1561, in response to "the vast majority of ... newcomers ... to London," to order a survey to be taken of the immigrants. Officials were instructed "to search out & learne the holl number of the Alyens & Straungers as well Denizens as other dwellinge and resiaunt at this [point]" (Yungblut 18). In January 1562/3, another London survey "apparently tried to correlate the motive of escape from religious persecution with the rising numbers of aliens in the realm" (ibid.). The government's efforts, however, did little to alleviate the concerns of native artisans and apprentices, who felt threatened by the skilled "aliens" who found success in their new country and who encouraged relatives and friends to immigrate. Opposition to immigration, not surprisingly, ran highest among those working in industries such as weaving and retail trade. In 1593, a bill designed to prevent "aliens from dealing in retail trade" was introduced into Parliament (Yungblut 41). Although the bill successfully passed the House of Commons, the House of Lords overturned the measure. The reaction among the London business community who had sponsored the bill, as one might suspect, was one of outrage and frustration. This anger, not surprisingly, was turned against the immigrants, and a campaign to drive them out of England ensued. Threats against the aliens, warning them "to leave England" or expect violence, had something of the desired effect, as a growing number of aliens did leave the country. Others, however, remained steadfast, looking to the government for protection.

Shakespeare's representation of England's sense of itself as a nation in his dramatic works evokes, with consistency, the parameters that define modern national identity: place of birth, common language, sense of community or belonging to a specific community, and an integrated political and social body (see Chapter 88, "Shakespeare's National Types"). From Falstaff's use of the term "English nation" in *Henry IV, Part 2*, to Cassio's use of the term "Englishman" in *Othello*, nation, as a political and social identity, is ideologically grounded in Shakespeare's canon. The exception to this commonplace usage is *The Merchant of Venice*, where it has a different connotation.

NATION OR RACE?

Of William Shakespeare's plays, only five are fully set in England: *The Tragedy of King Richard II, The Tragedy of King Richard III, King Lear, Cymbeline,* and *The Merry Wives of Windsor*. The remaining works move across geographic boundaries (real and invented) set outside the island and city where the dramatist worked and lived. The use of both English and non-English locales affords Shakespeare a degree of fictive license in creating his characters or depicting non-English peoples. Shakespeare's use of the word "nation" in this context seems unambiguous despite the settings he uses; that is, in reading the plays, we understand "nation" to signify a geographic locale inhabited by people born there and sharing common traits. Shakespeare's *The Merchant of Venice* is a bit of an exception. In act 1, scene 3, Shylock describes Antonio as one who "hates our sacred nation" *(MV 1.3.40)*. Two acts later, Shylock reiterates Antonio's animosity toward him: "he hath disgraced me and hind'red me half a million, laughed at my losses, mocked at my gains, scorned my nation ... heated mine enemies" *(MV 3-1.54-57)*. Whereas most of the references to himself and other Jews occur under the umbrella of "nation," like the Christians, Shylock occasionally refers to Jews as a "tribe" (for example, when he declares "cursed be my tribe / If I forgive him!" *MV 1.3*). The ideological and semantic difference between the two terms is striking. "Nation" usually denotes a structured political entity located in a specific place; "tribe," on the other hand, suggests a somewhat nomadic, loosely formed group of individuals linked by kinship or descent and, more to the point of this discussion, was invoked in reference to the division of the ancient Hebrews.

Shakespeare's use of "nation" and "tribe" as interchangeable generates a paradoxical image of Shylock and his community. On the one hand, the playwright appears to acknowledge the way Venetian society regulated non-Venetians, requiring English, French, Spanish, Germans, and others, including Jews, to live in homogeneous communities based on what we would consider to be national identity. The use of "nation" signals social and cultural homogeneity, and to some degree the Jewish community has this quality. Yet the theory of nation assumes political sovereignty linked to a geographic space - something lacking for the Jews in *The Merchant of Venice*. "Tribe," on the other hand, is semantically laden with notions of nomadic, agrarian, and patriarchal and kin-centered alliances. Tribes are often viewed as uncivilized—*Othello's* "base Indian" (first quarto) or "base Judean" (second quarto), who "threw away a pearl / Richer than all his tribe" (*MV* 5.3.364) - lacking an awareness of normative behaviors expected in a nation. That is, rarely do you see the word "tribe" used to invoke notions of civility. The traditional antithetical juxtaposition of nation and tribe becomes somewhat blurred in Shylock's self-description.

Shakespeare's language speaks to English culture's division of people along certain axes - skin color, geography, sex, religion - and the association of those divisions with particular descriptors (race, nation, gender, and Christian or non-Christian). Behind these divisions sit myriad ideologies and images, perceptions and misperceptions, truths and falsehoods, many of which Shakespeare captured in *The Merchant of Venice* and then reiterated in *Othello*. Although *Othello* does not make use of the word "race" as part of its depiction of racial tensions in the play, race is very much at the center of the tragedy. Othello's simultaneous incorporation into and alienation from Venetian culture mimics Shylock's position in the same city and Macmorris's status vis-a-vis Englishness in *Henry V*. These characters' racial identity inhibits their inclusion in a national identity, even if they use "nation" as a term of self-reference, as Shylock and Macmorris do.

What emerges in William Shakespeare's canon is an awareness that pre-1700 representations of race and nation were part of a systematic effort to foster social and political cohesion in England. What is more evident is that absolutes do not entirely work when reading Shakespeare's plays. We realize that sometimes race references a biological identity, whereas at other times it signifies national identity or social status. As Macmorris's question "what ish my nation?" implies, the question of national and racial identity in Shakespeare's works is very much an imagined existence.

RACE AND NATION POST-SHAKESPEARE

The complex histories of race and nation in the canon of William Shakespeare have been subject to scholarly scrutiny. Although both terms emerge as ways of describing familial or kinship relations or geographical identity, they follow different though at times overlapping ideological paths. Those who discuss race theory, such as David Theo Goldberg (2001) and Ivan Hannaford (1996), have illuminated the degree to which political and social institutions use race to shape ideas of nationhood, whereas Benedict Anderson's *Imagined Communities* (1991) offered theorists of nation-building a framework for assessing the use of race as one of the building blocks of national consciousness. Both approaches, however, envision race and nation as distinctly post-1700 or "modern" ideologies. Scholarship on pre-1700 England suggests that trying to fix a temporal start date for these ideologies may be an exercise in futility, especially since both terms were commonly used in medieval and Renaissance European cultures - becoming visible in England's lexical history around the twelfth century (the period when Anglo-Norman political control over Britain solidified).

Intellectual and critical analyses of a wide range of cultural phenomena (e.g., drama; art; philosophical, political, and religious discourse; travel writings) produced by Shakespeare and his contemporaries have provided a broad canvas of understanding for readers of Shakespeare's canon. More significantly, it is clear that Shakespeare's canon reflects the ways the idea and usage of nation parallels and intersects with that of race, with both concepts and terms shaping cultural discourse equally. Macmorris's "what ish my nation?," Othello's dissociation from the "wealthy curled darlings of our nation" (*Oth*. 1.2.68), and Shylock's "sacred nation" mark a discernible shift in the symbiotic relationship between race and nation. These usages speak to the necessary uncoupling of race and nation, marking each politically, ideologically, and semantically: Race and nation do not carry the same value. It would take the weight of time, geopolitics, science, and ideologies to ensure a complete break.

WORK CITED

The Moor of Venice, Or the Italian on the Renaissance English Stage"

"The Moor of Venice," Or the Italian on the Renaissance Stage,," was published in *Shakespearean Tragedy and Gender* eds., Shirley Nelson Garner, and Madelon Sprengnether Indiana University Press (1996), Copyright 1996. Reprinted with the permission of Indiana University Press.

References

Adelman, Janet. *Suffocating Mothers: Fantasies of Maternal Origin in Shakespeare's Plays, "Hamlet" to "The Tempest."* New York and London: Routledge, 1992.
Bartels, Emily C. "Making More of the Moor: Aaron, Othello and Renaissance Refashionings of Race." *Shakespeare Quarterly* 41 (1990): 433-54.
Berry, Edward. "Othello's Alienation." *Studies in English Literature* 30 (1990): 315-33.
Boose, Lynda E. "The Father and Daughter in Shakespeare." *PMLA* 97 (1982): 327.

—. "Othello's Handkerchief: 'The Recognizance and Pledge of Love.' "*English Literary Renaissance* 5 (1975): 360-74.

Braxton, Phyllis Natalie. "Othello: The Moor and the Metaphor." *South Atlantic Review* 55 (1990): 1-17.

Cantor, Paul A. *"Othello:* The Erring Barbarian among the Supersubtle Venetians." *Southwest Review* 75 (1990): 296-345.

Cavell, Stanley. *Disowning Knowledge in Six Plays of Shakespeare.* Cambridge: Cambridge UP, 1987.

Coryat, Thomas. *Crudities.* Glasgow: J. Maclehose and Sons, 1905.

D'Amico, Jack. *The Moor in English Renaissance Drama.* Tampa: U of South Florida P, 1993.

Garner, Shirley Nelson. "Shakespeare's Desdemona:' *Shakespeare Studies* (1976): 235-39.

Hale, John R. *England and the Italian Renaissance.* London: Faber and Faber, 1954.

Hall, Kim F." 'I rather would wish to be a Black-Moor': Beauty, Race, and Rank in Lady Mary Wroth's *Urania."* Women, "Race," and Writing in the Early Modern Period. Ed. Margo Hendricks and Patricia Parker. London and New York: Routledge, 1994. 178-94.

Hendricks, Margo. "Managing the Barbarian: *The Tragedy of Dido Queen of Carthage." Renaissance Drama* n.s. (1992): 165-88.

Howard, Jean E. "An English Lass amid the Moors: Gender, Race, Sexuality, and National Identity in Heywood's *The Fair Maid of the West." Women, "Race," and Writ ing in the Early Modern Period.* Ed. Margo Hendricks and Patricia Parker. London: Routledge, 1994. 101-17.

Jed, Stephanie. *Chaste Thinking.* Bloomington: Indiana UP, 1989.

Jones, Ann Rosalind. "Italians and Others: Venice and the Irish in Coryat's Crudities and *The White Devil." Renaissance Drama* n.s. (1987): 101-19.

Lacan, Jacques. *The Four Fundamental Concepts of Psycho-Analysis.* Ed. Jacques-Alain Miller. Trans. Alan Sheridan. New York: W.W. Norton and Co., 1978.

Levith, Murray J. *Shakespeare's Italian Settings and Plays.* New York: St. Martin Press, 1989.

Lewkenor, Lewes. *The Commonwealth and Gouernment of Venice. Written by the Cardinal Gasper Contareno, and translated out of Italian into English.*1599. Facsimile copy, Amsterdam and New York: Da Capo Press, 1966.

Lievsay, John. *The Elizabethan Image of Italy.* Published for the Folger Shakespeare Library. Ithaca: Cornell UP, 1964.

Little, Arthur L. Jr. " 'An essence that's not seen': The Primal Scene of Racism in *Othello.*" *Shakespeare Quarterly* 44 (1993) : 304-24.

McPherson, David C. *Shakespeare, Jonson, and the Myth of Venice.* Newark: U of Delaware P, 1990.

McWilliam, George W. *Shakespeare's Italy Revisited.* Leicester: Leicester UP, 1974.

Neill, Michael. "Changing Places in *Othello.*" *Shakespeare Survey* 37 (1984): 115-31.

--. "Unproper Beds: Race, Adultery, and the Hideous in *Othello.*" *Shakespeare Quarterly* 40 (1989): 383-412.

Newman, Karen. "'And wash the Ethiop white': Femininity and the Monstrous in *Othello.*" *Shakespeare Reproduced: The Text in History and Ideology.* Ed. Jean E. Howard and Marion F. O'Connor. New York and London: Methuen, 1987. 141-62.

Parker, Patricia. "Fantasies of 'Race' and 'Gender': Africa, *Othello* and Bringing to Light." *Women, "Race," and Writing in the Early Modern Period.* Ed. Margo Hendricks and Patricia Parker. London and New York: Routledge, 1994. 84-100.

Partridge, A. C. "Shakespeare and Italy." *English Studies in Africa* 4 (1961): 117-27.

Pocock, J. G. A. *The Machiavellian Moment: Florentine Political Thought and the Atlantic Republican Tradition.* Princeton: Princeton UP, 1975.

Ruggerio, Guido. *Binding Passions.* Oxford and New York: Oxford UP, 1993.

Shakespeare, William. *The Merchant of Venice.* New York: Viking, 1969.
— *Othello.* Ed. M. R. Ridley. London and New York: Routledge, 1958.

Snow, Edward A. "Sexual Anxiety and the Male Order of Things in *Othello.*" *English Literary Renaissance* 10 (1980): 384-412.

Traub, Valerie. *Desire and Anxiety: Circulations of Sexuality in Shakespearean Drama.* London and New York: Routledge, 1992.

What's Race Got to do with it?"

Published in *Approaches to Teaching Shorter Elizabethan Poetry*, eds., Patrick Cheney and Anne Lake Prescott. MLA publications. Copyright 2000 Reproduced with permission of the Licensor through PLSclear.

Race: A Renaissance Category

This essay was published in *A New Companion to English Renaissance Literature and Culture*, volume 1. Copyright 2010. Reproduced with permission of The Licensor through PLSclear.

1. Finally translated into English in 1634 as *The Works of that Famous Chirugeon Ambrose Parey*, the writings of Ambroise Paré were quite influential in the medical community in England throughout the late sixteenth century and all of the seventeenth century, those most late sixteenth- and early seventeenth-century readers read either the French or Latin versions. The edition of Paré's work cited in this essay was translated by Thomas Johnson and published in London in 1634.
2. See Allen 1997 for an excellent discussion of the links between early modern England's political economy, colonialism, and the emergence of whiteness as a definition of the notion of race.

References and Further Reading

Abercrombie, Nicholas, Stephen Hill, and Bryan S. Turner (1980). *Dominant Ideology Thesis*. London: George Allen & Unwin.
Adelman, Janet (1992). *Suffocating Mothers: Fantasies of Maternal Origin in Shakespeare's Plays, Hamlet to The Tempest*. New York: Routledge.
Allen, Theodore W. (1997). *The Invention of The White Race: The Origin of Racial Oppression in Anglo-America*, 2 vols. London: Verso.
Bartels, Emily C. (2008). *Speaking of the Moor: From Alcazar to Othello*. Philadelphia: University of Pennsylvania Press.
Barthelemy, Anthony Gerard (1987). *Black Face, Maligned Race: The Representation of Blacks in English Drama from Shakespeare to Southerne*. Baton Rouge: Louisiana State University Press.

Bovilsky, Lara (2008). *Barbarous Play: Race on the English Renaissance Stage*. Minneapolis: University of Minnesota Press.
Callaghan, Dympna (2000). *Shakespeare Without Women: Representing Gender and Race on the Renaissance Stage*. London: Routledge.
Casey, James (1989). *The History of the Family*. Oxford: Basil Blackwell.
Erickson, Peter and Clark Hulse (2000). *Early Modern Visual Culture: Representation, Race, Empire in Renaissance England*. Philadelphia: University of Pennsylvania Press.
Floyd-Wilson, M. (2003). *English Ethnicity and Race in Early Modern Drama*. Cambridge: Cam- bridge University Press.
Gillis, John (1995). *Shakespeare and the Geography of Difference*. Cambridge: Cambridge University Press.
Goldberg, David (1993). *Racist Culture: Philosophy and the Politics of Meaning*. Oxford: Blackwell. Goldenberg, David M. (2003). *The Curse of Ham: Race and Slavery in Early Judaism, Christianity, and Islam*. Princeton: Princeton University Press.
Hall, Kim (1996). *Things of Darkness: Economies of Race and Gender in Early Modern England*. Ithaca, NY: Cornell University Press.
Hendricks, Margo (1996). 'Obscured by dreams: race, empire, and Shakespeare's *A Midsummer Night's Dream*'. *Shakespeare Quarterly*, 47, 37–60.
Hendricks, Margo and Patricia Parker (eds.) (1994). *Women. 'Race' and Writing in the Early Modern Period*. London: Routledge.
Horowitz, Maryanne Cline (1992). *Race, Gender, and Rank: Early Modern Ideas of Humanity*. Rochester, NY: University of Rochester Press.
Huet, Marie-Helene (1993). *Monstrous Imagination*. Cambridge, Mass.: Harvard University Press. Hutner, Heidi (2001). *Colonial Women: Race and Culture in Stuart Drama*. Oxford: Oxford University Press.
Iyengar, Sujata (2005). *Shades of Difference: Mythologies of Skin Color in Early Modern England*. Philadelphia: University of Pennsylvania Press.
Jaffary, Nora E. (2007). *Gender, Race and Religion in the Colonization of the Americas*. Aldershot: Ashgate.
Loomba, Ania (1992). *Gender, Race, Renaissance Drama*, 2nd edn. New Delhi: Oxford University Press.

Loomba, Ania (2001). 'The colour of patriarchy: critical difference, cultural difference and Renaissance drama'. In K. Chedgzoy (ed.), *Shakespeare, Feminism and Gender* (pp. 235–55). Basingstoke: Palgrave.
Loomba, Ania (2002). *Shakespeare, Race, and Colonialism*. Oxford: Oxford University Press.
Loomba, Ania and Jonathan Burton (eds.) (2007). *Race in Early Modern England: A Documentary Companion*. Houndmills: Palgrave.
Macdonald, Joyce Greene (1997). *Race, Ethnicity, and Power in the Renaissance*. Delaware: University of Delaware Press.
Macdonald, Joyce Greene (2002). *Women and Race in Early Modern Texts*. Cambridge: Cambridge University Press.
Minsheu, John (1613). *A Dictionary in Spanish and English*. London.
Paré, Ambroise (1982). *On Monsters and Marvels*, trans. Janis L. Pallister. Chicago: University of Chicago Press.
Percyvale, Richard (1591). *Bibliotheca Hispanica, Containing a Grammar, with a Dictionary in Spanish, English and Latin*. London.
Rollins, Hyder (ed.) (1954). *The Renaissance in England: Non-Dramatic Prose and Verse of the Sixteenth Century*. Lexington, Mass.: D. C. Heath.
Singh, Jyotsna G. (ed.) (2009). *A Companion to the Global Renaissance: English Literature and Culture in the Era of Expansion*. Oxford: Wiley-Blackwell.
Smith, Paul Julian (1992). *Representing the Other: 'Race', Text and Gender in Spanish and Spanish American Narrative*. Oxford: Clarendon Press.
Sollors, Werner (1997). *Neither Black Nor White, Yet Both: Thematic Explorations of Interracial Literature*. New York: Oxford University Press.
Stolcke, Verena (1994). 'Invade women: gender, race, and class in the formation of colonial society'. In Margo Hendricks and Patricia Parker (eds.), *Women. 'Race' and Writing in the Early Modern Period* (pp. 272–86). London: Routledge.
Wilson, Thomas (1612). *A Christian Dictionary*, 2 parts. London.

Race and Nation

Sources Cited

Abercrombie, Nicholas, Stephen Hill, and Bryan S. Turner. *Sovereign Individuals of Capitalism*. London: Allen and Unwin, 1989.

Adelman, Janet. *Blood Relations: Christian and Jew in "The Merchant of Venice."* Chicago: U of Chicago P, 2008.

— *Suffocating Mothers: Fantasies of Maternal Origin in Shakespeare's Plays, "Hamlet" to "The Tempest." New* York: Routledge, 1992.

Anderson, Benedict. *Imagined Communities: Reflections on the Origin and Spread of Nationalism*. London: Verso, 1991.

Casey, James. *The History of the Family*. Oxford: Blackwell, 1989.

Goldberg, David Theo. *The Racial State*. Malden: Wiley-Blackwell, 2001.

Grabes, Herbert, ed. *Writing the Early Modern English Nation: The Transformation of National Identity in Sixteenth- and Seventeenth-Century England*. Amsterdam: Rodopi, 2001.

Hannaford, Ivan. *Race: The History of an Idea in the West*. Baltimore: Johns Hopkins UP, 1996.

Huet, Marie-Helene. *Monstrous Imagination:* Cambridge: Harvard UP, 1993.

Rollins, Hyder, ed. T*he Renaissance in England: Non-dramatic Prose and Verse of the Sixteenth Century*. Lexington: D. C. Heath, 1954.

Smith, Emma. "'Signes of a Stranger': The English Language and the English Nation in the Late Sixteenth Century." *Archipelagic Identities: Literature and Identity in the Atlantic Archipelago, 1550-1800*. Ed. Philip Schwyzer and Simon Mealor. Aldershot: Ashgate, 2004.

Yungblut, Laura Hunt. *Strangers Settled Here Amongst Us: Policies, Perceptions, and the Presence of Aliens in Elizabethan England*. London: Routledge, 1996.

Further Reading

Erickson, Peter and Clark Hulse. *Early Modern Visual Culture: Representation, Race, and Empire*. Philadelphia: U of Pennsylvania P, 2000.

Feerick, Jean. *Strangers in Blood: Relocating Race in the Renaissance*. Toronto: U of Toronto P, 2010.

Hall, Kim F. *Things of Darkness: Economies of Race and Gender in Early Modern England*. Ithaca: Cornell UP, 1996.

Knapp, Jeffrey. *Shakespeare's Tribe: Church, Nation, and Theater in Renaissance England*. Chicago: U of Chicago P, 2004.

Smith, Ian. *Race and Rhetoric in the Renaissance: Barbarian Errors*. New York: Palgrave MacMillan, 2009.

Thompson, Ayanna. *Passing Strange: Shakespeare, Race and Contemporary America*. Oxford: Oxford UP, 2011.

EARLY MODERN CRITICAL RACE STUDIES

THE ROMANCE OF SHAKESPEARE

President Lincoln (Oberon) and "Miss Virginia" (Titania):

Oberon—" I do but beg a little nigger boy to be my henchman."

Titania—" Set your heart at rest. The northern land buys not this negro child from me."

I came across this cartoon by John Tenniel, which appeared in London Punch on April 5, 1862, as I searched for an image for this section of the casebook. Seeing this image reminded me of the complex impact Shakespeare's play has wielded, for good and ill.
Source: Courtesy Allan T. Kohl/Minneapolis College of Art and Design.
There is a song "tall Doin's," published in the same issue as Tenniel's that speaks to the events leading up to the US civil war. See *Lincoln in Caricature* by Rufus Rockwell Wilson (ironically, one can purchase the print and a song as a piece of artwork).

http://www.historygallery.com/prints/PunchLincoln/1862oberon/1862oberon.htm

"OBSCURED BY DREAMS": RACE, EMPIRE, AND SHAKESPEARE'S A MIDSUMMER NIGHT'S DREAM

"There's no such thing as 'England' any more ...welcome to India brothers!"[1]

In July 1991 I was engaged as a textual advisor for a production of *A Midsummer Night's Dream* performed by the Shakespeare Santa Cruz repertory company (hereafter SSC). In a camp rendering of Shakespeare's text, director Danny Scheie sought to illuminate what he viewed as the sexual politics of the text. Featuring a variety of pop-culture motifs (ranging from 1950s American teenage attire and behavior to Disney's *Snow White*), the production obstructed any possibility of seeing the play as merely a romantic idealization of courtly behavior (though it did reinforce the centrality of marriage as a solution to social discord). While segments of the production were noteworthy for their playful disruption of tradition (particularly in treating the young lovers), the production also exhibited disturbingly unexamined acceptance of some sexual and racial stereotypes in its treatment of Titania and Hippolyta. Knowing that a camp Titania and Hippolyta would prove crowd-pleasers, the director was untroubled by the implications for the construction of race and gender of casting a black male as Titania and costuming him in a pink tutu and pink wig, or presenting Hippolyta as a stereotypic Wagnerian Valkyrie (thick blond braids, horned helmet, spear, etc.).

The director made a more radical and problematic decision with the Indian boy. Whether the Indian boy appears onstage at all is generally of little consequence, since he has no lines and would function as little more than a stage prop, part of the spectacle of Oberon and Titania's first meeting in the play. The director of the SSC production, however, chose to have the Indian boy make an appearance.[2] Normally this choice would scarcely merit a review note, let alone an entire essay. Yet, like the directorial decisions behind the representations and interpretations of Hippolyta, Oberon, Titania, and Theseus, the appearance and casting of the Indian boy bore ideological significance worth examining. First, the director, in a break with both textual and theatrical tradition, cast an adult male as the changeling: the "boy" was in his early twenties, six feet tall, tanned, and naked except for a gold lame loincloth. Second, in both the costume designer's drawings and on the stage, the Indian boy was culturally and racially marked: a turban (complete with feather), "Turkish" slippers, and jewelled dagger (see Figures 1 and 2). The Indian boy appeared on the Santa Cruz stage as a veritable Sinbad, a rich oriental "trifle" accessible to the gaze of predominantly white audiences for six weeks.

At the end of its run, this postmodern production of Shakespeare's *A Midsummer Night's Dream* might have gone the way of other small-repertory company productions of Shakespeare's comedy: the "part of the Indian boy played by" an inscription on the actor's resume; favorable or unfavorable reviews; and, after strike, the cast and crew moving on to other endeavors. But this history was not to be. The following year, while teaching a class on gender and theater, I was asked by students who knew that I had worked on the production to arrange a screening of the videotape. The students had heard that it was a lively, funny, and brilliant interpretation of Shakespeare's play. As I watched the videotape of SSC's *A Midsummer Night's Dream*, I meditated on the image of the Indian boy: was anyone other than me troubled by the oriental fantasy created by the director's political production? Did any of my students comprehend the unmistakably racist denotations of the representation? More important, was this particular representation of the Indian boy a directorial whim, or was the director constrained by something in a centuries-old playtext which inhibited any other possible reading of the Indian boy?

The director's attempt to infiltrate Shakespeare's text and subvert the long history of its theatrical production, as well as his commitment to challenge audience expectations about casting, I would argue, worked to engender not a radical rewriting of Shakespeare's text but merely another supplemental history of it. For in the representation of the Indian boy (and, in a different way, the figure of Titania), directorial subversion was instrumental in reaffirming an aspect of orientalist ideology: like the odalisque who became a favorite topos of Impressionist painting, the Indian boy of SSC's production silently conjured the template of eroticism and exoticism adumbrated in the West's vision of India and the East.[3]

The SSC production of *A Midsummer Night's Dream* sought to offer what Leah Marcus calls a "localized" Shakespeare: an attempt "to create an edge of defamiliarization about what has become too well known, engineer a set of encounters between disparate cultural situations in order to open up ways for audiences to rediscover the plays at the point 'where remoteness and accessibility meet.' " That is, the production, in part novel and in part familiar, endeavored to reveal "the cultural otherness of what we thought we understood."[4]

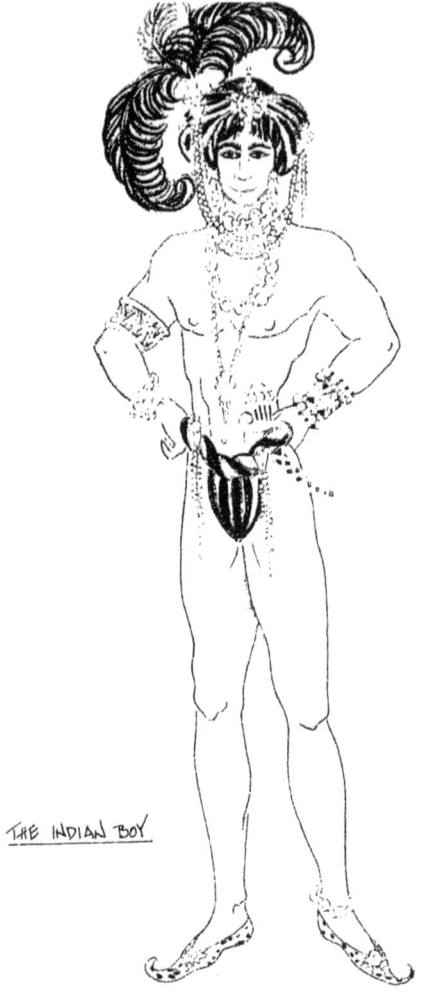

Fig. 1: Costume design for the Indian boy, created by B. Modern for the 1991 Shakespeare Santa Cruz production of *A Midsummer Night's Dream*.

Fig. 2: The Indian boy Jaime Paglia) in *A Midsummer Night's Dream*, Shakespeare Santa Cruz, 1991. Photograph by Ann Parker.

Yet, with contextualization, I want to offer an explanation as to why, in the SSC production, this "localizing" not only failed to "defamiliarize" but in fact colluded-and arguably could only collude- with an *a priori* racial ideology that imagines the Indian boy and what he signifies in early modern English culture.

The starting point for my reading of *A Midsummer Night's Dream* is a rudimentary query: what are we to make of the Indian boy? On the textual level the Indian boy is simply a plot device: he figures as the origin of the conflict between Oberon and Titania (a conflict that presumably begins in India). But why does he have to be Indian? Why not describe the boy as merely a changeling child? Or, if critical tradition is correct that all the fairies of *A Midsummer Night's Dream* are taken from English folklore, why not identify the changeling as the English boy? Obviously the dramatic structure and characterizations would not have been affected by such a change and, in fact, would have been made more definitively local. So once again it seems useful to ask: why does Shakespeare initially identify the child as "stol'n" from an "Indian king" and later expand on this identification with an elaborate narrative of the boy's maternal ethnic origins? Further more, what are we to make, culturally, of the fairies who fight for possession of him? Finally, what implications about race and early modern England's mercantilist and/or colonialist-imperialist ideology might we draw from Shakespeare's use of India?

Until recently explorations of early modern thinking about race meant recognizing early modern social discourse "to be about race ...when it employs a category which [we are] able to identify as having a referent corresponding to that designated by [our] own understanding of the term 'race.'"[5] In other words, such works as *Othello, Titus Andronicus,* or *The White Devil,* with their inclusion of a "black" character as a pivotal figure in the dramatic narratives of white European societies, have been taken as definitive signposts of early modern representations of race and racist ideologies. But what if our inferences, our understandings, are inaccurate? What if, in attempting to sort out the significance of early modern English literature to a post-World War II global political economy, we have misread, or not read at all, some of the signs of racial thinking present in that literature? Is it possible that a too narrow definition misrepresents and engenders an under-reading of the complexity and ambiguity of the word *race* and of its social and cultural articulation in sixteenth-century England? To ask these and other critically imperative questions about the ideological implications of any Renaissance text is also to be concerned with how audiences (then and now) might construe the concept of race and its linguistic inflections. In the whole of Shakespeare's dramatic canon the word *race* is employed only seventeen times, and generally it signifies genealogy. For example, in *2 Henry VI,* Suffolk tells Warwick,

> Thy mother took into her blameful bed
> Some stern untutored churl, and noble stock
> Was graft with crab-tree slip-whose fruit thou art
> And never of the Nevilles' noble race. (3.2.212-15)[6]

We find the same signification when the word is used in *Richard III* ("Live, and beget a happy race of kings" [5.3.157]), *Antony and Cleopatra* ("Have I my pillow left unpressed in Rome, / Forborne the getting of a lawful race" [3,13.107-8]), and *Cymbeline* ("a valiant race" [5.4.83]). There are only three instances when *race* seems to connote something different. The first occurs in *Measure for Measure* when Angelo remarks "And now I give my sensual race the rein" (2.4.161), where he is clearly referring to his personality. The second takes place in *The Tempest* when Miranda says of Caliban "But thy vile race ...had that in't which good natures / Could not abide to be with" (1.2.361-63), where *race* suggests type. And the third instance, somewhat ambiguous in its meaning, takes place in *Macbeth*, where Duncan's horses are called "the minions of their race, / Turned wild in nature" (2.4.15-16).[7]

In every usage there is a locus, an axis of determinism attendant upon a preconceived notion of fundamental distinctions, whether that locus is in a class-based concept of genealogy, in an essential nature, or in the ambiguity of ethnic typology. Race is envisioned as something fundamental, some thing immutable, knowable, and recognizable yet visible only when its boundaries are violated; thus race is also, paradoxically, mutable, illusory, and mysterious. Race is material (Duncan's horses) and immaterial (Angelo's nature). Race is language more than it is biology; yet without biology the language of race could not (and would not) exist.[8] Race is transmitted yet is viewed as essence. Race is ideology; race is ontology. Race is all this and nothing: a shaping fantasy.

It is this "shaping fantasy" in *A Midsummer Night's Dream*, a vision of race, which I intend to trace in my reading of Shakespeare's playtext. To begin with, I want to argue that literally and figuratively the playtext denotes cultural and temporal spaces that I shall refer to as "borderlands," spaces that are clearly marked for recognition. According to Gloria Anzaldua, "Borderlands are physically present wherever two or more cultures edge each other, where people of different races occupy the same territory, where under, lower, middle and upper classes touch, where the space between two individuals shrinks with intimacy."[9] While the most obvious instances of this phenomenon in *A Midsummer Night's Dream* occur in the social interactions between humans and fairies, male and female, Athenian and Amazon, I believe a borderland also coalesces on an ideological level in the concept of race. This concept is neither wholly the older (and more feudal) idea based on class and lineage nor wholly the more modern idea based only on physical appearance (i.e., skin color, physiognomy). Rather, the idea of race in *A Midsummer Night's Dream* is an uneasy mixture-the miscegenation, if you will-of these two views. My argument is that the figurative evocation of India localizes Shakespeare's characterization of the fairies in *A Midsummer Night's Dream* and marks the play's complicity in the racialist ideologies being created by early modern England's participation in imperialism. Moreover, it is my contention that this racialist ideology is not unique to Shakespeare's playtext but endemic to most textual representations of India contemporary with it.

As a way of situating this hypothesis, I begin with the literary tradition behind Shakespeare's use of Oberon and this character's link with India, in particular the medieval romance *Huon of Bordeaux*, Edmund Spenser's *The Faerie Queene*, and Robert Greene's *Scottish Historie of James the fourth*. I then examine two sixteenth-century travel narratives about India. Both the medieval romance and the two travel narratives, I argue, ideologically and lexically imagine a geographic region that becomes such a commonplace that the mere mention of the word "India" is enough to conjure a particular image, one figured in terms of skin color, geography, sexuality, and religion, and which instantiates a cultural subtext in Shakespeare's portrayal of fairyland. The final sections of this essay explore the ideological significance of these images, Shakespeare's use of India, and the lexicon both presuppose. In ways similar to yet different from descriptions of the New World, early modern accounts of India are marked by an emerging taxonomy of gender and linguistic difference. It is not unusual for the writer of an English Renaissance narrative to digress from topographical, mercantile, or political description in order to address a culture's sexual practices and behavior, especially the actions of women. Furthermore, what is striking in such digressions is the intrusive presence of an emerging racial lexicon tied to physical appearance and hybridity. By drawing a link between this lexicon, travel narratives, and Shakespeare's Oberon/Titania/Indian boy/ Bottom scenario, I want to highlight how dramatic invention intersects with lexical formulation in the reconceptualization of race. My argument, heuristically and philologically, endeavors to expand our understanding of the politics of race in early modern England. As Kim Hall suggests, modern concepts of "race are in large part the result of lingering notions of 'difference' that resided at the intersections of English travel and trade, plantation, empire, and science in the early modern period."[10]

I

Steven Mullaney has argued that a "map in the modern sense of the term is a guide to the present: a graphic index to the location of things in space, a traveler's aid which makes the passage from here to there less difficult."[11] *A Midsummer Night's Dream* might very well be considered a map of the sort Mullaney has described; in a number of its verbal and metaphoric expressions, the playtext offers a rather precise geographic index for identifying the location of spaces in the play. The comedy's action begins in Athens, moves to a wood outside the city (traditionally termed fairyland), and returns to Athens. One critic has argued, in a fine discussion of the anamorphic perspectives in *A Midsummer Night's Dream,* that the play compels us first to look straight on at Athens, then "shifts our perspective by obliging us to consider the forest, then brings Athens back in the third [perspective] and says, 'Look again'."[12] Yet the playtext's spatial layout is not so much a bipolar (Athens and Forest) as a tripolar configuration, with India sitting as the symbolic and ideological hub of departure and convergence for all the business of fairyland. That is, whatever exchange occurs, regardless of origin, is mediated through the discursive space that is India. Furthermore, "the routes of access" are "cultural and temporal as well as spatial."[13] It seems safe to assume that early modern audiences for *A Midsummer Night's Dream* came to the theater with a map for reading these local details of Shakespeare's dramatic world. The modern critic's dilemma is (and has been) how to reproduce that map so that its demarcations can be known more precisely.

Like a number of recent scholars, I have found extradramatic texts, travel narratives and medieval romances, useful in reading *A Midsummer Night's Dream* as Shakespeare's contribution to the literary invention of racial mapping.[14] I am not arguing that the play's audiences would have connected it directly to these texts. Rather, these works provide a means of recapturing a set of assumptions about India which were circulating in London at the time of the play's inscription, and with which Shakespeare's audiences could have been familiar. This familiarity did not necessarily require that all members of the audiences had read these narratives or even possessed the same degree of literacy.[15] For many Londoners knowledge of India (and Africa and the Americas) would have come orally, from seamen who served on the merchant and fighting ships traversing the Atlantic and Indian oceans.[16] These seamen were the most likely conduits for an image of India among those who could not read or, perhaps, afford to purchase the printed texts but who could afford to go to the theater.[17] In this manner the play's audiences might have been comprised not only of individuals acquainted with the medieval romance *Huon of Bordeaux*, Edmund Spenser's *Faerie Queene,* Robert Greene's *The Scottish Historie of James the fourth* (the literary sources for Shakespeare's depiction of Oberon), as well as manuscript and printed travel narratives, but also of people for whom India may have been the stuff of a sailor's tavern tale, a map made in the human imagination.

Let us begin to read our map of fairyland by turning to an index Shakespeare could have created for the lost traveler. Under the subject heading "Oberon," we might find the following citation: see Lord Berners, *Huon of Bordeaux*.[18] One of a number of medieval romances glorifying a culture no longer possible in late-sixteenth-century England, *Huon of Bordeaux* recounts the history of a young duke who unknowingly slays the son of Charlemagne and, for his crime, is sent to Babylon on a quest that Charlemagne believes will ensure Huon's death. Huon is told to return to Paris with a thousand bears, a thousand hawks, a thousand young men, and a thousand of Babylon's fairest maidens. He is also to bring Charlemagne a handful of the hairs and four of the teeth of Admiral Gaudys, Babylon's ruler. Huon's quest leads him to the East, where he meets Oberon, king of the fairies. Oberon, it turns out, is no ordinary fairy king, first, because he is mortal and, second, because his genealogy is notable. Oberon says that his father was Caesar (who was on his way to Thessally to wage war with Pompey when Oberon was begotten) and his mother "the lady of the privey Isle." Oberon, chronology notwithstanding, also claims as an older brother Neptanabus, king of Egypt, who is said to have "engendered Alexander the Great."[19]

Oberon explains that one fairy who was not invited along with the "many a prince and barons of the fair/ and many a noble lady" to attend Oberon's birth delivered the following curse: though Oberon would be the "fairest creature that ever nature formed," at three years of age he would cease to grow.[20] After recounting his genealogy, Oberon informs Huon that he is also "king of Momur, the which is [about] .iiii. C. leagues from hence" (that is, from where they stand conversing, which is itself two days' ride from Jerusalem).[21] With Oberon's help, Huon successfully, though at times painfully, completes his quest and, in addition, wins the "fair" Esclarmonde. At the romance's conclusion Huon comes to Momur, where a dying Oberon, having called together all his subjects, including Arthur, Morgan le Fay, and Merlin (who in this narrative is Morgan le Fay's son), transfers the fairy kingship to Huon (despite Arthur's vigorous objections). Not only is Huon made king of the fairies, but he also takes up residence in Momur, which is "in the far-reaching district that was known to mediaeval writers under the generic name of India."[22]

Lord Berners's translation of this thirteenth-century *chanson de geste* went through at least three editions during the sixteenth century and, significantly, provided a source not only for Shakespeare but also for Edmund Spenser and Robert Greene.[23] The romance was also adapted in 1593 by the Earl of Essex's Men and performed, according to Henslowe, as "hewen of burdoche."[24] Though this playtext is lost to us, Spenser's and Greene's texts survive; in their depiction of Oberon, they continue the associations begun in *Huon of Bordeaux* of the fairy king with the East in general and India in particular.

Book 2 of Spenser's *Faerie Queene* is the only section of the poem where *Huon of Bordeaux's* imprint can be easily discerned, for included in the narrative of Sir Guyon's adventure is an account of his genealogy. Toward the end of canto 9, Spenser writes:

> Sir *Guyon* chaunst eke on another booke,
>   That hight *Antiquitie* of *Faerie* lond,
>   In which when as he greedily did looke,
>   Th'offspring of Elues and Faries there he fond.[25]

Guyon's ancestry is derived from Elfe, the first man, created by Prometheus, and Elfe's union with "a goodly creature ...whom he deemd in mind/ To be no earthly wight" and names *"Fay."*[26]

As Sir Guyon continues to read, he discovers that "of these [Elfe and Fay] a mightie people shortly grew,/ And puissaunt kings, which all the world warrayd / And to them selues all Nations did subdew." The first mention of India comes not with Oberon but with Elfin, whom Spenser describes as "him all *India* obayd, / And all that now *America* men call."[27] The genealogy ends with Oberon, son of Elficleos and the younger brother of Elferon. When Elferon dies, Oberon inherits the "scepter" and the "rich spoiles and famous victorie" with which his father had advanced the "crowne of *Faery.*" And in his reign Oberon, "doubly supplide, in spousall, and dominion," surpassed the achievement not only of his father but of his ancestor Elfin in establishing the Faeries' "power and glorie ouer all."[28]

Robert Greene's *The Scottish Historie of James the fourth, slaine at Flodden. Entermixed with a pleasant Comedie, presented by* Oboram *King of* Fayeries offers a more three-dimensional portrait of the fairy king and one a bit closer to that presented in *Huon of Bordeaux*. Though in some ways an ancillary figure in the drama (the presenter of "a pleasant Comedie"), Oberon comes to have a significant role in *The Scottish Historie of James the fourth*. He is the first character to appear onstage, and throughout the play he surfaces as Bohan's confidant and (to some degree) protector. Like his romance counterpart, Oberon is a catalyst for change, for transformation in the human world. He appears to Bohan ostensibly as an auditor of Bohan's storytelling, but as the play progresses, we recognize the fairy king as the symbolic intervention of fate in Bohan's affairs, rescuing Bohan from his despair and saving the life of Bohan's son.

Relevant here is not Oberon's role in the action of the play but what his representation signals. At the end of the first act, Oberon says,

> I tell thee Bohan, Oberon is king,
> > Of quiet, pleasure, profit, and content,
> > Of wealth, of honour, and of all the world,
> > Tied to no place, yet all are tied to me.[29]

Despite his claim of being "tied to no place," Oberon does in fact tie himself to a specific locale. The dumb show Oberon paints for Bohan is marked by its Asiatic regionalism: the first scene depicts the defeat of Semiramis, "the proud Assirrian Queene," by Staurobates; the second treats of Cyrus's coronation and his death; and the third scene portrays the murder of Sefostris, a "potentate," by his "servants" (who, after slaying the king, continue to dine) at a banquet.

What is worth noting in these depictions of Oberon—in Spenser's brief genealogy, Greene's "pleasant Comedie," or the detailed narrative of *Huon of Bordeaux*—is the dense geographical umbra that stands at the imaginative center of the fairy king's literary history. Whether he appears in England, Scotland, or the outskirts of Jerusalem, Oberon enters each locale as an already "localized" (thus ethnic) entity. In other words, though all the world may be "tied" to Oberon while he claims to be "tied to no place," early modern writers insist that we recognize his claim as inaccurate, that we see him as clearly linked to the vast, undifferentiated region called India.[30]

By the time Shakespeare comes to write *A Midsummer Night's Dream*, images of an Asiatic or "Indian" Oberon are fairly well established as part of the literary imagining of the fairy king through the auspices of Spenser's and Greene's works. Undergoing something of a shift, however, was the nonliterary imagining of India. With the radical transformation of geographical knowledge produced by early modern mercantilism, Oberon's India gradually began to lose its quasi-mystical, quasi-mythical currency as a generic signifier of a distant imagined place and began to acquire a more precise delineation in terms of cultural and ethnic (or what we would call racial) taxonomies.[31] Though the mere mention of the word *India* still carried with it the figuration of an imaginative site of fabulous wealth, fantastic creatures, and other rarities in the English political consciousness, India also became representable as a real geographic and cultural space, capable of being partitioned, classified, conquered, and exploited. This transformation occurred through the early modern travel narrative.

II

The publication of travel narratives about India offered something of a corrective to the cultural mythology created by classical and medieval writers.[32] English (and other European) travelers no longer expected to find anthropophagi or Amazons in the East; these species now took up residence in the unexplored areas of Africa.[33] In addition, with the subdivision of the world into Old and New, and thus also an East and a West Indies, the ideological, literary, and cartographic topos of India had to be rewritten, had to be more precisely localized.[34] The "immense, unimaginable distance" adumbrated in medieval and classical accounts of India needed to be contained; and as ships set sail from England, Portugal, Spain, the Netherlands, France, and the Italian states, cartographers, soldiers, colonizers, and traders attempted, by producing more accurate demarcations of geographical space, to do just that.[35] Ultimately these inscriptions would set the stage for the modern ideology of race.

One narrative prototype for modern racial taxonomies is Richard Eden's *The History of Travayle in the West and East Indies, and other countreys lying eyther way, towardes the fruitfull and ryche Moluccaes.*[36] Eden's work contains a translation of Lewes Vertomannus's account of his travels in India. The text is meant to provide the reader with knowledge of the politics, customs, social relations, and physical appearance of the peoples of India, along with information about

India's topography. Interwoven with Vertomannus's narrative is a familiar (to our way of thinking) polarization of racial differences, with Europe at one end of the spectrum and Africa at the other. Vertomannus begins by declaring his intent to convey an impression of "the fruitfulness and plentifulnesse" of India.[37] His text is replete with descriptions of the regional rulers' wealth and state. "Marvelous rich" becomes a refrain, as does the minute detailing of a ruler's household: the sultan of Cambia "progresses" through all of India, taking with him "four thousand tents and pavillions, also his wife, children, concubines, slaves, four or five of the most courageous horses, monkeys, parrots, leopards, hawks." Of the king of Narsinga, Vertomannus writes that his "horse with the furniture [i.e., trappings] is esteemed to bee worth as much as one of our cities, by reason of innumerable jewelles of great price."[38] It is, however, in Vertomannus's description of the physical appearances of Indians that he employs the color-coded grid of what I will label modern racial distinctions. For example, he describes the people of Melacha as being of "blackish ashe colour. Their apparell is like to the Mahumetans of the citie Memphis....They have very large foreheads, round eyes, and Ratte noses." Of the people of Pego, he writes that the "inhabitants ...are like unto them of Tarnassari [another Indian city] but of whiter color, as in a colder region, somewhat like unto ours." In general, however, the people he meets are reported to be "of weasel colour, enclining to blacknesse, as are the most part of these Indians, being in manner scorched with heate of the Sunne."[39]

The physical appearance and wealth of the Indians are not the only matters subject to scrutiny. India's inhabitants, like those of Africa and Europe, profess a variety of religions and include Christians, Jews, and Muslims as well as what Vertomannus and others call "Gentiles," that is, Hindus and Buddhists. And, somewhat surprisingly, given the internecine struggles of early modern Christian Europe over dogma, Vertomannus often discusses these belief systems with considerable detachment. In the course of relating the cultural and religious behavior of India's peoples, the writer reveals a Eurocentric bias when describing those practices that deal specifically with gender relations. It is here, in that most contested of ideological spaces, that the early modern European traveler develops the racial denotations that later become familiar images not only of India but also of Africa and the Americas.

In the account of his visit to Calcutta, Vertomannus describes what he perceives as an extraordinarily peculiar custom: the king's wife is deflowered by the "Archbishop," though Vertomannus claims that "only the king of Calecut keepeth this custom." As we read through Vertomannus's text, however, we discover that this practice occurs in the city of Tarnassarie as well, with one significant difference; instead of the king's wife being given to "the priests to be deflowered," she is given to a "white man, as to the Christians or Mahumetans, for he will not suffer the Idolaters to do this. The inhabitantes likewise have not to do carnally with their wives, before some white man, of what so ever nation, have first the breaking of them."[40]

This deviation from marital norms, as Vertomannus sees it, is not limited to the rulers of Indian cities but, on the contrary, is found at nearly every level of society. Among the gentlemen and merchants, to exchange wives is seen as a matter of courtesy and friendship. Even so, Indian women are judged to have more freedom than their European counterparts. Vertomannus says that it is not uncommon for a woman to be "married to seven husbands, of the which every of them hath his night by course appointed to lye with her: And when she hath brought forth a childe, she may give it or father it to whiche of them she listeth: Who may in no case refuse it."[41] The idea of such sexual freedom among women, of course, violated nearly every ideological code of the European traveler, and the early modern European travel narrative became the space where sexual freedom could be simultaneously presented and condemned. For instance, the Dutch traveler Jan van Linschoten reports that it is common for "the women slaves ...[to] slip into some shoppe or corner ...where their lovers meet them, and there in hast they have a sport, which done they leave each other: and if she chance to have a Portingal or a white man to her lover, she is so proud, that she thinketh no woman comparable unto her." Van Linschoten, unlike Vertomannus, elides all religious, ethnic, and class differences among the women of India to generalize that they "are verie luxurious [i.e., lecherous] and unchaste, for there are very few among them, although they bee married, but they have besides their husbands one or two of those that are called souldiers, with whome they take their pleasures."[42]

The narrative and geopolitical mapping produced by early modern travelers to India was not just a cartographic reimagining of the world but an ethnographic interpretation of it. As part of the circulation of ethnographic taxonomies, maps were often reproduced in printed texts. In creating these maps and narratives, early modern travelers envisioned themselves as meaningful contributors to a new, global epistemology. More important, the narratives seemed authentic and accurate because the writers had visited the place described, had studied the indigenous peoples and their societies, and had published their findings in a written form that carried no taint of the "poetic."

Because the observer's status as a reliable informant is reified by this discursive strategy, even his reiteration of a medieval or classical fable acquires a veneer of authenticity. Hence, contrary to the writer's expressed aim, the narratives produce what might be termed a " 'poetics of displacement'"; that is, cultural imagery which simultaneously defines Asia, Africa, and the Americas in terms an early modern European could comprehend and offers new metaphorical terrains for the construction of difference.[43] In effect, the written and oral narratives circulating in sixteenth-century England reproduced images of India as a region of "such treasure and rich Merchandize, as none other place of the whole world can afford,"[44] even as they constituted it ideologically as a site of gender, ethnic, religious, and political differences.

The India of early modern English narratives is, as Thomas Hahn has argued, an " 'imaginative reality' ": a place where "explorers ...and their field of vision [were] framed by the imaginary [i.e., literary] landscape as much as by the real."[45] The poetic cartography of *A Midsummer Night's Dream* is a familiar one if we know how to read it. Like Africa and the Americas, India is a world where an Amazon and a fairy king can be lovers; a place where the visible signs of difference between Europeans and Indians can be remarked and similarities unacknowledged; a site where exoticism and difference are as conventional as trade and commodities—a place fit for exploration and exploitation. This is the India of *Huon of Bordeaux* and of the English Jesuit who, when "tolde that he could not want a living in the towne, as also that the Jesuites could not keepe him there without he were willing to stay," chose to reject the "Cloister, and opened shoppe, where he had good store of worke: and in the end married a Mestizos daughter of the towne, so that he made his account to stay there while he lived."[46] This is the India of Shakespeare's changeling boy.

III

At the beginning of Act 2, Puck informs one of the queen's fairies (and the audience) that Titania has a "lovely boy," allegedly the "stol'n" son of an "Indian king," whom Oberon desires to be a "Knight of his train, to trace the forests wild" (2.1.25). On a textual level Puck has little reason to establish the boy's identity beyond distinguishing him as a source of tension between the fairy queen and king; as I suggested earlier, the play's dramatic structure would not have been violated had this information been omitted or had Shakespeare identified the child as an English boy. Similarly, if the fairies are to be seen as English, there is no obvious reason for Shakespeare to specify India as Oberon's most recent place of resort. Titania demands,

> Why art thou here, Come from the farthest step of India,-
> But that, forsooth, the bouncing Amazon,
> Your buskined mistress and your warrior love,
> To Theseus must be wedded.... (2.1.68-72)

Though Titania answers her own question—"Why art thou here"—her words do not entirely explain Shakespeare's invocation of India.

Oberon is, of course, explicitly connected with India in the literary tradition from which Shakespeare draws. However, this explanation does not help us to address the query, why an Indian boy?, posed at the beginning of this essay. Perhaps another way to get at an answer is to examine Shakespeare's characterization in terms of his use of the lexicon engendered by early modern English mercantile activity in India. In this way we can make intelligible India's function as the center of linguistic and ideological exchanges between Athens and fairyland. Like Athens, India is an actual geographic place, and, like fairyland, it is still figured as a place of the imagination. This simultaneity permits the articulation of a racial fantasy in *A Midsummer Night's Dream* where Amazons and fairies signify an alien yet domestic paradox in an otherwise stable, homogeneous world.

When Titania offers Oberon the reason for her resistance to his wishes, in a poignant (and poetic) vision of female and mercantile fecundity, this vision is, in effect, a mapping of this reality:

> His mother was a votress of my order,
>   And in the spiced Indian air by night
>   Full often hath she gossiped by my side ...
>   Marking th'embarked traders on the flood,
>   When we have laughed to see the sails conceive
>   And grow big-bellied with the wanton wind;
>   Which she, with pretty and with swimming gait
>   Following (her womb then rich with my young squire),
>   Would imitate, and sail upon the land
>   To fetch me trifles, and return again
>   As from a voyage, rich with merchandise.
>   But she, being mortal, of that boy did die,
>   And for her sake do I rear up her boy;
>   And for her sake I will not part with him.(2.1.123-37)

Titania's words in this scene vividly reproduce the idealized imagery in the writings of travelers to India. The votaress embodies what India could (and would) represent to Europe as, like the merchant ships, she returns "from a voyage, rich with merchandise," to bring Titania the exotic "trifles" of an unfamiliar world.[47]

Her speech "rich" with the language of English mercantilism, Titania evokes not only the exotic presence of the Indian woman's native land but also the power of the "traders" to invade and domesticate India and, aided by the "wanton wind," return to Europe "rich with merchandise." In Shakespeare's "poetic geography," India becomes the commodified space of a racialized feminine eroticism that (to judge by the written accounts of such men as Vertomannus and van Linschoten) paradoxically excited and threatened the masculinity of European travelers. This racial subtext, which complicates the "shaping fantasy" of *A Midsummer Night's Dream*, is not obvious when Titania and Oberon first appear onstage. Their initial exchange is accusatory and fraught with erotic tension that masks their far greater conflict.

In response to Titania calling Hippolyta his "buskined mistress and warrior love," Oberon retorts: "How canst thou thus, for shame, Titania,/ Glance at my credit with Hippolyta, / Knowing I know thy love to Theseus?" (2.1.74-76). Oberon then lists the women Theseus has seduced and abandoned, apparently with Titania's aid.[48] Titania casually dismisses Oberon's accusation: "these are the forgeries of jealousy" (l. 81). The audience soon discovers what is really at the core of Titania's and Oberon's estrangement: she has refused to give him the child of her votaress, the "little changeling boy." As the text presents it, Titania's interest in the boy is sentimental, linked to her relationship with his mother and the promise the fairy queen made. Oberon's interest, on the other hand, is textually much more ambiguous. In fact, if both he and Puck are to be taken at their word, Oberon's interest in the Indian boy is primarily one of dominion: possession is linked to Oberon's political authority.

From the beginning both Oberon and Puck make clear that Oberon desires to have the boy as a "henchman" or "Knight of his train." Further more, Oberon's desire for the boy seems very much connected to desire for dominion over Titania. Hence I am inclined to view Oberon's quest for the boy less as the embodiment of fatherly love or pride than as the manifestation of a perceived prerogative to claim possession—to have "all ...tied to" him. The paternal interest that many critics argue lies at the heart of Oberon's desire is not evident in his words.[49] One finds in his exercise of paternalism the very ideology that made it "the smart thing for titled and propertied families in England to have a black slave or two among the household servants."[50] Like the growing number of non-European (particularly African) children who were imported into England to serve as badges of status for England's aristocracy, the "changeling boy" is desired as an exotic emblem of Oberon's worldly authority. Oberon's desire to claim the Indian boy as his servant should not be trivialized; in another century or so Asian Indians would become the household fashion.

But why the insistence on possession of the Indian boy? Dramatically, both Oberon's and Titania's obduracy is crucial to the plot structure but not dependent on the changeling's being Indian. The answer is to be found in Shakespeare's rewriting of the figure of Oberon and in the larger problem that *A Midsummer Night's Dream* explores in some detail: gender relations. And, as we shall see, a changeling is not always a mere changeling.

The idea of change (or transformation) is central to the dramatic plot and to the specific resolution of the dissension between Oberon and Titania. In order to dissolve the stalemate, Oberon must produce willingness in Titania to "amend" their "debate"; that is, he must persuade her to change her mind about giving up the Indian boy. The flower, "love-in-idleness," itself a product of change, enables Oberon to achieve his desire, the changeling child. The curious thing about this situation, and one worth exploring, is why Oberon feels it necessary to provide Nick Bottom as a substitute for the Indian boy.[51] Luce Irigaray suggests that men "make commerce *of* [women] …, but they do not enter into any exchanges *with* them," largely because "the economy of exchange—of desire—is man's business."[52] Because there is no other male of equal rank and power with whom Oberon can negotiate an exchange, and because the object he desires is not a wife but a page, he is forced to rewrite the rules governing this "economy of exchange" so that a direct transaction with Titania can take place. Importantly, the objects of exchange must be equivalents, and thus Oberon must provide a changeling for a changeling.

When Nick Bottom reappears from the brake, his head transformed into that of an ass, Snout declares, "O Bottom, thou art changed. What do I see on thee?" (3.1.96). Peter Quince considers Bottom "monstrous" and later declares that Bottom has been "translated" (11. 86, 98). Puck's alteration of Bottom enacts a familiar literary emblem.[53] Bottom, intriguingly, is "translated" into neither centaur nor satyr; it is not his body that is altered but his head: "An ass's nole I fixed on his head" (3.2.17). The alien(ness) Bottom represents is a mixture of the familiar and the foreign; with the exception of his head, Nick Bottom remains distinctly human. What is striking about Puck's trick and Oberon's exploitation of it is not only that it violates the sociocultural endogamy—the commerce that upholds patriarchal traffic in women—but that, in the substitution of the "translated" Nick Bottom for the Indian boy as the other male in the triangular relationship of desire, it irrevocably redefines both sexual and racial parameters in fairyland.

While the boy changeling may be viewed as the object of maternal affection, the adult changeling clearly invokes a different response in the fairy queen. In Titania's bower, Bottom, though subject to the fairy queen, clearly is not perceived as a mere child. On the contrary, as Titania's behavior indicates, Bottom becomes a substitute for Oberon as well. By employing Bottom as the erotic trap that permits him to "steal the boy," Oberon finds himself ensnared by the "hateful imperfection" of monstrous humanity that he has engendered: "For, meeting her of late behind the wood *I* Seeking sweet favours for this hateful fool, / I did upbraid her and fall out with her" (4. 1.60, 45-47). For Oberon, who is initially pleased with Puck's prank, the "sweet sight" (I. 43) of Titania embracing a "translated" Bottom in her bower eventually loses its charm. Once central to Titania's erotic desires, Oberon finds himself displaced twice: first by a changeling and then, in Bottom, by a monstrous "changeling" to boot. And while Oberon may now possess the Indian boy, it appears that the new changeling has become for the fairy king more than the "fierce vexation of a dream" (I. 66).

Change, rather than dreams, is the defining trope of *A Midsummer Night's Dream*. Whether in the changed story of the lovers Apollo and Daphne or in the "little western flower," in Lysander's drug-induced change or in Hippolyta's weariness with the moon, "Would he would change!" (5.1.238), change generates not something unintelligible and fundamentally alien but something that, because of its composition, is (paradoxically) differently the same. In effect, what is constituted is the hybrid. Even so, Hippolyta's moon, Hermia's Lysander, and the "little western flower" remain intelligible to all as moon, man, and flower despite their transformation. The change that Bottom and the Indian boy literally and symbolically register, on the other hand, is of a more particularized form—it is an ethnic (or racial) change that involves the forcible removal of a person from one culture to another and, in the case of Bottom, a change that produces a phenotypical transformation as well. And, not surprisingly, the ease with which change is accommodated, even accepted, produces general anxiety within fairyland.

At the center of this trope of change is a concept linked to the Spanish term *mestizaje*, or mixedness. The *Diccionario de Uso del Espanol* defines *mestizaje* as the *"cruzamiento de razas"* (crossbreeding of races) or the *"conjunto de mestizos"* (group of mestizos) and relates it to the verb *mestizar,* defined as *"adulterar la puerza de una raza por el cruce con otras"* (adulterating the purity of one race by mixing with others).[54] Both Bottom and the changeling child exemplify this hybrid state: in Bottom we see the *cruzamiento* of two species, human and equine (literally, the *mulatto*), and in the Indian boy the possibility of human and fairy mixedness (the *mestizo).*

It is, of course, critically problematic to label Bottom and the Indian boy in the terms of a racial lexicon that is not employed in Shakespeare's play. Yet I believe such a move is both theoretically and heuristically appropriate given Shakespeare's own framing of fairyland as a borderland between India and Athens. In this space, through his "translation" and incorporation into fairyland, Bottom becomes the figurative and literal instantiation of that newly engendered lexical hybrid, the *mulatto.* Similarly, while the Indian boy's enigmatic textual history must forever occlude the "facts" of his genesis (is Puck right when he declares the boy's father to be an Indian king, or is this merely one more of the mischievous sprite's fabrications?), Titania's narrative of the Indian boy's origins and her own behavior are so symptomatic of the accounts of Indian women by the travelers van Linschoten and Vertomannus that it is worthwhile linking these representations to the emerging linguistic taxonomy of cultural difference. Shakespeare's use of India calls attention to this parallel discourse; and if we look closely at its lexical and taxonomic matrices, we can shed light on the way race works in *A Midsummer Night's Dream.* As we shall see, the conflicting terrain of fairyland, with its easy violation of borders—both speciegraphical and geographical— adumbrates an ontological engagement with the linguistic complexities of *mestizaje.*

IV

Etymologically, *mestizaje, mestizo,* and *mestiço* trace their origins to the Latin *miscere,* as does the word miscegenation (*miscere* = to mix and *genus* = kind, sort, type). *Mulatto,* on the other hand, originates in the Latin word *mulus,* which describes the offspring born of an ass and a mare. Even so, *mulatto's* semantic genealogy includes *miscere,* for what produces the offspring is the mixing of what are perceived to be two different species or kinds. *Changeling,* unlike *mestizo, mestiço,* or *mulatto,* only indirectly traces its lexical and semantic genealogy to the Latin *miscere.*[55] *Changeling's* etymology originates in the Latin *mutare,* yet its semantic instantiations suggest a closer kinship to *miscere* and *translatio.*[56]

The lexicon of *mestizaje* was used politically and culturally to describe the offspring of a union between European males and non-European females (though with different configurations based on geography): the Spanish term *mestizo/a* referred principally to the offspring of Spanish men and American Indian women; *mestiço/a* described the offspring of Portuguese men and African or Asian Indian or American Indian women;[57] and *mulatto/a* identified the offspring of Spanish men and African women.[58] This racializing lexicon entered the English language largely via translations of Spanish and Portuguese travel narratives, though not until Richard Perceval and John Minsheu compiled their bilingual dictionaries was this lexicon codified as part of the English language.[59] Familiar modes of categorizing people (according to class or nationality) were no longer useful in the new world that European imperialism was beginning to create—a world suddenly comprised of hybrids, *mestizos,* and *mulattos.* Hence the appropriation of such words as *race, mestizo, mestiço,* and *mulatto* allowed the English to fill a cultural and lexical gap opened by the inadequacy of more familiar terms such as *changeling.*[60]

Predictably, what the new hybridity produced was not an orderly taxonomy but rather a state of lexical and cultural instability, mutability, and permeability. The Indian boy and the transformed Nick Bottom signal a new variant on the notion of race, a variant that silently but insistently calls attention to the details of its sociohistorical genesis. And while I would not insist that Shakespeare drew faithfully on the accounts of *mestizaje* in such narratives as those of Vertomannus or van Linschoten, I would point to the parallels between Shakespeare's account of the Indian boy's lineage and, for example, Vertomannus's terse report on the "deflowering" of the king of Calcutta's wife. Similarly, we find an analogy between Titania's refusal to give the Indian boy to Oberon and the obdurate Indian woman, who takes "pleasure in carrying [her *mestiço* child] ...abroad ...[and who] by no meanes will give it to the father, unlesse it should be secretly stollen from her, and so conveyed away."[61] Titania's unwillingness to give the boy to Oberon ("Set your heart at rest. / The fairy land buys not the child of me" (2.1.122)) may therefore be more than an example of maternal feelings; it may also echo the Indian woman's challenge to Eurocentric, patriarchal assumptions about control of the female body and about that body's ability to destabilize the idea of marking race solely through paternity. Generated in the face of such instability is an anxiety (exemplified in the behavior of both Oberon and the Europeans) about how best to handle such situations.[62] If we accept Nick Bottom **in** his "translated" state as emblematic of the *mulatto* and the Indian boy as emblematic of the *mestiço* child engendered in the deflowering of the king of Calcutta's wife, Oberon's vexation at the "sweet sight" of the *mulatto* in Titania's bower (and his earlier vexation with Titania's fondness for the *mestiço*) resonates with the European's growing anxiety about the definition of race in the borderlands.

The displacement of the changeling child and the substitution of the adult changeling foreground the problem of unregulated female sexuality and its effect on the existing concept of race. Nick Bottom might then signify a return to Irigaray's notion of "sociocultural endogamy," the other adult male in the "economy of desire," one who introduces an unexpected dimension into the equation. Just as the sexual relations of the Indian women expose as illusory the European notion of race within the borders of early modern India, so Oberon's knowledge of Titania taking pleasure in the transformed Bottom calls into question the possibility of sustaining absolute categories of difference. Oberon and his European counterpart each discover the general limits of patriarchal power and the specificity of his own fallibility. What we witness in India and fairyland is the fragmentation of patriarchal ideologies denoting race because women's erotic desires can displace and dispel the sexual continuum upon which race is constituted. It is for this reason that I find less than satisfactory the argument that "Fairy Land is an offstage kingdom, geographically and politically independent of any human territory."[63] Because fairyland is linked to India, a space of *mestizaje,* it sounds the discordant notes of shifting racial definitions even as it adumbrates a potential solution to the problems engendered by *mestizaje.* Furthermore, it is precisely because India has become the site where the concept of race (aristocratic genealogy) can easily be destabilized that race must be rewritten in order to posit an ideology capable of handling the superficial differences between Indians and Europeans.

The resolution, therefore, is not the eradication of the concept of race but its reformulation. The "new" idea of race, and its concomitant lexicon, must begin to reflect this possibility *(mestizaje)* and to contain it. Such containment is achieved, however, not by abandoning the imperial project but by redefining its lexical and ideological taxonomies when dealing with indigenous peoples. As we see in the descriptions offered by Vertomannus, van Linschoten, and others, the imperial project necessitates an essentialism (a "nature") that increasingly is linked to external appearance, in particular to skin color. Thus the image of the dark-skinned savage, the licentious and barbarous non-European, became the norm, instilling a sense of revulsion among Europeans for the sexual behavior that produces *mestizaje.* In words different from yet similar to those of the European travelers, Oberon insists that Titania look on the hybrid Bottom and abhor the image and reality of what she has hitherto embraced. Ironically, *this* changeling's genesis (or paternity) derives from Oberon, and Titania's relationship with the changeling therefore potentially violates two social taboos, incest and miscegenation—the former symbolically and the latter literally. Oberon's dilemma is resolved, even if temporarily, by the restoration of Bottom to his human appearance. The fact that Bottom and the Indian boy are the catalysts for a state of *mestizaje* in fairyland cannot be erased.

When viewed in the shifting context of early modern England's discourse of race, Oberon's "pity" may be tinged with a more complex emotion, as, in the moment of his victory, he discovers himself supplanted not only by a racially ambiguous male but by one of his own making. Though Bottom's expulsion from fairyland, as well as the Indian boy's expulsion from Titania's bower, may alleviate Oberon's vexation, it does not dispel the racial quandary their existence engenders. While Nick Bottom's return to both his human state and to Athens enacts the restoration of a class and gender hierarchy, it also leaves behind a new vision of a racial landscape, a "new world" where the image of humanity is not the European but a changeling—the *mestizo/a, mestiço/a, mulatto/a*. More important, Shakespeare's two changelings in *A Midsummer Night's Dream* are haunted by the ghostly presence of the historical condition of *mestizaje* which occasions both Shakespeare's dramatic representation of India and the modern Western notion of race.

V

My analysis has suggested that Shakespeare's comedy continues the racial discourses constituted by travel narratives that represented India as a "territory to be conquered and occupied," displaying its people as "rich trifles" to sate the European appetite for exotic novelty.[64] At the same time, *A Midsummer Night's Dream* constitutes race as an ideological fissure, producing a problematic dichotomy between race as genealogy and race as ethnicity or physical appearance.

It is this fissure, only recently visible to political criticism, that the director of the SSC production of *A Midsummer Night's Dream* failed to discern in his interpretation of the playtext.[65] Indeed, productions of the play become trapped in a historical conundrum whenever there is a decision to cast the Indian boy and put him onstage. The director (and, by extension, the play's readers) cannot avoid the culturally predetermined orientalism built into Shakespeare's geographic allusion. Furthermore, given the cultural role played by Shakespeare's canon in modern English imperialism, the SSC director's decision becomes even more problematic precisely because the Indian boy's presence on the modern stage engenders a localized reading where past and present historical discourses occasionally merge but more often collide. Shakespeare's evocation of India marks an ideological space where the colonizing impulse imposes a mode of representation suitable to the dynamics of an imperial project. Until directors, actors, textual advisors, and scholars begin not only to rethink their assumptions about the ideological purpose of Shakespeare's Indian boy but also to acknowledge the complex and varied images of race in Shakespeare's play, productions of *A Midsummer Night's Dream* may be destined to rehearse endlessly a racial fantasy engendered as part of imperialist ideology: the fantasy of a silent, accepting native who neither speaks nor resists.

The Indian boy is the most silenced of the play's characters, never given words to express his desires, his self-perception. What if he, rather than Puck, had been given the final word: what would the changeling child have said? What if, after four hundred years, his voice were restored to him? What would he say to the hybrid Bottom? Would the Indian boy declare, as a young white reggae fan in Birmingham, England, did, that

> there's no such thing as "England" any more ...welcome to India brothers! This is the Caribbean! ...Nigeria! ...There is no England, man. This is what is coming. Balsall Heath is the center of the melting pot, 'cos all I ever see when I go out is half-Arab, half-Pakistani, half-Jamaican, half-Scottish, half-Irish. I know 'cos I am [half Scottish/half Irish] ...who am I? ...Tell me who I belong to? They criticize me, the good old England. Alright, where do I belong? You know, I was brought up with blacks, Pakistanis, Africans, Asians, everything, you name it ...who do I belong to? ...I'm just a broad person. The earth is mine ...you know we was not born in Jamaica ...we was not born in "England." We were born here, man. It's our right. That's the way I see it. That's the way I deal with it.[66]

Somehow, giving our silent *mestizo* the voice of another *mestizo*, rather than that of an academic like myself, seems fitting. The words of this half Scottish/half-Irish changeling stand as a vivid reminder that it was in the "antique fables," the "fairy toys" produced in the colonizing dreams of Europeans, that the "shaping fantasies" of modern imperialism began. These words are a reminder that it will be the *mestizos*—the racialized descendants of those who framed the lexicon and practices of modern imperialism—who, dealing with it, will write the final epilogue to the shaping fantasy of race.

VISIONS OF COLOR: SPECTACLE, SPECTATORS, AND THE PERFORMANCE OF RACE

In the beginning was the image, and the word was race.

"Authenticating" Race

Anthropologist Agnes Smedley has argued that "race as a mechanism of social stratification and as a form of human identity is a recent concept in human history. Historical records show that neither the idea nor ideologies associated with race existed before the seventeenth century" (1998: 690). Smedley's assertion about the origins or emergence of a concept of race is not unique; on the contrary, the idea that race is a modern or post-Enlightenment notion has nearly universal acceptance within and outside the academy. Yet, especially among Renaissance and early modern scholars, there are voices crying out in the wilderness against this presumed universality, voices that seek to challenge presentist assumptions about the concept of race and its relation to pre-modern and early modern Western societies and the belief that earlier societies did not deploy race as a "mechanism of social stratification and as a form of human identity." This scholarship increasingly demonstrates that the concept wallowed in ambiguity, purified itself in practice, and infused itself into the daily discourse in Western cultures even before race's first registered (i.e., dictionary) appearance in the languages of Europe. Finally, voices that argue that race has shown itself, conceptually and linguistically, to be very adept at assuming, chameleon-like, whatever appearance its natural surroundings require.

Without question, use of the term *race* with regard to pre-1700 cultures clearly reveals an implicit semiotic schizophrenia: in this context *race* signifies this meaning and in that context it registers that meaning yet, in neither context, are these two meanings really elided. In his intriguing, but flawed, study, *Race: The History of an Idea in the West*, Ivan Hannaford acknowledges this semantic mutability when he highlights the various significations that surfaced with the word's initial usage. According to Hannaford, for the most part, when first used, the word *race* signified a person's genealogy, and so the lexicon of "descent" was associated with its definition – lineage, stock, pedigree. The late sixteenth and seventeenth centuries were pivotal moments in the transition of *race*'s shift in meaning from "lineage or continuity of generations in families, especially royal or noble families to ethnicity or physiological characteristics." In Hannaford's view, "it was not until the late seventeenth century that the pre-idea began to have a specific connotation different from that of gens (Latin, clan) and to be used in conjunction with a new term – 'ethnic group' " (1996: 5–6). While Hanford rightly draws attention to some of race's earliest predicates, I cannot entirely agree with his general hypothesis that the modern predicate of race was absent in pre-seventeenth-century cultures, especially if one of those cultures is England. The problem with Hannaford's dating is that he overlooks important works such as Edmund Spenser's *The Present State of Ireland* where the Irish are frequently referred to as a "race" – as are the English. Even Hannaford's "evidence" to support this contention contradicts his supposition; his discussion (albeit brief) of Raphael Holinshed's *Chronicles* and its use of the word race belies the multiple signification of race in Holinshed's text, including the discussions on various "races" such as Celts, Romans, Trojans, and so on. Hannaford's aim is to argue that race as ethnicity was not a factor in pre- and early-modern cultures; unfortunately, the very texts he uses undermine his claims.

As Hannaford acknowledges, *race* could refer to any number of things – human beings, horses, lines or marks on a surface, wine, or motion. However, as Hannaford's argument unfolds it becomes clear, despite his argument against a concept of a pre-seventeenth-century notion of race, the idea of race was an integral part of the fabric of premodern cultural thought. In fact, race was defined based on now-familiar assumptions about exclusivity, authority, ethical, and moral character, and, most importantly, belonging. *Race* denoted a membership in an elite "club" – the noble family, the *gens*, the *polis* or the nation. Membership, however, was limited to those whose claims of affiliation could be substantiated, and substantiation was inextricably tied to birth; hence, race also denoted a concept dependent to some degree upon bio-physicality. By birth I mean both the literal act of being born and the ideological sense of inherited rank and/or social position inherited from parents. An individual's first psychic affiliation, however, is not to a place, a group, a color, or an idea but to his or her parents – and more specifically because she is the locus of nourishment, to the mother. Yet claiming a racial identity in Renaissance and early modern Western cultures was rarely articulated through a relationship to the mother. Patriarchal hegemony dictated that racial membership in terms of family, *gens*, *polis*, or nation was primarily (though not always) determined through patrilineal descent.

Janet Adelman contends that "patriarchal society depends on the principle of inheritance in which the father's identity – his property, his name, his authority is transmitted from father to son . . . But this transmission from father to son can take place only insofar as both father and son pass through the body of a woman; and this passage radically alters them both" (1992: 106). In other words, children whose legitimacy can be called into question cannot make claims for the racial affiliation that would guarantee social status and/or financial success. These individuals have no privilege, under existing Renaissance codes of law, to a name, to political status (in some instances), to marriage, or to inheritance. Consequently, Marie-Helène Huet posits, "in a political culture where the notions of inheritance, name, title, and lineage

[were] reinforced by multiple rights (birthrights, rights to inheritance, entails, and so forth), the question of paternity [has] considerable urgency" (1993: 34). The concept of race was constituted to regulate human behavior, especially that of women, and as a corollary effect to avert the "confusion of blood" – a metaphor for race – that may occur as part of everyday gendered interactions (Abercrombie et al. 1989: 80).

By 1558 (the year of Elizabeth I's ascension to the English throne), the word *race* was firmly entrenched in the English language to aid in the construction of social and political hierarchy and differentiation. Elizabethans were quite likely to come across the word in a Shakespeare play, in a eulogy to a dead poet, in a history of Ireland, in a medical treatise, or in bilingual dictionaries – as well as in everyday speech. *Race* and its ancillary predicates ("a linage, a breed, issue of one's bodie, a progenie, a stocke, an offspring, a pedigree, stocke, or descent of kindred," nation, sex, tribe, and so on) were being used to categorize and differentiate among and between human beings, and such usage inevitably invited further distinctions (Percyvale 1591: n.p.). In using the word *race*, pre-1700 cultures clearly understood it to be an ordering principle to which predicates based on difference might be attached. The predicates for defining *race* were determined according to cultural or political need. For example, when *race* was used to differentiate within the human species, ideological predicates such as lineage, geographical locus, status or sex were created. If further differentiation was needed additional predicates might be conjoined with the initial ones; thus, in addition to lineage and locus, religion or physiognomy or social customs might be invoked to highlight racial difference.

Central to the arguments of Smedley, Hannaford, and others is that their intellectual and epistemological perception of race is not only dependent upon but also inevitably linked to an absolutist ontological belief that the primary predicate of race is skin color. Thus, the view that race was not a pre-seventeenth-century idea grows out of the presumption that there was extremely limited contact between Europeans and non-Europeans and that exploitative and oppressive elements that inform modern notions of race and its partner racism were absent from (or at least not documented in) these interactions. In other words, since evidence documenting deep and sustained social, political, and ideological interactions between these cultures does not exist, it is problematic to argue that pre-1700 cultures had a concept of race, especially one that includes color as a racial predicate.

What is not obvious in these arguments about the definition of race is the sense that race in pre- and early modern culture was also perceived as a performative act: that is, as a situational experience born not only of an individual's interpellation into a particular social formation but also as carried out or enacted by the individual. For example, when the term race was used to distinguish between social classes or to adumbrate social status, its visibility and definitiveness were manifested in the behavior of the designated individual. Hence, a person of "mean race" would never nor could ever exhibit the attributes associated with a noble race. No matter what the fabric of one's attire, the wealth in one's coffers, or the company one might keep, a "mean" person's racializing attributes would always reveal themselves to a "knowing" subject. Race in this context, in effect, always gestures towards the performative. When the word *race* is used to denote bio-physicality, and with all the assumptions about racial behavior it encodes, however, we rarely perceive this definition as performative, Yet, I would argue, it is precisely the perception of bio-physical stability that makes the performance of color – and blackness or whiteness in particular – a very real phenomenon that was as much a part of early modern society as it is today.

Performing Race

Recent theoretical and scholarly attention to "passing" has increased our awareness of the epistemological complexity of racial passing and its relationship to American literary and historical texts. Yet few social and cultural historians of Renaissance and early modern English culture, as part of the analysis of race, have explored the status and semiotics of color passing within the social and cultural fabric of sixteenth- and seventeenth-century England. In part, this reluctance derives from the ideological, political, and epistemological reasons I have outlined here: the persistent view that the modern predicates of race were not as important to sixteenth- and seventeenth-century English society; the overarching hold empiricism has on modern historiography and its methodologies; and a deeply-held sense that race is always visible. It is this final presumption, the infallibility of the eyes as the means to recognize and know a person's racial identity that we need to challenge if we are to grasp the significance of race as a performative act in Renaissance and early modern culture.

Julia Thomas remarks that "our eyes are not simple recorders or receptacles of information: they do not simply mirror a world that exists unproblematically outside them" (2000: 4). In fact, she continues:

> perception involves not just the act of looking but decision-making too: the brain searches for the best possible interpretation of the available data. And this idea of "interpretation" is of more than passing significance because in order for the brain to transform what is seen into something recognisable, to create meanings through sight, it relies on learnt assumptions about the characteristics of, and differences between, things. Such distinctions, however natural they seem, are not inherent in sight or even in the visualized world. But if these distinctions are not inherent to vision or the visual then where do they come from? Why do we see things differently and as separate entities?

For Thomas, linguistic and cultural knowledge is the tie that binds sight and its object.

Jonas F. Soltis makes a similar argument when he suggests that "seeing is neither simple nor plain but rather that our ordinary notions about seeing are complex, and though consistent, confusing" (1966: 140). Soltis offers a cogent reminder that seeing operates on multiple levels, some more successful than others. More important to me here, though, is Thomas's observation that

> it is more than biology that dictates how one sees. Seeing is bound up in value judgements (one assesses things by their appearance) and, because it is spatially and temporally limited (one cannot see

everything simultaneously but only a certain amount and at any one moment), it involves an element of choice. (2000: 4)

Thomas's point is especially cogent when we consider race and the essentially unstable nature of its predicates. In the context of race as ontological biophysical differences, passing arises as the cultural and ideological interlocutor of a concept that insists upon sight as the infallible medium of recognition and knowledge. Generally, one person sees another, he or she puts into a play a systematized, if unrecognized, set of values, which enable the viewer to read the other's physical appearance and so to decide whether, and in what ways, race may be an important predicate of identity. Of course, this system works well if one can be certain that the interpretation of what one is seeing will be validated. For example, a man racially designated as "white" sees a woman whose skin color is "dark brown." The man racially designated "white" draws upon a received body of cultural and linguistic codes designed to aid his interpretation of what he sees: assumptions about color, physiognomy, culture, status, and hierarchy, as well as a cultural lexicon to name what he is about to interpret. As a result, the man "sees" the woman as a "Black" woman, and thus as racially different and possibly inferior. Conversely, if the woman "seen" has "white" skin, then our "white" man undergoes the same reasoning process but reaches a different conclusion.

The telling epistemological problem is, I would argue, dramatized by the second scenario. Here, we need to recognize that the "white" man may be "reading" the woman's body both correctly and incorrectly; that the woman in fact was born to black parents yet by virtue of her physical appearance must be viewed as "white." If there is no other sign to indicate the woman's lineal "blackness," the man does not question what he sees. Should the woman be joined by two "black" individuals and she acknowledges a kinship relation or if through some other means the man discovers his mis-reading, then this relationship between seeing and knowledge, and the belief system that constitutes such seeing and its interpretation are thrown into question. Moreover, should the man remain ignorant of the woman's genealogy *and* the woman is aware of his mis-reading *and* she does not correct his assumption about her racial identity, then her action constitutes color passing. Similarly, even if the woman is unaware that racially she might be labeled "Black" – because her parents did not inform her of her lineage or that she had been adopted, or even because her parents were themselves "passing" – she still is constitutively engaged in the act of color passing and thus enacts a problematic subjectivity.

Modes of "passing," whether race is defined as gender, class, ethnicity, or color, occur in a symbolic economy predicated upon a presumed violation of social, political, and juridical norms. As a result, racial passing is always understood as a self-conscious "performative enactment" of those very norms; "performative" here signifies both its theatrical connotation and the gestural threat that the performance makes to an essential notion of blackness and, by extension, race. Harryette Mullen rightly argues that for individuals who pass, "passing is not so much a willful deception or duplicity as it is an attempt to move from the margin to the center [of social] identity" (1994: 77) so as to participate in the political economy denied to them on the basis of sex, color or religion. In the end, " 'passing' is, after all passing oneself off as a human person with all the rights and privileges thereof" (Sollors 1997: 248). In fact, as most critics of "passing" literature have inferred, economic and social inequality is often the primary reason for most types of passing.

Color passing, then, evokes not only a sense of power and privilege but also, simultaneously, duplicity and denial. In the end, Sollors offers this cogent reminder:

> these social rules have sometimes sanctioned a moral condemnation of passing on the grounds that it is a form of deception, hence dishonest. Yet this only works as long as it is taken for granted that partial ancestry may have the power to become totally defining. This aspect of passing distinguishes it from true masquerades in which an identity choice need not at all connect with any part of the masked person's particular background. "Passing" can thus justly be described as a social invention, as a "fiction of law and custom" (Mark Twain) that makes one part of a person's ancestry real,

essential, and defining, and other parts accidental, mask-like, and insignificant. (1997: 249)

The irony, of course, is that the belief in the inviolate visibility of color = race is what ultimately comes to undermine the power of the predicate itself.

William Shakespeare's tragedy *Titus Andronicus* stands as one of the earliest spectacles of what twenty-first-century spectators and readers would recognize as racial passing in the fullest sense of the word race as understood by Renaissance and early modern English theatre-goers. In the play, Shakespeare traces the political and social turbulence that ensues when the boundaries of racial identity are transgressed. Shakespeare's handling of race, it should be noted, is not limited to the love affair between Aaron and Tamora. Rather, the concept of race encompasses the filial and paternal connections between Titus and his sons, the marriage of Lavinia to Bassanius (the dead Emperor's son), and especially the playwright's representation of the conflict between the Romans and the Goths. This racial spectacle, however, is masked by the Aaron/Tamora liaison. As Guy Debord writes:

> since the spectacle's job is to cause a world that is no longer directly perceptible to be *seen* via different specialized mediations, it is inevitable that it should elevate the human sense of sight to the special place once occupied by touch; the most abstract of the senses, and the most easily deceived, sight is naturally the most readily adaptable to . . . generalized abstraction . . . Whenever representation takes on an independent existence, the spectacle reestablishes its rule. (1995: 17)

Nowhere is this observation more aptly demonstrated than in Act 4 Scene 2 of *Titus Andronicus*. Tamora, Queen of the Goths, is brought to bed and gives birth to the son of Aaron the Moor, whereupon she immediately sends the child to Aaron with orders for its death. Aaron refuses to slay his own child and offers instead a solution that will protect both Tamora's honor and his son's life:

> And now be it known to you my full intent.

> Not far, one Muliteus my countryman
> His wife but yesternight was brought to bed.
> His child is like to her, fair as you are.
> Go pack with him, and give the mother gold,
> And tell them both the circumstance of all,
> And how by this their child shall be advanced
> And be received for the Emperor's heir. (4.2.150–7)

With this advice, Aaron offers Tamora and her sons the means to further their political power and ambition and to save the life of his son.

Eldred Jones has argued in response to Aaron's inventive plan to save his child, that

> it is no diminution of Aaron's quickness of wit to suggest that Shakespeare intends this story of Muly and his white son to be taken as a complete fabrication. Indeed the speed with which Aaron devises the story is the supreme demonstration of his skill. The happy coincidence of the birth of a white child to a moor and a white woman with Aaron's desperate need for just such a child, would otherwise be the least credible of the chances which fortune presents to the villain in this play. That the child is white at all would have appeared nothing short of miraculous to an Elizabethan audience if they believed the popular idea that "in truth a blacke Moore never faileth to beget black children, of what colour soever the other be." (1965: 53)

Interestingly enough, the "fair" child of Muly receives no further attention from Shakespeare, thus seeming to affirm Jones's observation that the scene was invented to demarcate and highlight Aaron's "quickness of wit." In response, I want to suggest a different reading of the implications of Aaron's plan. To me Aaron's plan is less important as a signifier of character, as sign of innate wit or villainy, but as a sign of a larger cultural anxiety, an anxiety that is at once exposed by Aaron's scheme and elided by Jones's reading of it. I want to propose, then, a different representation of the play's articulation of itself as a racializing spectacle and what that represents to its spectators.

Very few critics have remarked on the performative gesture behind Aaron's proposed exchange, never asking why is it necessary for him to substitute one mixed child for another. Though Aaron offers a plan, in many ways (as Jones argues) he does not offer a rationale for the plan to exchange Muly's son for his own. Strictly in terms of the play's plot, Aaron would be better served if he were to exchange a Roman or Gothic child for his own. Francesca Royster has argued that Aaron's proposal is more than just a plan to save his child; it is also reflective of Aaron's "allegiance to his race, a commitment to establishing a foothold of power for Moors within the very heart of Rome" (2000: 453). Royster's point astutely captures the "politic" Aaron, yet it perhaps over-reads the motivation behind Aaron's proposal. More important for the character that Shakespeare has drawn is Aaron's ability to disrupt, disturb, define, and redefine how racial identity is to be understood. Muly's child "passing" among the Romans would become Aaron's "private joke" on the Romans. Aaron's attempt to "dispose" of his "treasure" among the Goths and to "bring up" his son "to be a warrior and command a camp" inevitably fails and the fate of the two mixed-race infants, linked as they are by their Moorish genealogy, appears to hang in the balance. Yet, only Aaron's son remains a dramatic force throughout the final scenes of the play. As spectators, we know the outcome of the infant's fate – his father having extracted a promise from Lucius that the newly crowned emperor would protect the child's life. No such promise exists for Muly's "fair" son. In fact, the infant ceases to be of import once Aaron and his son are captured by Lucius and his newfound allies, the Goths.

At the play's conclusion, all the various racial conflicts are resolved – Titus, Lavinia, Chiron, Demetrius, Tamora, and Aaron are dead, and Lucius becomes Rome's new emperor – except the one generated by Aaron's proposed substitution of Muly's son for his endangered "first-born son and heir" (4.2.94). Muly's son exists textually and dramatically as an unresolved tension, an ideological reminder of the dangers of relying too heavily on an inflexible concept of race. The specter of Muly's son dramatizes a fundamental incoherence in the play's understanding of race, as though Shakespeare either does not know how to resolve the racial spectacle he creates or he does not consider it significant enough to warrant resolution. The *Oxford English Dictionary* defines the word *spectacle* as follows: a "person or thing exhibited to, or set before, the public gaze as an object either (*a*) of curiosity or contempt, or (*b*) of marvel or view, esp. of a striking or unusual character; a sight"; or "an illustrative instance or example." Whatever the reason, Muly's son cannot help but serve as a paradoxically marked and unmarked spectacle whose body unknowingly gestures towards the performative that is race in *Titus Andronicus*.

Unlike Muly's son, Queen Anne, wife of James I King of England, and 11 of her ladies-in-waiting clearly understood the performativity that is racial passing. In 1605, the Queen and her women blackened their skin to take part in Ben Jonson's *Masque of Blackness*. The plot of the masque concerns the desire of 12 nymphs, "daughters of Niger," to restore themselves to their originary complexion – which once was "as fair / As other dames, now black with black despair," as a result of Phaeton's tragic ride. The masque represents the nymphs' journey to the West and their eventual restoration to a pre-Phaetonic state of whiteness. The Queen's performance in the masque generated quite a bit of commentary about the "blackening" of her "fair" skin. The problem was, aesthetically and ideologically, rectified in the masque's companion piece, *The Masque of Beauty*, where the "black" daughters of Niger are "washed" white by the River Thames. Kim Hall argues that the use of this trope derives from "actual contact with Africans, Native Americans and other racially different foreigners," rather than being solely dependent on literary or visual imagery, and so also indicates a greater engagement with "outsiders" during the reign of James I than in the reign of Elizabeth I (1996: 5). Thus, "the Jacobean royal engagement with blackness and foreign difference created strategies in representation for articulating and thereby solving the problem of difference in this court through the manipulation of blackness and gender" (1996: 5). In other words, Jonson's masques, and the Queen's performance in them, are very much linked to a shifting notion of race inside and outside the geographic boundaries of the island-nation.

The Queen's performance in *The Masque of Blackness*, to say the least, can be described as a spectacle of "color passing," even if it is passing under the guise of theatrical performance. In many ways, theatrical performance is an ideal way to project and contain the idea of color passing since, to perform a character, an actor must convincingly pass as that character. In other words, the actor theoretically must conceal, suppress or reduce all visible traces of her "actual" self in order to "pass" as the person called for by the script. Blackening her skin, the Queen undoes herself as a recognizable subject (including erasing her whiteness) in order to make recognizable her performative "self" as Niger's daughter. The fact that Niger's daughters also prove to be only temporarily black (their whiteness known to them even if concealed by sunburn) even heightens the Queen's act of passing. The literal restoration of the Queen and her women to their original color in *The Masque of Beauty* dispels the disruptive and disturbing effect that their color passing – no matter how symbolic – engenders. As any number of contemporary examples witness, passing as "Black," even if only onstage, is a highly fraught performance, especially when "racial passing" is coordinated with gender. As Dudley Carleton observed of the Queen and her women, "their black faces, and hands which were painted and bare up to the elbows, was a very loathsome sight" (1972: 68).

For male actors, passing for black was a less complicated though still problematic issue. Dympna Callaghan explores the relationship between the use of blackface and our understanding of the issue of race and Othello in her essay, "Othello Was a White Man: Properties of Race on Shakespeare's Stage." Callaghan begins her discussion by claiming that "this essay will investigate the obvious but none the less curious fact that in Shakespeare's plays there are histrionic depictions of negritude, but there are, to use Coleridge's infamous phrase, no 'veritable negroes.' There are, indeed, no authentic 'others' – raced or gendered – of any kind, only their representations" (2000: 193). Callaghan also calls into question the belief that these representations function as a form of mimesis: "mimesis entails an imitation of otherness, and its dynamism is a result of the absence of the actual bodies of those it depicts . . . Theatrical mimesis, however, involves the active manipulation of the body of the actor in the process of representation" (2000: 194). The question is whether this representation, this performative gesture towards blackness, can do all that it claims to do.

Blackface functions, according to Callaghan, as a "constitutive... articulation of racial difference: the display of black people themselves (exhibition), on the one hand, and the simulation of negritude (mimesis), on the other. These are the poles of the representational spectrum of early modern England" (2000: 194). In the theatrical performance, when "black" characters are incorporated into the script, what occurs is not the performance of blacks but, as Callaghan astutely argues, the exhibition of blackness: "people are set forth as objects, passive and inert before the active scrutiny of the spectator, without any control over, or even necessarily consent to, the representational apparatus in which they are placed" (2000: 194). When blackface is deployed as part of the representation of blackness, "race, crucially, *both* black *and* white, is articulated as an opposition on stage principally by means of cosmetics, burnt cork negritude projects racial difference against white Pan-Cake" (2000: 195). Early modern theatrical practices presumed an ontological identification, however temporary, between blackface and racial identity yet even though this performance was circumscribed by the stage and its two hours' traffic, staging race nonetheless focused an anxiety about the instability of race as a categorical predicate.

Nowhere is the "problem" of performance and race more deeply mired than in the study of Renaissance English culture, especially Shakespeare's plays. *Othello*, *Titus Andronicus*, *Antony and Cleopatra*, and to a lesser degree *The Tempest* have allowed for the centering of "race" as a performative issue in recent scholarship. The explosion of recent film adaptations of Shakespeare plays (*True Identity*, *O*) as well as filmed Shakespeare plays (*Titus*, *Othello*, *William Shakespeare's Romeo + Juliet*) similarly have moved "Shakespeare and race" to the forefront of Shakespeare cultural and performance studies. Of the recent essays exploring race and filmed versions/adaptations/ gestures towards Shakespeare's play-texts, Richard Burt's "Slammin' Shakespeare in Acc(id)ents Yet Unknown: Liveness, Cinem(edi)a, and Racial Disintegration" provocatively touches on the problematics of performing race even if Burt's "ending" is unsatisfying as spectacle.

Burt begins "Slammin' Shakespeare" by drawing attention to what he describes as the "mutual blindness" that marks "interest in Shakespeare and race": Shakespeare critics "interested in race" who have "largely ignored the citation and appropriation of Shakespeare in black films and other mass media" and "critics writing on race, cinema, and popular culture" who "have completely ignored the history of black actors either in Shakespeare films or films and related mass media that cite Shakespeare in racially marked contexts" (2002: 201). In this richly nuanced and complex analysis of what he describes as "cinem(edi)a" defined as "the circulation of all kinds of mass media in film (and vice versa)", Burt argues that "racial signifiers in filmed Shakespeare and other mass media need to be examined in relation to mediatization, which Fredric Jameson defines as 'the process whereby the traditional fine arts . . . come to consciousness of themselves as various media within a mediatic system' " (2002: 201). While Burt's essay does not explicitly articulate itself as a study in Shakespeare performance, this notion very much inflects the way in which Burt reads mass media Shakespeare.

Burt's essay raises a number of important questions about the role of "authenticity" and performance in the cultural discourse of race and in Shakespeare. Drawing upon Philip Auslander's notion of "liveness," the sense that "live performance and mass media are not ontologically distinct," Burt concludes that "race is now always a mediatized rather than a live performance." As Burt notes, Auslander's concept is indebted to "Baudrillard's theory of simulation as recreation of performances that never took place, representations without real referents" (2002: 203). In essence, "racial performances are no more 'unplugged' than Shakespeare performances are" (2002: 203). Burt's citation of "mediatized" examples of "black" engagements with Shakespeare (from Lauryn Hill's *The Miseducation of Lauryn Hill* to *The Cosby Show*) encourages critics to reflect on that often overlooked phenomenon the "black voice" or as Burt graphically reminds us in the essay's title "accent." For Burt, "sound" is as much a "racial signifier" as color. Ultimately, Burt contends:

in my examples of Shakespeare cinemedia, the simulation of liveness requires the synchronization of visual and aural racial signifiers (in order to achieve cinematic or televisual realism) as well as their integration of Shakespeare in relation to high and low culture, center and margin. Yet in each case the mediatization of liveness disrupts this dream of integration: a multicultural Shakespeare and a multimedia Shakespeare never coincide. (2002: 208)

Assuming that the notion of a "dream of integration" is valid, one must ask "for whom?" – for "blacks," "whites," "Asians," "Latinos," "Shakespeare critics"?

Burt's discussion highlights what is both illuminating and frustrating about cultural criticism and race, especially with respect to performance: that what is racialized is always already a performance whether live or mediatized, and that any notion of assumed authenticity is lodged not in performance but in the performative act or the Shakespeare play-text. As W. B. Worthen writes: "dramatic performance is not determined by the text of the play: it strikes a much more interactive, performative relation between writing and the spaces, places, and behaviors that give it meaning, force, as theatrical action" or, I would add, "filmic action" (2003: 12). It is this "performative relation" between race and text that Burt cogently makes references to in his essay but does not completely dislodge. My critique of Burt's essay should not be mis-read. "Slammin' Shakespeare" rightly takes issue with the presumed ontological status of a biological notion of race. What is not so obvious is how this essay helps us to move beyond the search for the "authenticity" of race as it promises. Here, I want to take up Burt's challenge and reflect on what Burt's observation about "race as a form of passing" and "sound as a racial signifier" can mean for the critical study of performance, Shakespeare's plays and the political engagement with the concept of race.

"Witnessing" the Spectacle

In her essay, "Brave New Bard," Courtney Lehmann argues

> that: whether classified as mainstream or radical. Loyal or loose, the cinematic adaptation of Shakespeare will always be the product of complex negotiations between text and screenplay, early modern and postmodern, live action and framed simulation. Consequently, the reception of filmed Shakespeare has historically been preoccupied with what gets "lost in the translation", a critical sensibility articulated through an inky rhetorical cloak of mourning for some violated conception of textual fidelity, historical accuracy, or artistic integrity. (2000: 2)

The desire for some authentic Shakespeare, dramatic representations that are "real" to us, for language that speaks to some inherently human element, haunts spectators of Shakespeare's plays – whether theatrically or cinematically performed. The desire for authenticity in performing "race" is even more profoundly framed by this sense of mourning. Despite the intuitive understanding that a "black" Shakespeare referent can never be an accurate representation of people of African ancestry, regardless of when the referent is performed, Shakespeare scholars continue to write as if blackness is an ontological state of racial being for millions of human beings.

Denise Albanese writes about the performance of Patrick Stewart as Othello:

> to accept the undeniably pale Stewart as black demands that the power of the script's fiction – what I've already termed the authority of the Shakespeare text – override all the cues to the contrary that the actor playing Othello is *not* black, nor is he making any somatic attempt to impersonate blackness, vexed, indeed, as that possibility would be.

Albanese claims, just as Burt does, the idea of an authentic black "race" (2003: 240). Nowhere in Albanese's discussion is there space for the person of African ancestry whose color is not "black." Would she have made the same argument had Patrick Stewart claimed African ancestry through a "passing" ancestor? Would his "whiteness" register the performance of blackness, of "race," in the same way as, for example, James Earl Jones's darker skin? If not, why not? More than any other factor, color passing wreaks havoc on the illusionary stability of the concept of race. Visibly registering normative expectations about racialized identity, the "white Moor" proves the permeability and the fragility of the idea of skin color as a predicate of race. To assume that the performance of race in a Shakespeare play-text is static, and one-sided, is to ignore the fact that being black is always already a performative act. There is no such thing as verisimilitude in the representation of "blackness."

I want to return to Richard Burt's insistence that sound be viewed as a racial signifier. As a preface, Burt argues that "like critics working on race (or 'race') in early modern culture, critics of filmed Shakespeare have attended to color rather than voice, accent, pitch, noise, and music soundtracks" (2002: 207). Baz Luhrmann's *William Shakespeare's Romeo + Juliet*, for example, figures prominently in Burt's analysis. Despite the "visual" predicates of "racial identity," none of the characters can be wholly read as emblematic of a race: "Can Mercutio be read as wholly African American when, seen from the perspective of Romeo on ecstasy, he lip-synchs a female vocalist's disco hit and crossdresses in white, calling up Ru Paul or possibly even Marilyn Monroe?" (Burt 2002: 207). Burt answers his question, contending "by not consistently opposing Montagues and Capulets racially either by color or accent, Lurhmann unsettles the idea that racial difference and racism drive their conflict" (2002: 207). While it is true that Luhrmann's film does indeed "unsettle," I am not so certain that the film unsettles in the area of race. In fact, I would argue that the film more solidly locates unmediated racial performances than Burt grants.

It is in Peter Greenaway's *Prospero's Books* (1991) that Burt finds that "sound and skin color can be "disintegrated racial signifiers, so that some films do not consistently link racial difference to exclusion" (2002: 208): "the dancer playing Caliban is white, but dance, sound, baldness, nudity, gay sexuality, and cosmetic covering from head to foot contribute more to his exclusion and marginalization than skin color, suggesting levels of difference beyond race" (2002: 208). The King of Tunis, on the other hand,

> is black, and we see him being washed by his servants after having deflowered Claribel, who is seen lying on a bed with blood on her abdomen. Here only the King's color defines his race (he has no lines), which is articulated by Ferdinand and Sebastian in (Prospero's) voiceover, who blame the shipwreck on Alonso's arrangement of the marriage. How much this scene represents the two villains' racist fantasy or Greenaway's own complicity in such fantasies is debatable, but the more interesting point, I think, is that, though the king is clearly raced, he is a master, like Prospero, not an excluded or marginal slave like Caliban. (2002: 208)

Here Burt becomes entangled in the performativity that is race as he is unable to "disintegrate" color from his notion of race to understand that the King of Tunis' "race" is not predicated upon his color but on his status.

It is this performative gesture that Burt's "Shakebites" occlude when color, and more specifically blackness, becomes the first-order predicate for race either as a manifestation of some textual referent by Shakespeare or as a matter of modern and post-modern ideologies. Yet this blackness cannot obscure the fact that all gestures and speech, identified as "black" are performative. And what Burt's essay does so eloquently is to remind us that in Shakespeare's plays sound functions as a racial signifier, even if at times the analysis engages in slippages that seem to construe black speech as *a priori* always already black. In other words, presumptions about the ontology of blackness as a racially marked predicate incorporate all aspects of physicality: skin color, hair, muscularity and body shape, and of course the speaking voice. The idea that one can always "tell" a black person by voice and speech assumes that there is a singularity in voice for all blacks. Variables in speech pattern, timbre, tone, and vocabulary are as great between "black" people as they are between "non-black" people. Among "non-black" speakers differences in speech are most commonly understood to signify class and education; so too with "black" speakers differences in speech patterns are predominantly the consequence of class rather than what we refer to as "race."

Like class, race as a performative act is founded upon behavior, biophysicality, and spectacle. In this context, passing becomes a useful theoretical framework for reflections on race, performance, and Shakespeare. Race in Shakespeare's plays is always located in the performative register: whether it is Prince Hal "passing" as an ordinary soldier or Portia "passing" as a man or Othello "passing" as a Venetian. To consider the performance of race in Shakespeare in this light is to recognize the instability of "whiteness" as a centrifugal force for racial identity, let alone "blackness" as a signifier for people of African ancestry. In an essay on black women's sexuality, Evelynn Hammonds frames her theoretical inquiry by asking a seemingly unrelated question: "how do you deduce the presence of a black hole? And, second, what is it like inside of a black hole?" The answer, she observes, is that "the existence of the black hole is inferred from the fact that the visible star is in orbit and its shape is distorted in some way or it is detected by the energy emanating from the region in space around the visible star that could not be produced by the visible star alone" (1994: 139).

The spectacle of "blackness" as a racial predicate in Shakespeare's plays is as much a product of critical discourse as it is a by-product of Shakespearean dramatic representations. This does not mean that these representations do not have ideological, cultural, and political implications for how "blackness" becomes constituted as a symbol for all that is wrong; rather, I want to argue that a search for authentic performances of blackness in Shakespearean performance is an exercise in futility, whether that performance is in the extraordinary "black talent" of theatrical actors such as Ray Fearon or James Earl Jones or Lauryn Hill's invocation of *Romeo and Juliet* in her *Miseducation of Lauryn Hill*. It is because there "ain't no such thing as blackness" that I make this claim. We would do better to examine the class issues that hide behind the representation of skin color in Shakespeare's plays if we truly want to understand how race comes to be (dis)authenticated within the Shakespearean performance.

GESTURES OF PERFORMANCE: RETHINKING RACE IN CONTEMPORARY SHAKESPEARE

In October 2002 I was invited to join a group of Shakespearean scholars and actors in a workshop organized by Lynette Hunter and Peter Lichtenfels held at the Globe Theatre, London. The workshop, "Fifth Wall," was conceived to foster conversations between theatre practitioners and literary scholars on a variety of issues often viewed as dividing the two groups, especially in the area of Shakespearean playtexts. The session I was involved in, "Gesture and Language," was lively, filled with contradictions, and, in the end, it fostered greater understanding of the complexities of Shakespeare's dramatic language and its performance. As someone intrigued by the performance of racial identities in general and in productions (theatrical and film) based upon Shakespeare's playtexts, I found great appeal in the idea of adding gesture to my theoretical exploration of race and Shakespeare. As is the case with nearly all intellectual conversations, there is a turning point when an elusive connection between ideas suddenly materializes, becoming solid, focused, and intelligible. This point occurred in the session when Alan Cox[1] spoke about improvisation as part of the rehearsal process, "what [he] called 'making rituals' that went on 'all the time'" (Arden, Hendricks, and Hunter, 63). It was not so much the notion of rituals but the making of them and the importance of gesture to that making that animated the conversation; it was the realization that, in the process of creating theatrical or performance cultures, writers, actors, directors, designers, and stage crews all participate in the making of rituals that become not only associated with Shakespearean playtexts but also become a necessary component of their performance.[2] The relationship between ritual and gesture, as Cox's observations throughout the workshop indicated, is a synergistic one, and this synergy is very much a manifestation of the actor's body.

"Gesture," Adam Kendon writes, "is a name for visible action when it is used as an utterance or as a part of an utterance" (Kendon, 7). By "utterance," Kendon means "any ensemble of action that counts for others as an attempt by the actor to 'give' information of some sort" (7). Furthermore, utterance "is any unit of activity that is treated by those co-present as a communicative 'move,' 'turn' or 'contribution.' Such units of activity may be constructed from speech or from visible bodily action or from combinations of these two modalities" (7). Gesture, then, "is the visible bodily action that has a role in such units of action" (7). More precisely, Kendon writes that gesture refers to "a movement of the body, or any part of it, that is expressive of thought or feel ing" (7-8). In other words, gestures are deliberate uses of bodily movements that add significance or meaning to spoken language. And, he concludes, "it is through the orientation of the body and, especially through the orientation of the eyes, that information is provided about the direction and nature of a person's attention," as well as "about the nature of their intentions and attitudes" (1).

Very few of the theatrical practitioners and scholars involved in the "Fifth Wall" workshop would disagree with Kendon's definition of gesture, or "that gesture is a vital aspect of communication," yet there was an acknowledgment of an "inbuilt difficulty of communication ... [on] the topic of gesture itself" (Arden et al., 61). As Annabel Arden reminded participants in the "Fifth Wall" workshop, a simple gesture can profoundly affect the way a performative moment is understood. Describing a moment in a production of Caryl Churchill's *A Number*, "a play about family relations, breakdown and divorce," Arden remarks that "at one point [Michael] Gambon simply glanced at the wedding ring on his hand and the audience thrilled to the suddenly charged air of that small detailed action." It was, Arden continued, "the 'perfect gesture' for that play. For the practitioner, the body itself is a gesture" (64). Arden went on to observe that "the body animates the text," to which I replied, "if the body animates the text, 'the text animates gesture'" (61).

The "Fifth Wall" workshop was the catalyst for this essay. In the process of reflecting on the ideas, comments, and challenges posed by Shakespearean actors and directors during the workshop, I began to consider the possibility that "racial identity" is more often than not a gestural act of performance, especially in Shakespearean playtexts; not only does gesture make visible a character's "intentions and attitudes," it also may make visible a race for the performing body (whether it is the actual actor playing a character or the character itself). Furthermore, I came to understand that both the theory and practice of colorblind (or nontraditional) casting, whether in theatrical or cinematic productions of Shakespeare's playtexts, cannot escape this gestural act. In the discussion that follows, I want to address two questions. First, how does one (actor, director, or costume designer for example) go about gesturing race into existence in a performance? And second, if I am correct in arguing that race is merely gestural, why do we continue to debate directorial decisions about casting Shakespeare's playtexts, whether on the stage or in film?

Sensing Race

In a course I taught on race, a student posed a simple query that kept the members of the class in animated discussion for some time: How does a blind person know race? The question is profoundly complex and perhaps incapable of truly being answered. Yet undaunted, we worried the problem until we reached something of a resolution that, in retrospect, seems apropos to the topic of this essay: in truth, a blind person could not know race as a sighted individual would, given that the current definition of race is predicated upon physical cues accessible through sight. Thus a blind person would have to be taught to use her auditory and tactile senses to recognize race (voice, facial features, and hair would have to be the basis for knowledge). Of course, there are problems with a tactile mode of racializing, as most people would not willingly allow themselves to be subject to an exploratory examination by a stranger so that the stranger could identify them "racially." In addition, one class member pointed out, there are people of African ancestry whose hair, skin color, and facial features are such that the blind person could mistakenly classify them as another racial category. So my class decided that the auditory sense would have to be the principal means by which a society guides a blind individual's initiation into racial consciousness and ideology. Listening to speech and discerning differences between individual speakers might be a better method for the sight-impaired person to categorize racially those around him. Hence, dialect, tonal timbre, pronunciation, and vocabulary would be the predicates for articulating racial difference. Noting and classifying the differences (in effect, recognizing accents and/or dialects) becomes part of the racial and ethnic taxonomy that allows a sight-impaired individual to know races without actually seeing race.

This method has its flaws, however, most notably in performance venues such as stage and film. In her insightful essay "False Accents: Embodied Dialects and the Characterization of Ethnicity and Nationality," Angela Pao illustrates that the "racial" or "ethnic" voice is a highly problematic proposition within performance spaces. Beginning with a discussion of an anecdotal account of the "dubbing" of "Oriental intonation" (i.e., that of American speakers of Asian languages) for "authentic" Chinese accents, Pao illuminates the ways in which contemporary performance media (television, film, and stage) help to sustain racist racializing practices (see Pao). The dialects or accents are nearly always of nonnative speakers of English, and the English is either unintelligible or comically "broken" (i.e., nonstandard). To many African Americans this terrain is quite familiar. In addition to the complication of skin color, linguistic patterns among a large segment of the African American population in the United States have also made racial identification appear relatively easy. In his article "Slammin' Shakespeare in Acc(id)ents Yet Unknown: Liveness, Cinem(edi)a, and Racial dis-integration," Richard Burt unwittingly falls into the ideological trap about language and race that Pao so cogently exposes in her article.

Burt's aim in the essay is "not only to fill a missing gap in Shakespeare and black film criticism but also to show that such materials invite theorizing Shakespeare, race, and film in terms of 'cinem(edi)a,'" especially the notion of "authenticity" in relation to Shakespeare's playtexts and their continued circulation within contemporary American culture (201). While Burt rightly criticizes those who assume an "authentic" Shakespearean performance (that is, a visually "correct" rendering of Elizabethan stage performance, albeit a performance that now includes women), he does undermine his own interrogation by arguing that sound is racially marked: "In my examples of Shakespeare cinemedia, the simulation of liveness requires the synchronization of visual and *aural* racial signifiers (in order to achieve cinematic or televisual realism)" (Burt, 208; emphasis added). As a reading of his essay reveals, what Burt means by "aural" racial signifiers in this context is the difference between English as spoken or pronounced by whites and English as spoken by blacks.

As I note in another essay dealing with Shakespearean performance, "The idea that one can always 'tell' a black person by voice and speech assumes that there is a singularity in voice for all blacks. Variables in speech pattern, timbre, tone, and vocabulary are as distinct between black people as they are between non-black people" (Hendricks, 521). Furthermore, as a result of the deep influence of hip-hop culture across the globe, the so-called black American speech pattern is increasingly heard internationally. Within the United States, many white, Asian, and Latino young people (suburban and urban) are "speaking" with what Burt would define as an "aural racial signifier." What is more striking is the fact that the so-called black voice has served as a political bridge across ethnicities and nationalities. In essence, the language of hip-hop culture is emblematic of what Pao describes as "what once would have been perceived as an unrealistic or 'unnatural' matching of body and accent has become or is in the process of becoming a common phenomenon" (Pao, 369). Pao continues:

> This is what has happened with British South Asians who speak English not with Indian or Pakistani accents, nor with the standard British accents, but with the regional accents of the industrial cities of the Midlands or with the ethnic Japanese from South America who speak English with a Spanish accent. It is what is beginning to happen with the children of Chinese immigrants who learn Irish before they have mastered English, or with Arab Americans who speak with regional rather than General American accents. (Pao, 369-370)

Pao's discussion of accents has serious implications for stage and film casting, especially the former. As she rightly argues, "As things stand in American theatre, unless experimental casting is being used as part of the production concept, racially authentic casting (sometimes rather broadly defined) has become the rule, with the character's ethnic identity being commonly constituted through empathy and an appropriate accent" (Pao, 369). The idea of colorblind or nontraditional casting, not surprisingly, has its more vocal critics among the groups that are most often marginalized in United States theatre. One voice, that of the late African American playwright August Wilson, stands out in opposition to the concept of colorblind casting. In a talk given at Princeton in 1996, Wilson raised the stakes on the idea of colorblind casting. His talk *The Ground on Which I Stand*, first printed by the Theatre Communications Group and reprinted in 1998 in the journal *Callaloo*, was, as two writers observed, "potent and provocative enough to transform a long smoldering brushfire into a flaming feud" (Saltzman and Plett 1997). About colorblind or nontraditional casting August Wilson argued:

> To mount an all black production of *Death of a Salesman* or any other play conceived for white actors as an investigation of the human condition through the specifics of white culture is to deny us our own humanity, our own history, and the need to make our own

investigations from the cultural ground on which we stand as black Americans. The idea of colorblind casting is the same idea of assimilation that black Americans have been rejecting for the past 380 years. For the record we reject it again. We reject any attempt to blot us out, to reinvent history and ignore our presence or to maim our spiritual product. (Wilson, 30-31)

Though Wilson acknowledged that playwrights such as Shakespeare influenced "the ground on which [he] stands," it is race that matters (11). For Wilson, colorblind casting does not disrupt but rather reiterates ideologies about black cultural inferiority.

Despite Wilson's concerns, the issue will not disappear, and such casting decisions remain fraught and much debated. For example, when the actor Bob Devin Jones was cast as Don John in Saint Petersburg, Florida's American Stage's Shakespeare in the Park production of *Much Ado About Nothing,* he was questioned about accepting a role as a villain: "A friend asked me 'so what I want to know is what does it feel like being the only African-American and also playing the villain?'" (quoted in Fleming). The unspoken concern behind the query, as Jones noted, was the potential for "negative racial stereo typing." Director Justin Emeka, a student in the University of Washington's School of Drama, took a different approach to the issue of nontraditional or colorblind casting. Emeka directed a multicultural cast in his production of *Macbeth* and deployed his cast "to incorporate race and culture into the telling of the story" (Wick). Emeka conceptualized his production in terms of the U.S. Civil War and its aftermath. He depicted the witches as "newly freed slaves" and Macbeth as a "fierce northern general"; Duncan was a "Lincolnesque figure hated by Macbeth's southern belle wife"; and "Banquo is an African-American soldier equal to Macbeth in merit who has been held back because of his race" (Wick).

Like many other directors, Emeka treated Shakespeare's playtext as a working palette, making "bold choices, bold edits" to tell a story about betrayal and a "nation divided" because of race. In making his decisions, the director sought to "go beyond so-called 'colorblind casting,' a system that encourages the casting of non-white actors in roles traditionally played by whites without any alteration in those roles" (Wick). Emeka argued:

> When colorblind casting began it was progressive, because it was letting people of color into the theater. But really what you're saying with that is, 'We'll let you be white and act like you are just like everybody else.' There's something that's kind of dehumanizing about that. This production for me was an experiment in saying, 'Let's not just let black actors in; let's incorporate their culture into the world, the telling of the story.' (quoted in Wick)

In essence, according to the writer of the article, Emeka viewed his casting decision as an opportunity for "black actors to play what he calls black roles" (Wick). One of the unknowns in Emeka's production is whether he retained Shakespeare's language intact—that is, whether the actors spoke Shakespeare's actual words, or whether the director modernized the play's language to reflect the modernity in which the play was set ("bold edits"). In other words, did the actors deploy Southern and black accents or dialects and American colloquial language, or did they adhere to the tradition of speaking the Jacobean verse that Shakespeare wrote?

What is striking about Justin Emeka's comments on his production decisions is that they are achingly familiar responses within the debates surrounding nontraditional and colorblind casting. On the one hand, the director seeks to validate the idea of Shakespeare's universality with a multicultural cast; yet, on the other hand, he also wants to repudiate that notion by localizing his production in "black" American culture. In many ways, productions of this type are weighed down by the still problematic discourse of race in theatrical performances of Shakespeare's playtexts. Race in this context is always a priori located in skin color, and with rare exceptions that color is "black." When a director seeks to disrupt what she or he sees as the racism that shadows both Shakespearean playtexts and their performances, more often than not the director disturbs the surface rather than disrupting it. The director's efforts (no matter how brilliant or diverse the cast) may not effectively redefine the language, gestures, and ideologies of the plays and their characterizations to achieve directorial aims. This is not to argue that Shakespearean language somehow transcends political agendas; rather, political agendas are often blind to their own limitations. The end result is a curious culturally schizophrenic position on casting that can satisfy neither side of the debate.

Even when a production is not explicitly framed in the familiar binary terms of black and white, race often becomes part of the conceptualization of the production. The Stratford Festival of Canada's 2003 staging of *Pericles* exemplifies this situation. In her review of the play, Margaret Jane Kidnie writes that "all modern productions of *Pericles* are challenged to find suitable, and suitably resonant, cultural and performance traditions within which to locate the figure of Gower" (Kidnie, 307). The director of the production Kidnie is reviewing "transposed and extended Pericles's journeys, originally along the eastern and northern Mediterranean coast to Arabia and India, to the far East" (311). How the playtext's "constantly changing locale" (and, I would argue, ethnicity or race) was conveyed was through costume design:

> Pentapolis, where the members of Simonides's court dressed in kimonos and geta sandals, was Japanese, while the bare-chested men wear ing white turbans and off-white lengths of cloth wrapped around their waists visually located Ephesus in Indonesia. Female actors draped head to foot in black chadors or burqas with full-faced views, and male actors dressed in kaffiyehs and loose robes with dark cloaks, belted and trimmed with heavy embroidery, created Antioch as a blend of Arab influences. (Kidnie, 311)

Props such as hookahs and "hand-held fans for the geishas" served to reiterate the ethnic or racializing process that marked the production.

Just as with the Saint Petersburg and University of Washington productions, the cast of Stratford's *Pericles* was "multicultural." In a footnote, Kidnie quotes from an e-mail sent by the director, Leon Rubin: "I decided early on to locate the play mainly in the Far East and I insisted appropriate actors would be cast. I wanted to use a richly multiculturally-influenced cast with diverse looks and cultural roots. I feel Stratford should be doing this" (317). Thus Kidnie writes, *"The Adventures of Pericles* told its audience a story about self and the foreign other. The neutral body was defined by the white male courtiers of this Greek Tyre, the place Pericles called home, and this body functioned as the normative perspective—the constructed I/eye—through which we read the exotic, often dangerous markings of race, gender, and ethnicity" (313). For Kidnie, Rubin's concept, while fascinating to watch, was troubling for its "miscues" and "heavily overdetermined in terms of [the] race and ethnicity" of bodies ("the kechak chorus in Ephesus or the kimonoed court in Pentapolis, for instance, seemed not Indonesian or Japanese but European or, equally distracting, African" [317]). In the end, Kidnie argues, "the conception shaping the exotic, marked body in this Ontario production presented a stereotyped and imprecisely executed treatment of race and culture that did little to challenge assumptions that the 'real' Shakespearean body is white and of European (preferably British) descent."[4]

Kidnie's essay, like Richard Burt's "Slammin' Shakespeare," represents a useful starting place for my consideration of race as a gestural act. In both essays, the performed body is a body to be read and, ideologically, made meaning of in relation to cultural intersections with Shakespeare's playtexts. How we read that body is very much determined by its movements, gestures, and its appearance—makeup, costume, and, of course, the actor's body. To illustrate this point, I want to turn to three films that draw upon or make reference to Shakespeare's playtexts: Julie Taymor's *Titus*, Baz Luhrmann's *William Shakespeare's Romeo + Juliet*, and Andrzej Bartkowiak's *Romeo Must Die*. Specifically, I will look at three instances of what would be viewed as highly charged moments in the films: the cinematic image of Aaron at the party celebrating the marriage of Tamora and Saturnius in Taymor's *Titus*; the opening scene of Luhrmann's *Romeo + Juliet*; and Han's entrance into Silk's Club in *Romeo Must Die*. My aim is to expand our understanding of these films as mediations of race in Anglo-

American culture.[5] More importantly, my reading of specific scenes in these films is my attempt to register the significance of the gestural performance of racial identity in contemporary productions of Shakespeare's playtexts.

"It's in the way that you use it"

One of the more striking figures in Shakespeare's *Titus Andronicus* is Aaron the Moor. In the playtext, Aaron sits as the ominous figure of doom, the Satanic instigator of Titus's fall, and the emblem of unbridled lust. Recent essays have dealt adroitly with the depiction of Aaron as a highly marked racial/racist figuration. What I want to explore in Taymor's film of Shakespeare's playtext is the importance of gestures to the construction of Aaron's racial identity. The African American body of the actor portraying Aaron (Harry Lennix) immediately localizes the relationship between Moor and skin color for the film's audience. Yet like Shakespeare's playtext, there is ambiguity about Aaron's racial identity that skin color cannot overwrite. Thinking about Aaron's status before his capture by the Romans, we must realize that we do not know much about Aaron and his relationship to the Goths, except that he is the lover of Tamara the Queen. This lack of knowledge provides Taymor and Lennix an opportunity to interject a "nobility" into Lennix's portrayal of Aaron. The result is a complex and paradoxical villain. Taymor's film, in ways not possible just with a reading of the playtext, highlights the complex range of racial signifiers the actor's—and through him the character's—body can project. During a panoramic shot of a wild party scene (clearly celebrating the union of Tamara and the Emperor Saturnius), the cinematic spectator catches her first glimpse of Aaron: he is standing alone, a glass of wine and a cigarette in hand, gazing out at the tableau before him, clearly an outsider yet very much part of the court. How the actor is positioned (above the crowd, on a step or a ledge) makes the specific object of his gaze somewhat mysterious: Is he merely a spectator of the excess of the Roman court, or is he studying his mistress with her new husband?

The shot of Aaron is extraordinary in that it is framed by erotic Greek vase paintings recapitulated on the walls of the chamber and in the excesses of the party, yet he is clothed in dark blue trousers (Turkish in design, loose-fitting but tapered at the ankles) and a robe or caftan of the same hue, belted with a sash and held together by a circle of gold. Aaron's garments and his tonsured look give him a priestly, ascetic image (one need only recall the costuming of *The Mission's* Jeremy Irons and Robert De Niro to know whence Aaron's clothing derives its Jesuit appearance). The clothing totally encompasses his body except for his face and hands, giving him a priestly air, disrupted only by the glass of wine held in his hand. What is notable about Aaron is the positioning and movement of his body. Aaron's right forearm is bent at the elbow and hidden behind him, almost as if he is hiding something. His body leans slightly to the right, as if he is a member of the party yet not entirely of it. What is most interesting about the moment is the gestural way in which Aaron holds his glass. Aaron's pinky finger, second finger, and thumb hold the glass, while his middle and first fingers hold the cigarette. The camera lingers briefly on the shot, Aaron's hand and the glass prominent in the spectator's gaze. What we notice almost immediately is the elegant length of the actor's fingers and the way they hold the glass.

Figure 10.1 Aaron's gesture. *Titus* (2000)

The hand animates our sense of who Aaron is, two fingers pointing upwards toward, but not directly at, his face, drawing attention to the contrasting blackness of his tie and the whiteness of his shirt, which in turn brings attention to his brown face. Were we to mask his face so that the only visible part of his body is his hand, we would find that the shade of Aaron's hand is quite similar to those of the server just below him and the woman seated near the server, and Aaron's racial identity would be relatively unintelligible. We do, however, see Aaron's face and with it the racializing effect of the hand's gesture, as, in the shot, the hand occupies almost the same visual space as his face.

The hand, in Taymor's film, is a profoundly racializing motif.[6] Aaron's hand directs the gaze to the predicates within the film that mark Aaron's blackness, his foreignness, his refusal to become assimilated into Roman society: on the one side is the room filled with white people (Romans and Goths), on the other side are his scarred face, his alien clothing, his brown-skinned hand elegant against the clear glass, the militaristic stance, the look of disdain on his face. When Aaron moves, it is to stand in front of a white pillar, a movement that heightens our awareness of the fact that he is the only dark-skinned person in the room. As Aaron repositions himself in front of the pillar and he crosses his arms, we realize that the glass is no longer in his hand—a cinematic gaffe, as we do not see him give the glass to another or put it down. What we do notice is that a flicker of uncertainty crosses his face as he watches his mistress being kissed by her new husband.

The effect of Aaron's gestures is both paradoxical and achingly familiar in the representation of people of African ancestry in the performance of racial identity. The bodily cues affirm his identity as an outsider, marginalized in both his color and position, as well as his powerlessness as he watches his mistress and her new husband. The paradox is that Taymor's and Lennix's vision of Aaron is one of nobility—in effect, the noble Moor that is Othello—and not the barbaric savagery that Shakespeare's playtext constructs and with which Taymor opens and concludes the film.. Aaron's villainy, then, becomes a study in contrasts for Taymor as, apparently, she seeks to ameliorate—or at least mediate—the problematic ideology that associates Aaron's blackness with evil. Unfortunately, her intervention is constrained by Shakespeare's playtext and the performative gestures Lennix uses that draw attention to and connections between his color and his identity as a racialized villain. Aaron's Moorishness (his racial identity) becomes located, interestingly enough, not in Lennix's skin color but in the actor's body and the way he uses it.

A similar tactic occurs in Baz Luhrmann's *William Shakespeare's Romeo + Juliet*. In the opening scene of the film, the rival Montague and Capulet "gangs" arrive at a gas station simultaneously. Because a van (filled with school girls and a nun) blocks each gang's view of the other, neither group is aware of the other's existence. Again gestures and costuming contribute to the defining of "ethnic" or racial differences: the Montagues are dressed in bright shirts with Christian iconography. In contrast, the Capulets appear as dark, menacing figures. The first figure we see, Abra, is dressed in dark clothing (black leather jacket and black trousers), his dark hair and beard giving him a very sinister appearance. Across the gas station, the rivals posture, flourishing guns and exchanging words. The exchange ends with Abra flinging his jacket off his shoulders and flashing a malevolent grin, his upper teeth encased in silver with the word "Sin" inscribed in the metal. One of the Montague boys, a frightened expression on his face, falls back into their car as Abra yells "Boo!" The confrontation escalates until Benvolio walks out of the restroom; he draws his gun and the two Capulets freeze. This scene is all about gestures: the constant waving of guns, the darting glances, and the woman's purse striking the head of a Montague. As the tension mounts between the Montague boys and the Capulets, all the audience hears are the clicks of the guns' safety catches being released, until the squeaking of a hanging metal sign overrides all other noises. In between the squeaks, a scratchy sound occurs and Benvolio turns toward it.

What Benvolio, and the audience, hears and then sees is Tybalt Capulet (played by John Leguizamo) striking a match and lighting a cigarillo. Just as with Aaron, what stands out are the hand gestures that draw attention to Tybalt's face. The match is held delicately in a vertical position between Tybalt's first and middle fingers; his thumb provides support beneath the two fingers to keep the match upright while the second finger is bent parallel to the middle finger and the little finger is vertical. The cigarillo is brown and creates a chiastic contrast between Tybalt's hand and his face in profile. Its brownness emphasizes the delicate, almost effeminate gesture Tybalt makes and, importantly, the dark tuft of hair just below his full lower lip. The next shot (and sound) is the match falling to the ground and hitting Tybalt's metallic heel as he turns toward Benvolio and the others. The actor's face occupies the left side of the screen, and a caption, "Tybalt CAPULET Prince of Cats Juliet's cousin," the right side. If in the initial shot Tybalt's racial identity was ambiguous, we are under no illusions with this second one. The dark eyes, the sideburns with a single curl, the shadow of a mustache, and the small goatee often seen on Latino men, as well as his suddenly slightly darker skin, all serve to mark him racially.

In a gesture that adds emphasis to his characterization, the actor smiles and slowly draws open his jacket. Like the lighting of the cigarillo, this gesture is crafted with exquisite elegance and deliberation. Tybalt's fingers become signifiers of meaning: they point simultaneously to an image of Christ (with stigmata) on a reddish brown shirt, and to Tybalt himself. The fingers of the right hand direct our gaze to Tybalt's belt even as they make clear he is drawing the jacket open. The fingers of the left hand, closed in a gesture of self-referential pointing, shift our gaze to the face of Christ, which bears a slight resemblance to the actor performing Tybalt in the color of his skin and his garment. Like the right hand, the fingers of the left hand are also performing the task of revealing what is inside the jacket.

Figure 10.2 Tybalt's gesture, *Romeo + Juliet* (1996).

The next two frames explode on the screen as Tybalt exposes the gun hidden inside his jacket pocket and its twin concealed at his waist. Again, his hands are the performative measure by which Tybalt's racial identity is marked. As the actor draws a gun and aims it, his hands dominate every movement he makes for the remainder of the scene. The shoot-out is vividly choreographed, leaving the audience breathless and knowing that what they are watching is a race war.

My third example is taken from the film *Romeo Must Die* (2000) staring Jet Li and the singer Aaliyah. Similar to Luhrmann's film, Birtkowiak localize the *Romeo and Juliet* plot in contemporary America. The film depicts the violent conflict between rival ethnic families in twentieth-century Oakland, California. One family is Asian (the father emigrated from China), and the other is African American. The conflict clearly is orchestrated by Mac (Machiavelli) the aide to the African American kingpin O'Day, and Kai, the aide to Ch'u, a Chinese American gang lord. Our hero Han Sing, a former police officer imprisoned in Hong Kong for crimes committed by his father, receives word that his brother Po has been murdered. Han escapes and travels to Oakland to find Po's killer. The film is primarily a showcase for Jet Li's martial arts skills. Thus, the storyline is neither original nor complicated. The screenplay by Eric Bernt and John Jarrell locates the narrative in a contemporary California city noted for its changing demographics (at the time of writing this essay, Oakland is approximately 36 percent African American, 24 percent white, 22 percent Latino/Hispanic, and 15 percent Asian). The white presence in the film, interestingly, is minimal, although it is clear that the economic power does for the most part reside with Roth (a white developer, though his name signals his potential Jewishness). Han successfully exposes the double dealings of Mac and Kai, and, after confronting his father with the fact that he (Han) knows that Ch'u is responsible for the murder of Po, Han wins the girl (Trish O'Day) and walks away.

What makes the film interesting to Shakespearean studies, as well as critical race studies, is its rewriting of the *Romeo and Juliet* narrative. Set in a violent world of guns, drugs, and class conflict, *Romeo Must Die* uses Shakespeare's storyline as an attempt to redefine our perceptions about race. Asian Han and African American Trish find themselves attracted to each other despite the emerging racial or ethnic conflict between the two families. Because Jet Li's martial skills are the reason for the film, the film's development of the romantic relationship between Han and Trish is at best superficial (much like that of *Romeo and Juliet*). Throughout the film "racial" identity is marked whenever there is interaction between Asian and African American. The actor's skin color and linguistic accent or dialect define each character's racial subjectivity in familiar and predictable ways. Yet there are two moments where the template for racialization is disrupted, and it is gesture that effects this disruption.

After her brother is murdered, Trish seeks Han's aid in finding the killer. Han shares with Trish information (a list of addresses) he has discovered in his investigation of his brother's death. One of the addresses is the club Po visited just before his death. Han persuades Trish to take him there. As the couple starts to enter the club, Trish stops Han and checks out his appearance. She removes her cap and places it on his head. With a slight grimace, she turns the cap around so that the brim is worn backward. "Now you're giving me some b-boy flavor," she says. Han looks puzzled and says "What?" As the two walk towards the club, Trish smiles, "Hip-hop." A serious expression on his face, Han repeats the phrase "hip-hop." Trish smiles again: "Yeah, hip hop." Han stops and takes gum from his pocket. The camera shot captures both Trish and Han, facing each other, as he clearly is about to offer her some. Their hands are close yet not touching, his slightly raised above hers, her fingers close ready to receive his gift. He gives her the gum and says, "I know hip-hop." In what is clearly to be read as parody, Han grabs his pants at the waist and readjusts them as he swivels his hips before engaging in a "black" swagger as the couple walk into the club. Han's gestures situate him simultaneously in two racial typologies, one ethnic (Asian) and one performative (African American). Han's performance as a "black man" can take place only through bodily gestures: wearing the cap backward, gum chewing, the walk, and facial expression. Gestures do not make Han Sing black; rather, what they do is allow him to perform black - where black is not skin color but gestural movement.

The second moment when race and gesture become indistinguishable occurs at the film's conclusion. Han's father has committed suicide after being confronted by his son. As Han walks slowly from the house, police rush past him. Standing next to a police car is Trish, only her face visible. She hurries up the steps toward Han;

when she reaches him, her hands are extended toward him as if to embrace him, yet she gently touches his hands; then her fingers move caressingly up his arms until they come to rest on his cheeks, her eyes dreamily gazing into his as she inquires about his well-being.

Figure 10.3 "I know hip-hop": *Romeo Must Die* (2000).

Figure 10.4 Blending differences: *Romeo Must Die* (2000).

The camera lingers on Trish's face, yet it is her fingers on Han's face (fuzzy in the image) that speaks volumes for the way race is simultaneously a factor and not. We cannot help but notice that the color of Trish's fingers virtually blends into Han's face. The film ends with Trish and Han embracing, then walking—hand in hand—away from Ch'u's. Our ability to use skin color to define and differentiate between the two lovers is rendered useless, and thus the race war is ended: Romeo and Juliet live, to beget a new racial model.

Unlike *Titus*, colorblind or nontraditional casting in *William Shakespeare's Romeo + Juliet* and *Romeo Must Die* serves to illuminate the performative nature of race. In each film gestures seem to override words, animating the body in directions that question the validity of our assumptions about the fixity of race in Shakespeare's playtext and, I would argue, in our world. Gestures such as Jet Li's "b-boy" moves make it clear that racial identity can be easily assumed and performed, rendering color a negligible element of that identity. Just as important, the hand gestures of Lennix and Leguizamo remind us that even when color and phenotype are deployed as predicates of race, they too must be performed. In other words, the physicality of race must be made visible if race is to have cultural and ideological weight. Simply stating that race is skin color without localizing and valorizing that statement renders the notion meaningless. To speak of a "black voice" or an "Asian dialect" or "traditional Shakespearean performances" is to ask an actor to physically gesture into existence or awareness that voice, dialect, or performance.

I have focused on three filmic engagements with Shakespeare's playtexts as a way of suggesting that perhaps it is moot whether colorblind or nontraditional casting should be undertaken. The cinematic (as well as other media) engagement with Shakespeare's playtexts has redefined the notion of "traditional" (i.e., as done according to Elizabethan and Jacobean theatre practices) performances of Shakespearean characters. What changes the dynamics of power in each film is a gesture that is at once metaphorical and racializing. By bringing Shakespeare's playtexts down from the stage into the audience by means of the cinematic eye, directors such as Luhrmann, Taymor, and Bartkowiak have shifted the level of meaning and knowledge that an audience must bring to bear on its apprehension of Shakespeare's dramas. What the cinematic eye reveals is that race in Shakespearean performance has no meaning until it is gestured. And this, rather than the merits of nontraditional or colorblind casting, is what makes Jet Li's performance so Shakespearean even if the screenplay is not Shakespeare's playtext.

To return to the workshop on gesture that gave rise to this essay, Lynette Hunter cogently argued, "Gestures cannot be 'aware' unless there is reciprocity, an answering gesture, so that actor and audience (or another actor...) engage in this process of bringing into intelligibility at their particular location in space and time, their situatedness" (quoted in Arden et al., 81). To animate the text, we must animate the body, and in animating the body we cannot help but gesture. Just as important, we need to understand the ways rituals associated with both the stage and cinema complicate how racial identity is and can be performed in productions of Shakespeare's playtexts (including their adaptation and evocation). What seems even more apparent now, when we consider the ways Taymor's, Luhrmann's, and Bartkowiak's films make use of Shakespeare's playtexts, is that gesture is to race what language is to Shakespeare: a necessary means to an end. And what that end is, not surprisingly, is what makes performing Shakespeare's playtexts exciting possibilities.

WORKS CITED

"Obscured by dreams": Race, Empire, and Shakespeare's *A Midsummer Night's Dream*
This essay was ublished in *Shakespeare Quarterly*, Vol. 47, No. 1 (Spring, 1996), 37-60 Published by: Folger Shakespeare Library in association with George Washington University. Copyright 1996 by Margo Hendricks.
I wish to thank Karin Magaldi-Unger, B. Modern, and Shakespeare Santa Cruz for permission to reproduce the costume drawing and photograph. I also want to express my deep gratitude to colleagues at UC-Santa Cruz, especially Deanna Shemek, Karen Bassi, Harry Berger Jr., Michael Warren, Donna Haraway, Vicki Pagani, and Judith Lopez. This paper has had a long run, including performances at Shakespeare Association and Renaissance Society of America annual meetings, the Columbia University Shakespeare Forum, University of North Florida, Indiana University, and in my Shakespeare seminar at Santa Cruz. I am especially indebted to Patricia Parker for sharing many of my ideas and reminding me that words are, in the end, the very heart of ideologies. Finally, despite my disagreement with a central feature of Danny Scheie's brilliant and hilarious production, I owe him a debt for provoking me to reconsider *A Midsummer Night's Dream* in the light of his directorial decision.
1. Quoted in Akhil Gupta and James Ferguson, "Beyond 'Culture':

Space, Identity, and the Politics of Difference," *Cultural Anthropology* 7 (1992): 6-23, esp. 10.

2. The Indian boy appears in a 1906 film version of the play, in Max Reinhardt's classic 1935 film, in two BBC video productions, and in the New York Shakespeare Festival's video production. In nearly all of these productions, the character's costume signifies ethnicity. Additionally, in the New York Shakespeare Festival's production a black actor plays the boy. Illustrations and paintings of Act 1, scene 2, also are eclectic when it comes to representing the Indian boy; for example, Fuseli includes the child while Boydell does not.

3. See Edward Said, *Orientalism* (New York: Random House, 1979). For a cogent engagement with Said's work, see Lisa Lowe, *Critical Terrains: French and British Orientalisms* (Ithaca, NY, and London: Cornell UP, 1991).

4. Leah S. Marcus, *Puzzling Shakespeare: Local Reading and Its Discontents* (Berkeley, Los Angeles, and London: U of California P, 1988), 40.

5. Frank Reeves, *British racial discourse: A study of British political discourse about race and race-related matters* (Cambridge: Cambridge UP, 1983), 8. Much work has been done, from a cultural-studies perspective, on theorizing race. Some of the best studies include: Kwame Anthony Appiah, *In My Father's House: Africa in the Philosophy of Culture* (New York and Oxford: Oxford UP, 1992); David Theo Goldberg, *Racist Culture: Philosophy and the Politics of Meaning* (Oxford: Blackwell, 1993); *The "Racial" Economy of Science: Toward a Democratic Future*, Sandra Harding, ed. (Bloomington and Indianapolis: Indiana UP, 1993); Donna Haraway, *Primate Visions: Gender, Race, and Nature in the World of Modern Science* (New York and London: Routledge, 1989); and the introduction to *The Bounds of Race: Perspectives on Hegemony and Resistance*, Dominick LaCapra, ed. (Ithaca, NY, and London: Cornell UP, 1991).

6. Quotations of Shakespeare plays other than *A Midsummer Night's Dream* follow *The Complete Works of Shakespeare,* ed. David Bevington, 4th ed. (New York: HarperCollins, 1992). Quotations of *A Midsummer Night's Dream* follow R. A. Foakes's New Cambridge edition (Cambridge: Cambridge UP, 1984).

7. This usage points to the ambiguity of the term, as in a few early

modern dictionaries "horse" is one of the definitions given for *race*. The word *race* was also used to describe the quality of wine. This type of lexical ambiguity about nature and appearance, as David Scott Kastan reminded me, is also at play in the Prince of Morocco's use of the word *complexion*-"*mislike* me not for my complexion,/ The shadowed livery of the burnished sun" (2.2.1-2)-in *The Merchant of Venice*.

8. See Donna Haraway's stunning essay "Universal Donors in a Vampire Culture-It's All in the Family: Biological Kinship Categories in the Twentieth-Century United States" in *Rein venting Nature*, William Cronon, ed., forthcoming.

9. Gloria Anzaldua, *Borderlands/ La Frontera: The New Mestiza* (San Francisco, CA: Spinsters/ Aunt Lute, 1987), preface [n.p.].

10. Kim F. Hall, "Reading What Isn't There: 'Black' Studies in Early Modern England," *Stanford Humanities Review* 3 (1993): 23-33, esp. 25. The parameters for engagement with the notion of race have been redefined by other recent work on the early modern period, including Ann Rosalind Jones and Peter Stallybrass, "Dismantling Irena: The Sexualizing of Ireland in Early Modern England" in *Nationalisms and Sexualities,* Andrew Parker, Mary Russo, Doris Sommer, and Patricia Yaeger, eds. (New York and London: Routledge, 1992), 157-71; *Women, "Race," and Writing in the Early Modern Period,* Margo Hendricks and Patricia Parker, eds. (New York and London: Routledge, 1994); Emily C. Bartels, "Making More of the Moor: Aaron, Othello, and Renaissance Refashionings of Race," *Shakespeare Quarterly* 41 (1990): 433-54; and Margo Hendricks, "Managing the Barbarian: *The Tragedy of Dido, Queen of Carthage,"* Renaissance Drama* n.s. 23 (1992): 165-88.

11. Steven Mullaney, *The Place of the Stage: License, Play, and Power in Renaissance England* (Chicago and London: U of Chicago P, 1988), 6.

12. James L. Calderwood, *"A Midsummer Night's Dream:* Anamorphism and Theseus' Dream," *SQ* 42 (1991): 409-30, esp. 410.

13. Mullaney, 6.

14. See, for example, Peter Hulme, *Colonial Encounters: Europe and the native Caribbean, 1492-1797* (London and New York: Methuen, 1986); and John Gillies, *Shakespeare and the geography of difference* (Cambridge: Cambridge UP, 1994). Though not directly exploring questions of race, Stephen Greenblatt's *Marvelous Possessions: The Wonder of the New World*

(Chicago and London: U of Chicago P, 1991) and Richard Helgerson's *Forms of Nationhood: The Elizabethan Writing of England* (Chicago and London: U of Chicago P, 1992) are thoughtful contributions to the discussion.

15. Yet I think we can, as Andrew Gurr suggests, assume that audiences of *A Midsummer Night's Dream,* comprised of nobles, artisans, apprentices, clerks, citizens, and day laborers, literate and illiterate Londoners, would represent a range of knowledge or awareness of what events, people, texts, and ideologies were being alluded to in the plays; see *Playgoing in Shakespeare's London* (Cambridge: Cambridge UP, 1987), esp. 80-85.

16. For example, Richard Hakluyt writes that in his "publike lectures [he] was the first, that produced and shewed both the olde imperfectly composed, and the new lately reformed Mappes, Globes, Spheares, and other instruments of this Art for demonstration in the common schooles, to the singular pleasure, and generall contentment of my auditory" *(The Principal Navigations Voyages Traffiques* & *Discoveries of the English Nation,* 12 vols. [Glasgow: James MacLehose and Sons, 1904], 1:xviii). While there is, of course, no empirical means of verifying the direct influence of orality in the circulation of these images, I consider Hakluyt's words to be convincing evidence of the validity of my point. On the relationship between oral and literary knowledge, see Walter J. Ong, *Orality and Literacy: The Technologizing of the Word* (London and New York: Methuen, 1982).

17. See Gurr, 82-86.

18. John Bourchier, Lord Berners, *The Boke of Duke Huon of Burdeux,* ed. S. L. Lee (London: Early English Text Society, 1887). I have modernized the spelling of quotations from this text.

19. Lee, ed., 72-73.

20. Lee, ed., 73. Oberon's other gifts include a magic horn and cup and the power to acquire whatever he desires merely by wishing for it.

21. Lee, ed., 74.

22. Lee, ed., I.

23. Editor S. L. Lee notes that it is difficult to determine the date of the second edition. He argues for 1570, however, because the colophon to the third edition (which Lee contends is "doubtless a reprint of the

first") states "that the book was translated by Lord Berners 'in the year of our Lord God one thousand five hundred three score and ten'." The third edition was printed in 1601 by Thomas Purfoot, "to be sould by *Edward White"* (Lee, ed., lv-lvi).

24 See *Henslowe's Diary,* ed. Walter W. Greg (London: A. H. Bullen, 1904), 16. Henslowe also lists the play under the titles "hewen of burdockes" and "hewen."

25. Edmund Spenser, *The Faerie Queene,* ed. A. C. Hamilton (London and New York: Long- man, 1977), II.ix.60.1-4.

26. Spenser, Il.x.71.5-6.

27. Spenser, II.x.72.1-3 and 5-6.

28. Spenser, II.x.75.3-5, 8-9, and II.x.76.1. In Spenser's allegory, Oberon figures for Henry VIII and thus becomes the father of Tanaquill or Glorian (Elizabeth). A. C. Hamilton notes that in Roman history Tanaquill was the wife of the first Tarquin, ancestor of Sextus Tarquinius, whose rape of Lucretia is often figured as the genesis of the Roman Republic. Spenser's link of fairy and Roman through the figure of Oberon mimics the account of Oberon's lineage in *Huon of Bordeaux* and thus continues the mythologizing of England's racial history. For a brilliant discussion of the relationship between Tarquin's rape of Lucretia, republicanism, and Renaissance humanism, see Stephanie H Jed, *Chaste Thinking: The Rape of Lucretia and the Birth of Humanism* (Bloomington and Indianapolis: Indiana UP, 1989).

29. Robert Greene, *The Scottish History of James the Fourth,* ed. J. A. Lavin (London: Ernest Benn, 1967), 1.3. [chorus] 4-7.

30. See Thomas Hahn, "Indians East and West: primitivism and savagery in English discovery narratives of the sixteenth century," *journal of Medieval and Renaissance Studies* 8 (I 978): 77-114. Hahn argues that *India* variously referred to "all of Asia, as Samuel Purchas declared in the seventeenth century: 'The name of India, is now applied to all farre-distant Countries, not in the extreeme limits of Asia alone; but even to whole America, through the errour ... in the Westerne world, thought that they had met with Ophir, and the Indian Regions of the East'" (78).

31. See Hahn, 79-88.

32. For another useful study of the ethnography of travel writing in

pre- and early modern Europe, see Mary B. Campbell, *The Witness and the Other World: Exotic European Travel Writing, 400-1600* (Ithaca, NY, and London: Cornell UP, 1988).

33. Here I am referring to Leo Africanus's *Geographical Historieof Africa* (London, 1600) and George Best's *A true discourse of the late voyages of discouerie...* (London, 1578).

34. See Gillies, passim.

35. Gupta and Ferguson, 10.

36. Richard Eden, *The History of Travaylein theWest and East Indies,and other countreys lying eyther way, towards the fruitfull and ryche Moluccaes* (London, 1577). Quotations from the narrative of Lewes Vertomannus follow this edition.

37. Vertomannus in Eden, 354v.

38. Vertomannus in Eden, 382r and 386v.

39. Vertomannus in Eden, 403v, 401v, and 382r.

40. Vertomannus in Eden, 388v and 399r.

41. Vertomannus in Eden, 390r.

42. *Iohn Hvighen van Linschoten. his Discours of Voyages into y' Easte & West Indies. Devided into Foure Bookes* (London, 1598), 62.

43. James Clifford, *The Predicament of Culture: Twentieth-Century Ethnography, Literature, and Art* (Cambridge, MA: Harvard UP, 1988), 10.

44. Van Linschoten, "To the Reader."

45. Hahn, 91.

46 ."The report of John Huighen van Linschoten concerning M. Newberies and M. Fitches imprisonment, and of their escape, which happened while he was in Goa" in Hakluyt, 5:512.

47. In an unpublished essay, Joan Pong Linton has noted that, within the early modern English lexicon, *trifles* was generally used to describe the type of exchanges between Native Americans and English sailors. For a different analysis of relations of exchange between the English and Native Americans, see Pong Linton, '*Jack of Newbery* and Drake in California: Domestic and Colonial Narratives of English Cloth and Manhood," *ELH* 59 (1992): 23-51.

48. One wonders whether this accusation might also imply that Titania

is the real object of Theseus's love, that it is for love of her that he left the other women.

49. In this I diverge from Louis A. Montrose, who reads this conflict in terms of the psychology of the nuclear family, where Oberon's efforts are seen as an "attempt to take the boy from an infantilizing mother and to make a man of him" ("A *Midsummer Night's Dream* and the Shaping Fantasies of Elizabethan Culture: Gender, Power, Form" in *Rewriting the Renaissance: The Discourses of Sexual Difference in Early Modem Europe,* Margaret W. Ferguson, Maureen Quilligan, and Nancy J. Vickers, eds. [Chicago and London: U of Chicago P, 1986], 65-87, esp. 74). Allan Dunn also sees the play in terms of this psychology, though he reads this familial conflict from the changeling's point of view, in his "The Indian Boy's Dream Wherein Every Mother's Son Rehearses His Part: Shakespeare's *A Midsummer Night's Dream," Shakespeare Studies* 20 (1988): 15-32. It seems to me that both monarchs operate within a feudal ideology about social responsibilities and status. Thus the Indian boy elicits from the monarchs very different interpretations of their social roles.

50. Peter Fryer, *Staying Power: The History of Black People in Britain* (London and Sydney: Pluto Press, 1984), 9. See also Folarin Shyllon, *Black People in Britain 1555-1833,* published for The Institute of Race Relations (London: Oxford UP, 1977); and James Walvin, *The Black Presence in Britain* (London: Orbach and Chambers, 1971).

51. The substitution of Nick Bottom as the object of Titania's affections, his regression to an infantile state, and the sexual significance of this new relationship have long received critical attention. For an insightful examination of sexuality, bodily functions, and shame in *A Midsummer Night's Dream,* see Gail Kern Paster, *The Body Embarrassed: Drama and the Disciplines of Shame in Early Modern England* (Ithaca, NY, and London: Cornell UP, 1993), esp. 125-43. 52 Luce Irigaray, "Women on the Market" in *This Sex Which is Not One,* trans. Catherine Porter (Ithaca, NY, and London: Cornell UP, 1985), 172 and 177.

53. For a discussion of Apuleius's *The Golden Ass* and Ovid's *Metamorphoses* as sources for Shakespeare's representation of Bottom, see Foakes, ed., 9-10.

54. Maria Moliner, *Diccionario de Uso del Espanol*, 2 vols. (Madrid: Editorial Gredos, 1967), 2:402.

55. See, for example, Thomas Middleton's and William Rowley's *The Changeling*. In its common usage in early modern England, *changeling* referred to a person put in place of another and, in particular, to a child secretly substituted for another child by fairies. It was also used to describe dramatic and inexplicable shifts in human behavior.

56. *Translation's* etymology originates with the Latin word *translatio*, which is derived from the union of *trans* and *ferre* (away from / across and to carry / to bear, respectively). *Translation* as Shakespeare uses it, however, seems to evoke a signification more akin to the semantics of *miscere-that* is, a mixing of two things to produce one-than to the notion of *translatio*, to carry or bear away. Peter Quince's use of the word *translated* insinuates this connection as it continues the pun created by Snout's use of the word *change*.

57. The Portuguese racial lexicon also included the term *castiço: castiço* referred to a Portuguese born in India, while *mestiço* described any Asian, African, or New World native who had a European ancestor.

58. The word *mulatto/a*, of course, immediately evokes an image of the animal, something the other two terms do not suggest. But, and this is crucial to our understanding of the link between language and sexual reproduction, the word *mulatto/a* also implies the inability to fix the idea of race, something the other two terms imply as well. I have generalized the gender of these relations not because Spanish and Portuguese women were absolutely uninvolved in the colonial process but because there is little evidence to indicate whether they were involved in miscegenous relations with native men.

59. In his 1623 *A Dictionary in Spanish and English,* John Minsheu offers his readers an "enlarged and amplified" version of Richard Perceval's 1594 *Biblioteca Hispanica*. Minsheu's aim was to provide "for the further profit and pleasure of the learner or delighted in this tongue." Minsheu's dictionary goes far beyond Perceval's not only in sheer number of words but also in its inclusion of words that mark racial identity.

60. I give both the Spanish and Portuguese spellings for *mestizo* to resist the totalizing of Spanish and Portuguese cultures as

homogeneous. While linguistically the two nations are quite similar, they are distinct entities. In both languages *mulatto* has the same spelling.

61. Van Linschoten, 62.

62. In 1510 Alfonso de Albuquerque, viceroy of the Portuguese settlement at Goa, instituted a policy prohibiting marriages between Portuguese men and "the 'black women' of Malabar in other words dark-skinned women of Dravidian origin, who were often termed 'Negresses' by the Portuguese" (C.R. Boxer, *Race Relations in the Portuguese Colonial Empire 1415-1825* [Oxford: Clarendon Press, 1963], 64-65).

63. Homer Swander, "Editors vs. A Text: The Scripted Geography of *A Midsummer Night's Dream*," *Studies in Philology* 87 (1990): 83-108, esp. 87. Swander's analysis is primarily concerned with the staging of the play rather than its internal geography. In an analogous discussion with different conclusions, Gary Jay Williams looks at a "semi-operatic adaptation" of *A Midsummer Night's Dream* performed in 1816. Williams argues that the "interesting and historically significant text of" this production is its "staging and the new pictorial scenery, whose vocabulary must be read in the light of empire," thus specifically recognizing the play's dependence upon a specific geographical and political "human territory" ("The Scenic Language of Empire: *A Midsummer Night's Dream* in 1816," *Theatre Survey* 34 [1993]: 47-59, esp. 47).

64. Patricia Parker, *Literary Fat Ladies: Rhetoric, Gender, Property* (London and New York: Methuen, 1987), 131.

65. Arguing that "the least interesting motivation behind the Indian Boy conflict would be the excuse that Oberon sincerely needs a page or 'henchman'," the director chose to highlight the sexual tensions of the play from a different angle (Danny Scheie, "Program Notes on *A Midsummer Night's Dream*" [Santa Cruz, 1991], 32).

66. Quoted in Gupta and Ferguson, 10.

Visions of Color: Spectacles, Spectators, and the Performance of Race

Published in *A Companion to Shakespeare and Performance*, eds., Barbara

Hodgson and W. B. Worthen. John Wiley & Sons Limited copyright 2007. Reproduced with permission of the Licensor through PLSclear.

References

Abercrombie, Nicholas, Hill, Stephen, & Turner, Bryan S. (1989). *Sovereign Individuals of Capital- ism*. London: Allen and Unwin.
Adelman, Janet (1992). *Suffocating Mothers: Fanta-sies of Maternal Origin in Shakespeare's Plays, Hamlet to The Tempest*. New York: Routledge.
Albanese, Denise (2003). "Black and White, and Dread All Over: The Shakespeare Theatre's 'Photonegative' *Othello* and the Body of Desdemona." In Lena Cowen Orlin (ed.) *Othello: Con- temporary Critical Essays*. New York: Palgrave/ Macmillan.
Burt, Richard (2002). "Slammin' Shakespeare in Acc(id)ents yet Unknown: Liveness, Cinem(e- di)a, and Racial Dis-integration." *Shakespeare Quarterly* 53: 201–26.
Burt, Richard & Boose, Lynda E. (1997). *Shakespeare, the Movie*. London: Routledge.
Burt, Richard & Boose, Lynda E. (2003). *Shakespeare, the Movie II*. London: Routledge.
Butler, Judith (1993). *Gender Trouble: Feminism and the Subversion of Identity*. London: Routledge.
Callaghan, Dympna (2000). *Shakespeare without Women: Representing Gender and Race on the Renaissance Stage*. London: Routledge.
Carleton, Dudley (1972). *Dudley Carleton to John Chamberlain, 1603–1624: Jacobean Letters*, ed. Maurice Lee, Jr. New Brunswick, NJ: Rutgers University Press.
Debord, Guy (1995). *The Society of the Spectacle*, trans. Donald Nicholson-Smith. New York: Zone Books.
Hall, Kim F. (1996). *Things of Darkness: Economies of Race and Gender in Early Modern England*. Ithaca, NY: Cornell University Press.
Hammonds, Evelyn (1994). "Black (W)holes and the Geometry of Black Female Sexuality." *Differences* 6, 2–3: 126–45.
Hannaford, Ivan (1996). *Race: The History of an Idea in the West*. Washington, DC: The Woo-drow Wilson Press Center Press/Baltimore, MD: Johns Hopkins University Press.

Hornback, Robert (2001). "Emblems of Folly in the First *Othello*: Renaissance Blackface, Moor's Coat, and 'Muckender.' " *Comparative Drama* 3: 69–99.

Huet, Marie-Helene (1993). *Monstrous Imagination*. Cambridge, MA: Harvard University Press.

Jones, Eldred D. (1965). *Othello's Countrymen: A Study of African in the Elizabethan and Jacobean Drama*. Oxford: Oxford University Press.

Jonson, Ben (1969). *The Complete Masques*, ed. Stephen Orgel. New Haven, CT: Yale University Press.

Lehmann, Courtney (2000). "Brave New Bard." *Cineaste* 26, 1: 62–6.

Mullen, Harryette (1994). "Optic White: Black- ness and the Production of Whiteness." *Diacritics* 24, 2: 71–89.

Percyvale, Richard (1591). *Bibliotheca hispanica. containing a grammar, with a dictionarie in Spanish, English and Latine, gathered out of divers good authors: very profitable for the studious of the Spanish toong. by Richard Percyvall gent. the dictionarie being inlarged with the Latine, by the advise and conference of Master Thomas Doyley doctor in physicke*. London.

Robinson, A. (1994). "It Takes One to Know One: Passing and Communities of Common Inter- est." *Critical Inquiry* 20: 715–36.

Royster, Francesca (2000). " 'White Limed Walls': Whiteness and Gothic Extremism in Shakespeare's *Titus Andronicus*." *Shakespeare Quarterly* 51, 453: 433–54.

Shakespeare, William (1988). *Titus Andronicus*. In *The Complete Works*, ed. Stanley Wells & Gary Taylor. Oxford: Oxford University Press.

Smedley, Audrey (1998). " 'Race' and the Construction of Human Identity." *American Anthropologist* 100: 690–702.

Sollors, Werner (1997). *Neither Black Nor White Yet Both: Thematic Explorations of Interracial Literature*. New York: Oxford University Press.

Soltis, Jonas F. (1966). *Seeing, Knowing, and Believing: A Study of the Language of Perception*. London: George Allen and Unwin Ltd.

Thomas, Julia (ed.) (2000). *Reading Images*. Lon- don: Palgrave.

Worthen, W. B. (2003). *Shakespeare and the Force of Modern Performance*. Cambridge: Cambridge University Press.

Gestures of Performance: Re-thinking Race in Contemporary Shakespeare

This essay was published in *Colorblind Shakespeare New Perspectives on Race and Performance,* ed., Ayanna Thompson. Routledge/ Taylor and Francis copyright 2006. Reproduced with permission of the Licensor through PLSclear.

1. Alan Cox is an actor and director who has worked in the Royal Shakespeare Company (RSC), National Theatre, and the Globe Theatre in London, England.
2. 1 have enlarged the list of usual suspects to include those who work behind the scenes because it is also their skill that enables the visual magic of the theatre.
3. I use both terms because, while nontraditional casting can include colorblind casting, it also refers to casting across gender, ethnic, and other categories of social identity. Colorblind casting refers solely to physical appearance.
4. Kidnie compares Rubin's efforts to those of the RSC and the National Theatre in London. She states that "so-called 'colorblind casting' is at the heart of a contested theoretical debate, some critics objecting that race on the modern stage is never invisible, others arguing that it tends to require actors, regardless of their racial and cultural backgrounds, to conform to a particular, supposedly 'neutral' accent and style of delivery. That said, it also allows talented black actors such as Ray Fearon and Adrian Lester to play lead roles once reserved exclusively for white actors" (318). She goes on to cite "racially and culturally diverse" productions at Stratford's Studio Theatre in 2003. About 7he *Swarrrre*'. Princess *Charlotte,* she observes that "sometimes race was dramatically significant" and at others it was not.
5. On Taymor's *Titus* and Luhrmann's *Shakespeare's Romeo + Juliet* see Lehmann 2001 and 2002. On *Romeo Must Die* see Beltran and Kim.
6. From the moment Lavinia's hands are severed, we are assaulted with visual reminders of the importance of hands throughout the film.
7. When the Goth captives are brought into Rome, Aaron is covered by a muddied fur mantle or cloak. At the film's conclusion, when he is about to be killed, he is naked except for a loincloth
8. Interestingly, the name "Romeo" is used only once in the film. It

occurs near the end when Mac is about to shoot Han and says, "Sorry Romeo, you gotta die." For the effect of the film's attempt at "racelessness" see Beltran's discussion, especially p. 57.

References

Hendricks, Margo. "Gesture, Language and the Body." In Shakespeare, Language *and the Stage*, edited by Lynette Hunter and Peter Lichtenfels. London: Arden Shakespeare, 2005.
Beltran, Mary C. "The New Hollywood Racelessness: Only the Fast, Furious, (and Multiracial) Will Survive." *Cinema* Journal 44 (2005): 50-67.
Burt, Richard. "Slammin' Shakespeare in Acc(id)ents Yet Unknown: Liveness, Cinem(edi)a, and Racial dis-integration." Shakespeare Quarterly 53 (2002): 201-226.
Fleming, John. "Much Ado About Race." St *Petersburg Times*, May 11, 2004,
Hendricks, Margo. "Visions of Color: Spectacle, Spectators, and the Performance of Race." in A *Blackwell* Companion fo Shakespeare *and Performance*, edited by Barbara Hodgdon and William Worthen. London: Blackwell, 2006
Kendon, Adam. Gesture.' Visible Action as Utterance. Cambridge: Cambridge University Press, 2004.
Kidnie, Margaret Jane. "'What world is this?': Pericles at the Stratford Festival of Canada, 2003." Shakespeare Quarterly 55 (2004): 307-319.
Kim, James. "The Legend of the White-and-Yellow Black Man: Global Containment and Triangulated Racial Desire in *Romeo Must Die*." *Camera Obscura* 55 (2004): 151–179.
Lehmann, Courtney. "Crouching Tiger, Hidden Agenda: How Shakespeare and the Renaissance Are Taking the Rage Out of Feminism." Shakespeare *Quarterly* 53 (2002): 260–279.
Lehmann, Courtney. "Strictly Shakespeare? Dead Letters, Ghostly Fathers, and the Cultural Pathology of Authorship in Baz Luhrmann's *William Shakespeare's Romeo + Juliet*." *Shakespeare Quarterly* 52 (2001): 189–221.
Pao, Angela C. "False Accents: Embodied Dialects and the

Characterization of Ethnicity and Nationality." *Theatre Topics* 14 (2004): 353-372. Saltzman, Simon, and Nicole Plett. "August Wilson versus Robert Brustein." *U.S. I Newspaper*, January 22 and April 16, 1997.

Wick, Nancy. "Shakespeare in Reconstruction: Classic gets Civil War Setting." *University Week*, February 3, 2005.

Wilson, August. *The Ground on Which I Stand*. New York: Theatre Communications Group, 1996.

PREMODERN CRITICAL RACE STUDIES

ME AND MR. FOLGER: 'WE GOT A THING GOIN' ON'

A MARGOH MEANDERING, AFTER A FASHION

[This is a MargoH early WIP draft. It was originally a chapter in what eventually became *Race and Romance: Coloring the Past* (2022) but written nearly a decade earlier. It is a draft, uncorrected writing, which means grammatical, discursive, and logic potholes exist. In other words, an example of how MargoH's brain works lol.)

Passing As Black

"I saw his visage in my mind" (*Othello*)

In his illuminating study, *Cities of the Dead: Circum-Atlantic Performance,* Joseph Roach writes that "genealogies of performance attend not only to 'the body' . . .but also to bodies—to the reciprocal reflections they make on one another's surfaces as they foreground their capacities for interaction. Genealogies of performance also attend to 'counter-memories' or the disparities between history as it is discursively transmitted and memory as it is publicly enacted by the bodies that bear its consequences."[1] In essence, "performance genealogies," Roach posits, "draw on the idea of expressive movements as mnemonic reserves, including patterned movements made and remembered by bodies, residual movements retained implicitly in images or words (or in the silences between them), and imaginary movements dreamed in minds, not prior to language but constitutive of it, a psychic rehearsal for physical actions drawn from a repertoire that culture provides" (26). "This repertoire," as defined by Pierre Nora, includes " 'gestures and habits,'" "'skills passed down by unspoken traditions, in the body's inherent self-knowledge, in unstudied [and studied I would argue] reflexes and ingrained memories' (13)." Crucial to Nora's theory is "the idea of 'places of memory' (*lieux de mémoire*), the artificial sites of the modern production of national and ethnic memory, in contrast to 'environments of memory (*mileux de mémoire*), the largely oral and corporeal retentions of traditional cultures." By "places of memory," Roach writes, Nora is referring to sites such as

> archives, monuments, and theme parks: "moments of history torn away from the movement of history, then returned; no longer quite life, not yet death, like shells on the shore when the sea of living memory has receded" ([Nora],12). "Living memory" remains variously resistant to this form of forgetting, however, through the transmission of gestures, habits, and skills (Roach, 26).

One "place" where "living memory" continues to assert its resistance to historical forgetfulness is the early modern English stage.

By early modern English stage I am referring not just to the performance space where the playtexts of William Shakespeare were originally performed (the Globe, the Rose or Blackfriars) but also to the 'environment of memory'—the continuing and complicated history of 'performance' of these scripts (including adaptations and literary analysis) that has spanned five centuries. As a "technological invention" for the instantiation and transmission of cultural and historical memory, the early modern English stage is a blend of both physical and metaphysical properties that work to sustain the "kinesthetic imagination" (Roach, 27) The "kinesthetic imagination," according to Roach, "inhabits the realm of the virtual. Its truth is the truth of simulation, of fantasy, or of daydreams, but its effect on human action may have material consequences of the most tangible sort and of the widest scope" (27). This definition aptly describes the genealogies of performance associated with the staging practice of color passing, or what is more often described as "blackface."

Inspired by the extraordinary wealth of recent studies examining the creation and/or representation of 'blackness' in performative scripts of the Renaissance and early modern English theatre, I want to explore the ways two theatrical scripts inscribe the phenomenon of color passing as a legitimate mode of performance, and thus, not surprisingly, simultaneously as a culturally acceptable and unacceptable "performative act." In other words, on the early modern English stage color passing is not only accepted but expected whenever a script calls for the depiction of Africaness (Moors, Blackmoors, Ethiopians, and Negroes) and non-Europeanness in general. In my use of the term "performative act" I am deploying Judith Butler's idea of the performativity of identity. However, as a theoretical framework for my analysis I want to make use of Judith Butler's conceptualization of performative and performativity. In order to make clear where we diverge, I believe it will be helpful to retrace her argument. In her groundbreaking essay, "Performative Acts and Gender Constitution: An Essay in Phenomenology and Feminist Theory," Butler contends

> gender is in no way a stable identity or locus of agency from which various acts proceeded; rather, it is an identity tenuously constituted in time-an identity instituted through a stylized repetition of acts. Further, gender is instituted through the stylization of the body and, hence, must be understood as the mundane way in which bodily gestures, movements, and enactments of various kinds constitute the illusion of an abiding gendered self.[2]

Constituting a "performance" that is repetitive, "gender is instituted through a stylized repetition of acts" which "must be understood as the mundane way in bodily gestures, movements, and enactments of various kinds constitute the illusion of an abiding gendered self " (519).

Furthermore, Butler argues, "the body is not a self-identical or merely factic materiality; it is a materiality that bears meaning, if nothing else, and the manner of this bearing is fundamentally dramatic. By dramatic I mean only that the body is not merely matter but a continual and incessant materializing of possibilities" (521) – in effect, social action. Because "social action requires a performance which is repeated," gender "is at once a reenactment and re-experiencing of a set of meanings already socially established" (526). Ultimately, Butler continues,

> As a public action and performative act, gender is not a radical choice or project that reflects a merely individual choice, but neither is it imposed or inscribed upon the individual, as some post-structuralist displacements of the subject would contend. The body is not passively scripted with cultural codes, as if it were a lifeless recipient of wholly pre-pen cultural relations. But neither do embodied selves pre-exist the cultural conventions which essentially signify bodies. Actors are always already on the stage, within the terms of the performance. Just as a script may be enacted in various ways, and just as the play requires both text and interpretation, so the gendered body acts its part in a culturally restricted corporeal space and enacts interpretations within the confines of already existing directives (526).

Taking Butler's argument as a framework, I propose that we should view 'racial' identity in similar terms, as a performative act.

Like gender, race is and has been constitutively defined in terms of perceptible biological differences: epidermal coloring, hair texture, the shape and size of the body, and other physiological attributes. In addition, a long list of cultural and social behavior has morphed into quasi-biological predicates of race – sexuality, intellect, and morality. Yet, for obvious and complex historical reasons, it is difficult to envision a theoretical discussion of race that does so without resorting to an analysis dependent on the physical appearance of the body that is 'racialized'. Even more to the point, it is nearly impossible to treat race in terms other than skin color, and as a racializing predicate ideologically ingrained in the collective cultural consciousness of European societies since the middle Ages.[3] If, as I am suggesting, that we view race as a "performative act" then we need to examine more carefully the ways in which transgressive racial identity, the 'color passing' subject, functions as a "corporeal field of cultural play" that "compels [us] to live in a world in which [races] constitute univocal signifiers, in which [race] is stabilized, polarized, rendered discrete and intractable" (Butler, 528).

The use of the word "performative" is not without its own set of issues, however. In *Shakespeare and the Force of Modern Performance* W. B. Worthen writes that "until fairly recently dramatic performance provided the paradigm of performance analysis;" however, "the salutary impact of the massive globalization of performance, and an energetic expansion of scholarly and critical practice in the fields of literary, theatre, and performance studies, have now displaced dramatic theatre as the paradigm of *performance*."[4] As a result of this expansion, innovative and radical modes of theorizing performance has shifted how even literary scholars approach the study of the Shakespeare script. Yet, more often than not, the materiality of performance becomes overshadowed by the linguistic or textual performative, i.e., "the terrain between language and its enactment" (Worthen, 3). And, the consequence is a "controversy about language, performance, and the performing subject" (3). Arguing for what he calls "'dramatic performativity' – the relationship between the verbal text and the conventions (or, to use Butler's term, 'regimes') of behavior that give it meaningful *force* as performed action,"[5] Worthen observes that we "must relinquish the notion that [dramatic performances] derive solely or directly from the authorial text" (10). In the end, Worthen writes that "a stage performance is not determined by the internal 'meanings of the text, but is a site where the text is put into production, gains meaning in a different mode of production through the labor of its agents and the regimes of performance they use to refashion it as performance material" (23).

Negotiating between Roach's notion of "performance genealogies" and Butler's concept of "performative act," while bearing in mind Worthen's insistence that "to consider dramatic theatre as an instance of the 'performative' requires a fundamental rethinking of the function of writing in performance,"[6] I want to explore the use of color passing in relation to theatrical scripts where blackface serves both a prosthetic device and an attempt to literally instantiate a "black" body on the Renaissance and early modern stage. In particular, because color passing simultaneously affirms and undermines the notion of color as an ontological condition of racial distinction, the performance of 'blackness' on the early modern English stage functions as both "a deconstruction of" class or status as the performative genealogy of racial identity "and the veiled assertion of a clandestine countermemory [color] in its stead."[7] To illustrate this hypothesis I shall begin with a brief look at three theatrical scripts where the prosthetic of blackface metamorphoses into a racial subject that is taken to be historical (i.e., representations based on actual people) and thus ontological: William Shakespeare's *Titus Andronicus* (1598), Thomas Dekker's *Lust's Dominion* (c1600) and Aphra Behn's *Abdelazer* (1670), an adaptation of *Lust's Dominion*.

The effect of these readings has been to reproduce the very binaries that the critics seek to disrupt. When, however, we look at two scripts that make use of blackface, Ben Jonson's *Masque of Blackness* (1607) and Richard Broome's *The English Moore, or the Mock Marriage* (c1637), we find that the use of blackface as a prosthetic device alters the way blackness and whiteness are to be understood. In my discussion of these two scripts, I engage most fully Virginia Mason Vaughan's *Performing Blackness on the English Stages, 1500-1800*. I do so because, of the recent work undertaken on race and performance in Renaissance and early modern English theatrical culture, Vaughan has attempted to offer a an in-depth analysis of the use of blackface. What goes unnoticed in Vaughan's exploration is the way color passing functions as both an elaborate plot device and an illustrative acknowledgement that racial "reality is performative which means, quite simply, that it is real only to the extent that it is performed" (Butler, 527). In effect, *Masque of Blackness* and *The English Moore* offer a dynamic counterdiscourse to the racializing ideologies depicted in the scripts by Dekker, Behn, and to some degree Shakespeare.

Bodily Inscriptions

. . .

Performative 'blackness' in Renaissance and early modern English theatre was not just a matter of an actor putting on blackface and de facto he or she 'becomes' 'black'. To effectively convey a character as a racially marked subject to the audience, the actor needed to conceal all traces of his own physical non-blackness and trigger the kinesthetic and cultural imagination of the audience so that all the spectators see is a 'black' person. Most likely, this concealment necessitates a negotiation on several levels: the physical, the psychic, the social, and the ideological. Thus spectators witnessing Renaissance and early modern performances of scripts such as *Titus Andronicus* or *Abdelazer* knew without question that the actor did not share the racial identity of the 'black' character he played just as these audiences knew the actor performing the characters Lear or Portia were not of Lear's royal status or Portia's sex. Yet, for the moment of performance, individuals were willing to accept the performance as a representative reality. While the space of performance (the theatre) is an ideal locus for such negotiations, the stage is also a problematic delineation of that performance. In as much as the performance is intended for a group of individuals, assumed to have some values in common but not all, the artificially constructed community that the theatre is produces a false sense of collectivity and identity that often goes unnoticed in critical studies of Renaissance and early modern drama.

On the surface, the use of black makeup does not seem constitutive of a performative act but rather a prosthetic device intended to 'mark' the body's recognizability, in essence a stage prop. Yet there is a fundamental ideological distance between the robe the actor performing Marc Antony dons and the black coloring the actor performing the character Aaron uses to render himself a "black Moor" – despite the fact that the makeup comes off almost as easily as Marc Antony's robe. In "Othello was a white man: properties of race on Shakespeare's stage," Dympna Callaghan makes this point from the very start: "this essay will investigate the obvious but none the less curious fact that in Shakespeare's plays there are histrionic depictions of negritude, but there are, to use Coleridge's infamous phrase, no 'veritable negroes'. There are, indeed, no authentic 'others' – raced or gendered – of any kind, only their representations" [8]. The belief that these representations function as a form of 'mimesis is called into question by Callaghan, who argues that performative "mimesis entails an imitation of otherness, and its dynamism is a result of the absence of the actual bodies of those it depicts. . . . Theatrical mimesis, however, involves the active manipulation of the body of the actor in the process of representation" (194) This "manipulation" includes not only the obvious staging devices of performative mimesis, costume and makeup, it also reflects the actor's gestural performance (which emanates from the actor's use of physical movements and voice).

Blackface functions, according to Callaghan, as a "constitutive . . . articulation of racial difference: the display of black people themselves (exhibition), on the one hand, and the simulation of negritude (mimesis), on the other. These are the poles of the representational spectrum of early modern England" (194). I would agree in as much as the blackness marks color difference which in turn is then used to establish 'racial difference'. In the theatrical performance, where characters whose epidermis is described or defined as 'black' are incorporated into the script, what occurs is not the performance of black subjectivities but, Callaghan astutely argues, the 'exhibition' of blackness: where characters depicted as black "are set forth as objects, passive and inert before the active scrutiny of the spectator, without any control over, or even necessarily consent to, the representational apparatus in which they are placed"(194).[9] When blackface is deployed as part of the representation of blackness, Callaghan concludes, "race, crucially, *both* black *and* white, is articulated as an opposition on stage principally by means of cosmetics: burnt cork negritude projects racial difference against white Pan-Cake."[10]

Felicity A. Nussbaum similarly highlights the ways in which blackface engages in projections of difference within a culturally articulated power dynamic. As Nussbaum argues,

> The metropole itself evolved into a contact zone where the empire persistently intruded into domestic affairs, and the consequences for the nation were palpable. One popular manifestation of this

penetration of people from elsewhere occurred in England's theatres. The drama incorporated colonial encounters onto the skins, gestures, and dialogue of white actors at once to fabricate the representation of racial difference to celebrate and worry it, and finally to grant it a recognizable reality. In particular impersonations in blackface helped formulate the racial politics that came to predominate around the Atlantic and later the Pacific.[11]

This "incorporation" enabled the eighteenth-century theatre audience to sit comfortably watching the performance of black masculinity, knowing that it was illusory. Moreover, Nussbaum contends, "in becoming black, the white man can participate in the sublime thrill of blackness, yet in the very act of presenting it, he exerts some control over its effects" (75).

In their analyses both Callaghan and Nussbaum, though looking at very distinct cultural moments in English theatrical history, highlight the "social privilege" that the inscription of blackness conveys to the dramatic impersonation. As Nussbaum writes, blackface "allow white men to inhabit black men's bodies, to shape and mold the culture's perceptions of them" (75). Tellingly, performative blackness also directs the audience's gaze to its "ephemeral" status as cork, paint, or whatever cosmetic is used to create the demarcation. The effect, both Callaghan and Nussbaum demonstrate, is not of essence but of "exhibition" or a "decorative" representation.[12] Yet, as Judith Butler remarks on the performative act of gender, "the body is not passively scripted with cultural codes, as if it were a lifeless recipient of wholly pre-pen cultural relations. But neither do embodied selves pre-exist the cultural conventions which essentially signify bodies" (Butler, 526). Whether spectators (and *readers* of Renaissance and early modern English theatrical scripts[13]) reflect on the fact or not, "actors are always already on the stage, within the terms of the performance. Just as a script may be enacted in various ways, and just as the play requires both text and interpretation, so the . . . body acts its part in a culturally restricted corporeal space and enacts [racializing] interpretations within the confines of already existing directives" (Butler, 526).

This performative temporariness, however, did nothing to alleviate cultural anxiety about the instability of the concept of race as color in Renaissance and early modern England. For example, in *Titus Andronicus* William Shakespeare raises the specter of color passing as a plot device when Tamora gives birth to a child whose father is a Moor. Tamora has the child delivered immediately to Aaron, with instructions that the infant is to be put to death; Aaron refuses. Instead, Aaron slays the nurse who brought the child and quickly devises a plan to save not only his child's life but Tamora's honor:

> And now be it known to you my full intent
> Not far, one Muliteus my countryman
> His wife but yesternight was brought to bed.
> His child is like to her, fair as you are.
> Go pack with him, and give the mother gold,
> And tell them both the circumstance of all,
> And how by this their child shall be advanced
> And be received for the Emperor's heir (4.2.150-157).[14]

With this advice, Aaron offers Tamora and her sons the means to continue their political ambitions while at the same time protecting the life of his son. Even though the plan does not succeed, it poses a bit of an obstacle for the ideological stability of racial identity.

Surprisingly, until recent very few scholars have explored at length the significance of this scheme beyond the internal narrative of the script. For example, in his analysis of *Titus Andronicus*, Eldred Jones comments that "it is no diminution of Aaron's quickness of wit to suggest that Shakespeare intends this story of Muly and his *white* son [emphasis added] to be taken as a complete fabrication. Indeed the speed with which Aaron devises the story is the supreme demonstration of his skill. The happy coincidence of the birth of a white child to a moor and a white woman with Aaron's desperate need for just such a child, would otherwise be the least credible of the chances which fortune presents to the villain in this play.[15] Francesca Royster argues differently, contending that Aaron's plan is more than a "demonstration of his skill." Royster argues that "Aaron's strategy is twofold: to use the white Moor child to infiltrate the imperial household while his own child is to be raised in the wilderness, beyond Roman surveillance, preparing for later invasion."[16] In essence, Aaron's scheme illuminates a highly subversive method for intervening in and destabilizing the Roman power structure in a fundamentally irrevocable way.

A white child, therefore, would not have the same ideologically transformative power, denoting, as Royster rightly contends, Aaron's "allegiance to his race, [and] a commitment to establishing a foothold of power for Moors within the very heart of Rome" (453). The script's ideological resolution offers a re-containment of both the performative blackness of [Richard Burbage, the actor performing the character of Aaron] and the performative act of 'whiteness' that Muly's 'moorish' son represents. *Titus Andronicus*' scripted performance of variegated racial identities, as Royster observes, may be indicative of the fact that, for Renaissance and early modern English culture,

> [color] passing suggests that skin pigmentation per se is not at issue in racial discrimination – that skin color is only the visible badge of some inner threat. The essence of Moorishness is not blackness of skin but an inner "foreign" wickedness that remains even though by some genetic accident the skin may be white. Insofar as hidden evil is more difficult to detect and combat than overt evil, a white Moor is even more threatening than a blackamoor (453).

Where this merits expansion, is of course, not in our reading of Aaron but in relation to his proposal to substitute Muly's son for his own.

Aaron's proposal illuminates the subversive performances that the linkage of color and the idea of race often engender. To raise the specter of the color passing subject is to acknowledge the instability of color as a racializing paradigm. While in the physical confines of the theatre this instability can be defused by reminding the audience that the white Moor, like the prosthetic use of blackface, is merely a plot device and what is 'inside' is essential (i.e., the inner blackness of the Moor or the actual 'whiteness' of the actor wearing blackface). Outside the theatre, the performative act of color passing (and by extension, racial identity) is not so easily resolved. Judith Butler's observation about transvestism is especially cogent here: "the various conventions which announce that 'this is only a play' allows strict lines to be drawn between the performance and life. On the street or in the bus, the act becomes dangerous...precisely because there are no theatrical conventions to delimit the purely imaginary character of the act, indeed, on the street or in the bus, there is no presumption that the act is distinct from a reality" (531). Clearly, Shakespeare's theatrical script acknowledges the potential instability that color passing produces and just as obviously attempts to reinscribe this performative act into its ontological state of blackness – at least on the stage. Yet it becomes equally clear that "if the 'reality' of [color passing] is constituted by the performance itself, then there is no recourse to an essential and [unrealizable concept of race] which [racializing] performances ostensibly express" (Butler, 531).

By the time Aphra Behn wrote *Abdelazer* (1676), theatrical and literary depictions of Moors and blackness were deeply interpellated in late seventeenth-century English dramatic culture. Revisions and adaptations of late sixteenth and early seventeenth-century dramatic scripts and fictional narratives with Moorish characters were quit fashionable and did much to sustain the emerging instantiation of color as a racializing signifier. Yet Behn is most noted for her critique of gender relations on the late seventeenth-century English stage than for engaging the matter of race. In fact, *Abdelazer*, Behn's adaptation of the late Elizabethan revenge tragedy *Lust's Dominion* (c1600), despite being her first theatrical engagement with the issue of 'race' has received very little critical attention. In her essay, "Gender, Family, and Race in Aphra Behn's *Abdelazer*," Joyce Green MacDonald opines" that "I believe that this play is particularly troubling to the feminist impulses that mark so much recent scholarship on Behn because in it we can observe her habit of literary revision working to produce much more rigidly patriarch views of gender and much more consistently whitened and Eurocentric formulations of racial identity than exist in *Lusts Dominion*."[17] Green MacDonald begins her discussion of Behn's play by noting "the conduct of my argument will draw on both Behn's placement within contemporary politics, specifically the mounting insistence in the 1670s on patrilineal sanctity, and on her play's treatment of notions of racial nature and identity" (68). Green MacDonald's reading of *Abdelazer*, appropriately enough, is linked not just to *Lusts Dominion* but also to *Titus Andronicus* as Behn's familiarity with Shakespeare's 'race' plays cannot not be underestimated; a factor Green MacDonald astutely highlights as she explores the dramatic conventions and characterizations that mark race and gender as intertwined threats to national stability.[18]

About *Titus Andronicus*, Green MacDonald writes that "racial difference is implicated in, and yet not truly organically related to, the crises of national and familial integrity the play depicts"(69). Clearly, while we are asked to taken skin color into consideration when categorizing the script's human taxonomy, it is also obvious that w are to view race as multivalent an ideology, allowing for ethnicity to be a racial predicate as well as skin color. Between the 'barbarous' Goths and the 'civil' Romans, Aaron the Moor becomes merely a third category of racial identity. In *Titus Andronicus*, race as color paradoxically achieves its omniscient status as a result of the erasure of an apparent racial crisis between Romans and Goths.[19] Each of the texts, Green MacDonald posits, serves as a "conservative endorsement of patrilineal succession" and this endorsement "is underwritten by its reactionary positions on the connections it sees between gender, sexuality, sovereignty, and race" (72) cannot be disputed. Like Shakespeare's Othello, Lusts Dominion's Eleazar and Abdelazer marry a non-Moorish and non-"black" woman, experiencing similar pangs of jealousy and betrayal as a result. While Othello's behavior is nearly always framed in relation to Othello's naivety in the face of Iago's duplicity and sophisticated machinations, Eleazar and Abdelazer are defined by absolutes – most evident in their erotic relationship with the Queen of Spain and their efforts to undermine (even destroy) the Spanish political structure.

These men are enmeshed thoroughly in the politics of the Spanish court – Eleazar is wedded to the dead King's daughter while Abdelazer is married to a Spanish noblewoman and both are trusted advisors (and lovers) to the Spanish queen. What links these representations to Shakespeare's "Moors" is their assimilation into the aristocratic and/or royal stratum of society, their concomitant alienation from that world, and the troubling gender dynamics that define both their subjectivity and their demise. With the exception of Aaron, the Moors who traversed the early modern stage were "converso" and had to either define themselves racially as "black" or accept such definition in pursuit of a desired revenge. For the actors performing the roles, this racializing identity has to be achieved not only in the language of the script but also, more importantly, in the performance of the character. As with Aaron and Othello, Abdelazer and his predecessor Eleazar are best understood as exempla of performative blackness as mediated through the performing body of a 'white' actor.[20]

Early modern English cultural ideologies presume an ontological relationship between blackface as a theatrical prosthetic device and the racial identity of a character labeled "Moor" for the duration of the performance. Both *Lusts Dominion* and *Abdelazer* enact the liminal space where text and blackface work to instantiate a racial subject. What the actors, mediating the language of the script, constitute in their performative presentations of both Abdelazer and Eleazar are not racial identities that can be considered African or Moorish but 'color passing' individuals who cannot help but figuratively project the white bodies inherently behind the prosthetic 'black' ones on display. In the end, what these stage Moors allow for is what Amy Robinson calls the "visibility of the apparatus of passing – literally the machinery that enables the performance."[21] Though the audience knows that the male actor, in these performances, can personate blackness, it is the female body that makes the color passing subject (I would argue) come face to face with the ideological and technical machinery that "enables" the pass. And, it is the color passing figure who most dramatically and irrevocably destabilizes the biological terrain upon which race, as an ideology, has been constructed.

Women and Blackface

. . .

In 1605 Queen Anne, wife of James I King of England, and eleven of her ladies-in-waiting blackened their skin to perform in Ben Jonson's *Masque of Blackness*. The masque recounted the desire of twelve nymphs, "daughters of Niger," to restore themselves to their originary complexion – which once was "as fair / As other dames, now black with black despair," as a result of Phaeton's tragic ride. The masque represents the nymphs' journey to the West and the promise of their eventual restoration to a pre-Phaetonic state of whiteness. The Queen's performance in the masque generated quite a bit of commentary about the "blackening" of her "fair" skin.[22] As Dudley Carleton wrote about the Queen's use of prosthetic blackness, "their black faces, and hands which painted and bare up to the elbows, was a very loathsome sight." [23] Blackening her skin, the Queen removes all traces of recognizability (including her whiteness) of her subjectivity in order to convey the subjectivity of Niger's daughter. Yet, as the narrative later reveals, the Queen's color passing seems prophetically to extend to Niger's daughters as they discover that their "blackness" masks a fairness destined to be revealed.

The fact that Niger's daughters also prove to be 'temporarily' black (their whiteness known to them even if concealed by sunburn) only heightens the significance of the Queen's performative act of color passing. The masque makes evident that the beauty of the Queen (and her ladies-in-waiting) is not affected by the performance of passing; Niger declares "that, in their black, the perfectest beauty grows." The textual ambivalence, of course, is whether black has a natural beauty or whether it is the Queen who, in passing, extends to blackness a claim to beauty.

Jonson's *Masque of Blackness*, despite the fact that it was performed only once and within a highly elite and circumscribed venue, increasingly surfaces as an iconic text in the study of blackness and thus race in early modern theatre. Though not a dramatic script in the same ways as *Othello*, *All's Lost by Lust*, or *Lust's Dominion*, *Masque of Blackness* is often discussed as if it were; and herein lies the difficult. Jonson's masques were not initially designed for 'public' consumption;

on the contrary, the masques came into existence at the behest of the royal court, performed by court members, and consumed by royal and aristocratic audiences. The 'public', as we understand it, were invited to consume the spectacle only in print form, not in dramatic performance. This distinction in audiences has important significance for understanding the masque's utility in the construction of a racial epistemology based on color. To explain this assertion I want to first look at recent studies that explore the issue of *Masque of Blackness* as constitutive of early modern English racial difference, if not racism.

With the publication of *Things of Darkness: Economies of Race and Gender in Early Modern England,* Kim Hall inaugurated a critical/theoretical reassessment of Jonson's *Masque of Blackness* and its implications for the study of early modern English culture and history. Forcefully, Hall raised the stakes for critical analysis of the script by asking "why such a landmark production involves bringing "Africa" (albeit a European version) to the English court?"[24] Hall seeks her answer by foregrounding the emerging reconfigurations of racial and imperial political formations taking shape within and without England, mediated by a familiar aesthetics of color. What Hall makes clear in her discussion is that, with an increasing presence of 'black' Africans in England – especially London – and 'white' English on African soil as a measure of the growing trans-Atlantic traffic in slaves, the English court developed a "renewed fascination with racial and cultural difference and their entanglements with the evolving ideology of the state" (128). It is in the tropes of blackness and whiteness, Hall observes, where we see "traditional notions of 'Englishness' and the concomitant issues of social [order] . . . being interrogated and threatened on all sides by the growing pains of imperialism" (140).

Bernadette Andrea similarly locates the masque's political and ideological effects in England's "investment" in imperialism in her essay "Black Skin, the Queen's Masques: Africanist Ambivalence and Feminine Author(ity) in the Masques of Blackness and Beauty." However, Andrea sees the masque as an indicator of the complex and often ambivalent participation by English women in their culture.[25] According to Andrea, the masques allows for the Queen's "unsettling representation of feminine 'blackness' as beauty while finally enabling the hegemonic dichotomy of racialized blackness and beauty that marks, as it were, subsequent eras." [26] Andrea reads the masques against the historical presence of African women residing in England and Scotland, in particular the "Black Queen of Beauty" Elen More who "presided over the Scottish court's entertainments in 1507 and 1508" (257). In its attentiveness to the idea of the dichotomy between dark and fair, black and white, Andrea's essay echoes much of the argument presented in Kim Hall's study of the script except in its conclusion. For Andrea, however, the queen's use of 'blackness' represents an attempted struggle for authorship and authority over and against the "material investments of the English aristocracy in the transatlantic slave trade" (281).

Other readings also insist upon the transgressive nature of the Queen's performance in the *Masque of Blackness*. For example, Clare McManus writes, "the relationship between the female performer and the linguistic dynamics of *Blackness* shows that the alignment of the feminine with the corporeal actually provided opportunities for a measure of female expression and autonomy with the masque, primarily since it was this very confinement of the female to the physical which allowed women to masque."[27] McManus further contends that

> the court masque, therefore, simultaneously demanded elite women's participation and the control of female representation during their performance. It is clear that the codes of social and gendered order and the court's demands of corporeal decorum and aristocratic community propelled the courtly woman into the masque, yet on her arrival on stage as a masquer she was trammeled by these very same codes of social convention and limitation. However, particularly in *Blackness*, these tools of control were also a means of expression for the masquing woman. The performative strategies of costume and face-paint opposed the requirements of court decorum, highlighting the ineffectual nature of female containment and emphasizing the pre-existent tensions within the structure and form of this masque (9).

Clearly, McManus considers the "pre-existent tensions" to be not only whose performing but the use of blackness and the "curtizan-like" garments the Queen and her ladies wore.

Hardin Aasand likewise finds the Queen's decision to be a reflection of her resistance to "a marginal existence in the Jacobean court."[28] Aasand finds Anne's performance creating a space, albeit momentarily, where *Masque of Blackness* paradoxically transforms the periphery of legitimate power into the center of a sustained work of transgression (272). According to Aasand, Queen Anne turns the conventional "representation of royalty" on its head, creating a "grotesque mockery of orthodox ideology that threatens the conventional image of beauty and dominance" (272). Yet, despite her resistance, Anne does not effect the degree of transformation that she seeks; her estrangement from James and her ultimate retirement from the court made clear the King's monarchical authority. Yet in the end, Aasand writes, "her death in 1619 underscored the mortality of James's monarchal power, however divinely invested it may have been in his royal figure. The *Masque of Blackness* had promised the kingly transformation of blackness to whiteness and corpse to redeemed life, but in death, Anne's pale body now had no need for the 'light sciential' to 'revive a corse.' She had become impervious to James's indifference, and in death, had entered into a more refined, more lasting *masque of beauty* [emphasis mine] (283).

More recently, Virginia Mason Vaughan examines the masque in her book, *Performing Blackness on English Stages, 1500-1800*. As Vaughan writes, "my emphasis . . . is on performance, on what audiences saw when they attended stage plays that featured black Moors. This study is but one piece in the puzzle as to how early sixteen-century inchoate notions about black Africans developed into rigid conceptions of racial difference and a global system of racial slavery by the late seventeenth century" (intro xi-xii). Vaughan's study is a testament to the firmly established sub-field of race studies within Renaissance and early modern English studies. Vaughan's engagement with the two texts at issue here, *Masque of Blackness* and *The English Moor, or the Mock Marriage*, in the end offers the most useful springboard for raising questions about how to reflect differently on the use of color passing in the English stage during the seventeenth century.

Tracing the 'place' blackness held in the Stuart royal household, Vaughan reminds us of the 'properties' associated with the masque, and their problematic status: "what is radical in Queen Anne's request is *her* desire to use black pigment" rather than the "coverings of lawn and velvet " and black vizards normally used to depict Moorishness. While the wearing of blackface was not uncommon within English early modern theatre, as Vaughan notes in her earlier chapters, "why, [she] wonders, would a Queen of England, six months pregnant, wish to appear in public, her face and arms coated with black grease" (65)? Vaughan's answer is that "a vizard would have concealed the Queen's features" and thus "the request for black paint was motivated instead by the desire to be recognized through the extravagant disguise" (66). In essence, Anne perhaps wanted to "experience her own 'to-be-looked-at-ness'." An act of subversion, an assertion of the Queen's identity, and "her authority as opposed to that the of the poet" is how Vaughan reads the Queen's decision. Ultimately, Vaughan contends, the masque serves to construct "white Englishness in opposition to African blackness, making room for a chromatic scale between" (68). Like Kim Hall, Vaughan sees the use of this trope has having derived from "actual contact with Africans, Native Americans and other racially different foreigners," rather than solely being dependent on literary or visual imagery, and indicates a greater engagement with "outsiders" during the reign of James I than in the reign of Elizabeth I. [29] In other words, Jonson's masque, and the Queen's performance in it, is very much linked to a shifting notion of "Englishness" inside and outside the geographic boundaries of the island-nation. And, Queen Anne's performative "blackness," not surprisingly, validates the ideological association (linguistically and culturally) of Englishness and whiteness as much as her later restoration to her 'natural' hue.

Vaughan ends her discussion by reminding us that "we should not underestimate the sheer beauty of this spectacle. The orient pearl used to deck the masquers' arms and necks provided a stunning visual contrast between textures of black and white. . . . To many of the courtiers assembled at James's court on 5 January 1605, the spectacle of the black-faced Queen and her ladies was a source of visual pleasure, with blackness the exotic focal point for the white, English 'gaze'" (69).

The problem of the Queen's color passing was, aesthetically and ideologically, deemed rectified in the masque's companion piece, *The Masque of Beauty*, where the "black" daughters of Niger are "washed" white by the River Thames. Not surprisingly, Vaughan approaches the script of *Masque of Blackness* as if it were a traditional dramatic script, i.e., a script with regular performances. Because *Masque of Blackness* was performed just once and under specific circumstances before it circulated in print form, any scholarly assessment of the scripts importance to cultural formations of racial identity is complicated. In particular, our reading of the script's contributions to emerging early modern conceptualizations of race must take into account the phenomenon of color passing and the ways in which it defines the Queen's masque, something that is missing from Vaughan's otherwise thoughtful examination.

Molly Murray's reading of the masque in terms of its relationship to devotional practices illuminates the impact that the Queen's decision had on the script's meanings. Murray considers the performance to be driven by the religious tensions shaping early seventeenth-century English politics. Murray finds in the nymphs' desires and in Niger's handling of his daughters' conflicted state of longing a political commentary on the larger devotional matters affecting the court. In an astute discussion of Niger's paternal response, Murray deems it to be problematic:

Niger's *volte-face*, although it ultimately reaffirms the conventional equation of chromatic and aesthetic "fairness," hardly inspires confidence in his own judgment, in the 'truth' of whiteness, or in his daughters' true color. To accept his newfound conviction, and to understand the ladies as merely temporarily black, is to acknowledge that their color has been changed in the past, and will be changed again in the future. Since the ladies have been blackened at some point before the action of the masque began, in other words, their second metamorphosis cannot entirely banish fears of recidivism.[30]

The literal restoration of the Queen and her women to their original whiteness in *The Masque of Beauty* signals an attempt to dispel the racial contradictions that color passing – no matter how symbolic-- engenders. Calling into question the idea of a stable notion of color as a racial predicate, color passing establishes a locus for an effective performance of racial identity for anyone whose appearance is not easily categorized. *Masque of Blackness*, as well as other color passing scripts, allow for the exposure and reintegration of these troubling bodies into an ideology of race increasingly being put to the test. The impact of the masque and the Queen's performance in it produces not just a fraught moment of kinesthetic displacement but also a troubling cultural memory. Even so, the cultural anxiety developing over color passing did not deter playwrights from making use of the phenomenon in their scripts. In fact, if anything, Queen Anne's performance seems to encourage more complicated moments of dramatic performativity where color passing and the female body structured a script's plot.

In 1638 Richard Brome's comedy *The English Moor, or The Mock-Marriage* was performed by Queen Henrietta's Men, most likely at Blackfriars Theatre.[31] Like many scripts that fall within the mode of city or citizen comedy, *The English Moor* has a convoluted structure where plot creates subplot which in turn produces subplot. Quicksands, an old wealthy Venetian Jewish usurer/merchant (aided and abetted by Millicent's uncle Testy) weds Millicent, a young Christian. Millicent, however, is in love with Theophilus Rashley, whose sister Lucy is beloved by Arthur Meanwel. Dionisia Meanwel hates the Rashelys and, disguised as a man, seeks to avenge her father, who she believes was murdered by the elder Rashley. Finally, there is Nathaniel, a friend of Theophilus, who seduce Phillis the daughter of Winlose ("a decayed Gentleman"). Just as with most city comedies, young love triumphs despite the complications brought on by the problematic desires of aged men. What makes this script worth exploring in a study of color passing is the way blackness as a prosthetic device becomes performative cues encoded in misperceptions about the ontological stability of skin color.

The English Moor begins with the unexpected arranged marriage of the aged merchant Quicksands to the youthful Millicent. To avoid consummating the marriage, Millicent feigns licentiousness when ordered by her Uncle Testy to shed her "maiden peevishness.". Millicent promptly shows Quicksands an exaggerated "cheerfulness" and promises to "kiss him, / Clap him, and stroke him" (1.3.53-54). Her behavior startles Quicksands, "she'll make me blush" and "She calls me chick and bird: The common names / With wives that Cuckold their old cravened husbands" (1.3.62-63). Disturbed by Millicent's actions, Quicksands wonders what type of wife he has taken. Millicent continues her performance until both her uncle and husband decide that sleep (rather the consummation of the marriage) is what she needs; and in her reply, Millicent makes clear the success of her ploy – "Hey ho, to bed, to bed, to bed. / No Bride so glad – to keep her Maiden-head" (1.3.226-27).

The following morning as Millicent, Quicksands and Testy talk, Quicksands receives a letter stating that "hundreds have taken oaths / To make thee false, and me a horned Monster" (2.2.25-27). Millicent uses the letter as bait to establish her own bargain with her husband. Stating that she will "take charge of my self, / And do fair justice, both on them and you," she requests that Quicksands allow her to "keep a vow" she made after Quicksands "flighted" or left her without consummating the marriage (1.143-44). She asks that she be allowed to remain chaste

> . . . for a month; and for so long
> I crave your faithful promise not to attempt me.
> In the meantime because I will be quit
> With my trim, forward Gentlemen, and secure you
> From their assaults; let it be given out,
> That you have sent me down into the country
> Or back unto my Uncles; whither you please. (2.2.75-81)

When Quicksands balks at the idea of her absence, she reassures him that she will not actually "leave your house, / But be locked up in some convenient room / Not to be seen by any, but your self / Or else to have the liberty of your house / In some disguise, (If it were possible) / Free from the least suspicion of your servants" (1.183-88).

Quicksands reaction is one of virtual glee, telling Millicent that he accepts the bargain and to leave the disguise to him. When the moment comes to put the scheme into place, Quicksands explains his plan to his wife: "first know, my Sweet, it was the quaint devise / Of a *Venetian* merchant, which I learnt / In my young Factorship" (3.153-55). Millicent intuitively grasps his purpose and exclaims, "That of the Moore? / The Blackamore you spoke of? Would you make / A *Negro* of me?" (3.156-58). Quicksands reminds her that she took a "vow / (For keeping this month your virginity) / You'll wear what shape I please" (3.159-62). Eventually Millicent acquiesces and allows Quicksands to "paint" her. As he undertakes Millicent's transformation into a color passing subject, Quicksands challenges her question –"would you blot out Heavens workmanship" – by interrogating her assumptions about the relationship between color and beauty: "has heaven no part in Egypt? Pray tell me, / Is not an Ethiops face his workmanship / As well as the fairest Ladies? Nay, more too. / Then hers, that daubs and makes adulterate beauty" (3.173-76).

As Kim Hall observes, Quicksands "uses a typical Petrarchan defense of the black beauty, insisting that her beauty is better than that of possibly painted beauties; however, he is quickly caught in a rhetorical trap because Millicent's blackness is in fact painted on and thus also 'blot[s] out Heavens Workmanship'" (3.1.70-71). As if the "painting" required further justification, Quicksands declares

> This (which is sacred) is for sins prevention.
>   Illustrious persons, nay, even Queens themselves
>   Have, for the glory of a nights presentment,
>   To grace the work, suffered as much as this. (3.1.96-97).

Accepting her situation, Millicent insists upon a "Maid for private service" as her "breeding has not been to serve myselfe" (3.1.153-55). Fortune smiles on the hapless wife and Phillis arrives at Quicksands door seeking employment. Quicksands listens to Phillis' story and decides to employ her as Millicent's maid.

As the time allotted Millicent draws to a close, Quicksands decides to revenge his wedding night humiliation by a group of gentlemen with an elaborate scheme designed to "display" his new wife (the merchant has put out that Millicent ran off and eventually died). When the gallants stop at his house, he tells the men that he is "mortified to beauty / Since [his] wife's death," and that he has taken an oath "not [to] keep a face / Better than this under my roof" (4.3.69-72). Quicksands then introduces the men to "Catelyna" his new wife. One of the men, Nathaniel (who it turns out seduced and abandoned Phillis), quickly becomes enamored, declaring that Catelyna "is the handsomest Rogue / I have ere seen yet of a deed of darkness" (4.3.85-86). Nathaniel's final words, of course, pun the action of Quicksands in trying to disguise his wife. And, as all too often happens in comedy, it is the aged husband who becomes the "butt" of his deception, In Brome's script, interestingly enough, Nathaniel becomes duped as well; for, as the night progresses, Millicent and Phillis devise a plan that allows the women to achieve the upper hand. Pitying the unhappy bride, Phillis offers to assume Millicent's identity, allowing the young bride to flee with Arthur who reunites her with Theophilus. Meanwhile, Phillis uses her "new" identity to re-kindle her erotic relationship with Nathaniel. The script ends with the return of the elder Meanwel, Rashley and Winlose, the dissolution of Millicent's marriage to Quicksands, and the betrothal of Nathaniel to Phillis. As for Quicksands, like Shakespeare's Shylock, the usurer is stripped of his property and the wealth he has acquired through his dealings with the gallants.

Brome's *The English Moor* joins the *Masque of Blackness* in being one of the few Renaissance and early modern text where the depiction of 'black' women is complicated by the assumption that color passing is containable.[32] In becoming "black women," Millicent and Phillis must not only prosthetically bear a different hue, they must also become convincing racial passers. In what is an unusual moment in scripts with 'black" characters, Brome has the two women use non-standard English in their exchanges with Nathaniel. When Nathaniel calls Millicent to come to him her reply is "No fee, O no, I dare a not a" (4.3.108). Nathaniel asks why and she tells him that "O noe de fine-a whit-a Gentillman-a / Cannotta a loue-a the black-a thing-a" (4.3.110-11).Virginia Mason Vaughan sees Millicent as responding "in the way she imagines a Moorish woman would speak, in pidgin English."[33] While I am in generally agreement with Vaughan's point that Brome uses the language to instantiation a very specific form of racialization, I would also add that the speech reflects a general pattern that we see whenever English playwrights want to caricaturize other European nations, especially in city comedies.[34]

Millicent's problematic English and self-effacement does not deter Nathaniel. In fact, his attraction to the "black" wife of Quicksands is in keeping with Nathaniel's personality. In an earlier conversation with Arthur Meanwel, Nathaniel boasts about his relationships with women:

> A dead one I nere coveted, that's my comfort:
>   But of all ages that are pressable;
>   From sixteen unto sixty; and of all complections
>   From the white flaxen to the tawney-Moor;
>   And of all statures between Dwarf and Giants;
>   Of all conditions, from the Doxie to the Dowsabel.
>   Of all opinions, I will not say Religious:
>   (For what make they with any?) and of all
>   Features and shapes, from the huckle-back'd Bum-creeper,
>   To the straight spiny Shop-maid in St. *Martins*.
>   Briefly, all sorts and sizes I have tasted (3.4.59-69).

Nathaniel is both incapable of discrimination in his sexual relations and of controlling his libido. Thus, the audience (and readers) are neither surprised nor wholly sympathetic when Nathaniel falls for the two women's subplot and eventually is coerced into wedding the woman he had seduced.

As color passing subjects, Millicent and Phillis exemplify the perception of sexual freedom that has come to characterize the black female body in early modern English cultural discourse. When Nathaniel suggests a "dance to a couch or a bed side" Phillis replies "I will doa my besta" (4.4.71-72). Her words indicate her clear comprehension of Nathaniel's intent, as well as her willingness to join in whatever activity he proposes. Passing as black, Phillis continues her illicit relationship with Nathaniel. It is as if she understands the intrinsic power that passing brings along with the dangers. Color passing allows her to circumvent the obstacles that 'whiteness' imposes upon the female body. In effect, she grasps the transgressive possibility that color passing offers and embraces the performative script that color passing requires. Her prosthetic skin and speech become part of the materiality of the dramatic performance and the means to achieve a re-defined performative ending: an ending that insists upon a demarcated zone where the script's internal meanings are not only put into production but also are revealed to be contestable.

In one of the few in-depth analyses of *The English Moor* and its conjoining of blackness, femininity and sexuality, Kim Hall writes that performative disguises in the script "are taken on to restore feminine 'honor,' gender-crossing is written as actual threat to the social order, while the racial crossing is not."[35] I would argue that both forms of 'crossing' are threatening. As Amy Robinson has argued, "the successful passer only disappears from view insofar as she appears [to her audience] to be the category into which she has passed" or, I would add, *from* which she has passed.[36] Because blackness is represented in the script as temporary and 'washable', it is easy to view its significance as moral commentary on Quicksands' lack of "patriarchal privilege" despite his wealth and marriage into the Christian community rather than a disruption of "patriarchal privilege."[37] Even if "whiteness" is restored the performance by Millicent and Phillis (as well as the actors performing the roles) leaves visible traces of the permeability of color as a racializing predicate. What is readily apparent in *The English Moor's* use of color passing is the fact that far from creating a sense of homogeneity the use of blackface reveals the permeability of the racial boundaries. When Millicent and Phillis enter "white-fac'd" it is with the full understanding, by both audience and the characters themselves, that racial identity is performative.

Nowhere is this more strikingly demonstrated than in Quicksands' masque. Determined to return the insult given him by the gallants (especially Nathaniel), Quicksands stages a wedding masque based on Heliodorus' novel, *Aithiopika*. The masque's storyline is loosely based on the story of Chariclea and the circumstances of her birth but with a twist. The masque begins with the spectacle of "Phillis (black and) gorgeously deck't with jewels' being led by an "Inductor like a Moor" into the gentlemen's presence. Unlike the spectacle of Jonson's *Masque of Blackness*, Quicksands' masque does not represent a longing for whiteness among the Ethiopians; on the contrary, there is a genuine anxiety about the color: "the Queen of Ethiop dreampt upon a night / Her black womb should bring forth a virgin white" (4.4.14-15). As the Inductor makes clear,

> For tis no better then a Prodegy
> To have white children in a black countrey.
> So 'twas decreed that if the child prov'd white,
> It should be made away. O cruel spight!
> The Queen cry'd out, and was delivered
> Of child black as you see: Yet Wizards sed
> That if this damsel liv'd married to be
> To a white man, she should be white as he (4.4.25-32).

Quicksands' masque is designed not just to entertain but also to reveal his authority over the gallants and his wife's sexuality.

The masque fails to provide Quicksand what he desires for two reasons: his wife escapes the marriage and Nathaniel's libidinous assault. Millicent, aided by a sympathetic Phillis, confounds Quicksands' plan to use his wife as a means to patriarchal privilege. Enlisting the aid of Arthur, Millicent, now in whiteface, flees both her marriage and the alienation that it imposed on her. Her departure also precipitates the restoration of Phillis's honor as well. Impersonating Millicent, Phillis is presented to the gallants by the Inductor, who declares that "The careful Queen, conclusion for to try, / Sent her to merry *England* charily / (The fairest Nation man yet ever saw) / To take a husband" (4.4.35-38). After rejecting each of the gallants, the Inductor selects Quicksands: "This is the worthy man, whose wealth and wit, / To make a white one, must the black mark hit" (4.4.59-60). In the end, it is not Quicksands who "the black mark hit" but Nathaniel who leads Phillis to "dance to a couch or a bed side."

The language of the masque (presumably written by Quicksands) clearly invites the type of punning interjections that exemplify the gallants', especially Nathaniel, ideological and social contempt for

Quicksands. When the Inductor recites that the Ethiopian Queen's "white dreame filld their [the King and his peers] with feares," Nathaniel appears to mishear "black heads" for "blockheads" (4.4.18-19). Brome does not allow the gallants to have the last word, as the Inductor's quick reply indicates, "Black heads I sayd. I'll come to you anon."[38] Brome seemingly does not trust the audience to grasp the pun or desiring to push it further as Testy interrupts, "he puts the blockheads on'hem grosly." The linguistic movement between "black heads" and "blockheads" occurs both visually (reading the printed text) and aurally (the actors' speech), the impact is quite different. The words are most likely uttered rapidly by the Inductor, and Nathaniel's declaration suggests that the short vowel sound in "black" as spoken by the Inductor may reflect a regional accent and thus produces the short vowel sound of 'block' for Nathaniel. Ideologically, both words indicate a lack: for the "block head" it is commonsense or quick understanding; for the "black head" it is the absence of whiteness, which in turn is indicative of a lack of quick understanding or commonsense. Nathaniel's "whoreson Blockheads" – assuming that the actors made certain that the pronunciations of the two terms were indistinguishable, becomes a defining comic moment as the theatre audience tries to discern who the true "blockhead" will prove to be, Quicksands or Nathaniel.

From the moment Quicksands chooses to use blackness as a defense against infidelity he sets himself up for failure and ridicule. Though his "black" wife is capable of producing a "white" child, Quicksands ultimately is deprived of that patriarchal pleasure. In the case of Nathaniel, despite his projected air of superiority, he becomes as much a dupe as his nemesis. When Quicksands' masque begins an "actor like a Moore [leads] in Phillis, black, & brauely deckt" (4.4.s.d.) Believing that the beautiful, bejeweled Moor to be Quicksands' 'new' bride, Nathaniel embarks on a plan of seduction.[39] The masque's use of dance as a concluding device allows Nathaniel to draw the passing Phillis aside while Quicksands deal with the unexpected arrival of his "bastard" son.[40] When Quicksands' 'bride' is discovered "lying together" with Nathaniel by the Inductor, the couple are brought before Quicksands. Nathaniel admits to Quicksands that he has bedded the Moor, loves her "and will justify my Act." Quicksands' ensuing despair is palpable and when asked confesses that the "Moor" "is my wife, Gentlemen." Prodded by the gentlemen in his house, he admits that he disguised her on purpose and declares that he will seek a divorce. Nathaniel, of course, is delighted – "Now I applaud my act, twas sweet & braue" (4.4.207).

Act Five of *The English Moor* brings resolution to the script's complicated plot lines and its use of color passing. Upon their return to London the elder Winlose, Rashley, and Meanwel discover the various crises that have come to afflict their individual and collective households and make their way to Quicksands the morning after Quicksands believes Nathaniel has made him a cuckold. Quicksands discloses to those present the details of his scheme to protect his honor. He also admits that his wife "lives, and is that strumpet" – most likely pointing to Phillis (5.3.44-45). The men's shock is evident in Meanwel's words, "That Moor, there? / Did you wed her since your fair wives decease?" ((5.3.46-47). Quicksands responds affirmatively and explains that her blackness "is but an artificial tincture / Laid by my jealousie upon her face" (5.3.49-50) Testy, believing the "Moor" to be his niece, orders that Phillis be removed and "instant trial be made / To take the blackness off" (5.3.57-58). While they wait, the men negotiate and determine her fate: Testy asks of Nathaniel, knowing that the gallant seduced the woman he every now believes to be Quicksands' wife Millicent, "are you content / To take this woman . . . If she be found no Moor to be your Wife, / In holy marriage to restore her honour" (5.3.70-73). Nathaniel agrees, even going so far as to promise that he is willing to "take her as she is, / Not as your Neece, but as his counterfeit servant, / Hoping he'le give me with her all shee beares about her" (5.3.84-87). Just after Quicksands agrees to Nathaniel's request, the stage directions state "Enter Phillis white."

A shocked Nathaniel curses and says, "the devil looks ten times worse with a white face, / Give me it black again" (5.3.100-101). In other words, he prefers Phillis' blackness to her "natural" hue. However, Nathaniel's words also highlights an unspoken anxiety over his inability to recognize what he assumed was a stable racial signifier. In asking for the devil's face to "black again," he not only displays his anger at being duped but also the faultline when appearance is expected to function as a safe and inviolable predicator of racial identity. In other words, Nathaniel assumed that he could trust his "eyes" – that what he sees is actual what is. Thus when Quicksands announces that the "Moor" is actually his wife Millicent, Nathaniel's frame of reference shifts ever so slightly. His belief that he has bedded the 'white' Millicent in her performance as a Moor allows him to accept the conditions laid down by Testy, "to take this woman now in question, / If she be found no Moor to be your Wife" (5.3.72) When the woman proves to be Phillis, Nathaniel reacts unconventionally – desiring the black woman and not the white, even with his final words. His verbal abuse of the woman he seduced continues until Testy introduces Nathaniel to Winlose, Phillis's father. At this point, Nathaniel accepts his fate and his future wife, declaring that "though Mr. Quicksands made a Mock-marriage with his English Moor, Ile not mock thee" (5.3.219-221). It is the "English Moor," the passing specter of Heliodorus' Chariclea, that marks Nathaniel's acceptance of Phillis.

The masque, not the prosthetic blackness of Millicent and Phillis, is the most troubling aspect of Richard Brome's *The English Moor*. Why did Richard Brome incorporate a storyline clearly drawn from Heliodorus' *Aithiopika*? That is, what purpose does a masque about an Ethiopian Queen, her dreams and fears of giving birth to a white child, and the reversal of the usual ending to the Queen's anxiety have to do with righting a wrong perpetrated by a pair of old men (Testy and Quicksands)? The answer may lie in the ideological message the masque is intended to convey. Brome makes clear that the audience has expectations about the dynamics of color as a racializing predicate. It is obvious that Quicksands' actions are based upon a culturally accepted view about "the biological constancy of" skin color and its knowability. However, Quicksands' use of blackface moves color passing from the metaphoric or supernatural realm that marks Jonson's *Masque of Blackness*, for example, to the everyday reality of English society. In effect, the color passing subject no longer exists in romances and idealized court drama: she walks, talks, and lives among English people.

Quicksands' manipulation of Millicent's whiteness assumes both the temporariness and ease of removal of the prosthetic device of blackface. That the device occurs as part of an actual theatrical performance and on stage before the gaze of the script's audience only reinforces this notion. What Quicksands' masque brings to light, however, is the unspoken acknowledgement is that only in fictive narratives, and only when the maternal imagination subject itself to patriarchal authority, can the biology of skin color can be contained. Otherwise, race is always inconstant. Quicksands' use of the Heliodorus' narrative offers a cogent reminder to *The English Moor*'s audience that it is only "on the uncertain terrain of . . . romance – where conditions are volatile and shifting, where acts are disturbing and disjoined from inner reality, and where words are uttered in order not to be believed – the stability imparted by the guarantee of race is crucial." [41] Brome's masque seeks to legitimate this idea and reiterate its premise that "belonging to the right race – as signaled by the biological constancy of" skin color – "guarantees the stability" of a patriarchal society. Unfortunately, the performative nature of color passing – so critical to Quicksands' plot – denies even the script's audience even this comforting thought.

Virginia Mason Vaughan writes about the masque that, "ironically, the marvelous scenario that" Quicksands envisioned "actually occurs, but not as he had planned. Phillis's sudden transformation from black to white, a tour de force for the make-up artist, is so quick as to seem miraculous. Her new appearance marks her transition from the blackened character of a fallen woman to the whitened status of gentle wife."[42] The script's conclusion sees Millicent and Theophilus reunited and the cross-dressing Dionisia restored to female clothing and committed to a "strict life . . . [that] shall render [her] / Some way deserving th'honour of a husband" (5.3.204-207). Blackness reveals itself to be a performative act, disruptive sexuality has been contained and the intruding other (the Jewish usurer/merchant) has been thwarted. Thus, Vaughan concludes, *The English Moor* "uses the

Moorish disguise to set up, in other words, a black-white binary and then, in a climatic moment, seemingly dissolve it, erasing blackness and constructing thereby a harmonious, homogeneous white community" (120). Would that it were so easy.

Quicksands' masque, as a theatrical device, a narrative of racialization, and a reaffirmation of patriarchal social order, reverses the details of Heliodorus' romance. In the *Aithiopika*, the baby is born white. The Queen entrusts the infant to her Eunuch who then flees Ethiopia. Eventually, the girl Chariclea is adopted by the Greek Caricles and raised as his daughter. In Quicksands' masque, the Ethiopian Queen gives birth to a child "as black as you see" and thus was not obligated to end the child's life. In addition, the Inductor reports a prophecy "that if this damsel liv'd married to be / To a white man, she should be white as he" (4.4.31-32). We should recall that while these words are being uttered, the Moorish Phillis is standing before the men invited by Quicksands. The prophecy, of course, represents what Amy Robinson describes as the "privileged knowledge" that those in the know (the "in-group") possess.[43] The Inductor, hired by Quicksands is aware that the Moorish woman involved in the entertainment is important in some way to Quicksands. Quicksands, author of the masque, "knows" that the female Moor's true color is "white." Framed as it is by the Heliodorus tale, the masque suggestively calls even that knowledge into question. The later unmasking of the Moor does little to alleviate the ideological problems invoked by the masque and its presentation of racial categories.[44]

Like many of the scripts crafted during the 1630s, Richard Brome's *The English Moor* evidences an on-going political concern with England's political and social stability. Not entirely free of its class divisions yet needing ideological cohesion if it is to embark on its imperial goals, English culture exploited physiological and phenotypic differences to engender a sense of national identity. While the *Masque of Blackness* openly situated the monarchy at the center of Englishness, *The English Moor* made color the defining predicate for national identity. Both scripts' prosthetic use of blackness, however, produced performance fractures that could not entirely be concealed. Again, Molly Murray's reading of the *Masque of Blackness* seems especially pertinent here. For, as she rightfully reminds us,

> Jonson proposes two equally unstable alternatives: we can either believe that the ladies were originally black and now seek to be whitened or that they were originally white, then by their own error were made black, and now wish to be whitened again. While the endpoint in both cases is an unobjectionable fairness, the process by which that fairness must be achieved underscores the disturbing idea that color can never be fixed.[45]

Consequently, even if the scripts "were written for the elite audiences of the indoor playhouses," as Vaughan asserts, their circulation in printed form ensured that the seeming performativity of blackness became engrained in the cultural attempts to stabilize skin color as part of an ideology of racial identity. Such dramatizations of color passing in Renaissance and early modern performances, at the least, illuminates a growing sense of unease within English culture about an unmitigated use of color as a dominant predicate of race.

Where traditionally the 'blackfaced' dramatic character appears linked to a moral or religious ontology, evil, Jonson's *Masque of Blackness* and Richard Brome's *The English Moor* suggestively intimate that blackness is best understood as a complicated and complex performance.[46] In addition, these dramatic scripts must be seen as paradoxes to the normative fetishization of blackness as negative or evil that occurs in other dramatic depictions of Moors or 'blacks'.[47] Both scripts engage racial identity as if it were a romance needing to be put to rest. In using color passing as a performative intervention in the symbolic negotiation of blackness, Jonson and Brome rewrite the history of the 'white" Ethiopian or Moor. In each script, the female body is idealized and made normative as the site for the restoration of this disruptive racial body to its appropriate locus. While blackface does not make a 'white' person 'black', it does de-center the binary so that racial identity can be re-examined and reinvented. What The *English Moor* and *Masque of Blackness*, as critical texts in the evolution of the idea of race, signal is that racial identity can never truly be more than a performance.

NOTES

[1] Joseph Roach, *Cities of the Dead: Circum-Atlantic Performance* (New York: Columbia University Press, 1996), 25-26. Roach formulates his concept of "genealogies of performance" in light of "Jonathan Arac's definition, applying Nietzsche and Foucault, of a 'critical genealogy' that 'aims to excavate the past that is necessary to account for how we got here and the past that is useful for conceiving alternatives to our present condition' (2)" (25).

[2] Judith Butler, "Performative Acts and Gender Constitution: An Essay in Phenomenology and Feminist Theory" *Theatre Journal*, Vol. 40, No. 4. (Dec., 1988), 519.

[3] For discussions of race and medieval culture see Geraldine Heng, Empire of Magic: Medieval Romance and the Politics of Cultural Fantasy (Columbia University Press, 2003),Thomas Hahn, "the difference the Middle Ages Makes: Color and Race before the Modern World," *Journal of Medieval and Early Modern Studies* (2001) 31:1, 1-37, and William Chester Jordan, "Why 'Race'?", *Journal of Medieval and Early Modern Studies* (2001) 31:1, 165-173.

[4] W. B. Worthen, *Shakespeare and the Force of Modern Performance* (Cambridge: Cambridge UP, 2003), 1.

[5] Worthen, 3. Summarizing the complex arguments of J.L. Austin, Judith Butler, Andrew Parker and Eve Kosofsky Sedgwick on performativity, Worthen highlights paradoxes that emerge in the theoretical use of 'performance', performative and performativity. In particular, Worthen reminds us that dramatic performance has a materiality that includes the script but is not exclusive to it; design, objects, practices, and most significantly the human body are equal measures of the dramatic performance.

[6] Worthen, 9.

[7] Roach, 20.

[8] Dympna Callaghan, "Othello was a white man: properties of

race on Shakespeare's stage," *Alternative Shakespeares*, vol 2, ed., Terence Hawkes (London and New York: Routledge, 1996), 193.

[9] What Callaghan describes as representation, however, I would argue constitutes passing. In other words, for the English actor to don blackface and come forth on the stage as Othello is to pass as a Moor.

[10] Callaghan then looks to the issue of "cosmetic practices" which she demonstrates, "bring into sharper focus the relation between race and gender in drama, showing how whiteness becomes visible in an exaggerated white, and crucially, feminine identity" (195).

[11] Felicity Nussbaum, "The theatre of empire: racial counterfeit, racial realism" in Kathleen Wilson, ed., A *New Imperial History: Culture, Identity and Modernity in Britain and the Empire, 1660-1840* (Cambridge UP, 2004), 71.

[12] Callaghan defines "exhibition" as the practice where 'people are set forth as objects, passive and inert before the active scrutiny of the spectator, without any control over, or even necessarily consent to, the representational apparatus in which they are placed" (194).

[13] Because printed versions of the scripts generated what I would define as a literary readership, we need to think about the ideological aspects that different modes of reception create. The individuals in the theatre will have an experience that cannot be replicated by the individual reader, sitting in the comfort of her/his home, reading the script.

[14] William Shakespeare, *Titus Andronicus*, in *The Complete Works*, eds., Stanley Wells and Gary Taylor (Oxford University Press, 1988).

[15] Eldred D. Jones, *Othello's Countrymen: A Study of African in the Elizabethan and Jacobean Drama* (Oxford: Oxford University Press,1965), 56

[16] Francesca T. Royster, " 'White-limed Walls: Whiteness and Gothic Extremism in Shakespeare's *Titus Andronicus*," *Shakespeare Quarterly* 51:4 (2000), 450.

[17] Joyce Green MacDonald, "Gender, Family, and Race in Aphra Behn's *Abdelazer*," in *Aphra Behn (1640-1689) Identity, Alterity, Ambiguity*, eds. Mary Ann O'Donnell, Bernard Dhuicq, and Guyonne Leduc (Paris: L'Harmattan, 2000), 67-73.

[18] Joyce Green MacDonald, see especially pages 67-73. The result,

as Macdonald illustrates, is a curious synthesis of *Othello*, *Titus Andronicus*, and *Lust's Dominion*.

[19] This hypothesis is true only if one defines race in terms of skin color; if one considered race to be multilevel, including the racial distinction initially constituted between the 'barbarous' Goths and the 'civil' Romans, one would reach a somewhat different conclusion. Aaron becomes merely a third category of racial identity and, as MacDonald rightly argues, not entirely clear what motives his 'revenge'—although the loss of his public place in Tamora's life might be a factor.

[20] For an extended analysis of *Abdelazer* see Green Macdonald's *Women and Race in Early Texts* (Cambridge UP 2002).

[21] Amy Robinson, 721.

[22] For detailed discussions of cultural, political and gender effect of *The Masque of Blackness* see Kim F. Hall; Stephen Orgel, Clare McManus, Bernadette Andrea etc.

[23] Dudley Carleton, *Dudley Carleton to John Chamberlain, 1603-1624: Jacobean Letters*, ed. Maurice Lee, Jr. (New Brunswick: Rutgers, 1972), 68. Bernadette Andrea's argument (*English Literary Renaissance*, (1999) 29:2, 246-281) that Kim Hall's reading of the masque as the politics of authority does not, in my view, hold much merit. Carleton's words reflect a racializing tendency that continues today. See also Mary Floyd-Wilson in *English Literary Renaissance*, 28:2 (1998),183-209.

[24] Hall, 129.

[25] For a different reading of this linkage of color and gender, see Gail Kern Paster, "The Unbearable Coldness of Female Being: Women's Imperfection in the Humoral Economy," *English Literary Renaissance*, Summer 1998 28:3, esp. 438-9. Paster's assertion that, "by comparison with sexual difference, skin color is a non-essential form of difference which can be removed by combined beneficence of ritual washing and the temperate warm of King James's sunshine," must of course be viewed as operating on a symbolic plane only, especially given the universal assumptions about the permanency of blackness that surface in the written discourses of Renaissance and early modern England.

[26] Bernadette Andrea, Black Skin, the Queen's Masques: Africanist

Ambivalence and Feminine Author(ity) in the Masques of Blackness and Beauty," *English Literary Renaissance* 29 (1999), 249.

[27] Clare McManus, *Women on the Renaissance stage: Anna of Denmark and Female Masquing in the Stuart Court 1590-1619* (Manchester UP, 2002), 11.

[28] Hardin Aasand, "'To Blanch an Ethiop, and Revive a Corse': Queen Anne and the *Masque of Blackness*," *Studies in English Literature*, 1500-1900 32:2 (1992), 271-285, 271.

[29] Kim F. Hall, *Things of Darkness: Economies of Race and Gender in Early Modern England* (Ithaca and London: Cornell University Press, 1995), 5.

[30] Murray, 438.

[31] Richard Brome, *The English Moore; or The Mock-Mariage*, ed., Sara Jayne Steen (Columbia: University of Missouri Press, 1983). All citations are from this text and noted parenthetically.

[32] While there are a number of scripts that include the representation or depiction of Moorish or black women as characters, these two scripts approach the phenomenon of color passing as co-exist with the intertwining of color and race.

[33] Vaughan, 118.

[34] For example, I would also question Vaughan's reading of Millicent's and Phillis's speech usage "as a burlesque of African dialects" when it is impossible for us to know how people of African ancestry spoke English. Vaughan offers no linguistic or historical evidence to support her assumption that Millicent and Phillis copied actual speech patterns of Africans.

[35] Hall, 174.

[36] Amy Robinson, Amy Robinson, "It Takes One to Know One: Passing and Communities of Common Interest," *Critical Inquiry* 20 (Summer 1994), 715-736, 718.

[37] I make this point in response to Hall's discussion. It seems to me that whether "color passing" is by choice, imposed or by accident, once it is assumed the performativity of race resists cultural containment.

[38] In her edition Sara Jayne Steen omits Testy's line, though it is in Brome's 1658 printed edition.

[39] In her introduction, Sara Jayne Steen describes this moment as "Phillis, beautifully dressed as an exotic Egyptian princess and wearing splendid jewels, is escorted onto the stage by a Moorish actor. Brome's script does not use the word "Egyptian" in reference to Phillis, only the word black. Strikingly, Steen's comments reflect the same practice of ethnic elision that we often find in texts such as Brome's.

[40] The arrival of Buzzard, Quicksands' former servant, and Arnold, Rashly's servant pretending to be Quicksands' bastard son is a plot conceived by Nathaniel. The confusion that ensues allows Nathaniel to slip away with the Moorish Phillis, using dance as an opportunistic moment.

[41] Geraldine Heng, *Empire of Magic: Medieval Romance and the Politics of Cultural Fantasy* (New York: Columbia University Press, 2003), 235. Though the subject of Heng's analysis is the medieval romance, her argument is applicable to Brome's script especially as it makes use of Heliodorus' Chariclea narrative.

[42] Vaughan, 120.

[43] Robinson, 720.

[44] Here, I am referring to the significance of a pregnant Queen. Queen Anne's performance in the *Masque of Blackness* generated aesthetic criticism among the court; what is not clear is whether there was an concomitant yet unarticulated anxiety about her unborn child – an anxiety exemplified in the Ethiopian Queen's fear recounted in *The English Moor*'s masque. The Queen's fear (and the Ethiopian community) and anxiety prove stronger than biology – effectively changing the potential whiteness of the child to a required blackness.

[45] Murray, 439

[46] In chapter four of *Performing Blackness on English Stages, 1500-1800*, Virginia Mason Vaughan offers a cogent discussion of the way dramatists writing during the reign of Charles I made use of the color passing female in dramatic scripts. Most of the dramatists wrote for either the theatre company Queen Henrietta Marie's Men or for court masques. In all likelihood, the use of the color passing female was inspired by Queen Anne's performance in *Masque of Blackness*.

[47] One of the more fascinating (and problematic) aspect of Vaughan's book is the way it organizes and differentiates between the

dramatic works that depict "actual" Moors – *Othello, Titus Andronicus, Merchant of Venice, The White Devil* and *Masque of Blackness* for example – and the scripts that depict "Europeans disguised as black Moors" – *The Lost Lady, The Parliament of Love, The Fatal Contract,* and *The English Moor,* when in fact what the performance audience sees are "Europeans disguised as black Moors." For all that Vaughan's analysis is guided by the desire to reveal the intersections between performative blackness and "real" blackness, her reading can only reiterate performative blackness bound as it is by theatrical practices.

COLORING THE PAST, CONSIDERATIONS ON OUR FUTURE

This essay is not one I thought to write when asked to contribute to this issue. My expectation was that I would submit a simple revision of "Coloring the Past, Rewriting Our Future: RaceB4Race" (the keynote lecture from which this paper emerges), only along scholarly lines. Yet, as history has long proven, what people intend and what they actually produce may be very different. I now find myself in a different writing space and less wedded to academic rhetoric. This essay, then, is a thought piece, a forward-facing reflection on the public humanities. It is also autobiographical in certain respects, since I am an academic who once struggled to find a place within the academy but no longer do. Thus, this meditation/mediation has two parts. Part One is retrospective: a look back at my place in an effort to decolonize my professional relationship to the academy and the discipline where my intellectual efforts are housed, the field of early modern English literature and culture (where I once landed not fully by choice). Part Two is a letter to and for Black, Indigenous, Peoples of Color (BIPOC), colleagues and allies.

On Periodization

. . .

My initial professional interest was in medieval culture with an end date of Elizabeth I's death. I was intrigued by the political, cultural, and literary dynamics generated by the emergence of a national literature in the wake of the Norman/French colonization of England. My doctoral institution had a somewhat traditional scheme for graduate work. A student chose a field (medieval, renaissance, eighteenth century, Victorian, modern, which included British and American literatures), a theoretical framework, and a topic. Of course, this occurred only after the study of the literature of all these eras. Despite my intent to study the Middle Ages, I ended up working on later periods. At the time, I assumed this was a result of my being an older Black woman who wasn't enamored with the trappings of the Ivory Tower or with the idea that literature could be so easily parsed, that there wasn't a degree of continuity beyond the shared use of English among the so-called periods.

Although it wasn't entirely clear to me at the time, I have since learned my decision was an effect of the often unquestioned form of academic gatekeeping known as periodization. The redirection nonetheless proved immeasurably valuable as it made me the activist-scholar/humanist that I have come to be. The gatekeeping also led to intellectual work and publications that contributed to the emergence of my commitment to the study of race in early modern English literature and culture. In a piece titled "Obscured by dreams: Race, Empire and Shakespeare's *A Midsummer Night's Dream*" (the only of my publications about which I will still unapologetically declare, "Damn, that was good"), I put it this way:

> Somehow, giving our silent *mestizo* [the Indian Boy] the voice of another *mestizo*, rather than that of an academic like myself, seems fitting. The words of this half-Scottish/half-Irish changeling stand as a vivid reminder that it was in the "antique fables," the "fairy toys" produced in the colonizing dreams of Europeans, that the "shaping fantasies" of modern imperialism began. These words are a reminder that it will be the *mestizos*—the racialized descendants of those who framed the lexicon and practices of modern imperialism—who, dealing with it, will write the final epilogue to the shaping fantasy of race.[1]

"Obscured by dreams" was preceded by *Women, "Race," and Writing in the Early Modern Period* (coedited with Patricia Parker for Routledge Press, 1994). *Women, "Race," and Writing* reflected, though we didn't conceptualize it as such at the time, an attempt to grapple with the emerging field of critical race theory and the idea of intersectionality while privileging our "own voices" (women). The collection of cross-disciplinary essays illuminated the intersection of gender, racial ideologies, and settler colonialism as the early modern embarked on a campaign of global expansion. Even now, the impact of that expansion remains visibly etched on the descendants of individuals and communities subjugated as part of colonial and racist practices.

The final piece in this triptych was a University of California Humanities Research Institute residency group, "Theorizing Race in Pre- and Early Modern Contexts." Faculty members of this group represented traditionally articulated periods and disciplines: classics, medieval, early modern, literature, history, and art history. What we quickly realized was that race and racial thinking didn't quite fit into those rubrics. Two decades later, the problem of race and periodization continues, largely due to academic gatekeeping. On the surface, it seems illogical to insist on rigid categories and temporalities when it comes to premodern cultures. As a doctoral student in English literature, I was expected to focus on a "century" or an "age" (sixteenth or seventeenth, Elizabethan or Stuart). Never one for conformity, I committed to something like a century—one that began circa 1560 and ended circa 1690. My rationale was one of continuity, especially since some writers and their careers spanned the reigns of at least two monarchs (the writings of William Shakespeare, John Donne, and Ben Jonson, for example, were Elizabethan and Jacobean). Also, I had discovered the writings of Aphra Behn. Periodization made no sense to me during my graduate school days, and it is definitely illogical when it comes to considering race in premodern cultures. Despite all efforts to construct monolithic historical narratives about race's origins (tied to the transatlantic trafficking of enslaved African peoples), transnational and cross-cultural permutations existed pre-

Enlightenment. In addition, the European construction of racial taxonomies was an ongoing process subject to fits and starts, evolution and entrenchment. My fascination with this process, itself a repudiation of periodization, has not waned. In fact, it calls into question the notion that periodization is the best structure for historical analysis. It is this questioning, this interrogation of centuries of arbitrary enclosures, that Premodern Critical Race Studies (PCRS) has made visible, and for those who want the "origins story," here it is.

Premodern Race Studies

Before the 1980s, the study of race in premodern cultures sat very much on the margins, localized by the focus on an isolated text or character. Traditional historiography's presumptions about the absence of peoples of color on the European continent fed the illusion of race's insignificance in premodern cultures. In addition, the argument that race is an Enlightenment concept—ideologically, scientifically, and politically linked to the enslavement and/or extrication of indigenous African and US peoples from their lands during European imperialism in the eighteenth and nineteenth centuries—led to an inattentiveness to premodern race-making and racism. The exception: characters like Aaron, Ithamore, or Othello were granted status as standard-bearers for an emerging ideology of racial thinking. What this meant for individuals arguing that race, racial taxonomies, and racism were fundamental to premodern European cultures was a form of academic pushback. The study of race in "medieval," "renaissance," or "ancient" literatures and history was viewed as an imposition of a modern sensibility, a political agenda. The study of pre-Enlightenment race was considered a "niche" topic, problematic when it came to publication, employment, and tenure or promotion. Non-white graduate students interested in studying premodern race were gently discouraged or openly denied. So we wrote about humanist values, literary conventions and tropes, and genres.

While there was no single cataclysmic explosion, several detonations silenced naysayers and signaled a fundamental theoretical shift in the study of the past: Martin Bernal's *Black Athena: The Afroasiatic Roots of Classical Civilization*, Kim Hall's *Things of Darkness: Economies of Race and Gender in Early Modern England*, and *Women, "Race," and Writing in the Early Modern Period*, eds. Margo Hendricks and Patricia Parker.[2] The publication of these books challenged a white-centric cultural, literary, economic, and philosophical vision of premodern cultures and the modes of periodization that defined the humanities. In essence, what these three studies did was expose the entrenched tenets of white supremacy inside the academy, especially during the heyday of the so-called Culture Wars. What emerged from this critical intervention was, I would argue, a theoretical foundation that would become premodern critical race studies.

What *Black Athena* brought to the table was attention to the fabrication of a white "Western Civilization" formation. *Things of Darkness* and *Women, "Race," and Writing* pushed the critique even further by insisting on the intersectionality of race, gender, and class as part of global capitalist expansion, especially with the advent of white settler colonialism and its anti-Black and anti-Indigenous campaigns. The genius of *Things of Darkness* and *Women, "Race," and Writing* as *analyses* was the "positional subjectivity" from which the authors and contributors approached their topics; that is, there was an authorial awareness/self-awareness of the intersecting threads of race, class, gender, and sexuality. What sets these works apart is how the authors situate themselves and their analyses in relation to a historical past and the sovereign bodies that make up that past—in essence, a bidirectional gaze.

A bidirectional gaze is one that looks inward even as it looks outward. As bell hooks observed, "Spaces of agency exist . . . wherein we can both interrogate the gaze of the Other but also look back, and at one another, naming what we see. The 'gaze' has been and is a site of resistance for colonized . . . people globally."[3] The tendency to dissociate from this mode of interrogation is, in my view, what differentiates PCRS from its "white" cousin, Premodern Race Studies

(PRS). What often goes amiss with PRS is the looking back and naming what the inquirer "sees": white supremacy and whiteness as a normative marker that somehow eludes race. This practice is most visible in the arguments for seeing blood, religion, gender, or ethnicity as racial taxonomies. These positions fail to consider capitalism's use of colorism, anti-Blackness, or anti-Indigeneity to further its economic and ideological (?) aims. The argument for seeing race as a trope does little to dismantle white supremacy as settler colonialism's hegemonic pulse. When somatic color becomes immaterial or just a difference to be noted in the same way as religion or gender or ethnicity, the exercise leaves intact an unexamined default. When deployed this way, gender or religion becomes a racial category. While race's premodern semantic fluidity is unquestionable, by the seventeenth century (at least in England) race as a purely biophysical label was establishing firm roots. What's lost in the premodern analyses of race as "fill in the blank" is the connection between a somatic, sovereign Indigenous body and the pernicious effects of settler colonialism and capitalism.

Under these conditions, PRS engages in a theoretical and political failure to "look back," to critically examine one's white subjectivity and positionality in relation to the non-white bodies that gave race its currency during the advent of settler colonialism. Instead, much of PRS operates in the same manner as white settler colonialism. The study of race requires no "oppositional gaze" or "intersectionality" because "race" is already captured as a "fill in the blank" "structural event."[4] Because the practitioners of PRS are generally white academics who either "shop" fixed figures of premodern anti-Blackness or redefine "race" as gender, blood, ethnicity, or (a personal favorite) "humoral" conditions, these individuals rarely dissect the white academic subjectivity they occupy—a position that serves as an uncontested normativity. In the end, PRS leaves in place whiteness in whatever form it appears (male, female, English, Catholic, humoral) while simultaneously claiming to illuminate the importance of racial taxonomies to premodern cultures. In these scholarly narratives, both academic and historical, Black, Brown, Indigenous, and Asian bodies become marginalized once again.

In my opinion, PRS is fundamentally written by and for white academics. Increasingly, scholars whose publication history shows no attention to "race" have suddenly become experts. While the focus on race is not a problem, what is troubling is the representation of this body of work as innovative or groundbreaking when, in fact, it is derivative. PRS assumes no foundational work on the study of race exists before it comes into play. If these scholars recognize the preexistence of a cohort of Black, Brown, and Indigenous scholars working on the subject since the 1980s, this preexistence is often relegated to a footnote surrounded by whiteness. Or worse, this body of scholarship is entirely ignored. What is left in place is a metanarrative that obliges academia's insistence on the sanctity of territoriality, periodization, genres, and a conceptualization of premodern individualism defined in terms of whiteness. In effect, this "logic of elimination" results in an affirmation of white supremacist thinking.

Premodern Race Studies (aka Intellectual Settler Colonialism)

Of course, the irony is that this logic accords with the ideologies of white supremacy and its insistence on what Lehua Yim described to me in conversation as the "arrogance of assumption" embedded in the inclusive "we." This "we" envisions itself acting inclusively, engaged in the political work of furthering PRS by structuring race as an event without actually confronting the presence of the non-white body. Nowhere is this better demonstrated than in Harvard University's Edx description for its online course "Shakespeare's Othello: The Moor": "In this course, we'll read William Shakespeare's *Othello* and discuss the play from a variety of perspectives. The goal of the course is not to cover everything that has been written on *Othello*. Rather, it is to find a single point of entry to help us think about the play as a whole. Our entry point is storytelling . . . . From lectures filmed on-location in Venice, London, and Stratford-upon Avon to conversations with artists, academics, and librarians at Harvard, students will have unprecedented access to a range of resources for 'unlocking' Shakespeare's classic play."[5] This online course is evocative of a white settler-colonialist move in the way it creates not a curated understanding of the implications of premodern discourses of race, anti-Blackness, or racial construction but a vision of white subjectivity. Through its "logic of elimination," this course decenters the theoretical, historical, and analytical work done by PCRS scholars to unpack the racism at the heart of Shakespeare's *Othello*. In effect, by focusing on the play as a matter of "storytelling" and framing it as a filmic piece, the film's professorial guide, Stephen Greenblatt, ensures that the spectatorial gaze is always white-centered. Othello's Black sovereignty becomes mediated through a white filter so that his enslavement is processed as a colonizing event: rinse and repeat, again and again.

What Greenblatt's presence and the course itself underscore is the problematic myopia that informs traditional engagements with premodern race—a failure to grasp a connective tissue between a resurgence of societal white supremacy and academic readings that envision race as a fluid trope capable of marking color, religion, ethnicity, gender, class or simply difference. Surprisingly, none of the proponents of race as a shifting trope recognize the troubling anti-Blackness and anti-Indigenous erasures their work does. Or perhaps they do.

To Protect and Serve: Periodization, Race, and Academic Gatekeeping

The phrase "To Protect and Serve" originally emerged in 1955. As part of its public relations campaign, the Los Angeles Police Department (LAPD) emblazoned the phrase on its vehicles, its letterhead, and its badges. While seemingly innocuous, the words proved to be contradictory over the ensuing decades. In 1965, the LAPD (and the National Guard) rolled into Watts "to protect and serve" Los Angeles in the face of Black anger over policing and racial injustice. In 1992 the LAPD rode in "to protect and serve" during an uprising that followed the police beating of Rodney King. For many communities, the idealization of police as protectors and servants has never been a reality, which is why we're now witnessing national and international uprisings in response to the problematic ideology of "to protect and serve." It may appear odd to suggest an analogy between a police state and the Ivory Tower, but, as I hope to illustrate, the impulse behind the phrase "to protect and serve" is very much evident in the academy. The difference: the choice of weapons. In what follows, I want to consider what academic gatekeeping means to the Black, Indigenous, Latinx, Asian, and marginalized voices at the forefront of premodern critical race studies.

In an open letter published in the Arizona Center for Medieval and Renaissance Studies' The *Sundial*, "It's Time to End the Publishing Gate-keeping!," the RaceB4Race Executive Board described the difficulty medievalists of color faced when, as a group, they proposed several sessions on race and antiracism to the International Congress of Medieval Studies (ICMS) in 2018. Their proposal was rejected and, after a public outcry, RaceB4Race, a series of conferences and a networking community, was convened in response to ICMS's rejection. Board members behind the RaceB4Race initiative received an invitation to submit a cluster of essays to *PMLA*. After review, the submission was rejected. The rationale: the proposal, while addressing "an important topic and . . . nicely framed . . . . would have benefitted from including some opposing perspectives to join in the debate." The letter writers' response is worth citing in full:

> We were disappointed and confused by this rejection, especially by the suggestion that the range of contributors was "constrained," given that our contributors' expertise ranges from the history of medieval studies to slavery in early modern England to 17th-century French court ballets. In what sense could our range possibly read as "constrained"? Perhaps "constrained" in that we did not include some older, more established white men to validate our calls for antiracist methodologies and pedagogies? But even more troubling was the suggestion that the editors were expecting and imagining "opposing perspectives" to an antiracist collection. What kind of "opposing perspectives" were

imagined exactly? The cluster's intervention pointed towards an entirely new direction for premodern studies, and its push for a radical transformation of the field was dismissed with a one-liner that hinged on ellipses and illogic. This second rejection felt eerily similar to the first by the International Congress of Medieval Studies.[6]

To argue for "opposing perspectives" or "rigorous debate" is a well-honed weapon designed to police BIPOC voices and careers and "to protect and serve" a privileged segment of the academy. My academic moments with this form of policing are not numerous, but they remain part of my psyche: the times when I was told (encouraged) to temper my analysis, to mute my anger, to acknowledge the important "white voices" in the field, to not criticize "white literary scholars" who erased the genealogy of non-white scholars who initiated the critical study of race in premodern studies. As many BIPOC researchers/scholars/faculty can attest, these moments come as parts of a complex academic gatekeeping system, including but not exclusive to publications. This system is far more insidious when it comes to employment and retention.

The gag order that is anonymity (peer reviews for essays, anonymous letters for tenure and promotion reviews, and the silence that often follows hiring decisions) has long served to protect not a system of fairness but a code of silencing and abuse within the academy. With the advent of social media, especially Twitter, the code has begun to unravel. During the summer of 2020, a Twitter hashtag, #BlackintheIvory, surfaced to document the experiences of Black faculty, students, and staff in academia. As a Black academic and a senior Shakespearean, I found the accounts painfully familiar and at times difficult to read. Particularly egregious was the degree of anti-Black behavior by non-Black IPOC academics. When a senior South Asian professor chooses to berate a senior Black American professor in public for the "race work" the Black woman does, it is obvious that academic privilege and anti-Blackness are at work. On a micro level, the critique has much more in common with white supremacist thought than postcolonial politics. Coupled with the ubiquitous academic Karens and Beckys who abandon allyship when their privilege is threatened, this type of policing of BIPOC faculty and academic fields becomes commonplace and not always restricted to early career scholars.

A sense of the need for political solidarity has probably led many to ignore the senior BIPOC and "white allies" who engage in "to protect and serve" acts of microaggression in the academy, and especially in premodern studies. We turn a blind eye to the non-Black faculty who quietly drive Black graduate students from their departments. We over- look the impact of the star system on Black, Indigenous, Latinx, and Asian scholars whose rise to the top is mercurial and often at the expense of another marginalized person. While some forms of "to protect and serve" come at the microlevel, more often they are openly visible and still not challenged. We need to ask ourselves: are we invested in protecting our professional cache if we become de facto allies to white supremacy through our anti-Black, anti-Indigenous, anti-Brown, anti-Asian micro and macroaggressions?

In addition, we need to consider whether we have lost sight of what it means to be marginalized, contained, denigrated, or niched for the work that made our careers. Have we done enough to protect BIPOC early career researchers and independent scholars from pernicious attacks or retaliation not just by white academics but by our BIPOC colleagues? Isn't it time for senior BIPOC scholars to "protect and serve" the BIPOC and other marginalized scholars whose decision to pursue an academic career is often a direct result of our visible presence? Have we taken a stand against the protective badge of anonymity, long a tool of academic white supremacy, not just in terms of publication but also in employment decisions (hiring, tenuring, and promotion)? Do we recognize that our silence implicates us as well in the policing of the academy?

The adage "Not all skinfolk are kinfolk" is an evergreen truth, and we need to remember that anti-Blackness and other forms of racism can and do appear in unexpected corners. It is also important to remember that allyship does not wear an "I support Black, Indigenous, and Peoples of Color" button. True allyship is a different kind of commitment to protect and serve all levels of a BIPOC's academic career. One of the most important allies to PCRS is and has been Peter

Erickson and Clark Hulse, whose *Early Modern Visual Culture: Representation, Race, and Empire in Renaissance England* (2000) shifted ground at a time when very few white pre and early modernists were engaged in critical race studies. I highlight this issue because, at this juncture in the history of PCRS, senior BIPOC and marginalized academics who consider themselves committed to the field must ask the most important question in their professional lives: who are we here to protect and serve if not the next generation?

A Brief Interlude titled *Desterrado*

Willoughby Plantation, Barbadoes 1649
   The young girl sat at the feet of her black nurse, entranced as the woman's aged fingers moved swiftly and certainly through the cane husks, bringing to life a past nearly forgotten. "Tell me once more, Nana. Tell me of the Negress Maria." "In the veins of the Negress Maria flowed the blood of kings. Both she and her sister (who was called Phillipa) were taken as young girls, no older than you. Maria was perhaps fifteen. The Spaniard who stole her kept her as his mistress. Her beauty bewitched an Englishman and it was he who taught her the secrets of love and hate. Francis Drake. El Draco," the old woman spat.
   The woman stroked the girl's dark hair. "Drake fathered Francisco, your mother's grandsire, on the Negress Maria then left her to die on an island with no women to care for her. None to bring the babe into the world. They lived, though. Mother and child. Francisco was always a wild seed, not African like his mother but not English like his father. The Spanish call them Mulattos, little mules. He was of that temper. When an English ship came to the island to take on food and water, Francisco persuaded the captain to take him on. Maria's son worked hard for the merciless white man and once the ship returned to England Francisco left the barbaric captain and went in search of El Draco, his father. Alas, 'twas not to be. El Draco was dead and with no mother, no father, nor lands, Francisco was lost, Desterrado."
   "Exile," the child mouthed.
   "Exile," the old woman repeated. "Drake's child begat a child and that child begat a child, you, and with each generation the Negress Maria's blood grew thinner and Drake's stronger. Francisco knew that those of his blood

would wear the whiteness of his father and pass among the English as one of them. Before his death, he made his daughter Elizabeth swear to remember his line. His daughter's daughter was to be called Afra. For the dark earth that nurtured her ancestors. Aphra. To remind her that, despite her whiteness, she was of the land, of Africa, was forever indigenous and mestizaje, forever desterrado."

This fictional account grew out of an archival/textual encounter with a footnote that has become indelibly etched in my memory and inspired a different writing path: romance fiction. In 1577, Francis Drake sailed along the coast of Central America, near Panama, towards Guatulco. On the way, he captured a Spanish vessel bound for Lima. The Spanish ship carried supplies for the colony and a Spanish nobleman, Don Francisco de Zarate. Holding the Don captive for three days, Drake showed de Zarate "much favour"—even going so far as to give the Spaniard "the poop to sleep in."[7] According to John Drake, the elder Drake's nephew, Francis Drake, delivered the Don safely to Guatulco and, as part of the ransom for the Don's release, Drake "took from Don Francisco a negress named Maria, and the pilot of said ship" (*N* 31). After replenishing his vessel, Drake "set sail with men of [his] own *nation*, the said negress Maria, a negro whom they had taken at Païta, and another they took at Guatulco, besides one they had brought with them from England" (*N* 31, emphasis mine).

From Guatulco, Drake sailed westward, eventually reaching the Indian Ocean. Coming upon the Moluccas islands, Drake "took in a supply of meat and provisions and lightened their ship by reducing their company to sixty men." From the Moluccas, the ship sailed north until it reached an uninhabited island, where, because of contrary winds, it remained for approximately six weeks. When the ship departed, three people were left behind: "the two negroes and the negress Maria, to found a settlement." In his generosity, the Englishman Drake left the three "rice, seeds and means of making fire" (*N* 32).

In *Francis Drake: The Lives of a Hero*, John Cummins refers to the incident twice. The first time, Cummins writes, "Drake retained from Zarate's ship a good-looking black girl called Maria, 'which was afterward gotten with child between the captain and his men pirats, and set on a small iland to take her adventure.'"[8] Nearly ten pages later, Cummins states, "When they sailed on 12 December they left behind the black woman Maria, now pregnant, and two negroes, 'to start a population.'"[9] As a biographer, Cummins does not see his purpose to create a revisionist history (i.e., looking at Drake's actions in light of the problematics of English settler colonialism) but to "document" Drake's actions as part of what is often viewed as a heroic and patriotic life. Thus, as Drake's biographer, Cummins does not perceive a need to comment on or explain away an unequivocally reprehensible act that exemplifies English colonialism. In words that seem intended to justify Drake's reprehensible action, Cummins comments only on Maria's looks—"a good looking black girl" (*N* 31).[10]

Though the historian who excavated John Drake's account (Zelia Nuttall) and the biographer of Francis Drake (Cummins) have quite different historical impulses in writing their books, both Nuttall and Cummins generate very similar ideologies in their handling of the Negress Maria situation—the marginality of her subjectivity and the glorification of masculinity. Cummins's work, in particular, reflects this tendency. Drake's exploits and career assume mythic proportions beneath Cummins's pen: "The aim of my book is not only to recount the facts of Drake's rise from battered ignominy to success and wealth; I hope also to examine the nature of his fame and the processes of his diverging roles in myth and legend; a figure who not only singed the King of Spain's beard, but could also warm the anatomy and fire the dreams of decent Spanish colonial women and haunt their menfolk with a draconian terror."[11] It is the "legend" Drake, not the man, who becomes preserved in Cummins's biographic account. Drake's commission of adultery and sexual assaults are insignificant in Cummins's worshipful biography compared to his successes against Spain's military might.

Zelia Nuttall's *New Light on Drake*, on the other hand, is reflective of the traditional historian's presumed objectivity; Nuttall approaches the Negress Maria incident with less "machismo" and more dispassion: "It also appears that the said John Drake said that after leaving the Islands of Crabs, where they left the negress and the negroes . . . they were driven by the wind out of their course" (*N* 98). Despite the "objective" quality of Nuttall's narration, her description is as problematic as Cummins's handling of Drake's abduction and rape of Maria. Nuttall's handling of John Drake's deposition on the surface seems unproblematic as it appears to be only a translation. What strikes me as unusual is the absence of any commentary on the incident with the Negress Maria, not even a footnote to indicate that Maria was pregnant. Nuttall surely must have known this fact because she cites the other texts that document the Negress Maria incident, *The World Encompassed*, and an anonymous account of Drake's voyage. In both texts, the authors make clear that Maria was "with child" or "very great" in her pregnancy when they describe her abandonment. Contrary to the historical visibility granted Maria by John Drake's deposition and the authors of *The World Encompassed* and the anonymous account of Drake's voyage, both Nuttall and Cummins manage to efface Maria's subjectivity in ways that none of the other texts could achieve. Like the existence so many women of African ancestry taken from their native lands either by force or voluntarily, Maria's is documented with little more than a footnote. What goes untold in all the written accounts of Drake's abduction and subsequent rape of Maria is the prehistory of her separation from her family, community, and homeland. Who was the Negress Maria? Did Maria leave from Africa or from a Spanish or Portuguese port where she had lived most of her life? Was she abducted by the Spanish Don, or did she enter into a relationship with the Spaniard of her own volition? Had she had previous contact with Europeans? What were her languages? Was she a product of miscegenation? Did her beauty draw the attention of first Zarate, then Drake (and thus substantiating Cummins's comments about her looks)? Did she die in childbirth after Drake left her on the island? Did the child survive?

Maria's marginality in Nuttall's and Cummins's narratives is, in my view, directly correlated with their valorization of Drake—the more significant he, the less important she; the more visible he, the more invisible she. Drake's stature within these particular examples of English historiography is untainted by his sexual abuse and ruthless abandonment of a pregnant woman of African ancestry. The Negress

Maria was by no means the only woman of African ancestry to have been taken from her homeland, nor was she the first to become (whether by force or choice) the sexual partner of a European. Had chance or bad fortune not brought her in contact with Francis Drake, Maria would not have been part of English history. What makes Maria "history" is that her life was entwined, even if for a brief period, with Francis Drake and recorded in historical accounts. In other words, what stops Maria from slipping into the nameless void that was the African slave trade, sadly, is also what produces her historical marginality: Francis Drake. Even so, Maria's dark body will forever contaminate the "purity" of Drake's legend; the nobility of his deeds becomes ever so tarnished by Maria. She is the inky marginal notation, the black speck, that historians and biographers cannot hide. As I was recently reminded, the silence of the enslaved and the marginalized does not go unheard.

Desterrado. Exile. Diasporic voices speak and yet are judged by the weight of their marginalia, citations, and historical evidence. This brief interlude is prompted by my curiosity about Behn's racial history, my foray into romance fiction, and my efforts to disrupt early modern race studies' business as usual.

Periodization and Premodern Critical Race Studies, a postscript

It is easy for institutionalized Shakespeare/early modern studies to suddenly declare 2020 the year of Blackness in Early Modern England/Britain. Yet graduate students are still told to avoid "niche" topics like "race" so as not to narrow their marketability. Intellectual policing of publications continues. Erasures continue. And while these backlashes may seem petty, the blind spots that British historians have for the longstanding work of literary scholars (especially those in the US) on early modern Black peoples in Britain is especially infuriating when they suddenly claim archival discoveries. Imtiaz Habib's *Black Lives in the English Archives, 1500–1677: Imprints of the Invisible* is the culmination of archival research begun in the late 1990s, while it is not amiss to declare that Hall's *Things of Darkness* had *been there and done that* in 1995.

If histories are reexamined, silenced voices framed so their narratives become visible, if non-Black, Indigenous, and Peoples of Color scholars are writing books, articles, thought pieces, holding conferences, and so on about the Black presence in early modern England, do origin stories really matter? My answer is, yes, they matter because they counter the erasure of the intellectual labor performed by a generation of Black and Brown renaissance/early modern English literary scholars who set in motion the study of race, of Blackness, of foreignness in sixteenth/ seventeenth-century Britain. Yes, origin stories matter because citation is not the same as foregrounding that scholarship.

Except for Habib, who is with his ancestors yet still watching over a field he helped see into the world, the generation of Black and Brown scholars who brought attention to Black lives in early modern history, literature, and culture are still active in the profession, still producing scholarship. Scholarly genealogies matter for the generation of Black and Brown scholars who initiated PCRS only to have the profession discount or resist their intellectual, political, and academic labor: professional advancement stymied, journal rejections, research funding denied, and institutional isolation. And yet, they persisted. This generation engaged with critical race theory, anti-Blackness, colonialism, the transatlantic enslavement trade, the genocide of Indigenous peoples, and the capitalist exploitation of human labor in literary and non-literary texts, labor many white scholars avoided or refused to consider because it was seen as ahistorical. This inattentiveness is also a matter of relational engagement with historical archives. Race, in all its permutations, didn't become a "presence" for many scholars of pre and early modern cultures until it became professionally profitable—in the first decade of the twenty-first century.

As I look to the future of PCRS, despite the obstacles thrown in its path by academic gatekeeping, I am encouraged by the academic voices of Black, Indigenous, Asian, and Latinx peoples who insist on decolonizing not just the present moment but also how we speak of the past, not just about the taxonomy of race but about white settler colonialism and its impact on indigeneity. I want to suggest that a crucial component of PCRS has to be greater attention to indigeneity and its implications for our work. The language of white settler colonialism—race, settlers, sovereignty, individualism, and destiny—remains terrain to interrogate, especially in the Americas and Africa. As we speak of the indigenous and the enslaved African's descendants, of their "ancestries" or genealogies, we would do well to bear in mind Kim TallBear's admonition in "Genomic Articulations of Indigeneity" that for "indigenous peoples 'ancestry' is not simply genetic ancestry evidenced in 'populations' but biological, cultural, and political groupings constituted in dynamic, longstanding relationships with each other and with living landscapes that define their people-specific identities and, more broadly, their indigeneity."[12] Leanne Betasamosake Simpson encourages us to pay attention to the implications of thinking about sovereignty outside the framework of white settler colonialism and what it might mean for our critical engagements with not just the past but the present when we consider what it means to be a sovereign individual on indigenous lands across the globe.[13]

For Maria Lugones, the importance of turning to a "decolonial feminism" that insists on our thinking about "the continuity between diasporic and nondiasporic subjects without ignoring questions of community as well as the continuity of both with people and communities indigenous to the Americas" is also to question the supremacy of "individualism" as part of a decolonizing theory.[14] Finally, as Patrick Wolfe reminds us, we need to pay attention to the gray areas between settler colonialism and genocide.[15] While not the same, these categories are not mutually exclusive—especially in the Americas. As it has done since its inception, PCRS continues to challenge a view of historiography that is white- centered, heteronormatively defined, and a continuous reaffirmation of white settler colonialism.

The failure to engage in deep intersectional analyses, to recognize generalizations about "women" or "religion" or "ethnicity" that privilege whiteness, and the semantic trap of seeking to pinpoint the exact moment "race became race" all exemplify Wolfe's notion of a "structural event." Whether deliberate or unintentional, PRS not only effaces the problem of colorism (black, red, brown, yellow, white) but upholds the centrality of white supremacy to premodern configurations of anti-Blackness and anti-Indigeneity as fundamental to the capitalist mode of production in the age of settler colonialism. From its inception, PCRS labored against two forms of resistance—institutional or disciplinary gatekeeping and dilution through what can only be viewed as "intellectual settler colonialism."

In my research and publications, critical race theory and Black feminist intersectionality inform the way I read early modern English literary texts, an analysis that insists upon both an oppositional and an insider definitional gaze. In other words, when I examine the premodern/early modern constructions of race as they manifest as white supremacy, that analysis is performed not just by me as a scholar of historiographies (literary, cultural, and economic). Rather, my analysis is mediated by my subjectivity, and this is crucial, as a US Black woman academic. What this means is that I don't divorce who I am from what I study. I am a product of the racial ideologies that began even before the enslavement of African peoples. My ancestors (African, white, and possibly indigenous) were further defined as racial beings by white settler colonialism in ways that mark how I see the world. My use of PCRS is strategic, intersectional, and political. It recognizes the capacity of the analytical gaze to define the premodern as a multiethnic system of competing sovereignties. PCRS not only insists on the "presence" of Black and Indigenous bodies that early modern white supremacy considered disposable, but also demands we focus on the sovereignty stripped from those bodies by settler colonialism.

What PCRS resists is the anthropological move of making Blackness and Indigeneity forms of academic ecotourism, a move very present in PRS. As an intellectual, political, and public deterritorialization of white supremacy's capacious erasure of the sovereignty of Indigenous peoples (whether in the Americas, the Pacific Islands, or the African continent), PCRS is the work of public humanists/scholars who recognize that the kinetic importance of their analyses cannot be reduced to a trope. Nor is the impact of critical race theory to be found by strolling through Venice or London, privileging a discourse of religion without attention to the impact of religion on a non-white body. Similarly, when anti-Blackness serves as the only narrative in premodern race studies (*Othello*), it refracts the critical lens from the anti-Indigenous strategies woven into white settler colonialism's anti-Blackness discourse.

When we look at anti-Indigeneity and anti-Blackness as intersecting acts, we recognize that white settler colonialism happens not just on the body but also through the mind. Enslaved Indigenous peoples removed from the continent of Africa were the first to undergo the ideological process of colonization. White settler colonialism stripped the enslaved of their right to sovereignty as an experiment for future use. This experiment involved the destruction of peoples' relationship to their land, their communities, and their very sovereignty. Indigenous Africans were removed from their lands, enslaved, and transported to the Americas. These individuals were deprived of land sovereignty and denied access to the land except as laborers. This initial Indigenous removal served white supremacy well once the "settling of the Americas" got underway.

By elevating the idea of individuality, a fundamental tenet of capitalism, and stripping Indigenous peoples of their relationship to the means of production, most importantly land, white settler colonialism ensured that not only descendants of the enslaved but all indigenous peoples remain locked in a capitalist experiment. It seems important to recognize the pre-enslavement indigeneity of African peoples removed from their lands. Too often, in our discussion of the enslavement of Africans and the legacy their descendants currently face, academics deploy the "master's tool" of white supremacy. To think of those enslaved between the fifteenth and nineteenth centuries solely in terms of anti-Black rhetoric elides their more complex sovereignty as Indigenous peoples.

This type of awareness is what informs PCRS. It is an awareness that refuses the individualistic models that come with periodization as tools of analysis. To commit to PCRS is to recognize we cannot just engage the problem of anti-Blackness. We must also examine the anti-

Indigeneity that goes hand in hand with anti-Blackness. It is not enough to investigate the role of gender within race-making. We must begin to look at the complications sexuality imposes on gender models and then further complicate the ways we engage "race." PCRS insists that to leave white subjectivity uncontested, unexamined, is to feed white supremacy. Finally, PCRS takes seriously Audre Lorde's injunction that white settler colonialism's ideological tools cannot be the ones to create a decolonizing resistance. An insistence on the intersectionality of race, gender, sexuality, and class is the only way to decolonize the academy's gatekeeping role in the furtherance of white supremacy. PCRS begins with a rejection of the periodization of the past and its implication for the study of race. PCRS's refusal to employ "medieval" or "renaissance" as markers signals a step away from a post-Enlightenment tendency to carve time, place, and human lives into discrete boxes. In essence, PCRS rejects gatekeeping in all its forms.

What PCRS marks is an insistence on intersectionality in scholarly analyses of the past. By decolonizing the past in terms of antiracist pedagogy and critical analyses, PCRS scholars expose the complex intersecting economic, gender, and somatic taxonomies that inform the policing of non-white subjectivity and sovereignty. Resistance to premodern critical race studies, whether in the policing of academic conference programming or in publications, or the efforts to sanitize (make white) the genealogy of PCRS, did not arise by happenstance. It takes a great deal of effort to "protect and serve" academic white privilege.

Epilogue: no estoy desterrado, or citational genealogies

In 2011 I gave a plenary talk at the Shakespeare Association of America's annual conference that hinted at the policing of the academy. The paper was supposed to be my "swan song" to the academic world, and it had no works cited page. As a Black woman with no intentions of becoming a university professor, my relationship with my university home and its insidious white deployment of "to protect and serve" had finally taken a toll. I was of an age to retire "early," even though an additional year would have brought financial benefits. The mental health costs were not worth the expenditure of time. I'm still of two minds on the academy, and once again I want to offer no works-cited page here. What I want to offer is a citational epilogue or genealogy. I will leave it to the reader to decide which best reflects the spirit of this essay.

Citational genealogy is an acknowledgment of the complex ways PCRS came into being: in essence, the intellectual, analytical, and archival mediations that had to take place for *race* to become a lens through which we gaze at premodern cultures. Citational genealogy is not a footnote or endnote. It is the awareness that mediations such as Shelley Haley's "Be Not Afraid of the Dark: Critical Race Theory and Classical Studies," or Geraldine Heng's *The Invention of Race in the European Middle Ages*, or Peter Fryer's *Staying Power: The History of Black People in Britain*, or Irene Silverblatt's *Modern Inquisitions*, or Hall's *Things of Darkness*, or Joyce Green MacDonald's *Women and Race in Early Modern Texts*, or Ayanna Thompson's *Passing Strange: Shakespeare, Race, and Contemporary America*, or Arthur Little's *Shakespeare Jungle Fever: National-Imperial Re-Visions of Race, Rape, and Sacrifice* laid not just the groundwork but the foundation for the study of race in pre and early modern cultures.[16]

These works not only questioned the value of periodization; they also interrogated academic disciplinary boundaries that insisted race was a post-Enlightenment matter. These studies insisted on the legitimacy of critical race studies as a methodological mode of inquiry into the past. PCRS is also intersectional. It is impossible for me to write about early modern racial taxonomies without attending to gender, sexuality, and class. Issues of performance, literariness, cultural interactions, and Indigenous resistance, whether in Africa, Asia, or the Americas, make intersectionality a necessity, not an afterthought.

Until the 2019 RaceB4Race invitation, I avoided academic events (I do owe Farah Karim-Cooper an in-person talk at some point) and focused on the mode of writing that, ironically, was an underlying reason for my decision to pursue an academic career in the first place:

romance fiction. What I hadn't imagined was the role critical race studies would come to play in this arena as well. What also has become quite clear is that PCRS isn't quite ready to release me. As I am crafting these words, I see the intellectual and personal genealogies embedded in the work I have produced during my academic career. Some are cornerstones of PCRS: Kim Hall, Arthur Little, Ayanna Thompson, Joyce Green Macdonald, Francesca Royster, Peter Erickson, Eldred Jones, Peter Fryer, Anthony Barthelemy, Jennifer Morgan, and Imtiaz Habib. Others are non-white postcolonialist and Marxist voices such as Stuart Hall, C. L. R. James, Walter Rodney, and Edward Said.

Emerging Black, Indigenous, Latinx, and Asian voices in PCRS inspire me: Lehua Yim, Dennis Britton, Justin Shaw, Patricia Akhimie, Ambereen Dadabhoy, Brandi Adams, Mira Kafantaris, Mary Rambaran-Olm, Ruben Espinosa, Carissa Harris, Sierra Lomuto, Noémie Ndiaye, Kyle Grady, Farah Karim-Cooper, David Sterling Brown, and Cord J. Whitaker, to name a few. If I've left anyone off, it's because I am just coming to know the next generation. Please forgive the oversight.

The original (OG) Black Shakespeareans who gave/give me sustenance and continually remind me of the importance of what we do: Ayanna Thompson, Arthur Little, Kim Hall, Joyce Green MacDonald, and Francesca Royster.

The ancestor who made it possible for Margo Hendricks to become the Black woman writing this thought piece was Zeola Culpepper Jones. The daughter of enslaved peoples, Zeola Culpepper Jones taught me the importance of family, genealogy, and intellectual integrity.

Finally, I am honored to be part of a group of Black, Indigenous, Latinx, Asian, and allied white scholars who radically changed and are changing the way we contend with the interconnections between capitalism, colonialism, and race, and "who tells the story." The story of the Negress Maria hasn't disappeared because of the academic Black women whose intellectual work focuses on early modern studies. Maria's history remains even when her African name has been erased. We tell the story of the enslaved, the Indigenous, and the marginalized whose voices have been silenced by white supremacy and settler colonialism. This telling, in my view, is the citational genealogy I choose to deploy. While the study of premodern race may become fashionable terrain for a type of intellectual settler colonialism, it is impossible to erase the foundation constructed and sustained by Black, Brown, Latinx, and Asian scholars' refusal to accept the limitations and silences periodization imposes on intellectual inquiry. Nor do we apologize when this refusal offends. We will be heard.

This is citational genealogy. This is Premodern Critical Race Studies.

University of California, Santa Cruz

[*This essay was intentionally written without endnotes/footnotes or a work cited page. The journal's stylistic format required otherwise.*]

This article first appeared in *New Literary History*, Volume 52, Numbers 3/4, Summer/Autumn 2021, pp. 365-384. Copyright 2021 Johns Hopkins University Press. Reprinted with permission.

NOTES

1. Margo Hendricks, "'Obscured by dreams': Race, Empire, and Shakespeare's *A Midsummer Night's Dream*," *Shakespeare Quarterly* 47, no. 1 (1996): 60
2. Martin Bernal, *Black Athena: The Afroasiatic Roots of Classical Civilization*, 3 vols. (New Brunswick, NJ: Rutgers Univ. Press, 1987, 1991, and 2006); Kim F. Hall, *Things of Darkness: Economies of Race and Gender in Early Modern England* (Ithaca, NY: Cornell Univ. Press, 1995); and Hendricks and Patricia Parker, eds., *Women, "Race," and Writing in the Early Modern Period* (New Brunswick, NJ: Rutgers Univ. Press, 1994).
3. bell hooks, "The Oppositional Gaze: Black Female Spectators," in *Black Looks: Race and Representation* (Boston: South End, 1992), 116.
4. See Patrick Wolfe, *Settler Colonialism and the Transformation of*

Anthropology: The Politics and Poetics of an Ethnographic Event (London: Continuum, 1999).

5. Stephen Greenblatt, "Shakespeare's Othello: The Moor," Harvard University Online Courses, accessed August 2, 2021, *https://online-learning.harvard.edu/course/shakespeares- othello-moor?delta=2*.

6. RaceB4Race Executive Board, "It's Time to End the Publishing Gatekeeping!" *The Sundial*, June 11, 2020, accessed August 2, 2021, https://medium.com/the-sundial-acmrs/ its-time-to-end-the-publishing-gatekeeping-75207525f587.

7. Zelia Nuttall, ed. and trans., *New Light on Drake: A Collection of Documents Relating to His Voyage of Circumnavigations, 1577–1580* (London: The Hakluyt Society, 1914), 31 (hereafter cited as *N*).

8. John Cummins, *Francis Drake: The Lives of a Hero* (New York: St. Martins, 1997), 112.

9. Cummins, *Francis Drake*, 121. Cummins, *Francis Drake*, 111.

10. Cummins, *Francis Drake*, 4.

11. Kim TallBear, "Genomic Articulations of Indigeneity," in *Native Studies Keywords*, ed. Stephanie Nohelani Teves, Andrea Smith, and Michelle H. Raheja (Tucson: Univ. of Arizona Press, 2015), 131.

12. Leanne Betasamosake Simpson, "The Place Where We All Live and Work Together: A Gendered Analysis of 'Sovereignty,'" in *Native Studies Keywords*, 23.

13. María Lugones, "Musing: Reading the Nondiasporic from within Diasporas," *Hypatia* 29, no. 1 (2014): 20.

14. Patrick Wolfe, "Settler Colonialism and the Elimination of the Native," *Journal of Genocide Research* 8, no. 4 (2006): 387–409.

15. Shelley Haley, "Be Not Afraid of the Dark: Critical Race Theory and Classical Studies," in *Prejudice and Christian Beginnings: Investigating Race, Gender, and Ethnicity in Early Christian Studies*, ed. Laura Nasrallah and Elisabeth Schüssler Fiorenza (Minneapolis, MN: Fortress, 2009), 27–50; Geraldine Heng, *The Invention of Race in the European Middle Ages* (Cambridge: Cambridge Univ. Press, 2018); Peter Fryer, *Staying Power: The History of Black People in Britain* (London: Pluto, 2018); Irene Silverblatt, *Modern Inquisitions: Peru and the Colonial Origins of the Civilized World* (Durham, NC: Duke Univ. Press, 2004); Kim F. Hall, *Things of Darkness: Economies of Race and Gender in Early Modern England*

(Ithaca, NY: Cornell Univ. Press, 1995); Joyce Green MacDonald, *Women and Race in Early Modern Texts* (Cambridge: Cambridge Univ. Press, 2002); Ayanna Thompson, *Passing Strange: Shakespeare, Race, and Contemporary America* (Oxford: Oxford Univ. Press, 2013); and Arthur Little, *Shakespeare Jungle Fever: National-Imperial Re-Visions of Race, Rape, and Sacrifice* (Stanford, CA: Stanford Univ. Press, 2000).

MARGOH, THE ROMANCE EXPERIENCE

DAUGHTERS OF SARIA

FATE'S MATCH

ELYSABETH GRACE

DEBATING THE OBVIOUS

This excerpt was originally published in *Race and Romance: Coloring the Past*. ACMRS Press copyright 2022. Reprinted with permission of the press.

In an odd twist of fate, for most of the twentieth and twenty-first centuries the romance genre is routinely subject to disdain or dismissal as *popular or genre fiction* rather than literary fiction. The tone of dismissal varies. Robert Gottlieb's sarcastic commentary is probably more biting than most:

> Regency, psychopaths, wedding planners, ranchers, sadists, grandmas, bordellos, dukes (of course); whips, fish tacos, entails, Down syndrome, recipes, orgasms — romance can absorb them all, which suggests it's a healthy genre, not trapped in inflexibility. Its readership is vast, its satisfactions apparently limitless, its profitability incontestable. And its effect? Harmless, I would imagine. (Gottlieb 2017)

Diane Callahan's efforts to explain the differences between genre fiction and literary fiction lack the vitriol of Gottlieb's, even if her observation seems to affirm the sentiments behind Gottlieb's dismissal of romance:

Beyond purpose and plot scale, to me the most distinctive marker between the two categories is writing style. *Genre fiction often uses more accessible prose* that reaches a wider audience and doesn't distract from the story being told. *Literary fiction values carefully crafted sentences* that can take more work to understand, but they attempt to capture precise images and feelings; they are often lyrical and layered. (Callahan 2020, original emphases)

In a *New York Times Books Review* interview, author Philippa Gregory denounces what she refers to as "lazy, sloppy genre novels" (Tamaki, 2017). Gregory ends her criticism by stating, "choosing to write a genre novel is like fencing the universe because you are afraid of space." Allison Flood, in a *The Guardian* response to Gregory's criticism, writes, "quite apart from[2] the fact that every piece of writing falls into one genre or another, the comment is bizarre first because of who Gregory is. The author of *The Other Boleyn Girl*, *The Taming of the Queen*, and most recently *The Last Tudor*, Gregory writes historical fiction — and is indisputably a genre novelist herself" (Flood 2017). In fact, as Flood observes, "[i]t becomes even more bizarre when, in the same interview, Gregory goes on to name her favourite fictional hero as a Georgette Heyer gent: Vidal, in *Devil's Cub*." Flood concludes her commentary by wryly noting, "So Gregory clearly enjoys reading 'lazy, sloppy' genre writing herself. It's also a miscalculation because I'd say the readers of her books include a vast swath of romance readers. Romantic relationships between the kings and queens of yore are generally at the heart of Gregory's novels."

Within the genre itself, "self-proclaimed" romance authors seem to have trouble avoiding the "genre fiction" pitfalls. Elizabeth Reid Boyd titles the essay she wrote for *The Guardian* on February 13, 2017, "Trashy, Sexist, Downright Dangerous? In Defence of Romantic Fiction" with a preamble of "Dr Elizabeth Reid Boyd spent publication day of her first romance novel in a darkened room. She has since discovered there's nothing to be ashamed of" (Boyd 2017). Even the romance genre's fiercest advocates appear to reinforce this logic with titles such as *A Natural History of the Romance Novel, Historical Romance Fiction, New Approaches to Popular Romance Fiction, Making Meaning*

Popular Romance Fiction, and *Happily Ever After: The Romance Story in Popular Culture*. Why not "romance genre" or "romance literature"? Why terms such as "fiction" or "story"? Of these titles, *A Natural History of the Romance Novel* is one that gestures toward the literary history of romance genre.

What is strikingly implicit in these academic book titles is an inescapable tie to academic ideologies about the cultural "purpose" of fictive writing. Often viewed as a guilty pleasure, for women only, and a misleading depiction of gender relations, romance has had more than its share of negative press over the course of its modern history. During the early modern period, the genre also received praise for its positive depictions of male and female virtue even as it was condemned for its frivolity. Caught between the rock, literature, and a hard place, genre fiction of the worst sort, the romance genre has had a contentious existence. Part of the issue lies in romance's generic fluidity: is it a genre, a literary mode [3], or merely a literary convention similar to metaphor or trope? Is romance an emotional state of being tied to relationships that are sexual in nature but inevitably lead to the protagonists "falling in love and enjoying a happily ever after" life? Or, is romance all of these and therein lies the problem?

Several factors contribute to the ways in which literary critics and academic scholars approach the romance novel. First, there is the implicit notion of literary canonicity and what texts are rightly labeled "literature" or "artistic" and what texts are relegated to the arena of popular fiction or "entertainment." The trivializing or belittling of the romance genre is not a recent phenomenon that occurs every February or when a "literary critic" or an author decides to mark territory. When we trace the historical debates about the complex relationships between epic, romance, and history, we find that writers themselves were not only ambivalent but also concerned as to the social or cultural value of romances. George Puttenham dismisses the romance as a "historical ditty," (Puttenham 1968/1589, 33) declaring that "[r]omances or historical rimes [are] made purposely for [the] recreation of the common people at Christmas dinners and bridals, and in taverns & alehouses and such other places of base resort" (83).

Torquato Tasso's *Discorsi dell'arte poetica* offered a challenge to those who claimed that romance and epic are distinct poetic forms, arguing "that since [he finds] no essential difference between the epic and the romance, it clearly follows that there is no generic distinction between them" (Rhu 1993, 121). For Tasso, "the romance (the name they use for *Orlando Furioso* and the like) is a kind of poetry different from epic, unknown to Aristotle, and therefore not bound by Aristotle's rules for epic" (Tasso 1973/1594, 68). Drawing upon Horace, Tasso contends that "those poems are better that win more approval from custom … And custom prefers the kind of poetry called romance, which therefore must be judged the better" (68). Clearly, Philip Sidney and Edmund Spenser in writing *The Arcadia* and *The Faerie Queene* respectively indicate a preference for Tasso and Ariosto over the dictates of theorists such as Puttenham.

Other Renaissance and early modern English writers also found the romance genre in prose form (especially in the romance novellas of Bandello [c. 1480–1562] and Cinthio [1504–1573]) to be a much more fruitful and lucrative source for their interventions in the production of literature. In its various modes, the romance provided plots and characters that English [4] writers often deployed in their drama and prose fiction. Works such as John Lyly's *Euphes* or George Gascoigne's *The Adventures of Master F.J.* helped to legitimate prose fiction as an acceptable heir apparent to the romance in poetic mode, and thus give rise to the modern novel. At least one twentieth-century scholar, A. C. Hamilton, laments this evolution: "Elizabethan prose fiction was succeeded by the novel. That devourer and confounder of all literary genres corrupts the taste for romance by setting up demands for realism, correspondence to every-day experience, and a serious criticism of life which the former [romance] cannot satisfy" (Hamilton 1984, 23). Even so, Hamilton continues, "of course, romance was never superseded" by the novel, it "only went underground" (24). What Hamilton alludes to in his condemnation of the novel is a long-standing tension about the romance genre, its nature, and its ideological or cultural purposes.

Throughout the sixteenth century, and even into the seventeenth century, the complicated and conflicting relationship between the romance genre and historiography — tension alluded to in Puttenham's description — remained relatively intact. That is, despite describing their texts as "trifles" or "toys," early modern writers of the romance often envisioned their texts as engaging in the practice of historiography, albeit a bit more imaginatively drawn than the type of factual histories produced by chronicle writers. Romance authors engaging the crux of history as epic and the nature of romance were no longer emphatically insisting that their romances fell squarely into place as History. Equally, with the growing popular interest in the novella, the verse epic mode of narratively creating storylines began losing ground as the privileged site for the romance genre. An emerging non-aristocratic readership, publication costs, and the constraints of verse form opportunity may have contributed to a rapidly shifting preference for the prose form of romance.

This cultural shift, however, did not deter writers and theorists from attempting to both define and construct the romance text as a continuation of epic historiography. For example, in his preface to *Parthenissa: A Romance in Four Parts* (1655), Roger Boyle writes,

> All the Readers of Parthenissa may wonder at my making of Spartacus and Perolla contempories, & that Artabbanes & Spartacus[5] should be the same Person &c. But I hope [they] will no longer do so, when I Mind [remind] them, that I write a Romance, not a History, and that therefore though *all* I Relate be not the Truth, yet if a Part be, I perform more than what the title of my Book does confine me to. (Boyle 1953/1655, a3–4)

Though not entirely abandoning its claim to historical narrativity, romance was deemed to be, as Pierre Daniel Huet would write in 1670, "Fictions of Low Adventures, disposed into an Elegant Style in Prose, for the Delight and Instruction of the Reader" (Huet 1970/1715, 46). Unlike Huet, Georges de Scudery seeks to retain romance's claim to historical narrativity (de Scudery 1952/1674). After a brief discussion of the structural rules associated with romance in his preface to *Ibrahim, or the Illustrious Bassa*, de Scudery highlights what he considers to be the most significant: "but amongst all the rules which are to be observed in the compositions of these works, that of true resemblance is without question the most necessary; it is, as it were, the fundamental stone of this building" (3). He then notes that, in his own work, he has "observed the Manners, Customs, Religions, and Inclinations of People: and to give a more true resemblance to things, I have made the foundations of my work Historical, my principal Personages such as are marked out in the true History for illustrious persons, and the wars effective" (4).

de Scudery's theoretical concept of the romance genre does not entirely settle the debates on its function, however. How is the reader supposed to comprehend a text that is described as a romance yet is also called a history? And what is the "verisimilitude" or "true resemblance" that writers presume or believe that they are invoking as history in their romances, and that the readers ought immediately or intuitively to comprehend? On the one hand, these questions are not entirely answerable as it is the very nature of romance to generate "error" and digression as the structural, even functional, principle of the romance mode (Parker 1979). Hence, most scholarly theories and analyses of romance accept that there is an inherent difficulty in attempting to define romance and instead address its "functional literary life," which involves a series of "generic transformations over time resulting in a kind of dynamic continuum"[6] (Brownlee and Brownlee 1985, 1). In his groundbreaking *Anatomy of Criticism*, Northrop Frye writes that

> the romance is nearest of all literary forms to the wish-fulfillment dream, and for that reason it has socially a curiously paradoxical role. In every age the ruling social or intellectual class tends to project its ideals in some form of romance, where the virtuous heroes and beautiful heroines represent the ideals and the villains the threats to their ascendancy (Frye 1957, 186).

To return to the question of definition, Patricia A. Parker cogently observes that one of the problems in discussing the form of romance has always been the need to limit the way in which the term is applied. I have chosen to approach the subject in a way which does not cover all the forms we call "romance" but may provide what a romance poet might call a "prospect" on them... Romance... therefore, is characterized primarily as a form which simultaneously quests for and postpones a particular end, objective, or object. (Parker 1979, 4)

Similarly, Corrine Saunders finds that "the genre of romance is impossible adequately to define," which "is not so surprising when we recall that the term finds its origins in the French word romanz, meaning simply literature written in the vernacular, the romance language of French" (Saunders 2004, 2). Nonetheless, Saunders astutely postulates, "perhaps it is not fanciful to view romance as a genre waiting to happen, a story already told, situated in those moments of classical writing, inherent in the earliest of fictions and fundamental to human nature" (2).

Romance structurally confounds as much as it organizes. In other words, romance is viewed as an adventure or quest located more often than not in "nature" and predicated upon the notion of a wandering heroic figure. Concepts such as salvation or redemption, realism, possibility, and punishment are thematic hallmarks of the romance plot, while love and a happily ever after are its generic conventions. In the end, what is important[7] in these studies of the romance genre is the idea of the social act. Or, as Fredric Jameson argues,

> as for romance, it would seem that its ultimate condition of figuration, on which the other preconditions we have already mentioned are dependent — the category of worldness, the ideologeme of good and evil felt as magical forces, a salvational historicity — is to be found in a transitional moment in which two distinct modes of production, or moments of socioeconomic development, coexist. (Jameson 1981, 148)

In essence, romance appears to be "bound up with a complex,

evolving, historical situation" and, consequently, "different romances in different historico-literary contexts call ... for methodological heterogeneity" (Jameson 1981, 148).

The reader of this chapter might well ask, in a book dealing with racism and colorism, why begin with a genealogy of scholarly theories on the romance genre? Does it really matter what form it takes if the conclusion is "different historico-literary contexts" create definitional ambiguity? Furthermore, if the genre's texts are "bound up with a complex, evolving, historical situation," then why view twentieth- and twenty-first romance fiction as outside the framework of Literature and cast the same cloak on pre-twentieth-century romance texts such as *Faerie Queen*, *Urania*, *Pride and Prejudice*, *The Blithedale Romance*, or the *Unfortunate Traveler*? Where in the canonical envisioning of Literature has literary scholarship failed with the romance genre?

I pose these questions not to answer them but to suggest that the romance genre has a longstanding and very complicated relationship to literary formation and its role since its inception in early modern English culture. One aspect of this relationship is how much the romance genre is bound up with racial capitalism, something most of the theorists ignore. When we look at early modern English romances, regardless of form, there is a pervasive engagement with race-making, whether it is tied to nation, ethnicity, or colorism — and sometimes all three. When we examine contemporary, i.e., twentieth and twenty-first century romances, there is no surprise in discovering that not much has changed.[8]

"The Grecians, Who Have Been Our First Masters"

In his treatise on romance, de Scudery argues that any writer of romance should look to "the Grecians, who have been our first Masters" (de Scudery 1952/1674, 2). One of the most influential of these "Greek masters" was Heliodorus, whose romance novel *Aethiopica* was translated and circulated in early modern English literary culture. Written between 230 and 275 CE, *Aethiopica* depicts the trials and tribulations of Charikliea, the daughter and heir of the monarchs of Ethiopia, and her beloved Theagenes, whose lineage is traceable to Achilles. Heliodorus is most likely indebted to the biblical account of the Ethiopian monarch Candace, which is taken up by Greek historiographers such as Pliny the Elder who writes

> They said that it [town of Meroe] is ruled by a woman, Candace, a name that has passed on through a succession of queens for many years At the present day there are reported to be forty-five other kings of Ethiopia. But the whole race was called Aetheria, and then Atlantia, and finally it took its name for Aethiops the son of Vulcan [universe vero gens Aetheria appellate est, deinde Atlantia, mox a Vulcani filio Aethiope]. (Pliny 1938/77 CE, 476–77)

The more famous Ethiopian princess who figures in *Aethiopica* and several adaptations of the romance novel is, of course, Andromeda.

For early modern romance theorists, Heliodorus's *Aethiopica* exemplifies all the conventions Renaissance and early modern English readers would come to love in their romance texts — pirates and armed men, caves and ambushes, dreams and visions, burnings, poisonings, and sudden deaths, battles and the triumph of virtue, and of course, love. The romance's depiction of virtues, such as chastity, honor, true love, and heroical figures, were consistently valorized as moral and ethical exempla in Renaissance and early modern English culture. As one Renaissance translator/editor observed: "not only many changes of fortune but also many images of virtue are here displayed. Among these is the description of Hydaspes, the king of Ethiopia, who is to be praised not only for his fortitude but also for his justice, clemency, and kindness towards those[9] whom he has subdued" (quoted in Doody 1996, 237). In fact, "both in morality and taste, this book [was considered] irreproachable" by translators of Heliodorus's text (235). Not only was the *Aethiopica* translated from Greek into Latin, but it also appeared in Italian, French, German, and English versions. In England, the novel enjoyed extraordinary popularity and clearly left its mark on a reading populace hungry for both romances and novellas that went on well into the eighteenth and nineteenth centuries.

The assimilation of Heliodorus's text into English literary and cultural discourses was remarkable. The romance surfaced in translations, adaptations, and/or the appropriation of the romance's protagonists, Charikliea and Theagenes. *Aethiopica* appears to have achieved its popularity with writers and readers for a number of reasons. First, the text's humanist translators apparently held a high regard for Heliodorus's "sophisticated way of exploiting the varied interpretive practices of readers of narrative fiction" (Mentz 2006, 48). The novel also provided "an alternative to chivalric romance and the Italian novella" (48). In effect, Steve Mentz asserts, the "opening scene models the diverse relations between the text and the diverse practices of its readers" (48). At this point this assertion needs to be understood as speculation but the popularity of *Aethiopica* suggests readers seemed to have found great delight in Heliodorus's skillful handling of love, magic, and the fantastic, elements which enable the narrative to move metaphorically from the realm of the impossible and fantasy (romance) to the realm of the believable (realism or history).

Heliodorus's romance sets into motion a generic and historical context that came to shape not only the way romance was conceptualized but also what constitutes legitimate plotlines within the romance genre. However, because the *Aethiopica* makes use "of the Manners, Customs, Religions, and Inclinations of People ... to give a more true resemblance to things," (de Scudery 1952/1674, 4), the text's storyline proves to be a double-edged sword — it is simultaneously engaging and believable and ideologically disruptive of Renaissance and early modern English race-making. With the first English translation, Thomas Underdowne's, readers and authors become immersed in a shifting discourse about colorism and its growing ties to modern racism.

The inclusion of the white-presenting Ethiopian as the raison d'être for a romance was an original touch in Heliodorus's narrative. As a genre[10] or mode that conventionalizes the fantastic or the supernatural, as well as the idea of happily ever after, romance was a fertile template for grasping the instability of race-making based on skin color. What theorists fail to consider is the way *Aethiopica* functions as an ideological conundrum that Renaissance and early modern European racism cannot entirely resolve. This is not to say that Heliodorus himself was free of what may best be described as racial prejudice; one has to only look at his representation of the Egyptians to discern his biases. Even so, the novel's aim seems not be the construction of an image of racial or ethnic negativity. Rather, the general purpose of the *Aethiopica* appears to be one of storytelling and the creative process of framing a readership. What the reader eventually discovers is that, had Charicles not insisted on arranging a marriage between Charikliea and his nephew, Charikliea's "Ethiopian" identity would most likely have remained a well-kept secret. Even when her true identity is revealed, no one evinces distaste or horror at Charikliea's Ethiopian-ness; for, as the novel makes clear, the Ethiopian people were held in high regard by the Greeks among whom Charikliea has lived.

At the novel's conclusion, Charikliea and Theagenes are wed and duly proclaimed heirs to the Ethiopian throne. Neither Charikliea's whiteness nor her parents' Blackness register as liabilities to Theagenes or, it appears, to Heliodorus and his readers. However, within the racializing taxonomy shaping sixteenth- and seventeenth-century England's view of the globe, such issues would prove problematic. Finally, and most importantly, what may have deeply intrigued and disconcerted English writers and readers of *Aethiopica* was the text's imaginatively constructed ideological dilemma and subsequent resolution with respect to Charikliea, a white-presenting Ethiopian.

Charikliea's Race

The appropriation and use of Heliodorus's *Aethiopica* as an illustrative text of idealized human behavior during the early modern period in England (and Europe) is not without irony. Despite the fact that Ethiopia had adopted Christianity as its principal religion in the early fourth century, "white" Europe did not truly take notice of the kingdom until the[11] twelfth century. Moreover, while Ethiopia was a major economic player within the eastern Mediterranean region, it was the legend of Prester John that brought the African nation-state to Christian Europe's attention. The myth of Prester John, coinciding as it did with the religious wars between Islam and Christian Western Europe (typically referred to as the "Crusades"), led to further contact between European and Ethiopian Christians, and fostered the dream of a unified Christendom aligned against the followers of Islam (Saracens). By the beginning of the fifteenth century, relations (political and economic) were well-established between the courts of European monarchs and Ethiopia and, as a consequence of embassies and mercantile interactions, the geography, culture, commercial value, and political and religious practices of the African state became fairly well known to Renaissance and early modern Europe.

One of the most widely circulated texts across Europe to offer a picture of Ethiopia was *A Geographical Historie of Africa, Written in Arabicke and Italian by Iohn Leo a More, Borne in Granada, and Brought up in Barbarie* (published in 1600), which offered its readers a detailed account of Ethiopia. Leo, more commonly referred to as Leo Africanus, has this to say about Ethiopia:

> The Abassins have no great knowledge of Nilus by reason of the mountains which divide them from it; for which cause they call Abagni the father of rivers. Howbeit they say that upon Nilus do inhabit two great and populous nations; one of Jews towards the west, under the government of a mighty king; the other more southerly, consisting of amazons or war-like women; whereof we will speak more at large in our relation of Monomotapa. (Leo, 1969/1600, 13)

What stands out about Leo Africanus's discussion of Ethiopia is that it is atypical in the brevity of his description of the physical appearance of Ethiopians: "The people are scorched with the heate of the sun, and they are black, and go naked: save only that some cover their privities with cloth of cotton or of silk" (395). The rest of Leo Africanus's account about the Ethiopians focuses on their complicated status (to European eyes) as Christians. Ethiopian Christianity held to a different set of apostolic[12] tenets including circumcision, adult baptism, holding the Sabbath on Saturday, and adherence to Coptic theology rather than that which governed the Vatican. In fact,

European Christians apparently were quite disturbed by "their [the Ethiopians'] alien Judaizing religious practices ... [which] were unmistakably heretical" (Quint 1993, 236).

While the medieval Christian nation of Ethiopia remained an ideal to be exploited in the grand struggle against the "infidel" or pagan, the word that described the inhabitant of the Renaissance and early modern east African nation, Ethiopian, had lost its privileged Christian denotation. With increased contact between Europeans and Africans, especially sub-Saharan Africans, and the advent of the slave trade to provide labor for European settler colonies, the word Ethiopian joined Moor, Negro, and, African as part of a collapsible lexicon of racial demarcation. Furthermore, when Leo Africanus penned his *Geographical Historie of Africa*, this lexical conflation to mark Blackness virtually overrode all cultural and ethnic distinctions between and among African peoples, as well as differences between Eastern and Western Africa.

This lexical erasure, aided and abetted by a combination of ignorance and policy among European nations about the continent of Africa, isolated a single determinate — skin color — to racialize any person native to the continent. Ironically, despite its shared "Blackness" with "Negroes" and "Moors," Ethiopia remained very much a part of Christian culture. The effect, not surprisingly, was a cultural and historical paradox within European geopolitics that acknowledged Ethiopia's adherence to Christian doctrine even as it allowed for the people of Ethiopia to be racialized into Blackness (where Blackness signified alienness, inferiority, savagery or incivility, and evil) alongside other Africans. This paradigm was very much in play when, in 1569, Underdowne published the first English translation of Heliodorus's *Aethiopica* as *An Æthiopian Historie*. So popular was the translation that after a number of printing runs, Underdowne decided to produce an edition "newly corrected and augmented with divers and sundry new additions" in 1587 (Underdowne 1967/1587, 107).

In his preface to the "gentle reader," Underdowne writes that he reviewed the first translation and decided to "make it as perfect as" he "could, and to reform it from those so many horrible escapes" or errors that marred the first edition (4). He then goes on to "commend the reading[13] of" his work, saying "If I shall compare it with other of like argument, I thinke none commeth near it. Mort Darthure, Arthur of little Britaine," and "Amadis of Gaule, etc, accompt violent murder, or murder for no cause, manhood: and fornication and all unlawfull lust, friendly love" (4). Heliodorus's text, Underdowne contends, "punisheth the faultes of evil doers, and rewardeth the well livers. What a king is Hidaspes? What a pattern of a good prince? What happy success had he? Contrariewise, what a lewd woman was Arsace? What a pattern of evil behaviour? What an evil end had she?" (4–5). Underdowne's commentary echoes sentiments articulated about Heliodorus's text.

Renaissance translations of *Aethiopica*, for the most part, adhered to the idea that a translation is merely the rendering of a foreign language text into the vernacular, and Underdowne's version was no different. When editors and translators of Heliodorus's romance intruded their views, it was generally in the form of an elucidation of a particularly difficult word or in marginal commentary on the ethical or moral lesson to be learned from a specific passage or chapter (as Underdowne's commentary makes clear). However, for English writers of fiction who later adapted portions of *Aethiopica*, or who "borrowed" from the work, the text's central premise may have presented them with something of a different quandary: do you leave intact the romance's representations of Ethiopia and Ethiopians, including the high regard with which they seem to be depicted by the Greek Heliodorus; or, do you "adapt" the image slightly so as not to completely denigrate Heliodorus's text yet making clear that the translator's culture holds a very different, and often ambivalent, view of Ethiopians? In other words, do you change Heliodorus's narrative to suit the generic aims of your own literary creativity and the cultural expectations of your society?

What goes unremarked in the cultural discourse surrounding *Aethopica's* inclusion into early modern English fiction is the problems posed by the white-presenting Ethiopian. Unlike the white-passing subject, the white-presenting subject may or may not engage in the performative process of color passing for the simple reason of ignorance. Inherent in racial capitalism is a campaign of anti-Blackness that requires individuals to see Blackness, not whiteness as a racializing trope. To identify, or mark, a person's race, we are taught to look at biophysical externalities,[14] skin, facial features, and, as if it is a genetic marker, geographical space. For Charikliea, none of her physical attributes (skin color and facial features) set her apart from the Greeks. Her father is Greek, his skin color is "white," and his socioeconomic status is enough to guarantee the perception and privilege of Charikliea's whiteness. Even when the "truth" of her birth and thus "race" become known, her white-presenting subjectivity is not a problem in Heliodorus's novel. However, the same cannot be said for adaptations and retellings of the romance of Charikliea and Theagenes.

In the next chapter, we will see what happens when early modern English racism meets Heliodorus's romance and the racecraft doesn't entirely mesh. Focusing on two seventeenth-century English texts that retell significant elements of *Aethiopica*, Edward Fairfax's *Godfrey of Bulloigne* (a translation of Torquato Tasso's 1581 *Gerusalem Liberata*) and William Lisle's *The Fair Ethiopian* (1631), I discuss the ways Renaissance and early modern English writers came to terms with the "white-presenting Ethiopian." In different ways, each verse romance reveals its literary descent and its ideological distance from *Aethiopica*. My reading of Fairfax's and Lisle's poems argues that Heliodorus's female protagonist, Charikliea, cannot function as an ambiguous signifier of race as she does in Aethiopica. England's political economy, with its settler colonialist ideologies and its involvement in the enslavement of African peoples, cannot tolerate such ambiguity. English racism requires not just a hierarchy of colorism; it also requires that the hierarchy centers an anti-Blackness ideology. In other words, what the adaptations of *Aethiopica* do is rewrite the conventions of romance according to white supremacist logic.

WRITING ROMANCE

This essay was originally published in *Race and Romance: Coloring the Past*. ACMRS Press copyright 2022. Reprinted with permission of the press.

In 2018 under the pen name Elysabeth Grace I published my first romance novel, *Fate's Match*. As I wrote in the author's note, the romance story of the main characters, Amina and Michael, had its roots in a historical and troubling narrative about a Black African woman ("the negress Maria") and the Englishman Francis Drake (Hendricks 2018). The series, *Daughters of Saria*, is indebted to a range of early modern English literary texts (John Milton's *Paradise Lost*, Ligon's *History of Barbados*, Shakespeare's *Richard III*, and, of course, the historical accounts of Francis Drake's voyages). The series owes a greater debt to Heliodorus's early modern English translators and adaptors, Milton's Lucifer/Satan, and to Aphra Behn for inspiring my scholarly and writerly interest in the intersection of racism and the romance genre. As authors whose fictional texts lay bare the racecraft at work in early modern English culture, these writers not only aided and abetted English racism, anti-Blackness, and white supremacy, they also exposed its fractures.

Fate's Kiss, Book 2 of my *Daughters of Saria*, is set during the reign of

Charles II, the world in which Behn lived. The Black female protagonist of *Fate's Kiss*, Anne Willoughby, is a shapeshifter who engages in white passing. She is fully aware of the performative nature of white passing and the dangers inherent in being caught out. Yet, just as [Beverly Jenkins] *Forbidden*'s Rhine Fontaine used his wealth and "whiteness" to ameliorate the plight of newly-liberated Black peoples following the United States Civil War, Anne uses her ability to become white to liberate or protect others, especially those who are targeted by racism and racial capitalism. While white-passing Anne not only positions her whiteness as a buffer against racism, she does not diminish who she is as a Black romance character. In essence, like Rhine, Anne makes a deliberate choice to disrupt white supremacist logic (albeit, because *Fate's Kiss* and all of the *Daughters of Saria* novels are paranormal romances, Anne's principal enemy is Satan and his rebellious co-conspirators).

Comparable to Clorinda, Anne is a warrior, although a supernatural one. She is an expert with swords and knives and uses them against her enemies.[104] Where the two women differ is in awareness of their origins and the outcome of their romance relationship. Anne is fully aware of her African-born matrilineal ancestry *and* the somatic skin coloring her white passing conceals. For Anne, whiteness is flesh she puts on and takes off as if it were a gown, something to be worn to protect herself and the women who make up the exclusive Holland's League brothel. Anne's concealed Blackness, however, is not the major conflict in *Fate's Kiss* that it is for Clorinda in *Godfrey of Bulloigne* and thus does not constitute an obstacle to an eventual happily ever after. Both Anne and the male protagonist, Gabriel, survive the violence that nearly costs them their lives and the novel ends conventionally and in line with Heliodorus's romance.

Similar to all romance fiction, from Heliodorus to Beverly Jenkins, my novels work within the parameters of the generic conventions of romance. The main protagonists overcome the obstacles that impede their the happily ever after, the villains face justice for their actions, and the storyline is recognizable as a romance. As an author of romance novels, I am part of a larger writing community (Romancelandia) very much shaped by limitations and possibilities that the romance genre has promised since its inception. The possibilities of the romance genre lie in its popularity and accessibility, and, despite the naysayers, romance novels have probably done more for universal literacy than the genres of poetry and drama. While storytelling is inherent in all genres of literary writing, the romance novel engages its readers not as adversaries, but as co-conspirators. What I mean by this statement is that readers do not have to "work" to grasp the stories, the themes, or the conflicts at play in romance fiction. There is meaning but one does not have to master Greek or Latin, prosody, or Aristotelian notions of tragedy to comprehend what is at work in a romance novel. This not to say there aren't expectations on the part of the author or reader. Rather, what exists is a consensual relationship between author and reader that mirrors the relationship between romance lovers. This is the gift the romance genre offers to its readership.

However, the romance genre has also been deeply imbricated in racial capitalism and white supremacy. As we witnessed with Fairfax/Tasso's reimagining of Heliodorus's *Aethiopica*, the female protagonist's Ethiopian genealogy, her Black parentage, is irreconcilable with her white-presenting[105] body. *Godfrey of Bulloigne* is the racecraft that allows us to see the racism at work in early modern English romance fiction. Because the world-building of *Godfrey of Bulloigne* is temporally, geographically, and culturally different from the world-building of *Aethiopica*, how whiteness, Blackness, and white-presenting work in the early modern English text must align with the racism operative in English social, political, and economic parameters. The forms of enslavement and colonialism present in Heliodorus's world are not identical to those at work in seventeenth-century England.

Therefore, to read or see the implications of Clorinda's Ethiopianness and the necessity for her death, we must attend to the anti-Blackness that maps cultural discourse and representations of Africans in early modern English cultures. The interchangeability of Black, Ethiopian, and Negro as signifiers of an ideology of colorism makes it impossible for any character who wears one of these labels to escape the effects of racism. While I am not arguing there is a direct literary genealogy between all the romance texts I've discussed in this book, I do believe the racecraft that necessitated Clorinda's death also set into motion one of the most pernicious and long-lasting cultural ideas within white Anglo-American romance fiction — the idea that Black people and happily ever afters are incompatible, that trauma, not love, is the definitive representation of Black peoples' experiences (especially in the United States). This view, sadly, shaped many of the nineteenth- and early twentieth-century African American novels even when authors placed Black love at the center of their storytelling.

At the end of the twentieth century, a sea change occurred in the romance publishing industry and in the romance genre as a whole. Technology enabled marginalized voices to circumvent the strictures of a largely racist publishing industry and produce romance fiction not bound by racism, misogyny, sexism, ableism, and classism. Within traditional publishing spaces, Black writers such as Brenda Jackson, Beverly Jenkins, and Francis Ray created romance fiction that not only centered Black romance happily ever afters but offered characterizations not steeped in trauma. These authors produced representations that reflected the complexities of Black American communities rather than a monolithic narrative rooted in Black trauma in the aftermath of enslavement, Jim Crowism, and white supremacist violence. While traditional publishing has been slow to embrace Black romance not designed for white readership of a certain age, class, and sexuality (primarily heterosexual or "cis-het") locked into a model of representation codified in white supremacist logic about what makes a "perfect" romance relationship, non-traditional publishing venues have supported the desires of romance authors and readers from a variety of marginalized communities.

Whether dealing with complex social issues such as white passing, economic class, sexuality, disability, interracial romances, and community, contemporary Black romance authors reject the naturalized conclusions about the inevitable failure of white-presenting Black protagonists such as Clorinda or the Phils to enjoy a happily ever after. Romance as a genre tends to resist absolutes except for the happily ever after. Importantly, it is the romance genre's flexibility as a literary form to accommodate whatever fictional premise or historically-based storyline an author wishes to create. Paradoxically, it is romance's flexibility that also permits the detection of a culture's racecraft. It is this watermark of racism, in all its variations, that permits a study like *Race and Romance: Coloring the Past* to exist.

AFTERWORD

If you've gotten this far, then know that I am a romance fiction writer who "passes" as an academic scholar. I believe I've "paid my debt" to academia with this imperfect book. So, dear gentle reader, if you wish to fully grasp the *Margo Hendricks Experience*, purchase any of the following books I've authored:

The Cock & Oyster Mystery Series: spicy historical cozy mysteries based loosely on some of William Shakespeare's plays. Imagine Dashiell Hammett's *Thin Man* meets Willie S and you'll enjoy these books.

Elizabethan Mischief: a Black historical romance set in the court of Elizabeth Tudor. Revenge is a dish best served cold, or with a glass of wine.

Your Heart Only: A contemporary Black romance with a secret, Shakespeare, and a measure of angst. It's the first book in the *Midsummer Sisters* series.

One Chance Only: A 'second-chance Black romance in the *Midsummer Sisters series*

Daughters of Saria: "Why would a Black woman involve herself in a white family's civil war, and an angelic one at that?" (*Fate's Consort*, Book 3). This series is equal parts Willie S's *Richard III* and John Milton's *Paradise Lost*, book I, if you know where to look. *winks*

You can buy my books at https://payhip.com/ElysabethGrace or on my romance website https://www.elysabethgrace.com/egs-bookshop.

> As always, romance is the key.
> *MargoH*

The
MIDSUMMER
SISTERS
Series

Your Heart Only

ELYSABETH GRACE

ABOUT THE AUTHOR

Margo Hendricks is Professor Emerita. Co-editor (with Patricia Parker) of *Women, Race and Writing in the Early Modern Period (1994)*, Margo has published essays on Shakespeare, premodern critical race, early modern women, and whatever strikes her fancy. Her book *Race and Romance: Coloring the Past* (ACMRS 2022). Other research projects include *From Cotton Fields to Shakespeare's Negress: An Academic Memoir. . . of sorts*. Under the pen name Elysabeth Grace, Margo is a Black romance author and a "Gooner" forever (IYKYK). Visit my website for "MargoH Musings" where I meander with abandon.
https://www.themargohendricksexperience.com/

www.ingramcontent.com/pod-product-compliance
Ingram Content Group UK Ltd.
Pitfield, Milton Keynes, MK11 3LW, UK
UKHW041952230426
12048UKWH00008B/284